# THE RULE OF LAW IN INTE
## COMPARATIVE C

CW01083854

# THE RULE OF LAW IN INTERNATIONAL AND COMPARATIVE CONTEXT

Edited by
ROBERT McCORQUODALE

**British Institute of International and Comparative Law**

Published and Distributed by
British Institute of International and Comparative Law
Charles Clore House, 17 Russell Square, London WC1B 5JP

© 2010

*British Library Cataloguing in Publication Data*
A Catalogue record of this book is available from the British Library

ISBN 978–1–905221–42–4

Typeset by Cambrian Typesetters
Camberley, Surrey
Printed in Great Britain by the MPG Books Group, Bodmin and King's Lynn

# Contents

*Contributors*                                                                    vii
*Preface*                                                                          xi
*Introduction*                                                                     xiii

1.  The Rule of Law in the International Legal Order                               1
    *Tom Bingham*
2.  Business and Human Rights                                                      21
    *Mary Robinson*
3.  Business, the International Rule of Law and Human Rights                       27
    *Robert McCorquodale*
4.  'Justice Delayed is Justice Denied': The Rule of Law,
    Economic Development and the Future of the European
    Community Courts                                                              49
    *Tim Cowen*
5.  Checks and Balances: European Competition Law and the
    Rule of Law                                                                   109
    *Philip Marsden*
6.  Investment Protection and the Rule of Law:
    Change or Decline?                                                            119
    *L Yves Fortier*
7.  Investment Protection and the Rule of Law:
    Change or Decline?                                                            137
    *Norah Gallagher*
8.  Benefits of Comparative Tort Reasoning:
    Lost in Translation                                                           149
    *Jane Stapleton*
9.  Comparing Tort Law: Some Thoughts                                             193
    *Duncan Fairgrieve*
10. International Cooperation and the Modern Prosecutor                           209
    *Keir Starmer*
11. International Cooperation: A Challenge for the Modern
    International Prosecutor                                                       217
    *Sarah Williams*

*Index*                                                                           243

# Contributors

**Tom Bingham (The Rt Hon Lord Bingham of Cornhill KG)** was the President and Chairman of the British Institute of International Law until his death in September 2010. Following an outstanding career at the Bar, he had an unprecedented judicial career, being the first judge to hold the three top judicial posts of Master of the Rolls, Lord Chief Justice and Senior Law Lord. His judicial and extra-judicial promotion of the rule of law led to the creation by the Institute, in his honour, of the Bingham Centre for the Rule of Law.

**Tim Cowen** is a Barrister and was General Counsel of BT Global Services until 2008. He is a member of the EU Business Affairs Council, Chairman of the Competition Panel at the Confederation of British Industry and the International Association of Commercial and Contract Management, is a Visiting Fellow of the British Institute of International and Comparative Law and a Fellow at ResPublica. He is also CEO of TRW Cowen Limited, a consultancy company that advises on policy, regulation, competition and commercial matters for the information technology industry.

**Duncan Fairgrieve** is Senior Research Fellow in Comparative Law and Director of the Product Liability Forum and the Tort Law Centre at the British Institute of International and Comparative Law. He is also Maître de Conférences at Sciences Po, Paris. He is a qualified French avocat and practises in the field of civil and commercial litigation in Paris and is a door tenant at One Crown Office Row, London.

**L Yves Fortier** is Chairman Emeritus of Ogilvy Renault, a leading law firm in Canada and from July 1988 until January 1992 he served as Canada's Ambassador and Permanent Representative to the United Nations in New York. He has acted as chair or party-appointed arbitrator on more than 100 arbitral tribunals, either ad hoc or constituted by different arbitral institutions, around the world and was a member of the Permanent Court of Arbitration in The Hague.

**Norah Gallagher** was Senior Research Fellow in International Investment and Trade Law and the Director of the Investment Treaty Forum at the British Institute of International and Comparative Law from January 2008 to December 2009, and is now a consultant to the Institute. Previously she worked in the International Arbitration Group of Herbert Smith LLP, where she advised on a wide range of issues relating to international arbitration.

**Philip Marsden** is Senior Research Fellow in Competition Law and Director of the Competition Law Forum at the British Institute of International and Comparative Law. He is a non-executive member on the Boards of the UK Office of Fair Trading and the Jersey Competition Regulatory Authority, and Visiting Professor at the College of Europe, Bruges. Prior to joining the Institute, Philip practised competition law in Toronto, Tokyo and London.

**Robert McCorquodale** is the Director of the British Institute of International and Comparative Law in London. He is also Professor of International Law and Human Rights, and former Head of the School of Law, at the University of Nottingham. His academic career includes posts at the University of Cambridge and the Australian National University, and, prior to this, he was a practising lawyer in large law firms in Sydney and London.

**Mary Robinson** served as seventh (and first female) President of Ireland and was UN High Commissioner for Human Rights from 1997 to 2002, after a career as an academic and Barrister in Ireland. She is currently the President of *Realizing Rights: The Ethical Globalization Initiative*, Honorary President of Oxfam International and President of the International Commission of Jurists, as well as being a member of The Elders, being eminent global leaders who seek to support peace building, help address major causes of human suffering and promote the shared interests of humanity.

**Jane Stapleton** is Research Professor of Law at the Australian National University College of Law, Ernest E Smith Professor at the University of Texas at Austin, and a Statutory Visiting Professor of Law and Emeritus Fellow of Balliol College, at Oxford University. She is a Council Member of the American Law Institute (the first foreigner to be honored in this way), an Adviser to the current Restatement (Third) of Torts project, an Honorary Bencher of Gray's Inn, London and a Fellow of the Academy of Social Sciences in Australia.

**Keir Starmer** is a Queen's Council and became the Director of Public Prosecutions and head of the Crown Prosecution Service in November 2008. Prior to this he was the head of Doughty Street Chambers, London, and was a leading human rights and criminal law Barrister, acting in a range of cases both nationally and internationally. As Director of Public Prosecutions, he is responsible for prosecutions, legal issues and criminal justice policy.

**Sarah Williams** was the Senior Research Fellow in Public International Law (Dorset Fellow) at the British Institute of International and Comparative Law from 2008 to January 2010. She is currently Senior Lecturer in the Faculty of Law, University of New South Wales, Australia. Previously she worked at the University of Durham, in legal practice and with the UK Foreign and Commonwealth Office.

# *Preface*

The first of the published lectures in this book on *The Rule of Law in the International and Comparative Context* is the Grotius Lecture given by Tom Bingham on 17 November 2008. His conclusion in that Lecture that the Iraq war was 'a serious violation of international law' not only electrified his audience but reverberated round the world, particularly in the Middle East. Here was the most senior and respected English judge, albeit recently retired, publicly telling his own government, in the presence of one of the Ministers most closely involved (Jack Straw, Foreign Secretary at the time) that the United Kingdom was in breach of the international rule of law.

Two particular reflections on this dramatic turn of events are perhaps appropriate. First, that there are, regrettably, many countries around the world where it would have been impossible or very difficult for such trenchant criticism of the political establishment to be voiced at all. Those of us based in countries where, broadly speaking, it is possible to exercise freedom of speech are uncomfortably aware that this is a privilege denied to many—perhaps even a majority—of citizens around the world. The fact that Tom Bingham's Grotius Lecture could be delivered at all was, in itself, a remarkable reaffirmation of both the existence, and the importance, of the rule of law.

Second, the lecture indicated the vulnerability, in some circumstances, of the rule of law, even in countries such as the United Kingdom with a long tradition in that regard. Indeed, there is a widespread understanding that even in Western countries the rule of law, as traditionally understood, has been and still is under increasing pressure. Examples include the counter-terrorism legislation, the advent of 'the surveillance society', the use of police powers, a perceived lack of access to justice, the increasing power of regulatory agencies of one kind or another, and the difficulty of holding the executive to account. In addition, many developing countries are still struggling to develop a durable culture of the rule of law, without which there is little prospect of investment or sustained economic development.

Yet for many 'the rule of law' remains an elusive concept. It is a principle that can be readily agreed upon but, when one tries to define it, to explain its content or to elaborate its often subtle texture, the analysis becomes more challenging. One of the few who have attempted that analysis is of course Tom Bingham himself, in the eight principles he articulated in the sixth David Williams Annual Lecture (2006), and in his subsequent writings.

It was against this background that, on the same evening as Tom's Grotius Lecture, on 17 November 2008, the British Institute of International and Comparative Law announced its intention to establish the Bingham Centre for the Rule of Law, and launched an Appeal to achieve that. The essential premise behind this initiative was, and is, that the rule of law is a concept of fundamental importance in itself, which needs and requires to be studied, debated, articulated and defended as a subject in its own right, across many different areas of law—whether human rights, investment treaties, antitrust or whatever —across national boundaries, and across different legal systems, whether domestic or international. The Institute, with its long tradition of scholarship in the sphere of international and comparative law, finds itself uniquely placed to establish the Bingham Centre, specifically dedicated to the study of the Rule of Law. What could be more appropriate than to create that Centre in honour of the President of the Institute, Tom Bingham himself, who readily agreed to guide the Centre through its early years.

Or so it was hoped and intended. On 6 December 2010, two years on from that Grotius Lecture, the official launch of the Bingham Centre for the Rule of Law, under its recently appointed Director, Professor Jeffrey Jowell QC, will take place co-incidentally with the publication of this work. To the great sadness of all, Tom himself, the inspiration of the project, will not be there. It is of some small comfort that, before his death on 11 September last, he knew that the launch of the Centre was imminent, and was able to congratulate Jeffrey Jowell on his appointment as Director.

The Centre, however, is determined to carry on the principles for which Tom Bingham stood, with an energetic programme of study, debate and promotion of the rule of law, both nationally and internationally, involving among others, judges, practitioners, academics, politicians, regulators, officials, those in industry and commerce, and the non-governmental and charity sectors. All those who wish to participate are cordially invited to do so; and, on a practical note, to contribute, if thought fit, to the Bingham Appeal by which the Centre is funded (see www.biicl.org/binghamcentre).

The lectures published in this book range across international law, human rights and business, issues affecting the European Union and competition law in particular, investment protection, tort, and international cooperation in criminal law enforcement. Such a broad canvas represents a preview of much hard work to come. As the work of the Bingham Centre for the Rule of Law goes forward, one might perhaps reflect on the wisdom of Lacordaire:

> Between the strong and the weak, between the rich and the poor, between the master and the servant, it is liberty that oppresses and the law that sets free.[1]

**Sir Christopher Bellamy QC**
**Chairman, Appeal Board of the Bingham Centre for the Rule of Law**

---

[1] Henri Lacordaire, Speech given at the *52e Conférence de Notre-Dame, Paris* (1848).

# Introduction

*Robert McCorquodale*

On 17 November 2008 the British Institute of International and Comparative Law celebrated its 50th anniversary. Its heritage was much longer, having been created by the merger of the Society of Comparative Legislation (founded in 1894) and the Grotius Society (founded in 1915 and named after the 16th century Dutch jurist Hugo Grotius, regarded as one of the founders of international law). This merger created an independent research body, unaffiliated to any university and also a charity, which is committed to the understanding, development and practical application of international and comparative law.

The Institute, of which I became the seventh full-time Director in January 2008, celebrated its 50th anniversary in two primary ways. First there was a major event on its birthday, being the Grotius Lecture given by its President, Lord Bingham, followed by a dinner open to the many members and supporters of the Institute. The dinner included a speech by Jack Straw MP, the Secretary of State for Justice, and he and Tom Bingham cut the birthday cake. Second, there were a series of evening lectures covering the main areas of the Institute's work by leading lawyers in the area, together with the Institute's Senior Research Fellows. These lectures were spread throughout the year and chaired by eminent persons.

The common theme across all these lectures was the rule of law. The rule of law in international and comparative legal context had been an implied (and sometimes express) theme underlying many of the Institute's activities—in its research, its events and its publications—during its 50 years. However, it was not always evident how this theme could be expressly dealt with across the various areas of expertise of the Institute's President, Director and Senior Research Fellows.

The starting point was Tom Bingham's own work.[1] In his judicial decisions and scholarly writing he had developed a clear and distinctive emphasis on the rule of law. These were set out by him in terms of eight sub-rules or principles:

---

[1] The connections between Tom Bingham's work and that of the Institute are explored in R McCorquodale, 'The Rule of Law Internationally: Tom Bingham and the British Institute of International and Comparative Law' in M Andenas and D Fairgrieve (eds), *Tom Bingham and the Transformation of the Law* (OUP, Oxford, 2009) 137–146.

1.  The law must be accessible and, so far as possible, be intelligible, clear and predictable;
2.  Questions of legal right and liability should ordinarily be resolved by application of the law and not by the exercise of discretion;
3.  The law should apply equally to all, except to the extent that objective differences justify differentiation;
4.  The law must afford adequate protection of human rights;
5.  Means must be provided for resolving, without prohibitive cost or inordinate delay, bona fide civil disputes which the parties themselves are unable to resolve;
6.  Ministers and public officers at all levels must exercise the powers conferred on them reasonably, in good faith, for the purpose for which the powers were conferred, and without exceeding the limits of such powers;
7.  Judicial and other adjudicative procedures must be fair and independent; and
8.  There must be compliance by the State with its international law obligations.[2]

He developed these in his superb book called *The Rule of Law*.[3] In the Grotius Lecture as part of the 50th anniversary activities, Tom Bingham applied the rule of law to the international legal system. This Lecture (reproduced in this book) was a magnificent and historic occasion as the leading judge of our time dealt with these issues carefully, coherently and incisively, including considering the consequences of applying the rule of law in terms of the illegality of the Iraq war. It led to front-page news across the British press. The untimely death of this wonderful, intelligent, humane and humble man has deprived the world of more of his insights. However, I am heartened by the fact that he knew that the Institute would continue his work in terms of the establishment within the Institute of the Bingham Centre for the Rule of Law.

Each of the lecturers in the 50th anniversary series then dealt with different aspects of the rule of law. The series was intended to showcase the broad scope of the Institute's work across a range of contemporary legal issues, inviting fresh thinking and debate. The series was as follows:

*The Rule of Law and EU Competition*
8 October 2008

Chair: Sir Christopher Bellamy QC, Senior Consultant, Linklaters LLP; former Judge, European Court of the First Instance; former President of the British Competition Appeals Tribunal

---

[2] T Bingham, 'The Rule of Law' 66 Cambridge Law Journal (2007) 67, 69–84.
[3] T Bingham, *The Rule of Law* (Penguin, Allen Lane, London, 2010).

Speakers:
Tim Cowen, General Counsel and Commercial Director, BT Global Services
Dr Philip Marsden, Institute Senior Research Fellow in Competition Law,
Director of the Competition Law Forum
This event was kindly sponsored by Linklaters LLP

*Business, the International Rule of Law and Human Rights*
26 November 2008

Chair: Jeremy Carver CBE, Senior Consultant Clifford Chance LLP,
Institute Trustee, Board member Transparency International; Trustee
International Rescue Committee–UK
Speakers:
Mary Robinson, former UN High Commissioner for Human Rights; former
President of Ireland, Founder, Realizing Rights: The Ethical Globalization
Initiative
Professor Robert McCorquodale, Institute Director; Professor of
International Law and Human Rights, University of Nottingham
This event was kindly sponsored by Linklaters LLP

*Investment Protection and the Rule of Law: Change or Decline?*
17 March 2009

Chair: Paula Hodges, Herbert Smith LLP
Speakers:
L Yves Fortier CC QC, former Ambassador for Canada and Permanent
Representative to the United Nations; Chairman, Ogilvy Renault, Montreal
Norah Gallagher, Institute Senior Research Fellow in International
Investment and Trade Law; Director of the Investment Treaty Forum
This event was kindly sponsored by Herbert Smith LLP

*Uses and Abuses of Comparative Tort Law*
23 April 2009

Chair: Lord Bingham of Cornhill KG, President of the Institute
Speakers:
Professor Jane Stapleton, Ernest E Smith Professor of Law at the University
of Texas School of Law; Statutory Visiting Professor and Member of the
Law Faculty of Oxford University
John Fleming Centre for Advancement of Legal Research, The Australian
National University College of Law
Professor Jeroen Kortmann, Professor of European Tort Law, University of
Amsterdam; Partner, Stibbe, Amsterdam
Dr Duncan Fairgrieve, Institute Senior Research Fellow in Comparative
Law; Director, Product Liability Forum

*International Co-Operation and the Modern Prosecutor*
2 June 2009

Chair: Professor Robert Sullivan Professor of Law, University College London
Speakers: Keir Starmer QC, Director of Public Prosecutions; former joint head, Doughty Street Chambers
Dr Sarah Williams, Institute's Senior Research Fellow (Dorset Fellow) in Public International Law

As the topics and the eminence of the speakers attest, this series shows the breadth and depth of the matters that encompass international and comparative law, and their relevance to contemporary practice. The Institute was deeply honoured to have such a selection of the leading lawyers and senior researchers who offered their thoughts on these matters and then agreed to have them published in this book. I thank them all. I also thank the members of Institute staff who enabled these events and publications to occur.

Throughout its 50 years the Institute has retained its mission to provide high quality research, education and informed discussion, and publications. This will continue to be developed and built on in the years ahead, including by the Bingham Centre for the Rule of Law. Indeed, when the Institute was founded, the Editorial in the Institute's world-renowned journal, the *International and Comparative Law Quarterly*, stated that:

> [I]t is intended that the Institute will become in time the principal British organisation for the encouragement of research and for exchange of views in the whole field of international and comparative law, and that it will be used as a source of objective data by all those concerned— lawyers, government officials, business concerns and others—both in this country and abroad ... [and] make a useful and indeed important contribution to international peace and understanding.[4]

As I hope this book attests, the Institute in its 50 years has achieved the aims of its founders, including in encouraging research, events and publication of exchanges of views in the field of international and comparative law, and making an important contribution to the rule of law internationally.

---

[4] Editorial, (1959) 8 ICLQ.

# CHAPTER 1

# The Rule of Law in the International Legal Order*

*Tom Bingham*

THE RULE OF LAW REQUIRES COMPLIANCE BY THE STATE WITH ITS OBLIGATIONS
IN INTERNATIONAL LAW AS IN NATIONAL LAW

I used to be much attracted by the description of public international law as 'The Law of Nations'. It seemed to reflect the lustre of Gentili and Grotius, to invest the subject with a grandeur and dignity separating it from the mundane concerns of everyday life, to conjure up a vision of proud and equal sovereigns, declining to bow the knee to one another but condescending to parley through the medium of their immune envoys. I now think, for very much the same reasons and others, that the expression, if not actually pernicious, is better avoided. For although international law comprises a distinct and recognizable body of law with its own rules and institutions, it is a body of law complementary to the national laws of individual States, and in no way antagonistic to them; it is not a thing apart; it rests on similar principles and pursues similar ends; and observance of the rule of law is quite as important on the international plane as on the national, perhaps even more so. Consistently with this, the current Ministerial Code, binding on British ministers, requires them as an overarching duty to 'comply with the law including international law and treaty obligations'.[1]

In his report of 23 August 2004 to the Security Council, the Secretary-General of the United Nations spoke of the rule of law as a concept at the very heart of the organization's mission. He continued:

It refers to a principle of governance in which all persons, institutions and entities, public and private, including the State itself, are accountable to laws that are publicly promulgated, equally enforced and independently

---

* Lecture as printed in *The Rule of Law* (Allen Lane, London, 2010). Reprinted with kind permission from Allen Lane.
[1] Ministerial Code, July 2007, para 1.2.

adjudicated, and which are consistent with international human rights norms and standards. It requires, as well, measures to ensure adherence to the principles of supremacy of law, equality before the law, account-ability to the law, fairness in the application of the law, separation of powers, participation in decision-making, legal certainty, avoidance of arbitrariness and procedural and legal transparency.[2]

Nothing in this formulation points towards a concept different from that familiar in the domestic sphere. Nor does the formulation of Professor William Bishop, who, having posed the question 'What do we mean by "international Rule of Law"?' proceeded to answer the question:

Without precise definition, I believe we could agree that the concept includes reliance on law as opposed to arbitrary power in international relations; the substitution of settlement by law for settlement by force; and the realization that law can and should be used as an instrumental-ity for the cooperative international furtherance of social aims, in such fashion as to preserve and promote the values of freedom and human dignity for individuals.[3]

He quoted a former president of the American Bar Association:

The rule of law within nations ... connotes the existence of the hundreds of legal rules, the legal procedures, courts, and other institutions which in sum total add up to order and stability, equality, liberty, and individ-ual freedom ... The rule of law among nations means the regulation of mutual intercourse of nations, and international contacts and relations of individuals, by legal concepts, standards, institutions and procedures.[4]

This would suggest that the rule of law in the international order is, to a considerable extent at least, the domestic rule of law writ large. Such an impression is fortified by two further sources. According to Professor Chesterman, ' "the international rule of law" may be understood as the application of rule of law principles to relations between States and other subjects of international law'.[5] In their Millennium Declaration the member states of the United Nations resolved to 'strengthen respect for the rule of law in international as in national affairs and, in particular, to ensure

---

[2] S/2004/16, 23 August 2004, para 6.
[3] W Bishop, 'The International Rule of Law' (1961) Michigan Law Review, 59, 553.
[4] C Rhyner, Opening Statement before Boston Conference on World Peace through Law, 27 March 1959.
[5] S Chesterman, 'An International Rule of Law?' (2008) 56 American Journal of Comparative Law 2, 355.

compliance by Member States with the decisions of the International Court of Justice, in compliance with the Charter of the United Nations, in cases to which they are parties'.[6]

The analogy, even if inexact, with the domestic situation makes plain, I suggest, why we should favour strict compliance with the law. However much any of us as individuals might relish the opportunity to live our lives free of all legal constraints—whether to pay taxes, observe the Highway code, obtain planning permission, discharge our debts or refrain from assaulting our next-door neighbour—we know quite well that acceptance of these constraints is the necessary price to be paid for their observance by others and that a society in which no one was subject to such constraints would not be a very congenial one. Then there might indeed be no such thing as society. The same is true in the international sphere. However attractive it might be for a single State to be free of the legal constraints that bind all other States, those States are unlikely to tolerate such a situation for very long and in the meantime the solo State would lose the benefits and protections that international agreement can confer. The rule of the jungle is no more tolerable in a big jungle.

The point is not infrequently made that there is no international legislature, which is, of course, strictly speaking true, and that international law, as a result, lacks the legitimacy which endorsement by a democratic legislature would give. This does not impress me as a very powerful argument. The means by which an obligation becomes binding on a State in international law seem to be quite as worthy of respect as a measure approved, perhaps in haste and without adequate inquiry, perhaps on a narrowly divided vote, by a national legislature. This is true of treaties to which, by signature and ratification, the State has formally and solemnly committed itself. It is true of 'international custom, as evidence of a general practice accepted as law', since the threshold condition—very widespread observance, as a matter of legal obligation—is not easily satisfied. It is true of 'general principles of law recognized by civilized nations',[7] since such principles carry strong prescriptive authority. The failure of a national legislature to annul a treaty, or reject a rule of customary international law, or disown a general principle of law recognized by civilized nations, may properly be relied on as evidence at least of acquiescence.

In his illuminating recent book, *International Law*, Professor Vaughan Lowe QC poses the question: 'Why do people comply with international law?'[8] I pause to draw attention to the premise of his question, which is that by and large people, including of course States, do comply with international

---

[6] Millennium Declaration, GA Res 55/2, UN Doc A/RES/55(2) (2000).

[7] I have followed the formulation in art 38 of the Statute of the International Court of Justice (1945).

[8] *International Law* (OUP, Oxford, 2007), 18.

law. This is a very important premise, since it is easy, not least for lawyers, to become mesmerized by breaches of the law and overlook the overwhelming mass of transactions which proceed smoothly, routinely and lawfully. In the domestic sphere, goods are bought and sold, land is conveyed, testamentary bequests take effect and people walk unmolested in the streets because the law is clear and departure from it is the exception, not the rule. So it is in the international sphere also, and international law is not, as sometimes supposed, a code more honoured in the breach than in the observance. Indeed, Professor Lowe observes that this 'view, particularly widespread among those whose vision is unsullied by any knowledge or experience of the matter, is hopelessly wrong'.[9] In answering his own question, the Professor relies on the fact that international law is not imposed on States by an external legislature,[10] and suggests that a powerful reason why States do comply, and always have complied, with international law is that they make the rules to suit themselves.[11] They are the rules of a members', not a proprietor's, club. He suggests other reasons also, among them the tendency to err on the side of caution, habit, and the similarity of outlook among many of those who govern the nations and among the high priesthood of international lawyers who advise the chancelleries of the world.[12]

Most potent of all reasons for compliance by States with international law is the sheer necessity of their doing so. The point was well made by Douglas Hurd, in a passage in a 1997 book quoted by Professor Lowe as the outside of his own book:

> [N]ation states are ... incompetent. Not one of them, not even the United States as the single remaining super-power, can adequately provide for the needs that its citizens now articulate. The extent of that incompetence has become sharply clearer during this century. The inadequacy of national governments to provide security, prosperity or a decent environment has brought into being a huge array of international rules, conferences and institutions; the only answer to the puzzle of the immortal but incompetent nation state is effective co-operation between those states for all the purposes that lie beyond the reach of any one of them.[13]

The earliest rules of international law can, I think, be attributed to the self-interest of States, the need to do as one would be done by (I have in mind rules such as those governing the duty to comply with treaty obligations, the equality and immunity of sovereigns, or the immunity of diplo-

---

[9] ibid 30.              [10] ibid 19.
[11] ibid.                [12] ibid 21–2.
[13] D Hurd, *The Search for Peace* (Warner Books, 1997) 6.

matic representatives) and recognition that there are some mischiefs which can only be effectively addressed if addressed by more States than one (such as piracy). But the passage of time has highlighted the number of situations in which a problem cannot be effectively regulated on a national basis. The international regulation of telecommunications, dating back to 1865, and mail services, dating back to 1874, are two examples. The international carriage of goods by sea provides another: shipowners, charterers, shippers and consignees must, to the greatest extent possible, enjoy the same rights and be subject to the same obligations at the port of loading, the port of discharge and any intermediate port of call, not rights and obligations peculiar to the national law of the port in question. Hence the Hague Rules of 1924, as amended by the Brussels Protocol of 1968. Hence too the Warsaw Convention 1929 on carriage by air, amended at The Hague in 1955 and further amended at Montreal in 1999. Hence also the CMR Convention on the Contract for International Carriage of Goods by Road made at Geneva in 1956 and now, no doubt, applying to the juggernauts from eastern Europe which familiarly thunder up and down the motorways of western Europe.

These are far from unimportant examples. They give effect to Lord Mansfield's insight (quoted in Chapter 3) that if commerce is to prosper investors and businessmen must know where they stand, not only in the UK but abroad. Important as they are, however, such examples scarcely scratch the surface of the current need for international cooperation in tackling problems which are national, in the sense that they afflict single States, but also international, in the sense that they afflict more States than one and can only be tackled jointly. I can make no more than cursory reference to some of these.

It is a matter of history that at the Bretton Woods conference, held in 1944 as the Second World War was approaching its end, the Great Powers sought to lay the foundations of international economic stability in the aftermath of war, a movement which led to establishment of the International Monetary Fund and the World Bank and, less directly, to the General Agreement on Tariffs and Trade. Here were serious, effective and strictly controlled international schemes to promote development, relieve poverty and raise living standards, reinforced by establishment of the International Centre for the Settlement of Investment Disputes and the Multilateral Investment Guarantee Agency. Regional international groups such as the European Union and the Caribbean Commercial Community have many of the same objects. It is hard to suppose that the traumatic market experience which followed the collapse of the American sub-prime mortgage market in 2007–2009 will not strengthen the hands of those who wish to stiffen such international controls as now exist of the conduct and lending practices of international institutions.

The propensity of criminals who have committed a crime in one jurisdiction to fly to another where they hope to escape apprehension is in no
way novel. Nor is the making of bilateral treaties for the extradition of such
criminals (usually, with some unfortunate exceptions, on a reciprocal basis).
But the need to apprehend and try serious criminals has been greatly
strengthened by a number of causes: among them are the increased ease,
with modern methods of business and means of communication, of
committing a crime in one State of which the effects are felt in another; the
utter abhorrence now felt for those who commit the most serious of crimes
such as genocide, torture and war crimes; and the international activity of
that special brand of criminals whom we stigmatize as terrorists, whose acts
of violence are not constrained by national boundaries. These cross-border
problems call for cross-border solutions, which can only be provided by a
coherent body of enforceable international rules. So it is not surprising, for
example, to find the Member States of the European Union devising a
streamlined means (the European arrest warrant) of procuring the surrender of criminals by and to each other, with much less formality and much
less scope for delay than was formerly the norm, a system described as
providing for the free movement of judgments.[14] It is not surprising that
agreement is reached to extend the jurisdiction of national courts to try the
most serious offences, such as genocide, torture and war crimes, wherever
the crimes were committed. It is not surprising to find the United Nations
establishing an International Criminal Court to try the most serious crimes
which will not be tried elsewhere, and ad hoc tribunals to try serious crimes
committed in the former Yugoslavia and in Rwanda. It is not surprising to
find the United Nations urgently calling on Member States to take measures
to combat the scourge of terrorism.

If international cooperation is the key to successful action against cross-
border criminal activity, it is also essential to secure effective protection of
the environment. That is so whether one considers the conservation of a
scarce natural resource such as fish, or the activity of one State which causes
pollution in another or, pre-eminently, the emission of carbon into the
atmosphere. In areas such as these the interests of different State are, in one
sense, inherently antithetical. All States want to maintain prosperous fish-
ing fleets, free to catch what they can. All wish to encourage profitable
activity without restrictive environmental controls. All wish to maintain,
and preferably enhance, their prosperity and the living standards of their
people. But of course they know that if fish stocks are depleted beyond a

[14] See *King's Prosecutor, Brussels, Office of the v Cando Armas* [2005] UKHL 67, [2006]
2 AC 1; *Dabas v High Court of Justice in Madrid, Spain* [2007] UKHL 6 [2007] 2 AC 31;
*Pilecki v Circuit Court of Legnica, Poland* [2008] UKHL 7, [2008] 1 WLR 325; *Caldarelli v
Judge for Preliminary Investigations of the Court of Naples, Italy* [2008] UKHL 51, [2008] 1
WLR 1724.

certain point, all lose; freedom to pollute may mean liability to be polluted; and each State knows (or ought to know) that other States will not take the stringent steps necessary to control climate change if it does not. None, I think, can doubt that if effective measures are not taken, on an international basis, to combat climate change, new meaning will be given to Keynes's aphorism that in the long run we are all dead.

Even a cursory and incomplete sketch such as this cannot ignore the international protection of human rights. Such international protection is significant, I suggest, for at least five reasons. First, it is founded on values which, if not universally shared, command very wide acceptance throughout most of the world. No other field of law, perhaps, rests so directly on a moral foundation, the belief that every human being, simply by virtue of his or her existence, is entitled to certain very basic, and in some instances unqualified, rights and freedoms.

Secondly, such international protection is relatively new, essentially a post-Second World War phenomenon inspired by the Universal Declaration on Human Rights of 1948 and followed by the International Covenants on Civil and Political Rights and Economic, Social and Cultural Rights of 1966, a string of later Conventions such as those on the Elimination of All Forms of Racial Discrimination against Women (1979) and that on the Rights of the Child (1989), quite apart from regional instruments such as the European and American Conventions and the African and Arab Charters. Such protection as existed before 1945 was largely extended on a national basis.

Thirdly, the closeness of the relationship between the international protection of human rights and the rule of law has been increasingly recognized. Not until 1996 did the Security Council make express reference to the rule of law in the operative paragraph of a resolution;[15] but it has done so very frequently since. By contrast, the European Court of Human Rights first referred to the rule of law in 1975,[16] and has done so with great consistency since. In 2007 28 judgments of the court referred to the rule of law, in January and February 2008 alone no fewer than 10.[17] In a judgment of 22 November 2007, the Court declared that 'the rule of law, one of the fundamental principles of a democratic society, is inherent in all the Articles of the Convention'.[18] After a slow start, the European Court of Justice referred in an obiter dictum in 1969 to 'the fundamental human rights enshrined in the general principles of Community law and protected by the

---

[15] Chesterman (n 5) 348.

[16] In *Golder v United Kingdom* (1975) 1 EHRR 524, para 54.

[17] Judge Mark Villiger, in a paper based on his oral contribution at the first International Law in Domestic Courts colloquium, held in The Hague on 28 March 2008, paras 2(a) and (b).

[18] *Ukraine-Tyumen v Ukraine*, 22 November 2007, para 49.

Court'.[19] Very soon the European Convention acquired a special and central role as a source for identifying fundamental rights,[20] and a judge of the European Court of Justice (Antonio Tizzano) has written of 'the defining characteristics of a Community that is first of all a community of principles and values at the heart of which are fundamental rights, constitutionalism, democracy and the rule of law'.[21]

Fourthly, the international protection of human rights is important to the rule of law internationally because of the extent to which national courts are drawn into the process of determining questions of international law. And, lastly, it is important because this is a field in which individual claimants feature very prominently, giving the lie to the old belief that the purview of international law is confined to the regulation of inter-state relations.

The notion that there is a great gulf fixed between national and international law is contradicted both by the osmotic absorption of customary international law into national law, as strikingly illustrated by the Court of Appeal's decision in *Trendtex Trading Corporation v Central Bank of Nigeria*,[22] upheld by the House of Lords in *I Congreso del Partido*[23] (General Pinochet's first appearance on the English forensic scene), but also and even more prominently by the involvement of the national courts, here and elsewhere, in deciding questions of international law. In his very interesting Michael Kirby Lecture in International Law delivered in Canberra in June 2008,[24] Professor James Crawford SC reviewed and compared the activity of the House of Lords and the High Court of Australia in this field over the period 1996–2008, almost the whole span of Justice Kirby's membership of the High Court. His survey showed that over that period the House of Lords had given judgment on questions of international law in 49 cases. The breakdown, on his analysis, of the aspects involved was as follows:

- Relation between treaty law and national law                                      7
- Relation between customary international law and national law       1
- Treaty interpretation                                                                              5
- State immunity                                                                                         4

---

[19] *Erich Stauder v City of Ulm-Sozialamt* [1969] ECR 419, para 7.
[20] A Tizzano, 'The Rule of the ECJ in the Protection of Fundamental Rights' in A Arnull, P Eeckhout and T Tridimas (eds), *Continuity and Change in EU Law: Essays in Honour of Sir Francis Jacobs* (OUP, Oxford, 2008) 138.
[21] ibid 138.
[22] [1977] QB 529.
[23] [1983] AC 244.
[24] 'International Law in the House of Lords and the High Court of Australia 1996–2008: A Comparison' The First Michael Kirby Lecture in International Law, Canberra, 27 June 2008.

- Refugee Convention obligations                          8
- Other international human rights                        12
- Extradition                                            6
- Extra-territorial jurisdiction                          3
- Miscellaneous                                          3

His last (miscellaneous) heading embraced compensation of the armed forces for injuries sustained abroad, challenge to an arbitral award and inconsistency between decisions of the European Court of Human Rights and domestic case laws. The total would have been significantly higher had decisions pertaining to European Community law been included.

For purposes of his comparison, Professor Crawford reviewed the response of the two courts to four problems which both courts addressed. The upshot of the comparison is not important for present purposes, but the problems addressed are, I think, of interest as showing the range of international law problems arising for decision in national courts. One turned on the meaning of 'a particular social group' as a ground of persecution under article 1A(2) of the 1951 Refugee Convention. On this point the House made what in my opinion (I was not a party to it) was a bold but correct decision in *R v Immigration Appeal Tribunal, ex p. Shah*,[25] followed more recently in *Fornah v Secretary of State for the Home Department*.[26] The first of these cases related to the treatment of married women suspected of adultery in Pakistan, the second to female genital mutilation in Sierra Leone. Those affected were held to be members of a 'particular social group'. A second question discussed by Professor Crawford, also arising under the Refugee Convention, was the applicability of the Convention where the persecution complained of is not by agents of the state. On that issue of interpretation of the Convention the House again ruled.[27] A third issue addressed by Professor Crawford was indefinite executive detention, on which the British courts made decisions relating both to derogation from the European Convention under article 15 and compatibility with article 5 ('the *Belmarsh* case')[28] and the justification under Security Council Resolution 1546 and article 103 of the United Nations Charter for detaining an Iraqi/UK national in Iraq (*Al-Jedda*).[29] The fourth of the Professor's examples examined the question, canvassed in both the High Court and the House of Lords, of whether unincorporated treaties

---

[25] [1999] 2 AC 629.

[26] [2006] UKHL 46, [2007] 1 AC 412.

[27] *Adan v Secretary of State for the Home Department* [1999] 1 AC 293; *Horvath v Secretary of State for the Home Department* [2001] 1 AC 489.

[28] *A v Secretary of State of the Home Department* [2004] UKHL 56, [2005] 2 AC 68.

[29] *R (Al-Jedda) v Secretary of State for Defence (JUSTICE intervening)* [2007] UKHL 58, [2008] 1 AC 332.

could give rise to legitimate expectations of a kind which could constrain official action, an issue on which an initial divergence of view between the two jurisdictions appears to have narrowed.[30] The cases chosen by Professor Crawford for purposes of comparison were, of course, a very small sample. The breadth of the field is made clear in Shaheed Fatima's interesting recent book, *Using International Law in Domestic Courts*,[31] in which the author lists the main practice areas where issues of international law may arise in national courts: they are aviation law, commercial and intellectual property law, criminal law, employment and industrial relations law, environmental law, European treaties, family and child law, human rights law, immigration and asylum law, immunities and privileges, international organizations, jurisdiction, law of the sea, treaties and, finally, warfare and weapons law. In recent years the British courts have ruled on questions arising in most of these areas. The interrelationship of national law and international law, substantively and procedurally, is such that the rule of law cannot plausibly be regarded as applicable on one plane but not on the other.

WAR

The last of Shaheed Fatima's headings points to what many, encouraged by Grotius, would reasonably regard as the most fundamental preoccupation of international law: the resort to war, the conduct of war and the rights and duties of an occupying power after a war is over (or, in the legal vernacular, the ius ad bellum, the ius in bello and the ius post bellum). In these areas above all, scrupulous observance of the rule of law may be seen to serve the common interest of mankind.

As Professor Sir Michael Howard has observed, 'war, armed conflict between organized political groups, has been the universal norm in human history'.[32] He quotes Sir Henry Maine, who in 1888 wrote that 'War appears to be as old an mankind, but peace is a modern invention.' Sir Henry spoke too soon. The Hague Conferences of 1899 and 1907, while seeking to humanize the conduct of war, recognized the use of force as an available option. The Covenant of the League of Nations discouraged resort to force, but did not prohibit it. Not until the Kellogg-Brand Pact of 1928 (ratified by Germany, the United States, Belgium, France, Britain and

---

[30] *Minister for Immigration and Ethnic Affairs v Teoh* (1995) 183 CLR 273; R *(European Roma Rights Centre) v Immigration Officer at Prague Airport (UNHCR intervening)* [2004] UKHL 55, [2005] 1 AC 1; R v Asfaw *(UNHCR intervening)* [2008] UKHL 31, [2008] AC 1061; *Re Minister for Immigration and Multicultural Affairs, ex p Lam* (2003) 214 CLR 1.
[31] (Hart Publishing, Oxford, 2005) ch 1, 3–26.
[32] *The Invention of Peace & the Reinvention of War* (Profile Books, 2002) 1.

its overseas Dominions, Italy, Japan, Poland, Czechoslovakia and Ireland) was there any renunciation of warfare as an option open to States as an instrument of national policy. But the making of the pact did not, over the coming decades, deter Japan from invading Manchuria, Italy from invading Abyssinia, Russia from invading Finland, Germany from invading most of Europe or Japan from invading large swaths of south-east Asia. Clearly it was necessary for the States of the world to make a further attempt to outlaw a practice whose evil results had been so amply demonstrated.

The Charter of the United Nations, adopted in 1945, to which 192 independent states have acceded, did just that. Having enjoined Member States to settle their international disputes by peaceful means, it required them in article 2(4) to 'refrain in their international relations from the threat or use of force against the territorial integrity or political independence of any state, or in any other manner inconsistent with the Purposes of the United Nations'. Primary responsibility for taking prompt and effective action for the maintenance of international peace and security was conferred on the Security Council, which was authorized to act on behalf of Member States.[33] Chapter VII of the Charter, covering threats to and breaches of the peace, provides in article 39 that 'The Security Council shall determine the existence of any threat to the peace, breach of the peace or act of aggression and shall make recommendations, or decide what measure shall be taken in accordance with Articles 41 and 42, to maintain or restore international peace and security.' Article 41 is directed to measures decided on by the Security Council which do not involve the use of armed force. Article 42 is directed to military measures and provides: 'Should the Security Council consider that measures provided for in Article 41 would be inadequate or have proved to be inadequate, it may take such action by air, sea, or land forces as may be necessary to maintain or restore international peace and security ...'. This provision has been interpreted in a way very similar to the right of personal self-defence in domestic law: there must be an armed attack on the State or a threat of imminent attack; the use of force must be necessary and other means of meeting or averting the attached unavailable; the response must be proportionate and strictly limited to defence against the attack or threatened attack. There is controversy whether force may exceptionally be used to avert an overwhelming humanitarian catastrophe, but otherwise the law under the Charter is clear: save in self-defence, force may be used if authorized by the Security Council but not otherwise. Unilateral resort to war is replaced by collective decision-making in the Security Council on behalf of all Member States.

Despite this apparently clear and unambiguous regime, an American academic author writing in 2005 recorded that in the past 25 years the

---

[33] Art 24(1).

United States had been involved in some 40 military actions, including wars in Iraq, Afghanistan and Yugoslavia; regime-changing invasions in Grenada, Panama and Haiti; military assistance to rebel groups in Angola, El Salvador and Nicaragua; and missile attacks in Lebanon, Libya, Yemen and Sudan.[34] Of these, by far the most contentious was the US-led invasion of Iraq in 2003.

It is not at all clear to me what, if any, legal justification of its action the US Government relied on. Prominent figures in the administration made clear their ambition to remove Saddam Hussein and replace his governmental regime,[35] and British officials gave assurances of the UK's support for regime change.[36] But the British Attorney General, Lord Goldsmith QC, was consistent in his advice that while regime change might be a result of disarming Saddam Hussein, it could not in itself be a lawful objective of military action.[37]

Sir Michael Wood, formerly the senior Legal Adviser to the Foreign and Commonwealth Office but now speaking in a purely personal capacity, has said that the British intervention in Iraq raised no great issue of principle: 'the legality of the use of force in March 2003 turned solely on whether or not it had been authorized by the Council. No one disputes that the Council can authorize the use of force. The question was simply whether it had done so. That turned on the interpretation of a series of Security Council resolutions.'[38] This was the approach taken by the Attorney General in his full written advice of 7 March 2003 to the Prime Minister (not made public at the time) and in his more summary statement published on 17 March 2003, a few days before fighting began.

In the earlier opinion the Attorney General addressed in some detail the interrelationship between three Security Council resolutions, respectively numbered 678, 687 and 1441. Resolution 678 was passed in 1991: it built on earlier resolutions calling for the withdrawal of Iraq from Kuwait following its invasion of that country and authorized the use of force to eject Iraq from Kuwait and restore peace and security in the area. This was the authorization of Operation Desert Storm, which drove the Iraqis out of Kuwait. Resolution 687 (1991) brought military operations to an end, imposing conditions on Iraq with regard to weapons of mass destruction and inspection. It suspended but did not revoke resolution 678. Resolution 1441 was adopted unanimously in November 2002. It recorded that Iraq

[34] R Peerenboom, 'Human Rights and the Rule of Law: What's the Relationship?', Georgetown Journal of International Law (2004–5) 36 936–937.
[35] P Sands, *Lawless World* (Allen Lane, London, 2005) 182.
[36] M Danner, *The Secret Way to War* (New York Review of Books, 2006), pp 129, 134.
[37] ibid 91; Advice to the Prime Minister, 'Iraq: Resolution 1441' 7 March 2003.
[38] Sir Michael Wood KCMG, Hersch Lauterpacht Memorial Lecture 2006, Third Lecture, 'The Security Council and the Use of Force', 9 November 2006, para 9.

had been and remained in material breach of its obligations under relevant resolutions, including 687. It offered Iraq a final opportunity to comply with its disarmament obligations. It established a stricter inspection regime and provided that further breaches would be reported to the Security Council for it 'to consider the situation and the need for full compliance with all of the relevant Council resolutions in order to secure international peace and security'. In his earlier opinion the Attorney General considered that resolution 1441 could in principle revive the authority to use force, but only if the Security Council determined that there was a violation of the conditions of the ceasefire sufficiently serious to destroy the basis of it. The Attorney General reviewed the competing arguments: on the one hand, that there was authority to use force if the Council discussed the matter, even if it did not reach a conclusion; on the other, that nothing short of a further Council decision would provide a legitimate basis for using force. He saw force in both arguments, but concluded that resolution 1441 left the position unclear and that the safest legal course would be to secure the adoption of a further resolution to authorize the use of force. A reasonable case could be made that resolution 1441 was capable in principle of reviving the authorization in resolution 678, but the argument could only be sustainable if there were 'strong factual grounds' for concluding that Iraq had failed to take the final opportunity. There would need to be 'hard evidence'.

In his summary statement of 17 March the Attorney General stated that a material breach of resolution 687 revived the authority to use force under resolution 678; that in resolution 1441 the Security Council had determined that Iraq had been and was in material breach of resolution 687; that resolution 1441 had given Iraq a final opportunity to comply with its disarmament obligations and had warned it of serious consequences if it did not comply; that the Council had also decided in resolution 1441 that any failure to cooperate in implementing resolution 1441 would be a further material breach; that it was 'plain' that Iraq had failed to comply and therefore was at the time of resolution 1441 and continued to be in material breach; and that accordingly the authority to use force under resolution 678 had revived and continued to that date. He ended: 'Resolution 1441 would in terms have provided that a further decision of the Security Council to sanction force was required if that had been intended. Thus, all that Resolution 1441 requires is reporting to and discussion by the Security Council of Iraq's failures, but not an express further decision to authorise force.'

This statement was, I think, flawed in two fundamental respects. First, it was not plain that Iraq had failed to comply in a manner justifying resort to force and there were no strong factual grounds or hard evidence to show that it had: Hans Blix and his team of weapons inspectors had found no weapons of mass destruction, were making progress and expected to complete their task in a matter of months. Secondly, it cannot be accepted that a determination whether Iraq had failed to avail itself of its final opportunity was intended to be taken otherwise that collectively by the Security Council. The revival argument itself has been ill-received. Lord Alexander of Weedon QC in his brilliant Tom Sargant memorial annual lecture for JUSTICE of 14 October 2003 (without access to the Attorney General's earlier advice) described it as 'unconvincing'.[39] Professor Sands QC has called it 'a bad argument'.[40] Professor Lowe has described the argument as 'fatuous': 'The whole point of the UN system is that when the Security Council is seised of a problem it is the Council, and not individual Member States, that has the right to control matters. If the Security Council had intended that the United States, the United Kingdom and others should invade Iraq in 2003 with its blessing and its mandate, it would have said so. It did not.'[41]

If I am right that the invasion of Iraq by the US, the UK and some other States was unauthorized by the Security Council there was, of course, a serious violation of international law and of the rule of law. For the effect of acting unilaterally was to undermine the foundation on which the post-1945 consensus had been constructed: the prohibition of force (save in self-defence, or, perhaps, to avert an impending humanitarian catastrophe) unless formally authorized by the nations of the world empowered to make collective decisions in the Security Council under Chapter VII of the UN Charter. The moment that a State treats the rules of international law as binding on others but not on itself, the compact on which the law rests is broken. 'It is', as has been said, 'the difference between the role of world policeman and world vigilante.'[42]

I should make it plain that Mr Jack Straw, Foreign Secretary in March 2003, and Lord Goldsmith, Attorney General at the time, strongly challenge the conclusions I have expressed,[43] and other may also do so.

Lord Goldsmith has emphasized that he believed the advice which he gave at the time to be correct—which I have not challenged—and remains of that view. On the issue of legality he has stressed three points in particular. First, the use of force in 2003 was (he has said) authorized by the United Nations because of the original authorization, which remained in force. He has pointed out that the revival argument had been relied on before, had been consistently supported by British Law Officers and had been endorsed by the Secretary-General of the UN in 1993 and by the then

---

[39] 'The pax Americana and the Law', first published in the JUSTICE journal in 2004, republished in extended form in 2007. In his oral presentation he used the word 'risible', which he later changed.

[40] Sands (n 35) 189.

[41] V Lowe, *International Law* (OUP, Oxford, 2007) 273.

[42] V Lowe, 'Is the Nature of the International Legal System Changing?—A Response' (2003) Austrian Review of International and European Law, 8, 72.

[43] In communications to the author.

Legal Advisor to the UN. Resolution 678 was not tied to expelling Iraq from Kuwait.

His second point is that the Security Council did set the conditions for the permission to use force to revive. Resolution 1441 made a finding of material breach and gave Iraq a final opportunity to comply. This did not require the Security Council to decide that there had been a further material breach. The negotiating history made this clear.

His third point is that the UK was justified in concluding that the final opportunity had not been taken. He had advised the Prime Minister that he had to be sure. Resolution 1441 was not about weapons of mass destruction. Under resolution 1441 Iraq had to cooperate fully and the British government judged that it had not done so.

Mr Straw has agreed with what Lord Goldsmith has said. The negotiating history and wording of resolution 1441 show, he has said, that it was not the intention of the Security Council, nor was it so expressed, that a decision on material breach had to be decided by the Security Council. This might be surprising, he comments, but it is true.

The question, then, is one of authority. This suggests three questions calling for an answer. First, who was authorized? Resolution 678 authorized 'the Member States cooperating with the Government of Kuwait'. That expression had a very clear meaning in 1991. But it could scarcely be read as a reference to a shrunken core of two of the former coalition partners, shorn of most of their former partners and against the strong vocal opposition of several of them. The multilateral application of resolution 678 was an important feature of it.

The second question is: what did resolution 678 give authority to do? The answer is clear. It gave authority to expel Iraq from Kuwait and 'restore peace and security in the area'. It is difficult to read this as authority to launch a full-scale invasion of Iraq in 2003 with the obvious intention of deposing its government and occupying its territory, the foreseeable consequence of causing widespread loss of life, and the potential to destabilize the area.

The third question is: when was authority given to invade? It cannot be plausibly suggested that authority was given by resolution 1441, for that gave the Iraqi government a final opportunity to cooperate. Clearly, therefore, an invasion could not have been launched the next day. But if not then, when? As soon as any Member State of the UN decided that the Iraqi government had had sufficient time to cooperate and had not done so? This, as I have already suggested, would subvert the collective decision-making process of the Security Council which lies at the heart of the Chapter VII regime. A decision as massive and far-reaching as one to invade and occupy a foreign sovereign State must be based on something very much more solid than a good arguable case. The inescapable truth is that

the British government wished for and tried to obtain a further Security
Council resolution authorizing the use of force, but was unable to do so in
the face of international opposition and went ahead without.

The legal duties of belligerents while hostilities are in progress and after
they have ended are very largely governed by the regulations annexed to the
1907 Hague Convention and by the four 1949 Geneva Conventions as
extended by Protocols adopted in 1977. These give effect to a wide international consensus that there are some methods of making was which are
impermissible (such as killing or wounding an enemy who is already
wounded or has surrendered, and the destruction of property without military necessity); that prisoners of war should be protected, and treated with
humanity and decency; and that civilians, non-combatants, the sick and the
wounded should be so far as possible protected from the military activity.
When hostilities are over, an occupying power 'shall take all measures in
[its] power to restore, and ensure, as far as possible, public order and safety,
while respecting, unless absolutely prevented, the laws in force in the country'.[44] Property and life must be respected.[45] The occupying power has no
mandate to transform the law and institutions of the defeated State, a somewhat anomalous rule given that the two most successful post-1945 occupa-
tions, those of West Germany and Japan, comprehensively transformed the
laws and institutions of those countries.[46]

The record of the British as an occupying power in Iraq has, as we know,
been sullied by a number of incidents, most notably the shameful beating to
death of Mr Baha Mousa in Basra.[47] But such breaches of the law were not
a result of deliberate government policy, and the rights of the victims have
been recognized. This contrasts with the unilateral decisions of the US
government that the Geneva Conventions did not apply to the detention
conditions in Guantanamo Bay, Cuba, or to trial of Al-Qaeda or Taleban
prisoners by military commissions,[48] that Al-Qaeda suspects should be

[44] Art 43 of the 1907 Hague Regulations.
[45] ibid art 46.
[46] This subject is valuably discussed by Professor Sir Adam Roberts in 'Transformative
Military Occupation: Applying the Laws of War and Human Rights' (July 2006) 100
American Journal of International Law 3, 580–622.
[47] See *R (Al-Skeini and others) v Secretary of State for Defence (The Redress Trust and
others intervening)* [2007] UKHL 26, [2008] 1 AC 153, para 6, case 6.
[48] Memorandum by John Yoo and Robert Delabunty to William Haynes of 9 January
2003; memorandum by Jay Bybee to Alberto Gonzales and William Haynes of 22 January
2002; memorandum by Alberto Gonzales to President George W Bush of 25 January 2002;
Memorandum by the President to the Vice-President and others of 7 February 2002: see K
Greenberg and J Dratel (eds), *The Torture Papers: The Road to the Abu Ghraib* (CUP,
Cambridge, 2005) 38–79, 81–117, 118–121, 134–135. The development of the adminis-
tration's policy on 'enhanced interrogation techniques' is traced by Professor Philippe
Sands, *Torture Team: Deception, Cruelty and the Compromise of Law* (Allen Lane,
London, 2008).

denied the rights of both prisoners of war and criminal suspects, and that torture should be redefined, contrary to the Torture Convention and the consensus of international opinion, to connote pain, where physical, 'of an intensity akin to that which accompanies serious physical injury such as death or organ failure'.[49] This is what underlay the abuses indelibly associated in the mind of the world with the photographs of Abu Ghraib but occurring elsewhere also, described in horrifying detail in reports of the International Committee of the Red Cross (February 2004 and February 2007),[50] General Taguba (March 2004),[51] Generals Fay and Jones (August 2004 and February 2007)[52] and the American Bar Association (August 2004).[53] Particularly disturbing to proponents of the rule of law is the cynical lack of concern for international legality among some top officials in the Bush administration. Thus in one memorandum the Deputy Assistant Attorney General (John Yoo), writing to the Counsel to the President, advised:

> Thus we conclude that the Bush administration's understanding created a valid and effective reservation to the Torture Convention. Even if it were otherwise, there is no international court to review the conduct of the United States under the Convention. In an additional reservation, the United States refused to accept the jurisdiction of the [International Court of Justice] (which, in any event, could hear only a case brought by another state, not by an individual) to adjudicate cases under the Convention. Although the Convention creates a Committee to monitor compliance, it can only conduct studies and has no enforcement powers.[54]

The British government did not adopt practices such as these, of which a number of prominent British ministers (including the Attorney General) were openly critical.

As I stressed at the outset, most transactions governed by international law proceed smoothly and routinely on the strength of known and accepted rules. I have perhaps dwelt disproportionately on the non-compliant tip of

[49] Memorandum by Jay Bybee (largely drafted by John Yoo) to Alberto Gonzales of 2 August 2002; see Greenberg and Dratel (eds) (n 48) 213–214; see also Jane Mayer, *The Dark Side* (Doubleday, New York, 2008) 151–152, 224, 231.
[50] Greenberg and Dratel (eds) (n 48) 383–404. *ICRC Report on the Treatment of Fourteen 'High Value Detainees' in CIA Custody*, www.nybooks.com.
[51] Greenberg and Dratel (eds) (n 48) 405–556.
[52] ibid 987–1131.
[53] ibid 1132–1164.
[54] Memorandum by John Yoo to Alberto Gonzales of 1 August 2002, quoted ibid 220–221.

the iceberg, illustrated by events in Iraq and elsewhere. But those events highlight what seem to me to be the two most serious deficiencies of the rule of law in the international order. The first is the willingness of some States in some circumstances to rewrite the rules to meet the perceived exigencies of the political situation, as the UK did in relation to the Suez crisis of 1956. The second is the consensual basis of the jurisdiction of the International Court of Justice (ICJ). Cases come before the Court only if the parties agree. While 65 of the 192 Member States of the United Nations have chosen to accept the compulsory jurisdiction of the ICJ, a majority do not, and it is a lamentable fact that, of the five permanent members of the Security Council, only one, the UK, now does so, Russia and China never having done so and France and the United States having withdrawn earlier acceptances. As HE Judge Rosalyn Higgins, then the President of the ICJ, said in a lecture at the British Institute of International and Comparative Law in October 2007, 'the absence of a compulsory recourse to the Court falls short of a recognisable "rule of law" model'.[55] The suggestion that the rule of law requires, in this day and age, a routine and obligatory recourse to the Court in matters connected to the UN Charter and related issues is obviously, she suggested, still a step too far. But it is, I think, a step which must be taken if the rule of law is to become truly effective in this area.

If events in Iraq and elsewhere highlight some of the deficiencies of international law, they may nonetheless yield a public benefit in the longer term. For while the lawfulness of earlier military interventions has attracted academic analysis (as, notably, by Geoffrey Marston on the Suez crisis[56]), I do not think the public at large has been much interested in whether the interventions were lawful or not. In the case of Iraq, perhaps because of widespread doubts in this country about the wisdom and necessity of going to war, the issue of legality has loomed larger than, I think, ever before. This has enhanced the importance of international law in the public mind, and Chapter VII of the UN Charter has come to be more widely recognized not only as a constraint on unauthorized military action but also as a guarantee that such action is necessary to maintain or restore peace and proportionate, traditional conditions of a just war. While prophecy is always perilous, it is perhaps unlikely that States chastened by their experience in Iraq will be eager to repeat it. They have not been hauled before the ICJ or any other tribunal to answer for their actions, but they have been arraigned at the bar of world opinion, and judged unfavourably, with resulting damage to their standing and influence. If the

---

[55] 'The Rule of Law: Some Sceptical Thoughts', 16 October 2007, 6–7.
[56] 'Armed Intervention in the 1956 Suez Canal Crisis: The Legal Advice Tendered to the British Government' (1988) 37 ICLQ 773.

daunting challenges now facing the world are to be overcome, it must be in important part through the medium of rules, internationally agreed, internationally implemented and, if necessary, internationally enforced. That is what the rule of law requires in the international order.[57]

[57] This chapter closely follows the text of a Grotius lecture ('The Rule of Law in the International Order') given on 17 November 2008 to mark the 50th anniversary of the establishment of the British Institute of International and Comparative Law.

# CHAPTER 2

# Business and Human Rights

*Mary Robinson*

It is a pleasure to be here in London and to join in celebrating the 50th anniversary of the British Institute of International and Comparative Law. I welcome this opportunity to reflect with all of you on the relationship between business, the international rule of law and human rights. It is a fitting moment to do so given that this year also marks another important anniversary—on 10 December 2008 we commemorate the 60th anniversary of the adoption of the Universal Declaration of Human Rights.

Ten years ago, as I was beginning my term as UN High Commissioner for Human Rights, my small office was preparing to mark the 50th anniversary of this foundational statement of the international human rights system. At that time, the debate over the proper roles and responsibilities of the private sector on issues relating to human rights was just beginning to take on a sharper focus and was moving up the agenda. As High Commissioner, I reflected on these issues initially by writing in the Financial Times that:

> [T]he drafters of the UDHR may not have foreseen the power and influence that business corporations would come to wield in our world, but they did allow for business, as part of the human community, to use its power with respect for human rights in mind … It is not a question of asking business to fulfil the role of government, but of asking business to promote and respect human rights in its own sphere of competence.

So where do we stand today on the issue of business and human rights? Before looking at this question specifically, let me step back just a bit and say a few words about some of the broader challenges we continue to face in making progress on human rights.

First, despite the fact that the Universal Declaration had been affirmed and reaffirmed by every government in the decades since its adoption, there are still questions in some quarters about what exactly was meant by the term 'human rights'. Human rights continue to be perceived by some as a Western agenda. For others, they remain confined to a narrow understanding of civil and political liberties, excluding the broad international framework embracing economic, social and cultural rights, which the Universal Declaration proclaimed. These continuing perception issues must be addressed if we are to make progress on protecting the full range of rights guaranteed under international law.

Second, it is evident that implementation of human rights obligations has fallen far short of commitments made. Tragically, the implementation gaps have arguably grown even wider in recent years. This has been due in part to the emergence of a more security-driven global political environment since the attacks against the United States in September 2001 which has had serious negative impacts on human rights around the world. Equally troubling, old Cold War divisions have given way to new forms of polarization between North and South on key areas of policy, including trade, aid, and the environment, in ways that are unhelpful to effective national action and international cooperation on human rights issues. It is my hope that, with a new administration taking office in the US and working with governments around the world, we can finally begin to regain the ground lost in recent years.

Third, and perhaps most sobering, is the recognition that the deepest challenges—of discrimination, oppression, injustice, disease, ignorance, exploitation and poverty—which the Universal Declaration pledges to overcome, are rooted in complex social and institutional relations. Beyond law and policy, if we are to make progress and truly protect human rights, we need effective institutions of government. Poorly equipped or corrupt institutions are a primary obstacle to effective action. Take as example the vast sums that have been invested to promote health in poorer countries in recent years by alliances of governments, the private sector, civil society actors and private philanthropy. Millions of people have benefited as a result. Yet those involved have recognized publicly that without greatly improved institutional capacity—meaning well-resourced and competent local and national health systems—further progress on improving public health will be limited.

Similarly, billions of people are today unable to access or protect their legal rights because judicial and law enforcement systems in many societies are impoverished or lack integrity. Changing this will require massive investment over long periods in courts, judicial officials, the police, prison systems, social ministries, and parliaments, as well as national human rights institutions and other official monitoring bodies.

With this broad context in mind, let me turn now to the question of business and human rights. As a new report titled 'Red Flags' by the UK based International Alert and the Norwegian based Fafo Institute[1] notes, business

---

[1]  http://www.redflags.info.

is facing an increasingly more complex legal and operational environment globally. The legal liabilities of companies operating overseas are no longer restricted to the national laws where they operate. Home government laws, and laws of third countries, may also apply. At the same time, new international standards are being incorporated into national laws; courts are taking a more expansive view of legal responsibility. Essentially, the web of corporate liability is expanding.

Companies face particularly high risks when operating in war zones, or where there is widespread violence, where human rights abuses are rampant, or where repressive regimes rule. Companies also face liabilities if they violate sanctions, operate in ways that violate financial regulations, or assist international crimes. Company executives themselves might face litigation. The Red Flags report, based on a review of existing international law and court cases, puts forward a number of examples of actions which may lead to significant legal risk. The red flags are warnings: it does not mean that a company will get sued; but the risk is high.

Some, actions, such as gaining access to operational sites through forced displacement of communities, or use of disproportionate force by government or private security forces acting on behalf of a company, has led to renewed attention to the issue of business complicity in rights violations. In this context, let me also point to another recent report, titled 'Corporate Complicity and Legal Accountability', prepared by an expert panel of the International Commission of Jurists.[2] This report, which was launched here in London just last month, makes clear that while standards of criminal law and civil law vary across jurisdictions, there is a threshold of conduct that a prudent company should avoid crossing so that they do not enter a zone of legal risk where criminal or civil responsibility could arise.

The lesson for corporate leaders is that, even in countries where the administration of justice may be poor, this does not give them the license to act in ways that expose them in assisting crime. I point to these two reports simply to make the point that the debates on business and human rights are entering a new level of detail and legal clarity that business leaders must be aware of in the years ahead.

My strong sense is that many more business leaders are doing just that and are today engaging with human rights issues and the implications for their companies in ways they weren't doing just a few years ago. Many of the business leaders I meet now see the 'business case' for respecting rights, including managing legal and operational risk and reputation, meeting shareholder and stakeholder expectations, and maintaining and motivating staff performance.

---

[2] www.icj.org/IMG/Volume_1.pdf.

They recognize that much of what they are already doing—whether striving for good workplace standards, ensuring equal opportunities for workers or engaging in dialogue with local communities—are all consistent with human rights principles. They just may not be using the term 'human rights' specifically to describe those actions. There is also a growing awareness that business is an increasingly important actor in development and the provision of public goods in many countries which has a direct impact on the realization of fundamental rights. This means coming to grips with a dynamic and changing relationship between State and non-State actors.

At the same time, I think it is clear that more determined efforts are still needed to develop greater clarity on what precisely the basic responsibility to respect human rights entails for business, and what steps companies need to take to satisfy themselves and others that they meet it. Voluntary initiatives on corporate responsibility, which have expanded enormously in recent years, and multi-stakeholder efforts which seek to clarify corporate responsibilities on a range of thematic issues—such as labour rights violations, threats to personal security and freedom of expression, among others—have still not been able to engage the vast majority of companies around the world and have generally not developed adequate reporting and accountability practices to ensure their legitimacy among stakeholders and the public.

Equally important, the effort needed to integrate human rights values into corporate culture obviously requires substantial resources for training programs and continuous improvement. Sending the message to employees that the company believes in the broad human rights agenda and that this should be a key part of business decisions at every level is much easier said than done. Even the most committed managers say they need more practical and authoritative guidance on what human rights mean for them and how these issues can be taken seriously within their day-to-day operations. These are all enormous challenges still to be addressed.

Governments working within the United Nations system have recognized these challenges as well. In 2005 they established a mandate of Special Representative of the UN Secretary-General to make progress on business and human rights issues. The Special Representative, John Ruggie of Harvard University, submitted his third report to the UN Human Rights Council earlier this year. In June, the UN Human Rights Council welcomed the policy framework for business and human rights put forward by the Special Representative and extended the mandate for another three years for the purpose of operationalizing the framework through concrete guidance to States and businesses.

The policy framework put forward by John Ruggie comprises three core principles: the State duty to protect against human rights abuses by third parties, including business; the corporate responsibility to respect human rights; and the need for greater access by victims to effective remedies.

John Ruggie's work has rightly highlighted the critical role governments must play in addressing ongoing questions around the role of business in the human rights field. He points out something I saw during my time in the UN—namely, that most governments, whether host or home States, continue to take a narrow approach to managing the business and human rights agenda. As John put it recently in an address at the Yale Law School:[3]

> Human rights concerns are often kept apart from, or heavily discounted in, other policy domains that directly shape business practices, including commercial policy, investment policy, securities regulation, and corporate governance. Inadequate domestic policy coherence, of course, is replicated at the international level.

My strong view is that the human rights obligations of governments need to be pushed beyond their narrow institutional confines. Governments need to consider more proactively human rights impacts when they sign trade and investment agreements, and when they provide export credit or investment guarantees for overseas projects in contexts where the risk of human rights challenges is known to be high. Such steps would address many of the governance challenges at the heart of questions relating to business and human rights.

Another important aspect of John Ruggie's analysis is the recognition that, as economic actors, companies have their own distinct responsibilities to respect human rights. If we don't achieve greater clarity on what those responsibilities are in practice we will continue to see them entangled with State obligations which will make it difficult if not impossible to address who is responsible for what in practice in an increasingly interconnected global economy.

The policy framework John Ruggie put forward earlier this year has been endorsed by the major international business associations and by leading international human rights organizations. Thanks to the efforts of the Special Representative, and the range of individuals, organizations and networks that have engaged constructively in his work, what we are seeing today is an emerging consensus on how to advance the business and human rights agenda in the years ahead.

I was happy to accept an invitation from John to serve with a number of other leaders from business, civil society and government on a leadership group which will advise him on the next steps in his mandate over the coming three years as he develops concrete recommendations to States, corporate and other social actors. The journey ahead will be long and difficult, but I am hopeful that we are now in a better position to reach greater

---

[3] See www.business-humanrights.org.

international normative clarity on the responsibilities of business in the field of human rights.

Part of that journey involves addressing difficult legal issues, but it also means learning from and developing further practical forms of cooperation between all stakeholders on a range of initiatives. Take as one example, the growing field of corporate sustainability reporting. More and more companies are reporting publicly on the environmental and social impacts of their operations as a form of transparency and accountability. This is an important development but there is still a good deal of work to be done on incorporating human rights issues more systematically in such reports.

A new project launched by my organization—Realizing Rights—in cooperation with the UN Global Compact and the Global Reporting Initiative to mark the UDHR 60$^{th}$ anniversary is encouraging more companies to include human rights in their annual sustainability reports. We want to obtain as many commitments from companies to include human rights in their next reports as we can over the coming months so we encourage you all to learn more about that project at www.globalreporting.org/humanrights.

Finally, let me briefly put on another hat I wear —as a member of The Elders—a group of leaders chaired by Archbishop Desmond Tutu which was formed last year under Nelson Mandela and Graca Machel's inspiration. We have been working this year with a range of partner organizations—including UNICEF, Amnesty International, CIVICUS, ActionAid and others, including companies taking part in the Global Compact and the Business Leaders Initiative on Human Rights—on the Every Human Has Rights Campaign to mark the 60$^{th}$ anniversary of the UDHR. We are calling on people to visit www.everyhumanhasrights.org and make their own personal commitment to human rights by signing a pledge to live by the principles of the Universal Declaration and then take action in their communities in support of human rights. We would welcome the help of British Institute of International and Comparative Law and its networks in spreading the word about this effort and in encouraging organizations large and small to use the campaign as an opportunity for dialogue and action on human rights during this anniversary year.

It seems clear that demands on companies to demonstrate responsible behaviour will only increase in the years to come. I believe business managers who view human rights and other social issues as just philanthropy, or as an afterthought—an extra—will face a growing number of risks. But I am hopeful that we will increasingly see the emergence of another kind of manager—one who is able to incorporate human rights and other ethical issues into her decision-making. That will not only be good for business, but it will also be a powerful force in realizing all human rights for all.

# CHAPTER 3

# Business, the International Rule of Law and Human Rights

*Robert McCorquodale**

## I. INTRODUCTION

[We do not like the fact that] the Nike product has become synony-
mous with slave wages, forced overtime and arbitrary abuse.

Nike CEO Philip Knight[1]

The perception of most of civil society, of many governments and of some
of the employees of corporations is that corporations do not care about
human rights or the rule of law.[2] Yet, as the statement above shows, it is in
the interests of business to uphold human rights and to work within the
law. It is also in their interests, as will be discussed, for there to be an international rule of law to enable them to operate effectively around the world.

There is a great deal of support for the rule of law. As will be shown, it
is propounded in national and international documents, asserted in
speeches and acknowledged in writings and case law. Yet, in the absence of
a clear definition, a national rule of law is derided as 'ruling class chatter',[3]
or dismissed as the 'jurisprudential equivalent of motherhood and apple
pie'.[4] These criticisms become even stronger when the possibility of an

* My sincere thanks to Mehnaz Yoosuf for her very helpful research and to Oliver R Jones,
who faithfully transcribed my lecture, and then added to it considerably in terms of research
materials and insightful comments.

[1] Quoted in B Herbert, 'Nike Blinks' *New York Times* (New York New York May 21,
1998).

[2] See, for example, the caption to cartoon by K Bendib for A Landman, 'Absolving Your
Sins and CYA: Corporations Embrace Voluntary Codes of Conduct' August 18, 2008 on
www.corporatewatch.org (and see http://www.prwatch.org/node/7724): 'Nothing like a good
corporate code of conduct, as long as it remains voluntary and one remains free to do with it
as one wishes'.

[3] J Shklar, 'Political Theory and the Rule of Law' in A Hutchinson and P Monahan (eds),
*The Rule of Law: Ideal or Ideology* (Carswell, Toronto, 1987) 1

[4] T Bingham 'The Rule of Law' (2007) 66 Cambridge Law Journal 67, 69.

international rule of law is raised. These issues are addressed by this paper and are applied to business in terms of their responsibilities in relation to human rights.

II. THE RULE OF LAW

The modern conception of the rule of law in the common law tradition centres on the work of Dicey, who identified three aspects of it: the absolute supremacy of the law over government power; equality before the law; and enforcement before the courts.[5] The civil law tradition has generally focused less on the judicial process and more on the nature of the state, in the form of *Rechtsstaat*, or the law-based state.[6] More recently Lord Bingham has encapsulated the core of the idea of the rule of law as being 'that all persons and authorities within the state, whether public or private, should be bound by and entitled to the benefit of laws publicly and prospectively promulgated and publicly administered by the courts.'[7]

The rule of law is most succinctly set out by Bingham in terms of eight sub-rules or principles:

(1)  The law must be accessible and, so far as possible, be intelligible, clear and predictable;

(2)  Questions of legal right and liability should ordinarily be resolved by application of the law and not by the exercise of discretion;

(3)  The law should apply equally to all, except to the extent that objective differences justify differentiation;

(4)  The law must afford adequate protection of human rights;

(5)  Means must be provided for resolving, without prohibitive cost or inordinate delay, bona fide civil disputes which the parties themselves are unable to resolve;

(6)  Ministers and public officers at all levels must exercise the powers conferred on them reasonably, in good faith, for the purpose for which the powers were conferred, and without exceeding the limits of such powers;

(7)  Judicial and other adjudicative procedures must be fair and independent; and

---

[5] AV Dicey, *An Introduction to the Study of the Law of the Constitution* (1885), (Macmillan, London, 1902) (2005 facsimile) Part II.

[6] See, for example, H Kelsen, *Pure Theory of Law* (2nd edn, University of California Press, Berkeley, 1970). See also the summary in S Chesterman, 'An International Rule of Law' (2008) 56 American Journal of Comparative Law 331.

[7] Bingham (n 4) 69.

(8)   There must be compliance by the state with its international law oblig-
      ations.[8]

These principles are necessary to ensure that there is legal order and stability in the state, equality of application of the law, protection of human
rights and settlement of disputes before an independent legal body. These
principles separate the rule of law from the rule by power and from the rule
by law (as having law by itself does not mean that it meets the requirements
of a *rule of law*).

  Bingham includes in his definition a requirement that the law afford
adequate protection to human rights.[9] Other definitions have tended to
emphasize the rule of law as involving procedural, rather than substantive,
protections, with a strong focus on judicial independence.[10] Bingham's
approach is adopted here, not least because the rule of law must include
justice in a substantive sense as part of its elements, and that part of modern
justice requires respect for human rights, including, for example, the right
to a fair trial, freedom from discrimination, rights to participation in public
life, and cultural rights.

  Additionally, many attempts to define the rule of law do so, if only
implicitly, by considering the rule of law as an 'all-or-nothing' concept. For
example, Bingham sees the rule of law as encapsulating the idea that the law
either binds a government and its subjects or it does not; Dicey wrote of an
'absolute supremacy' of law over government power; and Crawford refers
to the 'subjection of government to general laws, regardless of their character'.[11] However, the reality is that the existence of the rule of law is a
matter of degree, with all legal systems being on a spectrum with no rule at
all at one end and a complete actualization of the rule of law at the other.
For example, the 'Rule of Law Index', pioneered by the World Justice
Project, has sought to measure the *relative* compliance of legal systems
throughout the world with the ideals of the rule of law.[12] Therefore it is not

[8] ibid 69–84. See also R McCorquodale, 'The Rule of Law Internationally' in M Andenas
and D Fairgrieve (eds), *Tom Bingham and the Transformation of the Law* (OUP, Oxford,
2009) 137.
  [9] Bingham (n 4) 75. See, in support of this view, Bingham's successor as (now) President of
the UK Supreme Court, Lord Phillips: 'The Rule of Law in a Global Context', speech at the
Qatar Law Forum, May 2009.
  [10] Chesterman (n 6) 340, although arguably the procedural version also contains inherent
assumptions about substance, see H Charlesworth, 'Comment' (2003) 24 Adelaide Law
Review 13, 14.
  [11] J Crawford, 'International Law and the Rule of Law' (2003) 24 Adelaide Law Review 3
at 4.
  [12] World Justice Project, 'Rule of Law Index', available at http://www.worldjusticeproject.
org/sites/default/files/Index%202%200%20-%20Feb 6 2009.pdf; Mary Robinson, 'Why the
Rule of Law Matters', Keynote Address to the World Justice Forum, 3 July 2008.

possible to conclude if states *have* or *do not have* the rule of law.[13] To adopt an approach that only focuses on a complete actualization of the rule of law would be of no practical relevance and would be of limited conceptual value, especially in an international legal system where philosophical ideas are strengthened if developed by reference to the reality of international actions.[14]

Rather, the issue is the extent to which rule of law principles are operative within a particular system. While the objective must be towards complete actualization of the rule of law, the lack of this does not mean that there can be no rule of law at all. In the same way, a lack of compliance by all states with their national legal obligations in regard to criminal law enforcement by an independent judiciary does not mean that enforcement does not exist. Instead, the state is seen as being far from complying with the rule of law. Thus this paper will consider whether there can be an international rule of law for which relative compliance can be determined.

III. THE RULE OF LAW IN THE INTERNATIONAL SYSTEM

A. *Upholding National Rule of Law*

There are many international documents and statements that address the rule of law. For example, the Declaration on Principles of International Law concerning Friendly Relations and Cooperation among states in accordance with the Charter of the United Nations 1970 (which is often seen as clarifying the terms of the United Nations (UN) Charter) referred to the 'paramount importance of the Charter of the United Nations in the promotion of the rule of law among nations'.[15] Further, in matters of collective security, many UN peacekeeping operations have included the restoration or establishment of the rule of law as part of their aims, in the context of the overall purpose of enhancing peace and security.[16]

---

[13] cf I Brownlie, *The Rule of Law in International Affairs: International Law at the Fiftieth Anniversary of the United Nations* (Martinus Nijhoff Publishers, The Hague, 1998) 14.

[14] This is the approach of many third world, critical race theory, feminist and newstream international legal theorists. See, for example, J Gathii, 'The Contribution of Research and Scholarship on Developing Countries to International Legal Theory' 41 *Harvard International Law Journal* 263 (2000), Panel on 'International Dimensions of Critical Race Theory' 91 *American Society of International Law Proceedings* 408 (1997), H Charlesworth and C Chinkin, *The Boundaries of International Law: A Feminist Analysis* (Manchester Univ Press, 2000) and M Koskenniemi, *From Apology to Utopia: The Structure of International Legal Argument* (Finnish Lawyers Publishing Cooperative, 1989). Note also H Lauterpacht, 'The Subjects of the Law of Nations' (1947) 63 Law Quarterly Review 438 and (1948) 64 Law Quarterly Review 97.

[15] UN GAOR Res 2625 (XXV) (1970).

[16] See, eg, Security Council Resolution 152 (2004) (concerning Haiti) and Security Council resolution 1756 (2007) (concerning the Democratic Republic of Congo).

In economic and development matters the rule of law has also featured, with the World Bank considering that the practical application of the rule of law means that people in a society 'have confidence in and abide by the rules of society, and in particular the quality of contract enforcement, the police, and the courts, as well as the likelihood of crime and violence'.[17] This view was echoed in the World Summit Outcome Document 2005, which declared that 'good governance and the rule of law at the national and international levels are essential for sustained economic growth, sustainable development and the eradication of poverty and hunger'.[18] Indeed, the (then) UN Secretary-General, Kofi Annan stated that:

> [The rule of law is] a concept at the very heart of the [UN] Organization's mission. It refers to the principle of governance to which all persons, institutions and entities, public and private, including the state itself, are accountable to laws that are publicly promulgated, equally enforced and independently adjudicated, and which are consistent with international human rights norms and standards. It requires, as well, measures to ensure adherence to the principles of supremacy of law, equality before the law, accountability to the law, fairness in the application of the law, separation of powers, participation in decision-making, legal certainty, avoidance of arbitrariness, and procedural and legal transparency.[19]

These statements are strong and powerful. They reassert the need for a rule of law. Indeed, Annan's statement largely repeats the rule of law principles seen above, especially in terms of transparency, accountability, good governance and justice.

However, these statements are essentially about the rule of law in *national* systems. They demonstrate agreement at the international level by all states that the rule of law should operate in national systems.[20] They are intended to clarify why states should actualize the rule of law in their jurisdictions, as there are consequences for the state if the rule of law is not complied with. For example, issues of good governance, which are part of the rule of law, may affect the extent to which the state has access to international financial support.

Accordingly, few of these international statements assist in terms of understanding if there is an *international* rule of law. Indeed, existing definitions of

[17] World Bank, *A Decade of Measuring the Quality of Governance* (2006) 3.
[18] UN Doc A/Res/60/1.
[19] Report of the Secretary-General on the Rule of Law and Transitional Justice in Conflict and Post-Conflict Societies, UN Doc S/2004/616 (2004), para 6.
[20] See also the Statute of the Council of Europe 1949 where, in Article 3, each member state commits itself to accepting the rule of law.

the rule of law tend to be definitions created and refined within the national system. There is considerable difficulty in applying them directly to the international system, where there is no one binding court, no one executive or legislature, and where there is the sovereignty of states with which to contend.[21]

### B. Upholding the International Rule of Law

This does not mean that a rule of international law cannot be discerned. In fact, the UN Millennium Declaration 2000 urged states to:

> [S]trengthen respect for the rule of law *in international and in national* affairs and in particular to ensure compliance by member states with the decisions of the International Court of Justice, in accordance with the Charter of the United Nations, in cases to which they are parties.[22]

This demonstrates that there is an understanding of the existence of a national rule of law and an international rule of law. Nonetheless, relative compliance with the rule of law remains problematic at both the national and the international levels. Whilst the rule of law at an international level is very much, as Kofi Annan has stated, an 'unfinished project'—with the sovereignty of states seen as a particular obstacle[23]—it is evident that the international rule of law has been identified as a goal for the international system.[24]

It is argued here that the core elements of an international rule of law would still be essentially the same as for a national rule of law, being legal order and stability, equality of application of the law, protection of human rights and settlement of disputes before an independent legal body. Sir Arthur Watts, a former United Kingdom (UK) government legal adviser, expressed it this way:

> The protection of the interests of all states and the creation of international stability requires that state-to-state relations be subject to a long-term framework [of an international rule of law], which ensures that

---

[21] See H Correll, 'A Challenge to the United Nations and the World: Developing the Rule of Law' (2004) 18 Temple International and Comparative Law Journal 399 and R Higgins, 'The Rule of law: Some Sceptical Thoughts' in R Higgins, *Themes and Theories: Selected Essays, Speeches and Writings in International Law* (OUP, Oxford, 2009).

[22] UN Doc A/Res/55/2 (my emphasis).

[23] Note that P Allott, *Eunomia: New Order for a New World* (OUP, Oxford, 1990) s 16.49, comments that governments are 'generating an international Rule of Law, whilst still conceiving of themselves as masters of the Rule of Power'.

[24] 'We the Peoples: The Role of the United Nations in the Twenty-First Century' (UN Doc A/54/2000) at para 84.

international law is applied in conformity with principles of justice ... [and enables states to have a] stable, safe and predictable world in which they can better pursue their political and economic goals.[25]

This view corroborates some of the terminology about the rule of law at the international level, as seen above, which has tended to consider the rule of law at the international level in terms of order and stability, transparency, good governance, justice and accountability.

Evidence of acceptance of an international rule of law is seen in the doctrine of *pacta sunt servanda*. This is a rule of customary international law binding on all states (and part of *jus cogens* ie a binding constitutional rule of international law), which means that states must comply in good faith with legal obligations to which they have consented. In particular, if they consent to be bound by a treaty then they are legally bound to the terms of the treaty and, more generally, to the broader aims of the treaty, to which they must comply in good faith.[26] The benefit of this rule is for all states, so that each of them have confidence in reaching binding legal agreements to secure their own interest and to assist in attaining international peace and security.

This aspect of the international rule of law can be seen with the immediate decision by the new President of the United States of America (US) in 2009 to close the detention facilities at Guantanamo Bay and restore adherence to the Geneva Conventions 1949.[27] The aim was to show, as President Obama said, '[that] America will again set an example for the world that the law is not subject to the whims of stubborn rulers and that justice is not arbitrary.'[28] Indeed, the negative consequences for the lack of compliance with the international rule of law was shown when the US acted as it did at Guantanamo Bay, as other states sought to justify their lack of compliance with the rule of law by reference to the actions by the US.[29]

---

[25] A Watts, 'The International Rule of Law' (1993) 36 German Yearbook of International Law 15, 25, 41.

[26] B Simmons and D Hopkins, 'The Constraining Power of International Treaties: Theory and Methods' (2005) 99 American Political Science Review 623.

[27] M Mazzetti and W Glaberson, 'Obama Issues Directive to Shut Down Guantanamo' *New York Times* (New York New York 21 January 2009). See also the US Supreme Court's decision affirming the Geneva Conventions: *Hamdan v Rumsfeld* 548 US 557 (2006). The US has not yet acted fully on this intention but it is nevertheless a clear intention by the US government to comply with the international rule of law.

[28] American Society of International Law, 'Barack Obama Survey', Response to question 11, available at http://www.asil.org/obamasurvey.cfm.

[29] For example, the President of Zimbabwe, Robert Mugabe, used the US's actions at Guantanamo Bay as a shield to defend the many human rights abuses in Zimbabwe: T Otty, 'Honour bound to defend Freedom? The Guantanamo Bay Litigation and the Fight for Fundamental Values in the War on Terror' (2008) 4 European Human Rights Law Review 433, 450.

It may be difficult to recognize the principle of accountability in the international rule of law, at least in terms of the settlement of international disputes before an independent judicial or arbitral body. As noted, the International Court of Justice (ICJ) has a limited remit (eg primarily state-to-state disputes) and does not have compulsory jurisdiction, as states must specifically agree to allow it to decide on a dispute. Nevertheless, even in this voluntary context, 66 states (out of 192 members of the UN) have made declarations accepting the compulsory jurisdiction of the Court (under article 36(2) of its Statute).[30] Furthermore, almost all states that have had disputes before the ICJ have complied to a large extent with its decisions.[31]

Yet it is important not to focus solely on the ICJ when considering the settlement of international disputes. There are now a large number of international courts and tribunals that are deciding cases across a very wide area of international law. For example, the United Nations Convention on the Law of the Sea (UNCLOS), which has been ratified by over 150 states, specifically requires that disputes arising under it be settled by one of the methods set out in Part XV, which includes the International Tribunal for the Law of the Sea, the ICJ or an arbitral tribunal.[32] Also the dispute settlement systems in international economic, trade and human rights law are extensive at both the international and regional level, as will be referred to below.

The most advanced example of the operation of an international rule of law is the European Union (EU). In 1963 the European Court of Justice (ECJ) held that

> The European Economic Community constitutes a new legal order of international law for the benefit of which the states have limited their sovereign rights.[33]

This is an 'international order writ-small'.[34] Indeed, Jacobs has noted that the EU created a 'new order of international law', where states have stabil-

---

[30] 'Declarations Recognizing the Jurisdiction of the Court as Compulsory', International Court of Justice Website, available at http://www.icj-cij.org/jurisdiction/index.php?p1=5&p2=1&p3=3.

[31] C Schulte, *Compliance with decisions of the International Court of Justice* (OUP, New York, 2004) 271. Although the record for compliance by states with the ICJ's judgments on provisional measures is much worse.

[32] United Nations Convention on the Law of the Sea (UNCLOS), 10 December 1982.

[33] Case 26/62 *Van Gend en Loos v Nederlanse Administratie der Belastingen* (1963-02-05) (in the context of the formulation of the doctrine of direct effect).

[34] A van Staden, *Between the Rule of Power and the Power of Rule: In Search of an Effective World Order* (Martinus Nijhoff Publishers, Leiden, 2007) 212.

ity, economic benefits and judicial review.[35] They have also accepted the power of the ECJ to determine legal issues that bind the states, so that the 'veil of protection that the notion of sovereignty might otherwise provide' is lifted.[36] There are also many national law mechanisms that enable enforcement of international law.[37]

It is evident that there is now an extensive range of international dispute settlement mechanisms that can operate in a manner that is consistent with an international rule of law. This does not cover all areas of international law but nor is it restricted to small 'enclaves' of the rule of law.[38] These mechanisms are undoubtedly a patchwork but a patchwork that deals with many of the areas of greatest current activity in the international system.[39]

Therefore, there is sufficient evidence that there are principles upon which an international rule of law have been founded and developed. While the actualization of the international rule of law is still far from being completed, it is evident that:

[I]f the daunting challenges now facing the world are to be overcome, it must be through the medium of rules internationally agreed, internationally implemented, and if necessary, internationally enforced.[40]

This is a strong argument for an international rule of law, not just for governments but also for all those who participate in the international system. In particular, an international rule of law could be of relevance to transnational corporations and other business entities.

## C. Business and the International Rule of Law

There has been an understanding of the link between the rule of law and business for centuries, with Adam Smith noting:

---

[35] F Jacobs, 'The State of International Economic Law: Re-thinking Sovereignty in Europe' (2008) 11 Journal of International Economic Law 5.

[36] ibid 7. Note the concerns about the EU's rule of law in T Cowen, 'Justice Delayed is Justice Denied: The Rule of Law, Economic Development and the Future of the European Community Courts' (2008) 4 European Competition Journal 1, and reprinted in this publication (Chapter 4).

[37] For example, the cases under the Alien Torts Claims Act in the United States: see S Joseph, *Corporations and Transnational Human Rights Litigation* (Hart Publishing, 2004).

[38] cf J Crawford, 'International Law and the Rule of Law' (2003) 24 Adelaide Law Review 3, 12.

[39] JG Merrills, 'The Globalisation of International Justice' in D Lewis (ed) *Global Governance and the Quest for Justice* (Hart Publishing, Oxford, 2006) 89. See also B Zangl, 'Is there an Emerging International Rule of Law' (2005) 13 European Review 73.

[40] T Bingham, 'The Rule of Law in the International Order' Grotius Lecture of the British Institute of International and Comparative Law, 18 November 2008, reprinted in this volume (Chapter 1).

Commerce and manufactures can seldom flourish long in any state which does not enjoy a regular administration of justice, in which the people do not feel themselves secure in the possession of their property, in which the faith of contracts is not supported by law, and in which the authority of the state is not supposed to be regularly employed in enforcing the payment of debts from all those who are able to pay. Commerce and manufactures, in short, can seldom flourish in any state in which there is not a certain degree of confidence in the justice of government.[41]

While Smith was concerned primarily with the national rule of law, he used international examples extensively throughout his book and his insights are just as relevant in an international context today. The key factors that Smith recognized as being essential for the rule of law, and thus allowing for business to flourish, such as security, stability, good governance, justice and enforcement/accountability, are essentially the same factors that underpin support by states for an international rule of law, as shown above. Indeed, it is recognized this century, that the rule of law is essential for business in terms of 'securing investment, defining property rights, forming contracts, and preventing default on debts, and otherwise to aid in reducing the avoidable risks of investment',[42] which largely repeats the same factors noted by Smith in 1776.

The demands by business today that these factors be present in the international system in order for them to invest internationally is seen most clearly in the considerable developments in the international economic area. For example, the enormous growth in bilateral investment treaties (BITs) between states in recent years is primarily due to the demand by business to have more security of their investments, particularly when investing in less industrialized states.[43] These BITs create strong protections for its corporate national investors, as the host state wants to attract that investment, ostensibly to improve its economic development[44] and BITs 'maintain a stable framework for investment and maximum effective use of economic resources'.[45] These treaties are the umbrella under which international busi-

---

[41] A Smith, *An Inquiry into the Nature and Causes of the Wealth of Nations* (London, 1776) Book 5, ch III (his spelling).

[42] A Gerson, 'Peace Building: The Private Sector's Role (2001) 95 AJIL 101, 111.

[43] There are currently over 2, 400 BITs in existence: See UNCTAD, *Investor-State Disputes Arising From Investment Treaties: A Review* (United Nations, New York and Geneva, 2005), 3.

[44] See M Sornarajah, *The International Law on Foreign Investment* (CUP, Cambridge, 1995) 195.

[45] See Preamble, Treaty between the United States of America and the Argentine Republic Concerning the Reciprocal Encouragement and Protection of Investment, signed 14 November 1991, entered into force 20 October 1994. See also E Neumayer and L Spess, 'Do Bilateral Investment Treaties increase Foreign Direct Investment to Developing Countries? (2005) 33 World Development 1567 and M Busse, J Koniger and P Nunnenkamp, 'FDI Promotion

ness enters into contracts with a state to provide investment for a variety of projects, from state infrastructures to private endeavours. While there are distinct state-to-state treaty obligations, the resulting contracts have traditionally included two key provisions relevant to the rule of law: stabilization clauses and international arbitration requirements. Stabilization clauses are designed to ensure that the host state's government does not change its laws or procedures in such a way as to affect adversely the investment by the business. The purpose of such clauses is to protect business operations by requiring the host state to maintain its regulatory framework as it existed at the time the investment was made.[46] These contracts also give the business a right to take the host state to binding international arbitration to seek compensation should there be a dispute.[47]

These international arbitrations have increased rapidly, with many avenues available for disputes to be settled, including the International Centre for the Settlement of Investment Disputes and an ad hoc arbitration tribunal established under the UNCITRAL rules or through the International Chamber of Commerce. Any resulting award is usually enforceable under the New York Convention.[48] It is of note that these are contractual disputes between a state and a non-state actor (under a broad-based treaty) that are being settled by an international tribunal, with the decisions being binding on both parties. While the dispute settlement procedures in this particular area are still ad hoc, inconsistent, not necessarily free from bias, and not part of an institutional structure sufficient to create a norm of international law,[49] they demonstrate a number of the key factors for an international rule of law, including security, stability and accountability before an independent body.

In a related area of international trade law, there is now a clear institutional structure that supports the rule of law principle of independent legal dispute settlement. The Dispute Settlement Body within the World Trade Organisation (WTO) consists of a binding decision-making body, an appellate body, monitoring of compliance and a system of trade sanctions for non-compliance.[50] Rulings are automatically adopted by the membership

---

through Bilateral Investment Treaties: More Than a Bit?' Kiel Institute for the World Economy, Working Paper No 1403, February 2008.

[46] G Van Harten, 'The Public-Private Distinction in the International Arbitration of Individual Claims against the State' (2007) 56 ICLQ 371.

[47] P Muchlinski, *Multinational Enterprises and the Law* (2nd edn, OUP, Oxford, 2007).

[48] Convention on the Recognition and Enforcement of Foreign Arbitral Awards, 10 June 1958, entered into force 7 June 1959 (144 state parties).

[49] C McLachlan, 'Investment Treaties and General International Law (2008) 57 ICLQ 361.

[50] Understanding on the Rules and Procedures Governing the Settlement of Disputes, Annex 2 to Agreement Establishing the World Trade Organization, done at Marrakesh 15 April 1994, especially arts 6, 12, 16.4, 17 and 22.

of the WTO unless there is a consensus against doing so.[51] These dispute
settlement arrangements cover a broad scope, including international trade
in goods, services, finance and intellectual property. In addition, the dispute
settlement procedures under the Energy Charter[52] are expressly part of the
aim of the Charter, being:

> [T]o strengthen the rule of law on energy issues, by creating a level play-
> ing field of rules to be observed by all participating governments, thus
> minimising the risks associated with energy related investments and
> trade.[53]

These international rule of law principles directly and indirectly protect
businesses and enable them to participate effectively within the international system.

There are also broader economic arguments about an international rule
of law. There is economic research showing that entrenchment of the rule
of law will have beneficial economic results, and is critical to developing the
trust and certainty needed for entrepreneurship activity.[54] This also shows
that a functioning judiciary applying credible rules in the absence of corrup-
tion enhances the investment environment.[55] Indeed, the World Bank now

---

[51] G Evans, 'Issues of Legitimacy and the Resolution of Intellectual Property Disputes in the
Supercourt of the World Trade Organisation' (1998) 4 International Trade Law and
Regulation 81. Although these disputes are state-to-state only, business is also usually closely
involved. Examples of the driving role of business in directing litigation under the WTO
include Kodak and Fuji representatives being on the US and Japanese delegations on a case
affecting them, and the large banana corporations convincing the US and the EU to litigate
about the trade in bananas from the Caribbean, despite the very few bananas produced in the
US and the EU: see C Tietje and K Nowrot. 'Forming the Centre of a Transnational Economic
Legal Order? Thoughts on the Current and Future Position of Non-State Actors in WTO Law'
(2004) 5 European Business Organization LR 321, and C Brown and B Hoekman, 'WTO
Dispute Settlement and the Missing Developing Country Case: Engaging the Private Sector'
(2005) 8 J Int'l Econ L 861.
[52] Energy Charter Treaty and Energy Charter Protocol on Energy Efficiency and Related
Environmental Aspects, signed in December 1994 (entered into force April 1998).
[53] Energy Charter Secretariat, 'An Introduction to the Energy Charter Treaty', *The Energy
Charter Treaty and Related Documents: A Legal Framework for International Energy
Cooperation*, September 2004, available at http://www.encharter.org/fileadmin/user_upload/
document/EN.pdf#page=211.
[54] J Higbee and F Schmid, 'Rule of Law and Economic Growth' *International Economic
Trends*, August 2004, available at http://research.stlouisfed.org/publications/iet/
20040801/cover.pdf. It has also been suggested the 'rule of relationships' is a possible substi-
tute: R Peerenboom, 'Social Networks, Rule of Law and Economic Growth in China: The
Elusive Pursuit of the Right Combination of Private and Public Ordering', (2002) 31 Global
Economic Review.
[55] R Lensink and G Kruper, 'Recent Advances in Economic Growth: A Policy Perspective'
in M Oosterbann and others (eds), *The Determinants of Economic Growth* (Kluwer,
Massachusetts, 2000) at 254 and K Dam, *The Law-Growth Nexus: The Rule of Law and
Economic Development* (Brookings Institution Press, Washington DC, 2006).

regularly produces indicators that show correlations between real Gross Domestic Product (GDP) per capita and the rule of law, such that GDP per capita increases as the rule of law becomes more firmly entrenched in a state.[56] Indeed, *The Economist* has described the rule of law as the 'motherhood and apple pie of development economics'.[57]

Thus there is clear evidence that an international rule of law is necessary for both states and business, that it is accepted and being applied, and that there are incentives for it to be asserted by both these participants in the international system. Indeed, the incentives for business to press for an international rule of law and for the rule of law to be part of its decision-making processes may be even greater as foreign direct investment by businesses in developing states is now more than six times greater than investment by other states.[58]

### D. Business and Human Rights

While there are strong economic and institutional rationales for an international rule of law, as demonstrated above, there are also human rights elements to the rule of law that need to be taken into account. As noted above, human rights protections are within the principles of a rule of law. These apply equally in the international system, especially as every state has ratified (ie accepted that they have an international legal obligation) at least one of the major global human rights treaties.[59] Although no state complies fully with its international human rights legal obligations, and many states have reservations to aspects of some human rights treaties, all states have acknowledged that 'the promotion and protection of all human rights is a legitimate concern of the international community'[60] and all states have

---

[56] World Bank Governance Indicators are available at http://info.worldbank.org/governance/wgi/. See also the World Bank policy research papers: D Kaufman and A Kraay, 'Governance Matters: The "Development Dividend"' (2004) and D Kaufmann, A Kraay and M Mastruzzi, 'Governance Matters VI: Governance Indicators for 1996–2006'. For application in the context of Central and South America see Americas Society and Council of the Americas Working Group, Rule of Law, Economic Growth and Prosperity, July 2007.

[57] 'Economics and the Rule of Law' *The Economist* (London England 13 March 2008). See also T Cowen, (n 36) 6: 'good governance provides a framework for economic growth and prosperity; individuals feel safer and countries get richer the better the quality of the governance'.

[58] See the statistics quoted in D Kinley, *Civilising Globalisation* (CUP, Cambridge, 2009) 99–100.

[59] The major global human rights treaties include the International Covenant on Economic, Social and Cultural Rights, the International Covenant on Civil and Political Rights, the Convention on the Prohibition on Torture and other Cruel, Inhuman and Degrading Treatment and Punishment, the Convention on the Elimination of all Forms of Racial Discrimination, the Convention on the Elimination of All Forms of Discrimination Against Women and the Convention on the Rights of the Child.

[60] Vienna Declaration and Programme of Action 1993 32 International Legal Materials (1993) 1661, para 4.

accepted that the Universal Declaration of Human Rights 1948 is a legitimate universal standard by which to measure every state's performance of human rights under the Universal Periodic Review process of the UN Human Rights Council.[61]

In addition, under the current international human rights law structure, businesses (being non-state actors) do not have any international legal obligations; only states have these legal obligations. This means that states have international responsibilities with regard to any human rights abuses by businesses operating within their territory and, in some instances, in relation to businesses operating extra-territorially.[62] For example, the investigations after the discovery of prisoner abuse during the (illegal) occupation of Iraq have shown that some of these abuses were committed by employees of private contractors, which were businesses acting extraterritorially through governmental authority, and for which the state should be internationally responsible.[63]

Nevertheless, it is clear that businesses have some responsibilities with regard to human rights, as Mary Robinson has shown. For example, there has been very widespread support from the business community for the framework created by John Ruggie, the Special Representative of the UN Secretary-General on the Issue of Human Rights and Transnational Corporations and Other Business Enterprises (the Ruggie framework), in which business has a clear responsibility to respect human rights.[64] While there are a number of concerns about this framework,[65] this widespread support by the business community is consistent with the broad practice by almost all businesses operating across state boundaries to have some type of corporate social responsibility (CSR) policy, usually dealing with social, environmental and ethical issues. Indeed, many of these corporations see their CSR policies and their voluntary codes of conduct as being the equivalent to a human rights policy and/or as making them compliant with human rights norms.[66] Having a CSR policy is not the same as providing protection for all human rights, as a number of businesses with CSR poli-

---

[61] Human Rights Council Resolution 5/1, 18 June 2007, Annex, para 1(b).

[62] For a fuller discussion see R McCorquodale and P Simons, 'Responsibility beyond Borders: State Responsibility for Extraterritorial Violations by Corporations of International Human Rights Law' (2007) 70 Modern Law Review 598.

[63] See OR Jones, 'Implausible Deniability: State Responsibility for the Actions of Private Military Firms' (2009) 24 Connecticut Journal of International Law 249.

[64] Report to the UN Human Rights Council of the Special Representative of the Secretary-General on the Issue of Human Rights and Transnational Corporations and Other Business Enterprises, 7 April 2008. UN Doc A/HRC/8/5 ('Ruggie Report 2008').

[65] See R McCorquodale, 'Corporate Social Responsibility and International Human Rights Law' (2009) 87 Journal of Business Ethics 385.

[66] See, for example, the survey evidence of corporations in relation to human rights in A McBeth and S Joseph, 'Same Words, Different Language: Corporate Perceptions of Human Rights Responsibilities' (2005) 11 Australian Journal of Human Rights 95.

cies have been found to be acting contrary to human rights in a variety of cases worldwide.[67] Perhaps this is not surprising as essentially CSR policies[68] are management-driven and corporate-determined policies that focus on a few human rights only and are designed to assist the corporation's business, including in terms of its reputation, even if genuinely aimed for a positive social end. In contrast, human rights protections are person-centred, based on human dignity, are not voluntary, and have legitimate compliance mechanisms (even if these are not strong). Also, as the Ruggie Report 2008 makes clear, all human rights are relevant to corporations, including economic, social, cultural and collective rights, such as the right to education and labour rights, as well as civil and political rights. CSR policies could thus be considered to be part of the rule of economics and human rights as part of the rule of law.

With human rights as part of the international rule of law, businesses will continue to be affected by it. Three examples demonstrate this: the requirement to protect the right to health within the protection of the intellectual property of businesses; the impact of BITs based stabilization clauses on human rights; and the effect on businesses of counter-terrorism actions by states.[69]

## 1. *Intellectual property and the right to health*

In 1994 the WTO accepted the Agreement on Trade-Related Aspects of Intellectual Property Rights (TRIPS). This protects aspects of the intellectual property, including patents, of businesses worldwide, with the aim of having international legal rules to encourage businesses to develop new ideas. This includes patents in regard to medicines. However such patents can raise the costs of some medicines, with particular impacts on non-industrialized states.[70] This could have an impact on states' legal obligations under article 12 of the International Covenant on Economic, Cultural and Social Rights (ICESCR), which requires all state parties to take steps to achieve the full realization of every person's right to the highest attainable standard of physical and mental health.

---

[67] See the discussion in S Joseph, *Corporations and Transnational Human Rights Litigation* (Hart Publishing, Oxford, 2004).

[68] A useful definition of CSR policies is by H Ward, 'Corporate Social Responsibility in Law and Policy' in N Boeger, R Murray and C Villiers (eds), *Perspectives on Corporate Social Responsibility* (2008) 10: '[T]wo broad types of definitions of CSR: first, those that focus on outcomes—including outcomes in terms of "business impacts", "commercial success" and wider societal goals; and, second, those that stress the voluntary nature of CSR ("voluntary" in that CSR relates to business activity that is not mandated by legislation)'.

[69] My thanks to Oliver R Jones for the research on these examples.

[70] See J Greve, 'Healthcare in Developing Countries and the Role of Business: A Global Governance Framework to Enhance Accountability of Pharmaceutical Companies' (2009) 8 Corporate Governance 490.

A clear example of this problem arose in 1997 over the passage of the
*Medicines and Related Substance Control Amendment Act* in South Africa.
This legislation would have allowed the government to import or manufacture low-cost versions of branded anti-HIV medication that was protected
by patents.[71] A lawsuit was brought in 2001 by 39 pharmaceutical companies to challenge the legislation based on the TRIPS protections, though it
was eventually settled.[72] While it was evident that this action by the major
pharmaceutical companies damaged their reputation, the extent to which
the South African law would be able to overcome the TRIPS restrictions
was unclear.[73]

Eventually, the WTO passed the Doha Declaration in 2001 to try to
resolve this type of issue.[74] The Declaration reaffirmed both article 31(f) of
TRIPS, which states that each Member state has the right to grant compulsory licenses in cases of national emergency (limited to use in the domestic
market only) and that public health crises, including those relating to
HIV/AIDS, could represent a national emergency. The Declaration also
required the WTO TRIPS Council to take steps to resolve problems faced
by developing states who could not take advantage of compulsory licensing
provisions because they lacked the domestic capacity to manufacture
generic drugs. On this basis the Council issued a temporary waiver of article 31(f) on 30 August 2003 that allowed WTO Member states to issue
compulsory licences to export generic versions of patented medicines to
states with insufficient manufacturing capacity to do so themselves.[75] In
December 2005, WTO members reached an agreement to amend TRIPS to
make this temporary waiver permanent,[76] and a few states have availed
themselves of this waiver. [77]

[71] R Nessman, 'South Africa: Drug Companies Drop AIDS Suit' *Associated Press* (29 April
2001) available at http://www.corpwatch.org/article.php?id=121.
[72] BBC News, 'Aids court battle: Joint Statement' (29 April 2001) available at
http://news.bbc.co.uk/1/hi/world/africa/1285645.stm.
[73] S Joseph, 'Pharmaceutical Corporations and Access to Drugs: The 'Fourth Wave' of
Corporate Human Rights Scrutiny' (2003) 25 Human Rights Quarterly 423.
[74] Declaration on the TRIPS Agreement and Public Health, adopted on 14 November 2001,
Ministerial Conference, Fourth Session, Doha, WT/MIN(01)/DEC/2, available at
http://docsonline.wto.org/imrd/directdoc.asp?DDFDocuments/t/WT/Min01/DEC2.doc.
[75] Implementation of paragraph 6 of the Doha Declaration on the TRIPS Agreement and
public health, Decision of the General Council of 30 August 2003, WT/L/540 and Corr. 1,
available at http://www.wto.org/english/tratop_e/trips_e/implem_para6_e.htm.
[76] The amendment has been ratified by the European Community, bringing the number of
ratifying states to 55 as at 10 August 2009. 101 states are required for the agreement to enter
into force. See http://www.wto.org/english/tratop_e/trips_e/amendment_e.htm. The deadline
for ratification is 31 December 2011.
[77] For example, in July 2007 Rwanda became the first State to inform the WTO that it was
availing of the waiver to import cheaper generics made under compulsory licensing overseas.
Shortly after, Brazil issued a compulsory license to import an Indian-made version of the HIV
drug Efavirenz. See H Hestermeyer, 'Canadian-made Drugs for Rwanda: The First Application
of the WTO Waiver on Patents and Medicines' (2007) 11 ASIL Insights, available at

The problems created by the initial TRIPS system, combined with the proactive movement of states towards entrenching the outcomes of the Doha Declaration, demonstrate that it is in the interests of business to combine corporate strategy with social responsibility to create and enhance stable markets for investment. Indeed, internalizing the need to ensure public health needs are met in developing states can provide an opportunity for business to establish a trusted presence in emerging markets—markets that would be unlikely to be able to pay a premium for vital medicines in any event—to have clearer regulation of those markets[78] and improve their business reputations.[79] Thus, there can be a strong international rule of law that both creates the stability needed by business and protects human rights within it.

## 2. Stabilization clauses and labour rights

As noted above, stabilization clauses in contracts under BITs have been one method for business to ensure stability in their investments, as part of their activities in support of an international rule of law. However these clauses can hinder states that wish to improve human rights, environmental and/or labour standards in their own territory, for to do so requires a change to the regulatory environment in that state and could have an adverse impact on the investor's project, which would make the state in breach of its contract.[80]

An example of such a stabilization clause is contained in the Host Government Agreements between Chad and an oil consortium led by Exxon Mobil for the extraction of crude oil from Chad (and transported by pipeline to the Cameroon coast):

During the period of validity of this document, the state shall ensure that it shall not apply to the Consortium, without prior agreement of the Parties, any future governmental acts with the duly established effect of aggravating, directly, as a consequence, or due to their application to the shareholders of the Consortium, the obligations and charges imposed by

---

http://www.asil.org/insights071210.cfm and G O'Farrell, 'One small step or one giant leap towards access to medicines for all?' (2008) 30 European Intellectual Property Review 211, 213.

[78] Greve (n 70).

[79] Oxfam Briefing Paper 109, *Investing for Life: Meeting poor people's needs for access to medicines through responsible business practices*, November 2007, available at http://www.oxfam.org/sites/www.oxfam.org/files/bp109-investing-for-life-0711.pdf.

[80] International Finance Corporation, 'Stabilization Clauses and Human Rights' 11 March 2008, available at http://www.ifc.org/ifcext/sustainability.nsf/AttachmentsByTitle/p_StabilizationClausesandHumanRights/$FILE/Stabilization+Paper.pdf. This study also showed that stabilisation clauses are now being used less frequently.

the provisions of this Convention or with the effect of undermining the rights and economic advantages of the Consortium or its shareholders ... Only the Consortium shall be able to cite this stability clause, which is offered to it to the exclusion of any third party to this Convention.[81]

In its Report on the Chad-Cameroon Pipeline Project, Amnesty International alleged that, as a direct result of the pipeline project, villagers have been denied access to clean water, farmers have been denied access to their lands, and fish stocks off Cameroon's coast have been destroyed, and it thus called upon the parties to renegotiate their agreement in order to guarantee that Chad would be permitted to comply with its international human rights law obligations.[82] There have been no reports of such renegotiations taking place.

A consortium led by BP for the building and operation of the Baku-Tblisi-Ceyhan (BTC) pipeline in Turkey had a similar stabilization clause.[83] Yet it responded to similar criticisms[84] by agreeing to a 'Human Rights Undertaking' in September 2003.[85] The undertaking prevents the BTC company (created by the consortium) from asserting in legal proceedings an interpretation of the governing agreements that is inconsistent with the regulation by the host states of their obligations under human rights treaties. The Consortium also published a 'Citizens Guide' to assist the citizens of the host states to understand the commitments made by the Consortium companies.[86]

The power of stabilization clauses in investment agreements demonstrates that the rigorous judicial enforcement paths open to investors under BITs (as seen in the discussion of international arbitration above) often overwhelms the pull to compliance of international human rights law obligations on

---

[81] Art 34.3 of the agreement between the Consortium and Chad of 2004, as cited in Amnesty International, *Contracting out of Human Rights: The Chad-Cameroon Pipeline Project*, September 2005, 46, fn 67.

[82] Amnesty International, *Contracting out of Human Rights: The Chad-Cameroon Pipeline Project*, September 2005.

[83] The consortium members include, Amerada Hess, AzBTC, BP, Chevron, ConocoPhillips, Eni, INPEX, Itochu, Statoil, Total and TPAO. See BTC Co. Partners at http://www.bp.com/managedlistingsection.do?categoryId=9007998&contentId=7015010. For example, in its Host Government Agreement for the pipeline the Turkish government is prevented from requiring any consortium members to comply with labour standards 'that i) exceed those international labour standards or practices which are customary in international Petroleum transportation projects, or ii) are contrary to the goal of promoting an efficient and motivated workforce'.

[84] Amnesty International, *Human rights on the line: The Baku-Tbilisi-Ceyhan pipeline project*, May 2003, available at http://www.amnesty.org.uk/uploads/documents/doc_14538.pdf.

[85] The undertaking, made by deed on 22 September 2003, is available at http://subsites.bp.com/caspian/Human%20Rights%20Undertaking.pdf.

[86] http://www.amnesty.org.uk/content.asp?CategoryID=10128.

states, irrespective of whether one considers that these international obligations should take precedence over contractual obligations in private law.
However, the power of human rights arguments can have a significant
impact on some businesses and so strengthen the overall operation of the
international rule of law (being inclusive of human rights), as well as having
effects on the national rule of law in the state concerned.

### 3. Counter-terrorism sanctions

One of the many consequences of the 9/11 terrorist attacks was the passing
of national, regional and international regulations supporting counter-
terrorism actions by states. One example was the passing of resolutions of
decisions by the UN Security Council that established a Counter-Terrorism
Committee, with the power to make decisions imposing sanctions on individuals and organizations alleged to be involved in terrorist activity.[87]

This could have significant effects on business. If a business has given
money to an organization, individual or another institution that is alleged
to be involved in terrorist activity, even if that business is not aware of this,
then it is at risk of having its assets frozen. This could be disastrous for any
business. As the procedure by which the UN Security Council lists and
delists entities from the terrorist sanctions list is particularly opaque—
though the person, organization or business affected now must be informed
if they are placed on a sanctions list[88]—there is a real issue of procedural
fairness and breach of human rights.

As it is difficult for Security Council decisions to be judicially reviewed,
it is arguable that these procedures are contrary to an international rule of
law.[89] Indeed, decisions within Europe have indicated real concerns about
these procedures, and the ECJ has held that the Security Council process of
counter-terrorism listing of entities denies justice to those listed, because
'the procedure before the [Counter-Terrorism] Committee is still in essence
diplomatic and intergovernmental [which means that] the persons or entities concerned have no real opportunity of asserting their rights'.[90] The
European Commission is now working with states to create a new listing
procedure to protect human rights.[91] Interestingly, just prior to the decision

---

[87] Security Council Resolution 1373 (2001).

[88] See, for example, Security Council Resolutions 1730 (2006), 1732 (2006) and 1735
(2006).

[89] S Chesterman, '"I'll take Manhattan": The International Rule of Law and the United
Nations Security Council' [2009] Hague Journal on the Rule of Law 1.

[90] Cases C-402/05 P and C-415/05 *Yassin Abdullah Kadi and Al Barakaat International
Foundation v Council of the European Union and Commission of the European Communities*
(3 September 2008) paras 286–288.

[91] See http://www.europa.eu-un.org/articles/en/article_9369_en.htm.

of the ECJ, the Security Council resolved to require the Committee to provide summaries of reasons for listing on their website and to establish detailed procedures for representations for delisting.[92]

It is perhaps ironic that the Universal Declaration of Human Rights makes clear that 'it is essential, if man is not to be compelled to have recourse, as a last resort, to rebellion against tyranny and oppression, that human rights should be protected by the rule of law'.[93] These decisions may indicate that any attempt to create a rule of international law without regard to human rights is both contrary to business interests and is unsustainable.

## IV. CONCLUSIONS

The rule of law has been debated for centuries and it includes core principles of transparency, accountability, good governance, order, human rights protections, justice and independence of the judiciary. These principles have been shown to be equally applicable at the international level and have been so applied in a variety of contexts, from peace and security to trade and investment. The international rule of law is far from being complied with, however, it is a relative concept in which compliance by states is relative in terms of fulfilling the elements of the rule of law.

An international rule of law can create conditions of stability, certainty, accountability in decision-making, and independence and efficiency in the settlement of international (and national) disputes according to law. These are conditions that reduce the risks for business and render them more willing to invest. It is therefore appropriate that business has been working towards improving the international rule of law, at least in areas such as international economic and trade law, although these developments do not necessarily lead to international legal accountability of business for compliance with the international rule of law.

However, these developments cannot be seen as excluding human rights. As the three examples of intellectual property, stabilization clauses and counter-terrorism have showed, human rights form a necessary part of the international rule of law. They also show that it is in the interests of both states and business to support and comply with an international rule of law that includes human rights obligations. Indeed, the progression in relation to business and human rights shows the gradual move from voluntarism towards law. As Harold Koh, now US Legal Adviser at the state

---

[92] Security Council Resolution 1822 (2008).
[93] Universal Declaration of Human Rights 1948, Preamble.

Department, noted at a meeting about security and human rights between governments and business in the energy and extractive industries:

> The participants in this process have recognized that the goal of maintaining a secure operating environment is compatible with the goal of protecting human rights ... by supporting the rule of law, incorporating human rights into security arrangements, and working with NGOs, transnational companies can greatly strengthen and enrich the human rights environment in which they operate.[94]

This reasserts the crucial link between business, the international rule of law and human rights.

---

[94] Harold Koh was then US Assistant Secretary for Democracy, Human Rights and Labour: as quoted in 'Voluntary Human Rights Principles for Extractive and Energy Companies' (2001) 95 AJIL 636 637.

# CHAPTER 4

# *'Justice Delayed is Justice Denied': The Rule of Law, Economic Development and the Future of the European Community Courts* *

*Tim Cowen* **

## I. INTRODUCTION

This article looks at the recent changes in the European Union (EU) both under the Reform Treaty[1] and in relation to the recognized need to complete the Single Market. In essence, the political intent is agreed and the goals have been set. The Reform Treaty has set a way of working among Member States. By contrast, the EU system of law and the method by which agreed political intent is implemented has not been reviewed, and this is addressed below.

In this introduction the article highlights the importance of the rule of law and outlines the significant role of the European Community courts. Reference is made to recent reviews by the World Bank of the systems of

* Reprinted with kind permission from the European Competition Journal, in which this article first appeared in June 2008, Volume 4, No 1.
** Barrister, Chairman IACCM & Chairman Competition Panel CBI. This article has evolved over the past five years from discussions in many places, but principally at the British Institute of International and Comparative Law. The author would like to stress that the views expressed in this article are entirely his own and wishes to thank Lord Bingham, Sir David Edward and Dr Philip Marsden for their encouragement and comments. To Dr Brigitte Carbonare-Hartsleben for all of her contributions, assistance, encouragement and attention to detail, and Theodora Christou for her knowledge and patience. Without their help this article would never have been written.
[1] Treaty of Lisbon amending the Treaty on European Union and the Treaty establishing the European Community, signed at Lisbon, 13 December 2007, OJ 2007/C/306/01. It is due to come into force in 2009, if successfully ratified by all EU Member States, and would carry out most of the reforms previously proposed in the rejected European Constitution. The Treaty of Lisbon amends the Treaty on European Union (TEU) (essentially the Treaty of Maastricht) and the Treaty establishing the European Community (TEC) (essentially the Treaty of Rome), which is renamed the Treaty on the Functioning of the European Union (TFEU).

law in different countries. This has established that the legal system can itself enhance or undermine investment, productivity and growth. The idea of the rule of law is often recognized as one that underpins the fabric of democracy. In section I.A, the thinking on the rule of law that goes beyond merely an 'instrumental' view is canvassed. Simple legal 'instrumentalism' sees law only as a vehicle for implementation of political intentions. This can be contrasted with the view that the legal system is part of the culture of a society through which norms of behaviour are expressed and applied. One issue for investment and GDP growth which arises with the instrumental approach is that it can become a system of decrees and as unpredictable as political whims. States with written constitutions are likely to be more predictable for investment provided basic rights, such as property ownership and personal freedom, are written into the constitution. There is also a worry that even elected representatives can contravene constitutional principles; in States with written constitutions the courts are often called upon to adjudicate between the application of a statute and the application of the law more generally. The instrumental view has also been described as 'rule by law' and contrasted with the rule of law since the latter presupposes a more stable system and a societal view that looks at the law in its cultural context and as a sociological tradition based on precedent and practice. Even a system of law with an unwritten constitution can be described as operating within the rule of law. The common law approach is one where precedent is found in the cases and statutes are imposed from time to time but cannot take precedence over certain well-established constitutional principles. The explanation of the rule of law by Lord Bingham in 2007 is now taken as a starting point and the middle ground between the differing points of debate.[2] The essence of the discussion is that the greater certainty and security that can be derived from a predictable system is probably the key when considering investment and GDP growth.

A short analysis of the role of the European Community courts in light of key European policies and principles (with a particular focus on the Lisbon objectives, the EU Reform Treaty and the aims of the Single Market) is also presented. The article takes an investment and business perspective. The Reform Treaty has increased Member State coordination and judicial cooperation in criminal matters under Title V, which covers freedom, security and justice. These aspects are without doubt important and will act as a further impetus for increasingly speeding up the system, but are not addressed further.

---

[2] Lord T Bingham, 'The Rule of Law' (2007) 66 Cambridge Law Journal 67; BZ Tamanaha, On the Rule of Law: History, Politics, Theory (CUP, Cambridge, 2004); BZ Tamanaha, Law as a Means to an End: Threat to the Rule of Law (CUP, Cambridge, 2006).

Section II ('The Issues—Why is There a Need for Reform?') provides a critical analysis of the functioning of the current system, and identifies the main aspects of procedure where improvements are necessary. It has a particular focus on the lack of speed in the application of European Union law and how the European Community courts' workload affects the timeliness of its decisions. The analysis of this particular problem justifies why this aspect of the rule of law is such an important issue and the main focus of this article.

Section III ('Options for Reform') first reviews previous analyses and thoughts for reform of the EU court system and commentaries of the European Community courts before outlining certain options for future reform.

### A. The Important Role of the European Community Courts within the Framework of the Rule of Law[3]

The EU is built on the principle of the rule of law and a single coherent system, at the heart of which lie the European Court of Justice (ECJ) and the Court of First Instance (CFI). These interrelate with the domestic courts of the EU Member States and coherence is achieved, primarily through a system of references on issues of law as well as substantive decisions on many subjects.

It is well established that the rule of law is a cornerstone of democracy and fundamental to the operation of a free and just society. Many have identified freedom and liberty as ultimately intertwined with the precondition of law and justice.[4]

---

[3] See generally, T Carothers, *Promoting the Rule of Law Abroad: In Search of Knowledge* (Carnegie Endowment for International Peace, Washington, DC, 2006); Indepen Consulting, Productivity, Growth and Jobs: How Telecoms Regulation Can Support European Businesses (London, Indepen Consulting, 2008); T Friedman, *The World is Flat* (New York, Farrar, Straus & Giroux, 2005); D Kaufmann, J Isham and LH Pritchett, 'Civil Liberties, Democracy, and the Performance of Government Projects' (2005) 11 World Bank Economic Review 219; D Kaufmann and A Kray, 'Growth without Governance' (2002) World Bank Policy Research Working Paper No 2928; D Kaufmann, A Kraay and M Mastruzzi, 'Governance Matters IV: Governance Indicators for 1996–2006' (2007) World Bank Policy Research Working Paper, available at http://papers.ssrn.com/sol3/ papers.cfm?abstract_id=999979 (accessed on 12 May 2008); F Hayek, Law, Legislation and Liberty, Vol I (University of Chicago Press, 1973); R La Porta, F Lopez-de-Silanes, A Shleifer and R Vishny, Law and Finance (University of Chicago Press, 1998); Lord Bingham (n 2); D North, Institutions, Institutional Change and Economic Performance (Cambridge University Press, 1991); D Rodrik, A Subramanian and F Trebbi, 'Institutions Rule: The Primacy of Institutions over Geography and Integration in Economic Development' (2002) NBER Working Paper No 9305; A Sen, *Development as Freedom* (OUP, Oxford, 1999); A Smith, *An Inquiry into the Nature and Causes of the Wealth of Nations* (1776), available at MetaLibri Digital Library: http://metalibri.i ncubadora.fapesp.br/portal/authors/AnInquiryIntoTheNatureAndCausesOfTheWealthOfNations (accessed on 12 May 2008); Tamanaha 2004 (n 2); Tamanaha 2006 (n 2).

[4] Smith ibid defined freedom as 'every man so long as he does not violate the laws of

A clear and predictable system of law is generally accepted as a precondition for personal freedom and the central growth of human rights in a democratic system. Predictability and clarity for human rights, however, have tended to overshadow the importance of predictability and clarity for investment. However, it has been a key purpose of the law that it should protect freedom and rights to property. Protection of property rights and security for investment was noted in the 17ᵗʰ century:

> Commerce and manufactures can seldom flourish long in any state which does not enjoy a regular administration of justice, in which the people do not feel themselves secure in the possession of their property, in which the faith of contracts is not supported by law, and in which the authority of the state is not supposed to be regularly employed in enforcing the payment of debts.[5]

It is perhaps obvious that arbitrary government creates risks for investors; however, empirical evidence has now been gathered to support the relationship between the two.[6] This is further outlined in Figures 1 and 2.

Figures 1 and 2 illustrate the relationship between GDP per capita and the rule of law index that has been established by World Bank economists. This allows a comparison to be made between a number of countries and correlates the GDP growth per capita with the rule of law.

One question raised from the graphs is the extent to which the correlation can be improved within the EU. As trade barriers have been reduced or eliminated, so the restrictions on trade have changed. Simple restrictions such as tariff barriers were eliminated under the GATT [7] and various WTO 'rounds'. Indirect barriers have been eliminated in various parts of the

---

justice [being] left perfectly free to pursue his own interests in his own way'; see also Hayek (n 3):

> Since the value of freedom rests on the opportunities it provides for unforeseen and unpredictable actions, we will rarely know what we lose through a particular restriction of freedom. Any such restriction, any coercion other than the enforcement of general rules, will aim at the achievements of a particular result, but what is prevented by it will not usually be known.

See, more recently, K Dam, *The Law-Growth Nexus: The Rule of Law and Economic Development* (Brookings Institution Press, Washington DC, 2006), who criticizes the approach toward building of the rule of law by transplanting but accepts the importance of the rule of law for economic growth.

[5] Smith (n 3).

[6] D Kaufmann and A Kraay, *The World Bank*, available at http://www.worldbank.org/wbi/governance. Also available at http://www.govindicators.org (accessed on 12 May 2008).

[7] General Agreement on Tariffs and Trade functions (GATT). The functions of the GATT were taken over by the World Trade Organisation (WTO), which was established during the final round of negotiations in early 1990s.

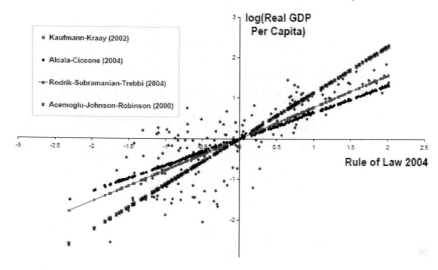

*Figure 1    Government Matters: The 'Development Dividend' Isolating Causality: From Governance to Income. Source: Kaufmann and Kraay (n 6)*

world, for example through to the establishment of a European Single Market. The gradual elimination of indirect or disguised restrictions has highlighted new areas not perhaps previously thought of as having a significant or material effect on the market. Access to justice and speedy enforcement of the regulatory system may be just such a newly discovered barrier.

Very recently the rule of law has become 'a big idea in economics'. This was, for example, noted in *The Economist*:

> The rule of law is usually thought of as a political or legal matter ... But in the past ten years the rule of law has become important in economics too ... The rule of law is held to be not only good in itself, because it embodies and encourages a just society, but also as a cause of other good things, notably growth ...[8]

Leading the way in quantifying the benefits in terms that many can understand has been the work done by the World Bank, described above. This includes and is especially concerned with 'governance' and the accountability of government for its actions as well as the rule of law in terms of the quality of justice and the nature of the legal system. Put simply, good governance

---

[8] 'Economics and the Rule of Law: Order in the Jungle' *The Economist* (13 March 2008) available at: http://www.economist.co.uk/finance/displaystory.cfm?story_id=10849115 (accessed on 12 May 2008).

54    *Tim Cowen*

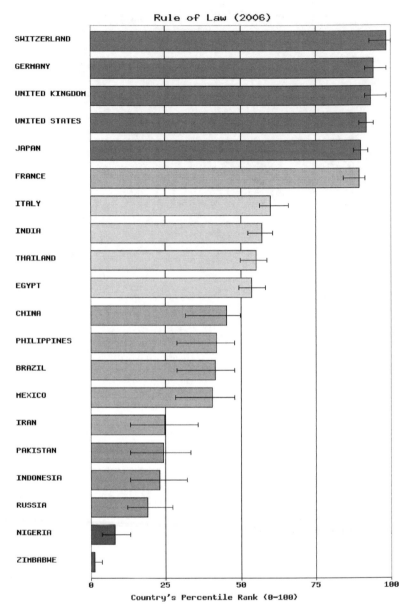

*Figure 2 Governance Indicators for 1996–2006. Source: D Kaufmann, A Kraavy and M Mastruzzi, 'Governance Matters VI: Governance Indicators for 1996–2006' (2007), World Bank Policy Research Working Paper No. 4280, available online at: http://papers.ssrn.com/sol3/papers.cfm?abstract_id=999979 (accessed on 12 May 2008).*

provides a framework for economic growth and prosperity; individuals feel safer and countries get richer the better the quality of governance. Indeed, the World Bank has assessed this as a '300 per cent dividend' since, in the long run, a country's income per capita rises by roughly 300 per cent if it can improve its governance by one standard deviation on the World Bank scale.

Most recently, leading thinkers in development economics and those concerned with establishing laws and regulations have pointed to the deficiencies of transplanting legal systems without establishing a culture of behaving within the law.[9] Leaving aside for the moment the discussion on legislation being the creature of instrumentalism and the importance of enshrining constitutional principles as the basis for an enduring application of the system, a critical analysis of the effectiveness of the legal system in enforcing the law is in itself vital for the efficient functioning of the economy. This is necessarily a matter that needs to be considered in some detail in the EU Single Market, where other trade barriers have been reduced or eliminated.

This introduction identifies the importance of the efficiency of the legal system in two ways: its importance to underpin basic concepts of justice in a free and open society, and its importance to economic development. This is more than the establishment of an idea that 'something must be done' on a reasoned basis. As we will see, there is a broad consensus on the need for change and the importance of reform to speed up the EU legal system. Also, the intention in referring to the rule of law at the outset is also to refer to the inherent idea within the rule of law idea of self-limiting principles. So, reform is needed but care must be taken.

There are currently a number of groups attempting to define the rule of law.[10] I consider that one of the simplest and clearest explanations has already been provided by Lord Bingham,[11] who identifies eight principles as being central to the rule of law:

---

[9] See, eg Carothers (n 3). Sir John Latham, former Chief Justice of Australia, drew a distinction between continental legal systems and the English common law.

'It is not the English rule of law that whatever is officially done is law, a view adopted by some jurists on the continent of Europe—on the contrary, the principle of English law is that what is done officially must be done in accordance with the law' (*Yates and Co Pty Ltd v The Vegetable Seeds Committee* [1945] 72 CLR 37).

One question that arises is whether the English position has been affected by the EU Reform Treaty and its entrenchment of constitutional rights in its Human Rights provisions, or whether, in accordance with Lord Bingham, certain rights are guaranteed by the common law and safeguarded under the Constitution of Reform Act 2005, where in s 1 it states that it does not adversely affect the existing constitutional principle of the rule of law.

[10] ABA/IBA World Justice Project (WJP), an initiative to strengthen the rule of law worldwide. The WJP uses four working definitions of the rule of law. Available at http://www.abanet.org/wjp/ (accessed on 12 May 2008).

[11] Lord Bingham (n 2).

- accessible, intelligible, clear and predictable rules;
- the application of law is prime over the exercise of discretion;
- law should apply equally to all, unless objective justification allows otherwise;
- law must allow adequate protection of fundamental human rights;
- a means of resolving (without prohibitive cost or inordinate delay) bona fide disputes;
- officials must exercise powers reasonably and in good faith, for proper purpose and without exceeding the powers' limits;
- the State's adjudicative powers must be fair (eg, independent and impartial judiciary; adequate time to prepare cases etc);
- the State complies with its international law obligations.

The above list addresses a number of factors that are important for the efficient functioning of the system. This article focuses on the 'mechanisms' of the rule of law and in particular the need to ensure that the means are in place for resolving disputes without unreasonable delay.

Before turning to speed of process or the lack of it, the first principle of accessibility and intelligibility, clarity and predictability is particularly worth touching on for a moment. For example, in a series of studies the detailed procedures and clarity of a single EU regulatory system, that of the EU telecommunications (telecoms) legalization, have been looked at and reviewed for their effect on the economy and therefore their effect on investment.[12]

Figure 3 compares regulatory performance as measured by the ECTA's Regulatory Scorecard against investment records from the Organisation for Economic Co-operation and Development and shows that investment in telecoms is substantially lower where the regulatory approach is weaker. The economic correlation analysis is striking, and it benefits from the 'control' that the EU telecommunication regime starts with an identical set of laws; what differs is the national system of law that operates on the application of the same EU legislation.

While the coherent application of law is, as a matter of legal policy, a cornerstone of the European system, different national rules, court traditions and procedures mean that the EU will always have a degree of differential enforcement, which inevitably gives rise to some inconsistency.[13]

---

[12] European Competitive Telecommunications Association (ECTA), Regulatory Scorecard (Brussels, ECTA, 2007). The ECTA study compares the regulatory environment in 18 EU Member States and Norway in the electronic communications sector and its effectiveness in promoting the objectives of the EU regulatory framework. Available at http://www.ectaportal. com/en/ basic651.html (accessed on 12 May 2008).

[13] For a study in the telecommunications area on the extent to which national procedural rules and dispute resolution mechanisms impact on the availability and effectiveness of the

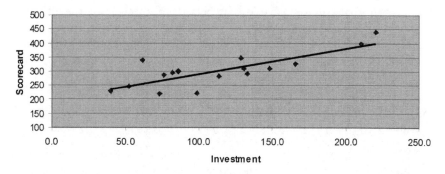

*Figure 3 Relationship between Scorecard and Investment per Capita: 2005. Source: ECTA Regulatory Scorecard (2007) (n 13)*

However, provided that enforcement operates within the accepted margin of appreciation, coherent policy implementation can eventually be achieved. In the ordinary course there are countless legislative and other changes made every year across the EU. While some policies can be implemented over time, with national authorities choosing both the form and method of implementing secondary legislation, urgent economic policy initiatives and the imperatives of improving productivity and further enhancing economic progress (in particular, to achieve the revised Lisbon goals) make the speed of implementation and the coherent enforcement of legislation a much greater priority for the future than it has perhaps been in the past.

This is a significant issue. One recent study has shown that the beneficial impact on the economy of modern business communications systems, if EU rules were consistent and correctly applied, amounts to a net present value of €68 billion over seven years (rising to €193 billion over 10 years and between €1,100 billion and €1,300 billion over the next 20 years) in the EU (in line with the EU's strategy and 2007 Spring Council declaration on completing the Single Market).[14] Following this logic, and the logic behind

underlying substantive telecommunications rules and, ultimately, the creation of a single European telecommunications market, see: British Institute of International and Comparative Law (BIICL), 'Effective Access and Procedure in Telecommunications Disputes in Europe' (BIICL, London, 2004), available at www.biicl.org (accessed on 12 May 2008). The study assesses the law and regulatory practice in selected EU Member States with a major focus on the interaction of the domestic legal systems with the European framework legislation for telecommunications and Internal Market rules.

[14] See Indepen Consulting (n 3). The study highlights the importance of 'ubiquitous access'. Ubiquitous access refers to supply conditions such that pan-European communications services providers are able to purchase wholesale access services at competitive supply conditions and offer seamless access to multiple business sites. The study estimates that ubiquitous access—ie provided on a competitive supply basis right across the EU—together with complementary measures, would generate benefits with a net present value of between €1,100 billion

the Lisbon goals, it is probable that better enforcement of the EU legal system would have significant, positive and wider economic benefits.

When considering a system of law, it is also possible to consider each component of the judicial system of oversight as a mechanism for the perfection of the regulation or a control of the discretion in the application of the law. One of Lord Bingham's 'sub principles' is 'that questions of legal insight and liability should actually be resolved by appreciation of the law and not the exercise of discretion' and,

> the broader and more loosely textured discretion, whether conferred an official or judge, the greater the scope for subjectivity and hence for arbitrariness, which is the antithesis of the rule of law. The consequence is that discretions should be narrowly defined and the exercise capable of reasoned justification.

These principles, however, require assessment in a time period that is reasonable and applicable to the pace of the modern economy. What is a reasonable timeframe depends on a number of factors, not least the pace of the economy. Individual examples at a personal level serve as a reminder that modern business decisions proceed in electronic time, not in real time.

This has led, as Bill Gates suggested, to 'business at the speed of thought'.[15] As, for example, famously described by Tom Friedman in 'The World is Flat',[16] a Dell laptop computer is created, shipped and delivered from the moment that an order is received in only four days. The total supply chain for a single laptop computer, including suppliers of suppliers, involves about 400 companies in North America, Europe and primarily Asia, with about 30 key components from 44 different companies operating in 130 different countries.[17]

---

and €1,300 billion over the next 20 years. To put these estimates in context: (i) while it might take a decade for the EU economy to feel the full effects of ubiquitous access and complementary measures, the full effect would be to increase EU GDP by 1.6–2 per cent each year from then on; (ii) this increase is equivalent to an increase in wealth of €430–510 per person per year in the long term. These estimates do not include additional potential benefits such as improved macroeconomic stability from better supply chain integration and management, and the potential for businesses to reduce their carbon footprint through better ICT connectivity.

[15] B Gates, *Business at the Speed of Thought* (New York, Grand Central Publishing, 1999).
[16] Friedman (n 3) 414–419.
[17] Friedman ibid:

> In an average day, we sell 140,000 to 150,000 computers' (explains Dick Hunter, one of Dell's three production managers); 'Every two hours the Dell factory in Penang sends an email to its suppliers nearby, telling each one what parts and what quantise of those parts they want delivered in the next 90 minutes and not one minute later within 90 minutes trucks from the various supplier logistic centres around Penang pull up to the Dell manufacturing plant and unload the parts needed for all those notebooks ordered in the last two hours, this goes on all day every two hours.

The above example shows how many decisions can be coordinated on a truly multi-national basis to produce everyday items. It is remarkable to note that it takes only four days to produce a single laptop computer from many different parts of the world, but that a decision in a legal case spends on average seven months in translation before the ECJ. Surely, with the application of modern communication infrastructure and a more modern approach to the decision-making process, the system can be speeded up?

According to UNCTAD, 77,000 transnational firms span the global economy today, with some 770,000 subsidiaries, countless affiliates and associates, and millions of suppliers.[18] As John Ruggie, the UN Secretary General's Special Representative for Business and Human Rights, Kirkpatrick Professor of International Affairs, Director, Center for Business and Government, Kennedy School of Government, Harvard University, has noted:

> For many corporations going global has meant adopting network-based operating models involving multiple corporate entities spread among and within countries. Networks by their very nature involve divesting a certain amount of direct control over significant operations, substituting negotiated relationships for hierarchical structures. This organisational form has enhanced the economic efficiency of firms...

This comment notes a general change that is taking place worldwide and which is a collaborative organizational model required to adapt modern businesses to internationalization or globalization. It has been described as the major event of our time, with the mechanisms that underpin and facilitate interdependence being a major challenge.[19]

One challenge which globalization faces is whether the legal systems facilitate or impede the agreements that underpin international supply chains. While jurisdiction and the choice of law clauses and arm's-length contract law have allowed many organizations to contract out of and avoid the deficiencies of arbitrary or deficient legal systems, this is increasingly difficult to achieve when investments are truly multinational and non-transitory, and where submission to local laws is unavoidable. Exposure to many different local laws and procedures is a major challenge for any organization operating across the world, but is a particular issue in operating

---

[18] UNCTAD, World Investment Report 2006, available at http://www.unctad.org/en/docs/wir2006_en.pdf (accessed on 12 May 2008). WalMart alone is reported to have more than 60,000 suppliers. The WalMart statistics came from H Lee Scott, CEO, Cambridge University Programme for Industry; also available at http://www3.cpi.cam.ac.uk/pdf/BEP%20London%20Lecture%202007.pdf (accessed on 12 May 2008).
[19] 'Clinton Charms Albert Hall Audience' *BBC News* (26 September 2006) available at http://news.bbc.co.uk/1/hi/uk/5383214.stm (accessed 12 May 2008).

across the 27 EU Member States. In the EU the possibility exists for a system of law to become more effective and to help support the modern economy. The particular issue today is that, following the accession of the new EU Member States, there is both an opportunity and a need to build a coherent legal culture and rule of law, based on consistent EU decisions, under a single Court of Justice. It is important that this is addressed now since the opportunity for divergence, inconsistent application of the law and incoherent implementation of policy and agreed intent has never been more important.

At present legal systems, traditions and cultures vary widely, and the delays that are experienced in different Member States could impede progress toward agreed political and economic goals. However, one of the preconditions for economic progress in a globalizing world is good governance.[20]

As recognized by Lord Bingham, 'means must be provided for resolving without prohibitive cost or inordinate delays, bona fide civil disputes which the parties we are ourselves unable to resolve'. The principle is also known as 'justice delayed is justice denied'.[21] The issue that then arises is how much the justice system can be speeded up to operate within the principles of the rule of law in a modern economy.

### B. *The European Community Courts in Light of Key European Policies, the Reform Treaty and Lisbon Goals*

The experiences of many businesses operating in a multi-domestic or multinational way across the EU indicate that there is growing concern, particularly about the speed in the application of European Community law.[22]

---

[20] As noted by Friedman (n 3).

[21] William Gladstone (1809–1898).

[22] See section II.A for statistics on the speed of court proceedings in front of the ECJ and CFI. Furthermore, see (oral/written) evidence by Rufus Ogilvie Smals, Alex Nourry, Tim Cowen, James Flynn QC, Confederation of British Industry; Onno Brouwer, Georg Berrisch, CCBE Permanent Delegation to the Court of Justice and the Court of First Instance of the European Community and the EFTA Court; Dr William Bishop, CRA International; Sir Christopher Bellamy QC, Charles Dhanowa, Competition Appeal Tribunal; Sir David Edward QC; M Michel Petite, Philip Lowe Director General, DG Competition, European Commission; Allen & Overy; BDI (Bundesverband der Deutschen Industrie); Competition Commission; Competition Law Association; Department of Trade and Industry; International Bar Association; International Chamber of Commerce; Joint Competition Law Working Party; MEDEF (Mouvement des Entreprises de France); Office of Fair Trading; Peter Roth QC, Monckton Chambers; Svenskt Naringsliv (Confederation of Swedish Enterprise); John Temple Lang and Robert O'Donoghue. See House of Lords, European Union Committee, 15th Report of Session 2006–2007, An EU Competition Court—Report with Evidence (London, The Stationery Office, 2007), HL Paper 75 (hereinafter House of Lords report). The report is also available at http://www.parliament.uk/parliamentary_committees/lords_s_comm_e.cfm (accessed on 12 May 2008).

This concern is growing despite the fact that the principles of direct effect[23] and supremacy[24] of European law are well established within the EU.

Under the Treaty establishing the European Community (EC Treaty), national courts have a duty to cooperate with the ECJ.[25] These procedures allow the ECJ to ensure uniform application of European law at the national level and help to promote equal treatment among citizens, reduce distortion of competition and promote economic efficiency.

A coordinated approach is in line with the approach adopted in the Lisbon Treaty. Through the negotiations for the Lisbon Treaty a centralized federal system was rejected in favour of a negotiated relationship. Instead of adopting a system analogous to that of the US, the EU has chosen to move forward in a coordinated and harmonized manner, preferring to increase reliance on the national systems of the Member States. A greater degree of coordination may also be appropriate for the EU court system.

This is recognized as a possibility in the Lisbon objectives,[26] which state the need for a further reform of the European Community courts in order to achieve more democracy, legal certainty, transparency, accountability and efficiency, as well as the aims of the Single Market (particularly in the context of references for preliminary rulings, which are a key factor in the proper functioning of the internal market).

In the 2007 Annual Report, President of the Court of Justice, V Skouris notes as follows:

> The year 2007 will doubtless also remain engraved on the memory as the year in which the Treaty of Lisbon was signed, an instrument which is designed to endow the European Union with more effective legislative and administrative structures enhancing its ability to meet the challenges of the beginning of the 21st century.

---

[23] It is a well-established principle of European Community law that provisions of the Treaty can have a direct effect and create individual rights which national courts must protect. See Case 26/62 *van Gend en Loos* [1963] ECR 1.

[24] The doctrine of primacy has existed in European law for over 40 years and can be traced back to the judgment of the ECJ in *Costa v ENEL*. See Case 6/64 *Costa v ENEL* [1964] ECR 585.

[25] Art 234 of the EC Treaty enables the Community court, on a reference from a national court, to give preliminary rulings on the interpretation of Community legislation and on the validity of the acts of the institutions of the Union and of the European Central Bank. This jurisdiction provides a mechanism of judicial cooperation between the Community court and national courts, and is particularly important in maintaining certainty and consistency in the application of Community Law.

[26] The Lisbon Strategy, also known as the Lisbon Agenda or Lisbon Process, is an action and development plan for the EU. Its aim is to make the EU 'the most dynamic and competitive knowledge-based economy in the world capable of sustainable economic growth with more and better jobs and greater social cohesion, and respect for the environment by 2010' set against the background of productivity in the EU being below that of the US. It was set out by the European Council in Lisbon on March 2000.

The European courts could be reformed to fall in line with this fresh framework of negotiated and collaborative engagement.

It is probable that the political expectation for the completion of the Single Market is that enforcement exists or can be expected. In competition law, which is central to economic development, the expectation is that rigorous application of competition law will deliver growth, productivity, innovation and jobs. There is a level of concern that this is not happening fast enough, that the regime is unbalanced and that the legal system unfairly favours the defendants as enforcement appears to be ineffective.[27]

In the competition law area, the response to the lack of effective enforcement appears to be to consider the issue as one of sanction. Consequentially, the focus, in the EU[28] as well as in the UK,[29] is on the level of sanction and enforcement.

Little time is being spent on the process, or on the speed of enforcement and access to justice.[30] Furthermore, in looking to increase the sanctions and hence the enforcement of competition law, the assumption is that increased sanctions will mean increased compliance with the law. However, the opposite may be an unintended consequence. Where sanctions are

[27] Recent reviews of competition law have noted the differences at national level as an impediment to effective redress. See European Commission, Green Paper—Damages Actions for Breach of EC Antitrust Rules, Brussels, 19 December 2005, COM(2005) 672 final, as well as European Commission, White Paper on Damages Actions for Breach of the EC Antitrust Rules, COM(2008) 165, published on 2 April 2008. See also the study by law firm Ashurst, Conditions of Claims for Damages in Case of Infringement of EC Competition Rules, Comparative Report (Brussels, prepared by D Waelbroeck, D Slater and G Even-Shoshan, 2004), available at http://europa.eu.int/comm/competition/antitrust/others/actions_for_damages/study.html (accessed on 12 May 2008). The study found that levels of private enforcement through damages claims in Europe are very low and found that is not only 'total underdevelopment' of actions for damages for breach of EU competition law, but also 'astonishing diversity' in the approaches taken by the Member States.
[28] See European Commission, White Paper on Damages Actions for Breach of the EC Antitrust Rules, ibid. It sets out for public comment a new model for achieving compensation for consumers and businesses which have suffered loss due to breaches of the EC Treaty rules on restrictive agreements and abuse of a dominant market position. The key recommendations of the White Paper are: (a) single damages; (b) collective redress; (c) disclosure (it advocates an EU-wide minimum level of disclosure between the parties in an antitrust damages claim); and (d) binding effect of final decisions (in order to avoid the time and cost of re-litigation, final decisions of Member States' competition authorities should be considered sufficient proof of an infringement in subsequent actions for damages).
[29] Office of Fair Trading, Private Actions in Competition Law: Effective Redress for Consumers and Business: Recommendations from the Office of Fair Trading (London, OFT916resp, November 2007), available at http://www.oft.gov.uk/shared_oft/reports/comp_policy/oft916resp.pdf (accessed on 12 May 2008).
[30] It may also well be that increasing the enforcement powers of administrative authorities, and in particular the current proposal by the White Paper on Damages Actions for Breach of EC Antitrust Rules (n 27) that final decisions of Member States competition authorities should be considered sufficient proof of an infringement in subsequent actions for damages, offends the principle of separation between the administrative and judiciary powers, as well as the principle of judicial independence.

increased, defendants would have a greater incentive to challenge the decisions (particularly of an administrative authority) instead of negotiating the payment of the fine, settling and/or complying. To let an administrative decision stand could leave companies vulnerable to 'follow-on' damages actions. This may also increase the workload of the courts and lead to enforcement delays.

Finally, the effective enforcement of the law may also be undermined by the enforcement system itself.[31]

## II. THE ISSUES—WHY IS THERE A NEED FOR REFORM?

### A. Procedural Delays

The European Court of Justice became a victim of its success.[32]

From the start, the ECJ took an active and important role in the creation of the constitutional order of the European Union and at the same time made every effort not to alienate national courts.[33] That success, however, has its disadvantages.

The Court's wide jurisdiction is a positive force for greater economic convergence and is central to the fulfilment of the economic goals described as the Lisbon goals. The large volume of law of which it is the sole authoritative interpreter has not only increased confidence in the ECJ, but also resulted in an increased workload of cases and consequent delays in the

---

[31] This may, for example, be the case in relation to the operation of the Commission's leniency programme, which grants immunity from Commission investigation but not from national court actions. Increased risk of sanction can be expected to make organizations think very carefully before making leniency applications, and may reduce the willingness to compromise. Any documentation disclosed in leniency applications may be discoverable in national proceedings. Furthermore, the increase in the opportunity for windfall claims that class actions would bring might increase close scrutiny of a wide range of agreements, many of which may legally be borderline in terms of their compliance with art 81(3) EU Treaty, but of limited economic consequence. There is a prospect for a dangerous unintended consequence: legally borderline but economically unimportant cases were not a problem in a system where borderline was capable of being safeguarded through a notification process. Without notification there is no safe harbour from the national court process, and borderline cases are more likely to be reviewed in courts and undermine the enforceability and certainty of contracts. This might also increase the risk to businesses considering how to innovate.

[32] See, eg P Jeney, 'Victim of Its Own Success—the EU Court in Need of Reform' available at http://www.eumap.org/journal/features/2002/aug02/eucourtreform (accessed on 12 May 2008).

[33] See BIICL, 'The Role and Future of the European Court of Justice' A report by members of the EC Section of the British Institute's Advisory Board chaired by the Rt Hon the Lord Slynn of Hadley (BIICL, October 1996; hereinafter BIICL report), stating that the ECJ is 'in many ways, the most successful international court in the world community; its fundamental function in the Community legal order is now well established'.

disposal of cases over the years before the Community courts.[34] These developments also threaten ultimately to undermine institutional confidence.

There are at least four factors which have led to the increase in the caseload of the Community courts and which particularly affect the timeliness of procedures. First is the enlargement of the EU; second, the expansion of the areas over the which the EU has competence; third, the very success of EU harmonization initiatives requiring increased judicial clarification and thereby generating work for the Community judicial system; and fourth, the growing awareness of EU law by lawyers.[35]

In response to the increased workload of the ECJ, a new court, the CFI, was created in 1989 with jurisdiction to hear certain direct actions. The rationale behind this was to set up a court which would be better placed to hear complicated cases in technical areas of law, enabling the ECJ to focus on exercising its unifying jurisdiction under the preliminary reference procedure.[36] This was one of the important institutional reforms of the Single European Act in 1986. Initially it had a limited remit, but over time the CFI's jurisdiction has, in response to demand, been increased,[37] resulting in significant delays also in front of the CFI.[38] Excluding staff cases and special proceedings, the number of cases introduced before the CFI increased by 33 per cent[39] in 2006, from 291 in 2005 to 387 in 2006, and by another 20 per cent in 2007, from 387 to 464.

The number of procedures conducted by the Community courts increased steeply in the mid-80s and 90s, and as a result the number of actions handled by the ECJ and CFI doubled between 1990 and 2000. It is worth noting that there are also significant cross-country and subject matter variations, which themselves also vary from sub-period to sub-period.[40] Since the accession of 10 more Member States to the EU in May

---

[34] See BIICL report, ibid 23.

[35] See P Craig, 'The Jurisdiction of the Community Courts Reconsidered' in G de Burca and JHH Weiler (eds), *The European Court of Justice* (OUP, Oxford, 2001) 177, 184.

[36] See, eg Case C-344/98 *Masterfoods and HB v Commission* [2000] ECR I–11369, para 54, stating that judicial review in the field of competition deals with decisions involving 'complex technical and economic assessments which, if they are to be correct, require exhaustive review of the substance by a specialised judicial authority. In order to meet that need ... Community legislature on constitutional matters was led to set up the Court of First Instance'.

[37] In 2007, the CFI closed 397 cases (436 in 2006), received 522 new applications (432 in 2006) and ended the year with a backlog of 1,154 pending cases (1,029 in 2006).

[38] See House of Lords, European Union Committee, 6th Report of Session 2003–2004, The Future Role of the European Court of Justice, 10, para 13.

[39] This increase can be divided into two figures: one, regarding trademark cases, is up 46 per cent and the other, regarding all the other cases together, is up 25 per cent. See oral evidence by B Vesterdorf in House of Lords report (n 22), 'Minutes of Evidence', 89, questions 364 and 365.

[40] Figures by A Stone Sweet and TL Brunell, *Data Set on Preliminary References in EC Law* (Robert Schuman Center, European University Institute, San Domenico di Fiesole, 1999) show

2004 and a further two in 2007, the ECJ is now the presiding court for 27 different countries. The courts of the new Member States are also less famil-iar with EU law and hence request more preliminary rulings from the EU courts. This rapid expansion in size of the EU has also led to the severe delays in the proceedings being recognized as a significant weakness of the system.

As stated by Bo Vesterdorf, the former CFI president: 'The main prob-lem with our current system of judicial review is not its effectiveness in terms of how closely the Courts scrutinize the Commission's decision, but in terms of the speed of that review'.[41] With regards to preliminary rulings, it can be said that article 234 of the EC Treaty is the most important proce-dural provision in the Treaty as it facilitates the dialogue between the national courts and the ECJ.[42] By providing the meeting point between Community and national law, it facilitates access to justice by making it clear that Community law is to be applied not only by the ECJ but also by national courts, thus enabling citizens to enforce their Community rights within a national jurisdiction.[43]

The ECJ was from the start very eager to encourage national courts to refer matters for interpretation. It facilitated preliminary rulings by, for example, broadly interpreting the notion of a 'referring court or tribunal'[44]

that Germany made the largest number of references per year, almost twice as many as the next country (France). On the other hand, Ireland and Luxembourg made the smallest. Stone Sweet and Brunell attributed the growth of references and the cross-country and subject matter vari-ations to demand by private litigants, and offered empirical tests to support this. The essence of their argument is that, as national laws were not designed to resolve disputes arising from transnational transactions, which generate demand for dispute resolution, the void is filled by Community law. National courts recognize the relevance of Community law in facilitating transnational economic activity and accept the competence of the Community courts. Hence, as the volume of economic transactions among the EU countries grows, conflicts between national law and EU law will increase and, consequentially, so will the demand for a proper system of dispute resolution. Moreover, their hypothesis accounts for the cross-country and cross-subject variation in references. See A Stone Sweet and TL Brunell, 'The European Court of Justice and the National Courts: A Statistical Analysis of Preliminary Reference 1961–95' (1998) 5 Journal of European Public Policy 66. See also G Tridimas and T Tridimas, 'National Courts and the European Court of Justice: A Public Choice Analysis of the Preliminary Reference Procedure', 13 December 2001, available at http://polis.unipmn.it/epcs/ papers/ tridimas.pdf, 7 (accessed on 12 May 2008).

[41] Emphasis added. B Vesterdorf, 'Judicial Review in EC Competition Law: Reflections on the Role of the Community courts in the EC System of Competition Law Enforcement' (2005) 1 Competition Policy International 2 22.

[42] Art 234 is even regarded as the 'jewel in the crown of the existing regime'. See Craig (n 35) 181.

[43] For an analysis of the inter-related functions of art 234, see Tridimas and Tridimas (n 40).

[44] See, eg Case 61/65 *Vaassen-Goebbels v Beambtenfonds voor het Mijnbedrijf* [1966] ECR 377, refined in Case 54/96 *Dorsch Consult* [1997] ECR I–4961, 4992–96; Dutch Professional Chamber of Dentists 246/80 *Broekmeulen v Huisarts Registratie Commissie* [1981] ECR 2311; also Case 61/65 *Vaassen-Goebbels v Beambtenfonds voor het Mijnbedrijf* [1966] ECR 377. Danish industrial tribunal hearing labour disputes case 19/88 *Handels-og Kontorfunktionaererernes Forbund i Danmark* [1989] ECR 3199.

and by widening the scope of Community Acts that may be the subject of interpretation.[45] In general, the ECJ treated references in a very flexible manner and rarely turned down references.[46] While this proactive judicial purpose of the ECJ to enhance its role in the interpretation of Community law has been a real success story, a significant side effect has been an increasingly burdensome caseload, which has resulted in delayed proceedings.

The recent case law of the ECJ indicates an attempt by the ECJ to reduce its workload by turning down references which it would have accepted in the 1990s. Whilst this might certainly lead to a decrease in the workload and an improvement in the response time by the ECJ, a significant side effect could be the undermining of benefits achieved in terms of cross-border consistency and hence a reduction in ECJ-sponsored harmonization which may give rise to increased barriers to cross-border trade. This diverges from the ECJ's previous case law and, if it becomes a trend, it would impact negatively on legal certainty and harmonization.[47]

As at the end of 2007, the average time for preliminary rulings in front of the ECJ is 19.3 months; for direct actions 18.2 months and for appeals 17.8 months.[48] In the year 2007 the average number of months taken for a case to be completed by the CFI was 29.5 months in ordinary proce-

---

[45] Case 322/88 *Grimaldi* [1989] ECR 4407; Case 181/73 *Haegeman* [1974] ECR 449; Case C–11/70 *Internationale Handelsgesellschaft Gmbh* [1970] ECR 1125.

[46] P Craig and G de Búrca, *EU Law: Text, Cases and Materials* (2nd edn, OUP, Oxford, 1998) 433–436.

[47] See, eg decision by the ECJ regarding referral of the Austrian National Regulatory Authority for Telecommunications (Telekom-Control Kommission), [2006] OJ C 10/7. The ECJ decided not to answer to the request for a preliminary ruling by the Austrian regulator and declared that it had no jurisdiction to answer the regulator's question about the validity of the Commission's veto decision on the wholesale market for transit services in the fixed public telephone network (market 10) because there was no lawsuit pending that would have required the Court's judicial decision. In another recent case, the ECJ also found that it has no jurisdiction to answer the questions referred by the Greek Competition Commission. See Case 53/03 *Synetairismos Farmakopoion Aitolias & Akarnanias (Syfait) and Others v Glaxo-SmithKline* [2005] OJ C 182/06. The ECJ held that the Greek Competition Commission is not a 'court or tribunal' within the meaning of art 234 of the EC Treaty. According to the ECJ, the Greek Competition Commission does not have certain characteristics necessary for it to be classified as a 'court or tribunal', namely independence and the fact of being called upon to give judgment in proceedings intended to lead to a decision of a judicial nature. This will result in a regrettable delay in the final interpretation of Community competition law as national competition authorities cases may now only reach the ECJ when courts reviewing decisions of the national competition authorities refer questions to Luxembourg. Needless to say, this recent approach by the ECJ may also affect the consistent application of European Community law.

[48] ECJ statistics (end of 2007): the number of cases pending increased by about 1.4 per cent and the number of cases brought to a close increased by approximately 4 per cent (570 cases closed in 2007, 580 new cases, 741 cases pending at the end of 2007). See further European Court of Justice, 2007 Annual Report, available at http://curia.europa.eu/en/plan/index.htm (accessed on 12 May 2008).

dures.[49] In 2006 the average number of months taken for a case to be completed in expedited procedures was 13 months (nine months in merger cases, with the shortest merger case taking just under seven months).[50] In that year, the CFI delivered two judgments under the fast-track procedure: one took 19 months[51] and the other seven months. This clearly indicates that the expedited procedure in itself does not represent a solution to the problems of timeliness of CFI reviews.

In general, it is agreed that this is too long and that such delays deter particularly references of points of Community interest from national courts.[52]

Furthermore, one point in the evidence before the House of Lords was the effect of a slow system on the number of cases brought to appeal. In effect, the lack of cases on appeal could be a sign of the failure of the system to work effectively.[53]

The effect of these procedural delays can have a particularly harmful effect on business and the economy in competition cases. Needless to say, these delays are particularly critical in the field of mergers, where speedy adjudication is of crucial importance and where, given the time for appeal, only a few companies can keep the deal alive for such a length of time. For a merger appeal to have any value for business, the maximum time taken to deliver a judgment should be six months.

---

[49] CFI statistics (end of 2007): pending cases: 1154 (competition: 197, state aid: 165); new cases: 522 (competition: 62, state aid: 37); completed cases: 397 (competition: 38, state aid: 36). Appeals: competition: 13 (appeals dismissed), 1 (appeal allowed), 1 (removed from register); state aid: 5 (appeals dismissed). For further statistical information, see European Court of First Instance, 2007 Annual Report, available at: http://curia.europa.eu/en/instit/presentationfr/index.htm (accessed on 12 May 2008). From its establishment in 1989 up to 31 December 2006, 743 competition cases (excluding state aid cases) were introduced before the CFI, of which 559 have been closed. Those 559 cases may be broken down as follows: 428 cases concerning the application of art 81 EC and 65 ECSC, which have given rise to 160 appeals before the ECJ; 68 cases concerning the application of art 82 EC, which have given rise to 19 appeals before the ECJ; 58 cases concerning merger control, which have given rise to three appeals before the ECJ; five cases concerning the application of the competition rules, together with art 86, 87 or 88 EC, which have given rise to three appeals before the ECJ. See, in particular, written evidence by B Vesterdorf, 'Minutes of Evidence' of the House of Lords report (n 22), 17 January 2007, 102 ff.

[50] Case T–87/05 *EDP v Commission* [2005] OJ C 281, 22 (action was lodged with the CFI on 25 February 2005).

[51] Case T–464/04 *Independent Music Publishers and Labels Association (Impala) v Commission* [2006] ECR I–2, where the CFI annulled the European Commission's clearance of Sony/Bertlesmann, took 19 months to complete.

[52] See, eg *R v Minister of Agriculture Fisheries and Food ex parte Portman Agrochemicals Limited* [1994] 3 CMLR 18 (QB). Anecdotally, correspondents suggest that this delay acts as deterrent even in the art 234(4) courts of last instance, where a point is not truly acte clair.

[53] According to the CFI Statistics (end of 2007), there were a total of 397 cases completed and a total of 76 appeals, of which 72 were dismissed. See CFI, 2007 Annual Report http://curia.europa.eu/ en/instit/presentationfr/index.htm (accessed on 12 May 2008).

There is no doubt that mergers play an important role in a market economy and can bring benefits to competition and, in turn, consumers. The importance of mergers for the competitiveness of European industry is also recognized in the Merger Regulation 139/2004.[54] And as the EU Commission has said, combining the activities of different companies may allow the companies to develop new products more efficiently, for example, or to reduce production or distribution costs. Through their increased efficiency the market becomes more competitive, and consumers benefit from higher-quality goods at fair prices.

The world moves swiftly and delays incur huge opportunity costs; for example, in one case alone the business loss of an unconsummated transaction amounted to £100 million per month.[55] There are numerous examples of judicial review of merger decisions that took too long and final judgments came about when the envisaged transactions could no longer be implemented (or no longer made economic sense). In Kali and Salz, the ECJ annulled the Commission's decision authorizing a concentration with remedies four years later. The Airtours judgment came about almost three years after the Commission decision. Also, the Schneider/Legrand case serves as a reminder of the lack of effectiveness of the EU system, taking over six years to finally be resolved.[56] Furthermore, the Microsoft deci-

---

[54] Preamble, para 4.

[55] See British Telecommunications plc/ AT&T Corporation, where the business benefits were set at this level.

[56] Joined Cases C–68/94 and C–30/95, *France v Commission* (Kali and Salz) [1998] ECR I–1375; Case T–342/99 *Airtours plc v Commission* [2002] ECR II–2585. Case T–77/02 *Schneider Electric SA v European Commission* [2002] ECR II–4201 (Schneider II). The same day, the Court of First Instance decided also on the case arising on 13 December 2001 (Case T–310/01 [Schneider I]), annulling the decision on separation: Case T–310/01 *Schneider Electric SA v Commission of European* Community [2002] ECR II–4071. Background: on 11 July 2007, the CFI delivered its long-awaited judgment in the appeal of Schneider Electric SA against the decision of the European Commission. The CFI ruled for the first time that a merging party can be compensated (at least in part) for losses sustained as a result of the illegal prohibition of its merger. The case dates back to 2001, when in February of that year Schneider and Legrand, two large French industrial groups, agreed that Schneider would acquire control of Legrand through a transaction that required clearance by the Commission. Subsequent to Schneider's acquisition of Legrand in August 2001, the Commission blocked the merger on the grounds, inter alia, that the merged entity would significantly impede effective competition in a number of markets in France. These include the electrical panel-board components sector and various downstream electrical equipment market segments. The Commission also adopted a separate decision ordering the divestment by Schneider of Legrand. Schneider subsequently brought an action for the annulment of both Commission decisions. At the same time, Schneider prepared its divestiture of Legrand. By its judgments of 22 October 2002, the CFI annulled the Commission's prohibition decision. The court held that the Commission had failed to have regard to Schneider's rights of defence, since the Commission had advanced for the first time in the decision an objection to the merger that Schneider had not had an opportunity to comment upon. The objection alleged that Schneider would leverage its dominant position in the electrical panel-board components sector into Legrand's leading position in downstream electrical equipment market segments in France. According to the court, the alleged reinforcement of a dominant position through the dominant firm's position in related

sion[57] was finally decided by the ECJ in 2007 referring to a factual situation that existed in 2004.

What is important to the companies concerned is not only speed but also finality and legal certainty. It must therefore be predictable for those entering negotiations whether—and, if so, when—their deal can go ahead without further possibility of challenge.

Given these issues, it is clear that something needs to be done in order to avoid a 'serious crisis where the average length of proceedings ... would grow to completely unacceptable levels'.[58]

To 'reduce procedures as much as possible while maintaining quality' is also a target and top priority for new CFI president Marc Jaeger,[59] who has already taken the first step in addressing the delays by spreading the tribunal's 27 judges to eight chambers (instead of the original five).[60]

However, there are various additional factors that will increase the Court's caseload over the next years, suggesting that national governments need to make the Court more efficient sooner rather than later.

First, the Charter of Fundamental Rights[61] could potentially generate a great deal of litigation in order to test out its limits, interpretation and meaning;[62] Member States have certainly increased the chances of liti-

---

markets (facilitated by its ability to provide a portfolio of products) had not been raised in the Statement of Objections earlier in the proceedings. Accordingly, the Commission had not afforded the merging parties the opportunity to counter such allegations, nor to craft remedies that could address the Commission's concerns arising from the 'portfolio' effect created by the merger. The Commission, however, had not closed its procedure until after the date on which the sale of Legrand had been contractually agreed to take place. This led Schneider to divest Legrand. Subsequently, Schneider brought an action for damages before the CFI.

[57] Case T–201/04 *Microsoft Corp (The Computing Technology Industry Association Inc and Others, intervening) v Commission of the European Communities (Software & Information Industry Association and Others, intervening)* [2007] OJ 2007/C 269/80.

[58] B Vesterdorf, 'The Community Court System Ten Years from Now and Beyond: Challenges and Possibilities' (2003) 28 European Law Review 309.

[59] M Jaeger took over from B Vesterdorf, who retired after leading the court for nine years, on 17 September 2007.

[60] See M Jaeger, 'New EU Court Head Says Priority Cutting Case Backlog' *Bloomberg* (October 2007) available at: http://www.bloomberg.com/apps/news?pid=20601085&sid=ayYfhR7ueZyw&refer=europe (accessed 12 May 2008).

[61] Charter of Fundamental Rights: the Presidents of the Commission, European Parliament and Council, signed and solemnly proclaimed the Charter in Strasbourg, 12 December 2007, IP/07/1916.

[62] Through the EU Reform Treaty (or Lisbon Treaty—see n 1) the Charter of Fundamental Rights becomes binding, having the same legal value as the Treaties, although its text will not be in the Treaties (art 6(1) TEU; Declaration 1); EU law is to be interpreted in compliance with the Charter. Protocol 7 to the Reform Treaty introduces specific measures for the UK and Poland, seeking to establish national exceptions to the justiciability of the Charter (Protocol on the Application of the Charter of Fundamental Rights to Poland and to the United Kingdom; Declarations 61 and 62). The Treaty also provides a new legal basis for the accession of the Union to the European Convention on Human Rights (art 6(2) TEU and Protocol on the Accession of the Union to the European Convention on the Protection of Human Rights and Fundamental Freedoms; Declaration 2). It is worth pointing out that the UK has been

gation by making the operation and interpretation of the Charter unclear.[63]

Secondly, the complex format of the newly signed Lisbon Treaty,[64] as well as the reforms it sets out, could for a time make the overall EU legal framework more uncertain, which could in turn lead to an increase in disputes requiring the adjudication of the Community courts. History has shown that constitutional engineering on such a scale almost always leads to a period of uncertainty when the new framework comes into operation.

One example of the uncertainty that may arise is the agreement reached by the EU Member States in June 2007 to remove the competition phrase contained in article 3(1)(g) of the EC Treaty[65] from the Lisbon Treaty and create a 'competition protocol' that includes the words from article 3(1)(g). Some academics have argued that this is likely to have a number of damaging consequences for EC competition law as Member States might seek to use the Lisbon Treaty to weaken the crucial impact of competition law (by expanding the scope for lawful State aid on social and social market grounds, by permitting merger clearance on broader industrial policy

---

adamant that the Charter does not have legal force. This is reflected by UK's opt-out in Protocol 7 to the Reform Treaty which states as follows:

> Art 1: 1. The Charter does not extend the ability of the Court of Justice of the European Union, or any court or tribunal of Poland or of the United Kingdom, to find that the laws, regulations or administrative provisions, practices or action of Poland or of the United Kingdom are inconsistent with the fundamental rights, freedoms and principles that it reaffirms. 2. In particular, and for the avoidance of doubt, nothing in Title IV of the Charter creates justiciable rights applicable to Poland or the United Kingdom except in so far as Poland or the United Kingdom has provided for such rights in its national law. Article 2: To the extent that a provision of the Charter refers to national law and practices, it shall only apply to Poland or the United Kingdom to the extent that the rights or principles that it contains are recognised in the law or practices of Poland or of the United Kingdom.

Essentially, it does not extend the powers of any court—domestic or European—to challenge UK employment and social legislation. The rights vis-à-vis the UK remain enforceable through existing international and European obligations and domestically through the Human Rights Act, the common law and relevant legislation. Protocol 7 clearly states that it does not prejudice the UK's other duties and obligations under EU law. Nor does it exempt the UK from abiding by the ECJ's judgments seeking to ensure uniform application of EU law. Fundamentally it appears to the authors that the Protocol is more of a face-saving step to satisfy the eurosceptics at home, since as has already been stated that most of the rights contained in the Charter can be enforced through other routes.

[63] See A Townsend, 'Can the EU Achieve an Area of Freedom, Security and Justice' Centre for European Reform, available at: http://209.85.129.104/search?q=cache:Xw1192jcg68J: www.cer.org.uk/pdf/opinion_at_jhaoct.pdf+A+Townsend+Can+the+EU+achieve+an+area+o f+freedom,+security+and+justice+Centre+for+European+Reform&hl=en&ct=clnk&cd=1&gl = uk (accessed on 12 May 2008).

[64] Treaty of Lisbon amending the Treaty on European Union and the Treaty establishing the European Community, signed at Lisbon, 13 December 2007 (n 1).

[65] The provision of 'a system ensuring that competition in the internal market is not distorted'.

grounds and by weakening the pressure for market liberalization, particularly in energy and network services).[66]

In light of the fact that the ECJ has developed a 'purposive interpretation' tradition to deal with conflicts,[67] time will tell whether the ECJ will provide the protocol with the same interpretative status in its case law as an article of principle or an objective in the treaty itself,[68] but what is certain is that the changes in the new treaty will raise many questions and hence litigation to test out its meaning and limits.

Thirdly, under the Lisbon Treaty the jurisdiction of the ECJ (renamed under the Lisbon Treaty as 'Court of Justice')[69] will be expanded to all the activities of the EU with the express exception of common foreign and security policy.[70] However, the Court will have oversight in the case of a breach of procedure or a conflict over competence (in effect, patrolling the frontier between the first and second pillars). It will hear appeals against restrictive measures and give an opinion about an international treaty.[71] Where the opinion of the Court is adverse, the agreement envisaged may not enter into force unless it is amended or the treaties are revised.[72] There are a number of other amendments, beyond the scope of this article but of general relevance to improved governance, which may have an indirect effect on the speed of the system.[73]

---

[66] See A Riley, 'The EU Reform Treaty and the Competition Protocol: Undermining EC Competition Law' (September 2007), CEPS Policy Brief, No 143. Furthermore, Antonio Bavasso, visiting professor of competition law at University College London and a partner with law firm Allen & Overy, said the following about the changes as a consequences of this deal: 'the political significance of the change cannot be overstated ... The foundations of competition enforcement are now weaker.' For more details on the current status of the discussion, see House of Commons debate on the Treaty of Lisbon, 4th allocated day provisions relating to the Single Market, 6 February 2008. Furthermore, the BIICL hosted a conference on the new European treaty, the Treaty of Lisbon, on 29 February 2008. Speakers included academics, practitioners, political scientists and politicians (Michael Connarty MP; Sir David Edward KCMG QC; Andrew Duff MEP; Xavier Lewis of the Legal Service of the European Commission; Professor Steve Peers; Timothy Kirkhope MEP; Michael Patchett-Joyce of Monckton Chambers; Professor Richard Whitman; Professor Alan Dashwood CBE).

[67] That means that the ECJ considers the objectives and purposes of the EU in deciding which of the conflicting arguments should be given greater weight.

[68] Professor Alan Riley (n 66) raises his doubts as follows: 'No mere protocol can achieve the same interpretative status as the preamble and the first few articles'.

[69] Note: the CFI will be renamed 'General Court', and the term 'Court of Justice of the European Union' will officially designate the two levels of jurisdiction taken together.

[70] Arts 9f and 11(1) TEU (n 1).

[71] Art 240a TFEU (n 1).

[72] Art 188 n (11) TFEU (n 1).

[73] Further changes worthy of mention: the appointment process for judges and Advocate Generals of the European Court of Justice will change: a panel will be set up to give an opinion on the suitability of the candidates proposed by the Member States. The panel will comprise seven persons appointed by the Council from among former judges of the European Court of Justice and the General Court, justices of national supreme courts and lawyers of recognized competence, one of whom must be proposed by the European Parliament. The rules of procedure of the panel will be established by the Council. A serious further innovation

Finally, as the Single Market broadens its scope and reach into the new Member States, the volume of court cases with a cross-border element is increasing, leading to an increase in the Community courts' workload.

## B. Language

The linguistic regime is a surprisingly important constraint on the productivity of the Court and the understanding of its judgments.[74] The Court's language regime is laid down in the Rules of Procedure (RP).[75] All languages are treated as being equal, and judges and Advocates General are entitled to use any language and to require translation of any document into the language of choice.

Furthermore, the European Community courts have a special linguistic status compared to the other European institutions because the Rules of Procedure provide the possibility to use a language which is not one of the official languages of the EU in the oral proceedings in the examination of witnesses or experts if the Court's permission is granted.[76] Hence, an article 234 reference from a Latvian court to the ECJ could therefore be conducted (partially) in Russian (despite the fact that Russian, unlike Latvian, is not an official language of the EU).

is a change to art 226 to enable the European Court of Justice to impose a lump sum or penalty payment on a Member State that has failed to implement a directive without first obtaining a declaratory judgment to that effect. In addition, there's a change to the standing requirements in art 230 §4 for individuals to challenge acts of the institutions. First, any act will be open to challenge if addressed to the plaintiff, not just decisions. If the act is not addressed to the plaintiff, the plaintiff must show that the act is of direct and individual concern. Secondly, in the case of a regulatory act (a measure of general application), the plaintiff must show that the regulatory act is of direct concern (dispensing with the need to show individual concern) and that the act does not entail implementing measures. The above-outlined change could also lead to a further increase in the Court's caseload. Finally, amendments to the Statute of the Court of Justice will be possible by the ordinary legislative procedure provided the Court is either the initiator of the amendment or is consulted on the amendment.

[74] Also highlighted by D Edward, 'The Preliminary Reference Procedure: Constraints and Remedies', in CCBE, College of Europe Colloquium Bruges, 19–20 November 1999, 12, revising the EU's judicial system, assessing the possible solutions, revising the preliminary ruling mechanism.

[75] See Rules or Procedure of the Court of Justice, arts 29–31. Rules of Procedure of the Court of Justice of the European Communities of 19 June 1991, [1991] OJ L 176, 7 and [1992] OJ L 383 (corrigenda). Latest version: Amendments to the Rules of Procedure of the Court of Justice of European Communities of 15 January 2008, [2008] OJ L 24, 39. See arts 35–37, Rules of Procedure of the Court of First Instance of the European Communities of 2 May 1991, [1991] OJ L 136; corrigendum published in [1991] OJ L 317, 34. Latest version: Council Decision of 18 December 2006 amending the Rules of Procedure of the Court of First Instance of the European Communities with regard to languages on 18 December 2006, [2006] OJ L 386, 45. The concept of official languages and working languages was introduced in art 1 of Reg 1/1958. The Council, in determining the language regime, an indication of an awareness of the importance of the issue, based the Regulation on art 217 of the EEC Treaty, which provides for unanimous voting.

[76] Art 29 (4) of the Rules of Procedure, ibid.

Internally, the Court uses a single working language, which is, largely for historical reasons,[77] French (although this is not specifically stated in the Court's Statute or Rules of Procedure). The difficulties resulting from this are becoming increasingly serious, in particular because French is not widely spoken in the new Member States, which are mostly Central or Eastern European Countries, where English is the prevalent second language. This has led to the fact that English is currently the 'unofficial' working language of the Community courts, and in practice many cases heard by chambers in the ECJ will use a reduced number of languages depending on the circumstances and practical requirements. This more or less informal practice is set to grow.[78] During 2006–2007 (at least) one chamber of the CFI worked in English for the practical reason that much of the documentation was in English. Since the CFI was established in 1989, 49.3 per cent of merger cases were introduced in English, 22.5 per cent in French and about 10 per cent each in German and Spanish.[79]

It has also recently been recognized by the European business lobby UNICE that English is 'the language of business'.[80] Ideally, this reality should be reflected in a modern court system.

The Court published a report on the 23 March 1999 highlighting that the volume of documents to be translated is not under the control of the Court and is rising at an alarming rate. This problem is now exacerbated by the expansion in size of the EU, which has created 12 additional working languages, bringing the total to 23. Consequently, there are over 380 possible different linguistic combinations, as all pleadings, included those submitted by a Member State in its own language, still have to be translated into the language of the case and into the working language of the Community courts.

In broad terms, each additional language involves the recruitment of about 30 translators, interpreters and secretaries.[81] In front of the ECJ, translation is required at approximately five separate stages of the procedure, which

---

[77] When the Court was created in 1953, the procedural rules and the grounds for judicial review in the Treaties were closely aligned on the rules in French administrative law and at that point in time French was the language in which most legal texts and articles intended for an international audience were written. This changed when Denmark, UK and Ireland joined in 1973.

[78] See also M Horspool, 'Over the Rainbow: Languages and Law in the Future of the European Union' available at http://www.sciencedirect.com/science?_ob=ArticleURL&_udi=B6V65-4GV9SM6-5&_user=3962339&_rdoc=1&_fmt=&_orig=search&_sort=d&view=c&_acct=C0000 61901&_version=1&_urlVersion=0&_userid=3962339&md5=e928b98ff8cd9fdaa764fc3f8ca8c565#bfn6 (accessed 12 May 2008).

[79] See also oral evidence by B Vesterdorf, the House of Lords report (n 22) answer to question 429, 17 January 2007.

[80] See 'Chirac Flees Summit in a Fury over Use of English' *The Times* (London England 24 March 2006).

[81] Edward (n 74) 12.

cannot proceed to the next stage until the necessary translations have been completed.

On average, translation consumes about seven months of the total time taken to process a reference.[82]

There were in the past various attempts to acknowledge this problem. For example, in 1994, the French Minister of Foreign Affairs, Alain Lamassoure, citing the example of the European Trade Mark Office, which works in five languages (English, French, German, Italian and Spanish), proposed that the same practice should be followed in the internal workings of the European Institutions.[83] The European Parliament, however, opposed it, referring to article 6 (now article 12) of the EC Treaty, which prohibits any discrimination on grounds of nationality, and to article 128 (now article 151) of the Treaty, which refers to the Community's duty to 'contribute to the flowering of cultures of the Member States' and, in particular, to the Community's duty to 'take cultural aspects into account in its action ... in particular in order to respect and promote the diversity of its cultures'.[84]

The linguistic regime is established by article 29 of the ECJ Rules of Procedure[85] and article 35 of the CFI Rules of Procedure,[86] which both state that the language regime may only be changed by unanimous decision of the Council under article 64 of the Statute. While recognizing the political sensitivity, the economic costs of delay will be significant, quite apart from the damage to the credibility of any legal system arising from a basic lack of access to justice.[87]

## C. Decentralization

Recognizing the expansion of the EU and the need for swift access to justice in competition cases, the Commission took the step of decentralizing by granting greater powers to National Competition Authorities (NCA) and national courts. With effect from May 2004, Regulation 1/2003[88] intro-

---

[82] ibid 8.
[84] Art 151(4) EC Treaty.
[86] See (n 75).
[87] For an analysis of various reform options, see section III.
[83] Horspool (n 78).
[85] OJ 1991, L176/7.
[88] Council Reg (EC) No 1/2003 of 16 December 2002 on the implementation of the rules on competition laid down in Arts 81 and 82 of the Treaty [2003] OJ L 1/1 (hereinafter Reg 1/2003]. The main pillars of modernization are the harmonization of the substantive competition rules and the decentralized application of European competition law. For the European business community the harmonization of European competition law has significant advantages. In particular, companies that are active on a pan-European basis benefit from the fact that their contracts no longer need to be assessed on the basis of national laws but that it is sufficient that their contracts are compatible with European competition law. Also, the country in which the agreement or practice is assessed should not be of importance, because all authorities and courts need to apply the same standard. It therefore needs to be ensured by all

duced a system of parallel competences with respect to competition authorities such that a competition case affecting trade between Member States
can be dealt with by either the European Commission or a single national
authority, or various national authorities acting in parallel. Such a system
allows the Commission to concentrate its resources on important cases and
generally leads to better cooperation and coordination between national
authorities and the Commission.

Furthermore, the procedural delays in preliminary ruling proceedings
before the ECJ and in direct competition law annulment actions before the
CFI encourage recourse to national courts. Hence, greater powers have
been given not only to the European Commission and National
Competition Authorities, but also to the national courts.

There is a strong claim that a centralized court system is necessary to
ensure a common legal culture and uniformity, consistency and coherence
in light of the differences in national procedures.[89] The question therefore
is whether recourse to national courts driven by decentralization necessarily means less uniformity and consistency in the application of European
law. This will be further analysed below.

Looking at the role of the EU Commission itself, its role to ensure the
consistent application of European law is recognized in the Notice on the
Cooperation within the Network of Competition Authorities,[90] the EU
Treaty itself and Regulation 1/2003, and is secured by the tools at the
disposal of the Commission. In this respect, it is worth noting the
Commission's training programme for judges, the exchange programme for
officials working in the competition authorities, the obligation of the
Member States to inform the Commission at least 30 days before a decision
is taken of the intended course of action[91] and the possibility for the
Commission to make use of a number of instruments, such as taking up
cases that raise new issues under article 10 of Regulation 1/2003.

authorities and all courts that European competition law is applied in a consistent manner in
all Member States. See P Lowe, 'The Role of the Commission in the Modernisation of EC
Competition Law' speech at the UKAEL Conference on Modernisation of EC Competition
Law: Uncertainties and Opportunities, 23 January 2004, 2, supporting this advantage for the
European Business Community. For reform in the field of mergers, see Council Reg (EC) No
139/2004 on the control of concentrations between undertakings [2004] OJ L 24/1 (hereinafter Merger Reg).

[89] For example, the area of private competition enforcement (eg burden and standard of
proof) is currently not fully harmonized throughout the EU.

[90] Commission Notice on Cooperation within the Network of Competition Authorities
[2004] OJ C101/43.

[91] See art 11(4) of Reg 1/2003, (n 88).

## D. Limited Role of Judicial Review in Administrative Competition Law System

The European Court of Human Rights has held that decision-making powers can be entrusted to administrative authorities as long as they are subject to effective judicial review by an independent and impartial tribunal.[92]

Hence, it is up to the Community courts to ensure that the administration's decisions are subject to comprehensive judicial review by an independent external tribunal.

Article 230 of the EC Treaty gives the Community courts the competence to review the legality of acts adopted by the institutions, including acts of the Commission. It allows any natural or legal person to seek the annulment of a Commission Decision that is addressed to that person or is of direct and individual concern to it. Hence, appeal of the Commission's Decisions before the CFI and then, on grounds of law only, to the ECJ is possible.

Judicial review under article 230 of the EC Treaty is limited in scope as there is no full appeal on the merits possible.[93] This reflects the fundamental principle of the institutional balance provided for in the EC Treaty, according to which the, 'division of powers between the Commission and the Community judicature ... do not allow the judicature to go further, and ... to enter into the merits of the Commission's complex economic assessments or to substitute its own point of view for that of the institution.'[94]

Furthermore, the grounds for annulment are limited and are those stipulated in article 230 EC Treaty.[95]

The CFI may not substitute its own decision on the merits but must 'remit' the case back to the Commission for re-examination. This leads to a situation that is unsatisfactory for both the applicant and the Commission. First, this can lead to a new examination, with the applicant facing the uncertainty of a new review as well as consequential procedural delays. Secondly, it is often not clear what measures the Commission must take following annulment, although there is a general obligation to draw the necessary conclusions from the consequences of the Court's judgment

[92] See art 6 of the European Convention of Human Rights as well as, eg Case A/73 *Ozturk v Germany* Judgment of the European Court of Human Rights of 21 February 1984.

[93] One exception to this restricted role of Community courts in the EC system of competition enforcement is in the case of decisions imposing fines. Art 229 EC enables the grant of unlimited jurisdiction to the courts in the determination of penalties. This is reflected in both the merger field, in art 16 of the Merger Reg (n 88) and the antitrust field, in art 31 of Reg 1/2003 (n 88).

[94] See Case C–12/03 P *Tetra Laval v Commission*, AG Opinion, para 89.

[95] These are namely lack of competence, infringement of an essential procedural requirement, infringement of the Treaty or of any rule of law relating to its application, or misuse of powers.

having regard not only to the operative part but also to the Court's reasoning.[96]

The need for an administrative review, court review and then another administrative review and decision all takes time. There would ultimately be greater speed of enforcement, certainty and effectiveness of judicial control if a system of full jurisdiction, ie the ability to retake a decision on the merits rather than simply annul the Commission's decision, was introduced. In particular, in the area of mergers,[97] it would be more effective if closure to the litigation could be achieved by the CFI. Such changes might necessitate a change in the provisions of the EC Treaty (in particular articles 229 and 230 of the EC Treaty).[98]

### III. OPTIONS FOR REFORM

### A. Introduction

Before considering detailed proposals, it is important to outline the overall aims for any reform process.

The starting point for any reform must be that any changes do not have a negative impact on the effective administration of EU justice. All proposals for reform and ideas on the future of the Community's judicial system must take into account three fundamental requirements,[99] which are important aims in any judicial system:

- the need to secure the unity of Community law;[100]
- the need to ensure that the judicial system is transparent, comprehensible and accessible to the public;
- the need to dispense justice without unacceptable delay ('justice delayed is justice denied').

Any reform proposals or changes that damage the Community courts' ability to resolve disputes, ensure consistency in interpretation and remedy

---

[96] See art 233 EC, which reads as follows: 'The institution . . . whose act has been declared void . . . shall be required to take the necessary measures to comply with the judgment of the Court of Justice'.

[97] This is in particular important in the light of the Merger Reg, (n 88) stating in its art 10(5) that the administrative procedure before the Commission restarts, and that the examination must take into account current market conditions. These might have changed in the meantime.

[98] For further reform proposals see section III.

[99] See proposals by the ECJ and CFI, The Future of the Judicial System of the European Union (Proposals and Reflections) (Brussels, May 1999), 17

[100] The ECJ and CFI, ibid, stated in their proposals that the unity of Community law should be secured 'by means of a supreme court'. I do not fully share this opinion, as further outlined in my reform proposals below.

breaches will fundamentally undermine the EU, and this is clearly undesirable in economic terms.

Reform proposals to date fall into two distinct categories: those which involve only procedural changes[101] and those which go further and require changes to the judicial structure.[102]

Outlined below are the first summaries of proposals put forward by others. These are then followed by the consideration of some options and recommendations of possible future changes that would enable the European Community courts to deal more effectively and expeditiously, and resolve some of the current failings as outlined above (see above, section II).


*B. Overview on Previous Reform Proposals and the Status of Discussion*

*1. BIICL Report*[103]

The British Institute of International and Comparative Law (BIICL) published a seminal report into 'The Role and Future of the European Court of Justice', which was presented by the Rt Hon Lord Slynn of Hadley in 1996. This report considered a number of alternatives that would have improved the administration and working of the Court and the administration of justice on European legal matters more generally across the EU.[104]

The report reviewed the composition and administration of the ECJ, its jurisdiction, procedure, interim measures, enforcement of judgments and mechanisms for reviewing the Court's decisions. It recognized that the Court is a victim of its own success and

> in many ways, the most successful international court in the world community; its fundamental function in the Community legal order is now well established. That success, however, has its disadvantages. The Court's wide jurisdiction, the large volume of law of which it is the sole

---

[101] The solutions outlined in the BIICL Report (n 33) which would not have involved a new judicial structure, included, for example, an increase of the number of judges, Advocates General and other staff of the Court, a use of chambers and plenum, the possibility of dispensing with or curtailing the hearing, a review of process of infringement cases, a broadening of the locus standi under the former art 173 of the EC Treaty and a general modification of the preliminary reference system. For a summary of the BIICL Report see section III.B.2.

[102] See in particular the BIICL Report (n 33) which reviewed measures adopted to improve the efficiency of the ECJ and identified possible solutions within the judicial structure existing at the time, then considered solutions involving a new judicial structure. For an analysis of the BIICL Report, see below section III.B.3.

[103] See BIICL Report (n 33).

[104] Note that references in the report are to the articles of the European Treaty at the time, not the latest version of the Treaty; the Treaty articles remain the same but some numbers have changed.

authoritative interpreter and the relatively effective enforcement of its judgments have made it a popular forum for litigation. This has led to an increasing caseload and consequent delays in the disposal of cases over the years both before the ECJ and the CFI.[105]

The report reviewed measures adopted to improve the efficiency of the ECJ and identified possible solutions within the judicial structure existing at the time, before considering solutions involving a new judicial structure.

Solutions which were canvassed in the review that would not have involved a new judicial structure included[106] an increase in the number of judges, Advocates General and other staff of the Court;[107] the use of chambers and plenum;[108] the possibility of dispensing with or curtailing the hearing;[109] altering the role of the Advocate General;[110] possible extension of the jurisdiction of the CFI;[111] a review of the process of infringement cases;[112] the modification of the preliminary reference system;[113] and broadening the *locus standi* under article 173.[114]

Solutions which were canvassed in the review which would have involved a new judicial structure included:

## a) Option 1—Reform along the Lines of the US Court System[115]

This reform proposal dealt with a possible restructuring of the EU judicial system to create parallel European and national competence. The best known example of a court system acting as umpire between centralizing and separatist tendencies is that of the US, with the State courts and the Federal courts having parallel competence. The State courts control State functions, the Federal courts control federal functions. The present court system of the European Community already numbers this task amongst its functions.

By contrast with the US system, a different approach has been adopted by the EU. The national courts may handle any cases involving Community law, except for those cases where the Community courts have been given original jurisdiction. This means that national courts are frequently called upon to apply and enforce Community law at the national level.

The principal method adopted to achieve the objective of uniform interpretation and application of Community law is the preliminary reference procedure. The US's equivalent procedure is the certification procedure for the US Supreme Court.

---

[105] See BIICL Report (n 33) 23.
[107] ibid 43–47.
[109] ibid, 51–53.
[111] ibid 55–60.
[113] ibid 68–87.
[115] ibid 98–101.

[106] ibid 43–96.
[108] ibid 48–51.
[110] ibid 53–55.
[112] ibid 61–67.
[114] ibid 94–96.

The report reviewed Option 1 and recognized that the European system had chosen a different path from the United States. In particular,

> [b]y an act of faith, which has been found to be largely justified, it entrusts its application and enforcement to the National Courts and uses the reference mechanism as the principal method to achieve unity. This system works well subject to the problem of the delay between the reference and the ruling.[116] It is this problem which must be tackled and there is no reason in principle why solutions should not be found.

The report concluded that major restructuring of the Community judicial system along the lines of the US court system was not, in practical terms, necessary.

b) Option 2—System of Community Regional Courts[117]

Under this option, the proposal of a genuine restructuring of Europe's judicial architecture by introducing a system of Community regional courts was reviewed (this had previously been reviewed prior to the inter-governmental conference in 1990). The central idea was to propose that the ECJ remains at the apex of the system and is renamed as the European High Court of Justice. Direct access would be limited to a number of specific articles of the treaty. Four or five new Community regional courts could be created to serve a grouping of Member States. Each regional court would have a regional jurisdiction relating to applications by private parties under (former) article 173 or 175 or non-contractual liability under (former) article 215 of the Treaty.[118]

The regional courts would receive preliminary references from and issue preliminary rulings to national courts, and a number of other specific procedural and jurisdictional matters were also considered.

The BIICL report listed as the advantages of the regional court system that it would[119] bring justice nearer to the likely parties, be more familiar with the legal, economic and social systems of the regions, adopt a simple linguistic regime, function more efficiently and speedily and raise the profile of Community law.

The disadvantages of a regional court system highlighted by the BIICL report were that it might[120] jeopardize the unity and coherence of the community legal system, cause issues of the status of decisions and jeopar-

---

[116] Emphasis added.
[117] See BIICL Report (n 33) 101–104.
[118] Now arts 230, 232, and 288 of the EU Treaty.
[119] See BIICL Report (n 33) 102.
[120] ibid 102–104.

dize uniform interpretation and application of Community law, increase delays in preliminary references, increase administrative complexity as well as costs and expenses falling on the Community budget, and create regional groupings of Member States.

The report concluded that the creation of a regional court system could not be supported.

### c) Option 3—A Two-tier ECJ[121]

One of the critical problems in the court's workload was identified as the delay in deciding (former) article 177[122] references. This was identified as an issue requiring further resolution under Option 1.[123] An alternative to reducing the number of references was the establishment of a second tier of judges (with no Advocates General) in the ECJ. The idea was that a lower tier of judges would decide most preliminary references, therefore leaving to the higher tier those cases that are currently decided by plenary session. The higher tier of the ECJ would decide important issues—for example, questions of validity of general community legislation or where the law requires clarification in the light of previous decisions.

Advantages that might be achieved from such a system included speed and access to justice, while enabling judges on the higher tier to concentrate on the more important cases. Disadvantages included the fact that it would be seen to be creating a three-tier structure of courts which might be too elaborate, whilst a two-tier structure would involve considerable expansion of the ECJ and add considerably to the complications of administration and costs of the ECJ.

The report considered that an expansion of the CFI would address the issues identified in this option more effectively.

### d) Option 4—Creation of Specialized Courts/Tribunals or Specialized Chambers[124]

This option reviewed the development of the CFI into an ordinary administrative court specializing in the judicial protection of private parties against illegal administrative acts by Community institutions, and the parallel development of specialist tribunals, such as the establishment of a staff tribunal to hear at first instance all staff cases, and the establishment of a competition, State aid and anti-dumping tribunal.

---

[121] ibid 104–10.
[122] Now art 234 of the EU Treaty.
[123] See above, in particular the quotation in italics.
[124] See BIICL Report (n 33) 106–110.

The report considered that such a development had a number of disadvantages, in particular the difficulty of defining a structured relationship between all the different tribunals, but also the concern that specialist tribunals would proliferate and would ultimately jeopardize the uniform interpretation and application of EC law.

e) Option 5—New Distribution of Jurisdiction between the Community Courts and National Courts[125]

This option reviewed a change to the division of jurisdiction between the domestic courts and the ECJ and CFI. One fundamental difficulty with this approach is that the Community legal system is part of the national legal system. The balance of jurisdictions was reviewed, but the conclusion was that this option would not work in practice and, if adopted, would cause more problems of coordination and uniformity than it would solve.

f) Option 6—Should the Community Courts be Able to Refuse Jurisdiction?[126]

The benefits and disadvantages of this option were reviewed, and the conclusion was that the introduction of filters or selection mechanisms for the ECJ would be undesirable and difficult to achieve.

In conclusion, the BIICL report's recommendations were that no radical changes to the present judicial structure should be introduced. However, it acknowledged that the ECJ needs to be enabled to cope more efficiently with its actual and prospective caseload, that the CFI should be expanded and that generally proceedings of the Community courts need to be improved.

## 2. House of Lords Sub-Committee Report[127]

The House of Lords Sub-Committee inquiring into the viability of establishing an EU Competition Court issued their full report at the end of March 2007.[128] In its report, the Sub-Committee rejected the idea of establishing either a separate court or chamber dedicated to competition law. Whilst it accepted that the delay was a significant problem, it felt that the main causes (language and case overload) would continue to plague any new court/chamber.

---

[125] ibid 110–13.          [126] ibid 113–19.          [127] See (n 33).
[128] While the Sub-Committee reviewed evidence that established that delay is a serious issue, no reform proposals were considered that would resolve the problem. I have clustered the report 'something remains to be done', as it was well established before the enquiry that 'something must be done'.

The Sub-Committee concluded that adding another level of appeal would not be the answer and may in fact lead to further delays. The Sub-Committee stated that its recommendations focused on how to first improve the existing system and procedures. It also emphasized the need to guarantee quality over expediency. Whilst it did not entirely dismiss the possibility of its establishment at a later date, it should be noted that the creation of a new court depends on a proposal from the Commission or on the request of the ECJ. On the basis of the responses by various witnesses to the Sub-Committee during the consultation, and without strong encouragement from Member States, it now appears unlikely in the near future.

The basis of the inquiry was the June 2006 CBI brief proposing the creation of a European Competition Court (on the basis of article 225a TEC) with specialist judges and tailor-made procedures.[129]

The first chapter[130] of the Sub-Committee report, introducing the issue, focused in particular on the problem of delay. Together with statistical analysis of the caseload and time frames, the evolution of the EC merger control procedures was also set out. The agreed conclusion was that delay in hearing appeals in merger cases is a problem but that there is no agreed solution.

The second chapter[131] considered the causes of delay, namely the language issue and the question of overload, and set out the proceedings before the CFI, the written procedure, and the oral hearing and fast-track procedures.

In the third chapter[132] the advantages and disadvantages of a new competition court were considered and rejected.

Instead of a new court, it was suggested by some witnesses that a new chamber should be established within the CFI.[133] However, the Sub-Committee noted that without more judges there would be no advantage over the existing structure and that it could therefore lead to further delays and reduced flexibility overall.

Appointing more judges and creating additional chambers would appear to be the obvious response; however, the Sub-Committee noted that there would be serious political difficulties with this proposal.[134]

The Sub-Committee believed that a greater level of autonomy should be given to the CFI and ECJ to changing their rules (accepting that a change of the official language would require political endorsement). It identified several ways in which the practice of the courts under the existing rules could help speed up the process. These included firmer case management by

---

[129] CBI Brief of 15 June 2006, reproduced in the 'Minutes of Evidence' of the House of Lords report (n 22) 1–3.
[130] See House of Lords report ibid, 9–16, paras 1–24.
[131] ibid 16–23, paras 24–53.     [132] ibid 24–31, paras 54–85.
[133] ibid 36–38, paras 110–23
[134] For a summary of the conclusion, see ibid 38, para 122.

the judges as well as the recommendation to abolish the 10 day 'delai de route' when lodging an appeal. Furthermore, third-party interveners should have the right to request an accelerated procedure and that the CFI should have the discretion to take a final decision itself (eg no substantial alteration in circumstances).

Appeals against fines imposed by the Commission are time-consuming. The proposal to introduce a system of plea bargaining was welcomed by both the Sub-Committee and Bo Vesterdorf. Whether plea bargaining promotes justice is, however, questionable.

Appeals to the CFI concerning trademarks are proliferating, thereby increasing the Court's workload. Intellectual property cases were an area identified as clearly distinguishable cases suitable for transfer to a judicial panel. This proposal received a positive response from the Commission and the Court, with the former stating that first an evaluation of the transfer of staff cases would need to be carried out.[135]

Whilst acknowledging the time sensitivity of merger cases, the UK government[136] doubted whether the creation of a competition court or chamber would address the delay issue. Either option would only add another layer of appeal without addressing the true causes of delay, namely language and the need for tighter practice procedures. It could not see the merit of initially submitting summary applications, and was hesitant to fully support proposals which would alter the CFI's jurisdiction, where the CFI itself is better placed to decide or requires fuller evaluation on a political level.

The UK government did, however, respond positively to the Sub-Committee's other recommendations and stated in particular the need for firmer case management by the judges, which included the proposal for them to decide on a case-by-case basis whether to conduct the internal deliberations in the language of the case and to prioritize time-sensitive cases. Furthermore, the UK government stressed the importance of speeding up the lodging and acceptance of cases, of granting a right to third-party interveners to request an accelerated procedure and of allocating trademark cases to a judicial panel.

In terms of the next steps, the UK government stated that it will discuss the options with the Commission and the European Community courts to determine the best way forward.

---

[135] See also ibid 47, para 173: 'The transfer of trademark cases could lead to a marked decrease in the CFI's workload and we encourage the Commission to give urgent consideration to this suggestion'.

[136] See the response of the UK government, available at http://www.parliament.uk/documents/upload/govrespeucomp.pdf (accessed on 14 May 2008).

## 3. *Other Submissions*

### (a) Sir David Edward

In his evidence to the House of Lords Enquiry, the report of which I have summarized above, Sir David Edward further commented on the difficulty in defining the scope of any specialist competition court in stating that 'in Luxembourg, 'competition cases' do not come neatly packaged and labelled'.[137]
He went on to say that

> some discussion of a Competition Court misunderstands the place of competition law in the context of EU law as a whole. Jean Monnet is reputed to have said that 'The whole Treaty is about competition'. Articles 81 and 82 form part of a wider Chapter that includes the rules relating to public undertakings, services of general economic interest, revenue producing monopolies and, especially, state aids. That Chapter is in turn integrally related to the rules on free movement and other policies. EU competition law is not a self-standing legal discipline to the same extent as US antitrust law or even UK competition law which has its own statutory framework.[138]

In his words,

> References from national courts under Article 234 EC relatively rarely pose questions that are confined to the competition rules in a narrow sense. More frequently, they pose questions about the competition rules combined with other questions about free movement, state aids, transport, social or industrial policy, etc.
> [5.4] Courage v Crehan, to which reference is made in the call for evidence, was not just about 'competition law'. The primary issue was a more fundamental 'constitutional' one: Does Community law require a national court to set aside a rule of national law that precludes a party to a contract from pleading the unlawfulness of that contract as a basis for seeking damages from the other party?
> [5.5.] In short, EU competition law is not an isolated 'specialist' subject and 'competition questions' do not come to Luxembourg in neatly parcelled and labelled packages. In this respect, competition cases are different from staff cases and patent cases (even if there is an overlap between intellectual property rights and free movement).[139]

---

[137] See Minutes of Evidence to the House of Lords report (n 22) written evidence by Sir David Edward, page 47, para 1.2. It is worth to note that Sir David Edward is a former judge at the ECJ as well as a former judge at the CFI (from 1989 to 1992).
[138] See ibid 50, para 5.1.          [139] See ibid 50–51, paras 5.3–5.5.

On the question of delay, Sir David Edward highlighted the fact that it is not an exclusive problem of the Community Court system but that 'the antecedent investigation and decision-making process before the Commission is itself a source of delay and uncertainty'.[140]

He was therefore sceptical about the need for, or the desirability of, creating a specialist competition court. It seemed, however, 'logical' to him that, as the scope of the CFI's jurisdiction expands, its chambers should become more specialized. Within that context, judges who have substantial knowledge and experience of competition law could be assigned to chambers dealing with competition cases without it being necessary to define precisely what constitutes a 'competition case'.

As general points, Sir David Edward stated the need for the European Community courts to be able, on their own initiative, to test out new procedural methods and expedients that would go some way towards achieving greater speed and efficiency.[141] This would help in resolving the current problem that the scope for proactive case management by the Court is extremely limited, as the Rules of Procedure cannot be changed without the approval of the Council.[142]

As regards the possibility of developing 'competition references' under article 234 to the CFI, Sir David Edward favours assigning to the 'CFI references where the questions posed by the national court are confined exclusively to questions concerning the interpretation and/or application of Articles 81 and/or 82'. He analysed that he would

> favour such a solution for the following reason: a reference whose subject matter is exclusively confined to interpretation or application of Article 81 or 82, is likely to arise in the context of a dispute between private undertakings. It is likely (though not certain) that the issue will turn on the particular facts and circumstances of that dispute, and will be analogous to the issues arising in actions to annul Commission decisions, already devolved to the CFI. If, exceptionally, such a reference were to raise questions of general importance, the First Advocate General could propose that the ECJ should review the decision of the CFI on the ground that 'there is a serious risk of the unity or consistency of Community law being affected' (Article 62 of the Statute). This seems to us to represent a rational and workable division of labour between the ECJ and the CFI.[143]

These comments recognize the difficulty of competition from other cases

---

[140] See ibid 47, para 1.4.                     [141] See ibid 51, para 6.3.
[142] This is a majority approval (with the exception of the language regime).
[143] See 'Minutes of Evidence' to the House of Lords Report (n 22) written evidence by Sir David Edward, 51, paras 5.8–5.10.

while also recognizing the fact that the process of decision making before the Commission carries issues of delay.

## (b) Bo Vesterdorf

During his time as President of the CFI, but in his own capacity, Bo Vesterdorf wrote widely about the functioning of the European Community courts and areas for reform.

One of his recent articles[144] aptly summarizes his views. He first states that, although the courts have exercised their judicial review function effectively, a review of their work reveals certain shortcomings in the current system that lead to thoughts for improvements to the system. In this context, he highlights two aspects of the current system that from his personal point of view may diminish the effectiveness of judicial review: the facts that the CFI lacks full jurisdiction (except in respect of fines) and that judicial review is not always timely.

Having identified speed as the main aspect of the CFI's procedure that could be the subject of improvement, he outlines some avenues of possible future changes which would enable the CFI to deal more effectively and expeditiously with competition cases. Whilst acknowledging the advantages of both a specialized competition tribunal as well as specialized CFI chambers,[145] Vesterdorf favours as a 'more practical and realistic solution' the removal of other cases, in particular civil service cases and trademark cases, which together would reduce the caseload by 37 per cent.[146]

Highlighting the important role played by the Community courts, he concluded by quoting Advocate General Cosmas from the *Ladbroke* case:

> [A] comprehensive review as to the substance ... does not, of course, supplant the administrative work of the Commission but constitutes a correct exercise of judicial tasks in a legal order-like the Community legal order-governed by the principles of legality and the rule of law.[147]

The preceding sections of this review consider the following:

- The importance of the judicial system for securing justice and fulfilling the political goals of the EU and the rule of law, as well as improving economic progress.

---

[144] See Vesterdorf (n 41) and quoted throughout this article.
[145] For Vesterdorf's analysis of the advantages and disadvantages of the specialized competition tribunal and the specialized CFI chambers, see ibid 25 and 26.
[146] The statistics provided were based on the number of cases pending at the end of 2004 (in terms of judgments delivered in relation to civil service cases, which accounted for 30 per cent, and intellectual property cases, which accounted for 22 per cent); ibid 26.
[147] Case C–83/98 P France v Ladbroke [2000], ECR I–3271, para 16.

- The fact that the existing system simply 'takes too long' to achieve a result, whether from court statistics, identified procedural issues that require reform, language, the increased collaborative and decentralized nature of the EU, and proposals for reform of the competition law system.
- Various proposals for reform have been canvassed and all are deficient in different ways in failing to fully achieve the EU's goals while speeding up the system of justice.

All of the witnesses from a widely drawn community[148] have established agreement that 'something must be done'.

What might be done to address the issues that have been identified needs to be seen in the context of the EU Reform Treaty and a prevailing political environment which supports a sharing, collaborative and decentralized approach, while ensuring coherence through a single unified system of justice.

### C. Is it Time for a Long-term Change to the Judicial Structure? A 'Nomination System'

#### 1. The Impact of Regulation 1/2003

For some 40 years, enforcement of the Community's competition rules was centralized. While the competition rules in articles 81 and 82 could be enforced by national competition authorities (pursuant to article 84) and applied by national courts (by virtue of direct applicability), the Commission was in practice the principal and almost sole enforcement agency, its procedure being governed by Regulation 17 of 1962. A major change occurred in May 2004, when modernization of the application of articles 81 and 82 was effected by Regulation (EC) No 1/2003 on the implementation of the rules on competition laid down in articles 81 and 82 of the Treaty.[149]

It is widely expected that the impact of Council Regulation 1/2003 and the trend to increased decentralization will result in a significant increase in private litigation and consequentially national courts being confronted with complex (competition) law questions. This might be expected to result in a potential increase in preliminary proceedings in front of the ECJ.

---

[148] See witnesses who provided written and oral evidence listed in House of Lords report (n 22).

[149] Responsibility for applying the competition rules is now shared between the Commission, national competition authorities (NCAs) and national courts. The main features of the regime introduced by Reg 1/2003 are: (1) the end of the notification of agreements to obtain exemption under art 81(3) and the introduction of self-assessment; (2) decentralization of enforcement with greater involvement of national courts and competition authorities in enforcing Community competition rules; and (3) a strengthening and clarification of the Commission's enforcement powers.

Furthermore, former CFI President Bo Vesterdorf stated that,

> it may be more coherent to allow the CFI the power to deal with such preliminary rulings as is possible under Article 225(3) EC. This would, however, inevitably increase the workload of the CFI even further and would be an additional factor to be considered in any discussion of changes with the aim of improving speed in the adjudication of competition cases before the Community courts.[150]

Taking competition cases, but bearing in mind the comment of Sir David Edward that competition cannot be separated from other provisions of the Treaty, if the CFI is to be granted jurisdiction over competition references from national courts, which would be possible under article 225 (3) of the EC Treaty, the opportunities for speeding up its proceedings in competition cases will be considerably improved. In light of the competition cases the Community courts have dealt with, I assume that the level of experience with specific competition law cases must be statistically lower at the ECJ than at the CFI. Hence, it would indeed be more coherent to allow the CFI the power to deal with such preliminary rulings. Such a possibility for a preliminary reference to the CFI would depend primarily on how important and time sensitive the case is (which is particularly critical in merger as well as antitrust cases, but perhaps less so in cartel cases).

In light of the European Commission's White Paper on the desirability of encouraging private enforcement actions in the national courts,[151] the role of the national courts and the need for maintaining consistency of interpretation and uniformity in application of EC competition law are becoming even more crucial. The main reform proposal in the form of the 'nomination system' embraces this new role of the national courts.

Indeed, the role of private enforcement actions highlights the need for a new approach to the organization and structure of the European courts. For example, in competition matters, the European Commission shares the administrative powers of enforcement of EC competition law with the national competition authorities through the European Competition Network, with its system of allocating cases to the best placed national competition authority (or the Commission itself).

This new system of directly applicable EC competition law enables the national courts to exercise powers equivalent to those of the European Commission and/or their national competition authority within the scope of their jurisdiction.

---

[150] Vesterdorf (n 41) 27.

[151] European Commission, Green Paper—Damages Actions for Breach of EC Antitrust Rules and White Paper on Damages Actions for Breach of the EC antitrust rules (n 27).

With the new emphasis on private enforcement and damages claims, the national courts will have a parallel, if not more important, role to that of the Community judicature in competition enforcement in Europe. However, divergence of national processes, different procedures and delays could give rise to different application, which would threaten to splinter the system of enforcement and, in turn, the system of law.

A more radical reform may be needed to fully acknowledge this ongoing trend of cooperation and collaboration between Member States of the EU Reform Treaty and decentralization, as well as to maintain consistency of interpretation and uniformity in the application of European law.

## 2. *The Impact of the Nice Treaty*

In general, changes to the judicial structure have now been made possible by the Nice Treaty.[152] Serious consideration is now needed to speed up the court process if the economic goals, and gains, are to be achieved.

The implementation of a number of the reforms made possible by the Nice Treaty has already begun. Article 225 of the EC Treaty now provides that the CFI is to have jurisdiction to hear and determine at first instance all direct actions with the exception of those assigned to a judicial panel and those reserved in the Statute for the ECJ.[153]

The European Council has amended the Protocol on the Statute of the Court of Justice and adopted provisions for the establishment of such a 'judicial panel'.

First, on 26 April 2004, the Council amended[154] articles 51 and 54 of the Protocol on the Statute of the Court of Justice in such a way that from 1 June 2004 direct actions for annulment and for failure to act brought by a Member State against an act of, or failure to act by, the Commission fall within the jurisdiction of the CFI. The same is true for actions brought by

---

[152] The Nice Treaty entered into effect on 1 February 2003.
[153] 153 art 225A stipulates as follows:

The Council, acting unanimously on a proposal from the Commission and after consulting the European Parliament and the Court of Justice or at the request of the Court of Justice and after consulting the European Parliament and the Commission may create judicial panels to hear and determine at first instance certain classes of action or proceeding brought in specific areas. The decision establishing a judicial panel shall lay down the rules on the organisation of the panel and the extent of the jurisdiction conferred upon it. Decisions given by judicial panels may be subject to a right of appeal on points of law only or, when provided for in the decision establishing the panel, a right of appeal also on matters of fact before the Court of First Instance.

[154] Decision 2004/407/EC, Euratom, amending arts 51 and 54 of the Protocol on the Statute of the Court of Justice, [2004] OJ L 132/5; corrigendum at [2004] OJ L 194/3.

Member States against decisions of the Council concerning State aid, acts of the Council adopted pursuant to Council regulation concerning measures for trade, acts of the Council by which it exercises implementing powers and acts of the European Central Bank.

Secondly, on 2 November 2004, the Council established the EU Civil Service Tribunal.[155] This new tribunal, consisting of seven judges, is responsible for hearing disputes involving the EU Civil Service. Its decisions will be open to appeal, limited to points of law, before the CFI and, exceptionally, subject to review by the ECJ in the circumstances prescribed by the Protocol on the Statute. The EU Civil Service Tribunal was duly constituted into law on 2 December 2005.

This establishment of the EU Civil Service Tribunal, resulting in the expected removal of civil service cases and reduction of the current caseload of the CFI by approximately 25 per cent,[156] also indicates the need to consider the removal of other cases from the CFI's workload. For example, the creation of a trademarks tribunal[157]would result in the removal of approximately 33 per cent[158] of the CFI's current caseload and would enable the CFI to use the expedited procedure more effectively in time-sensitive cases (such as merger cases).

As a result of these changes, only approximately 5 per cent of the ECJ cases were transferred to the CFI in 2004.[159] The CFI has been relieved of about 25 per cent of the cases brought each year, proving that the approach of establishing specialist tribunals and removing workload from the CFI really works.[160]

On the other hand, these low figures (in particular, in relation to the ECJ) also indicate that there is still an urgent need for reform in order to enable the Community courts to deal more effectively and expeditiously with pending cases.

### 3. Introducing a 'nomination system'

This section suggests that swifter justice does not need to be 'summary justice' and that greater effectiveness lies in addressing the procedural issues and delays in the system, in addition to any increases in sanction (if any is

---

[155] Decision 2004/752/EC, Euratom, establishing the European Union Civil Service Tribunal, [2004] OJ L 333/7.

[156] For an overview on the cases pending in front of the European Union Civil Service Tribunal, see http://www.curia.eu.int/en/content/juris/index.htm (accessed on 12 May 2008).

[157] The author will propose such a reform solution at section III.D.(5).

[158] Excluding staff cases and 'special forms of procedure' cases, 33.7 per cent of all total claims in front of the CFI are trademark cases.

[159] In 2004, 25 cases pending before the ECJ were transferred to the CFI, mainly concerning state aid and the European Agriculture Guidance and Guarantee Fund.

[160] Furthermore, the ECJ was relieved of hearing appeals relating to staff cases accounting for about 10 per cent of its annual caseload.

really needed). Also, increases in sanctions without addressing the nature and shape of the system are unlikely to achieve lasting results.

From recent discussions three possible alternatives might be considered that would make the system more workable on a pan-European basis. These are: first, a wholesale reform of national legal procedures; secondly, a federal system of courts, which, as an attractive option, has been discussed extensively in the past but not supported at all levels across the EU;[161] and finally, a nomination system, by which each Member State could nominate an existing court to sit as a chamber of the Community courts.

The analysis below focuses on the latter, the nomination system, as it would—in contrast to other reform proposals—go not only part way in reforming or addressing the problems with the current European judicial system but provide a definitive solution. For example, improvements in the system of translation will not finally address the Community courts' capacity problem in the longer term. The issues with the current system as outlined above are particularly regrettable in the case of references for preliminary rulings, which are a key factor in the proper functioning of the internal market.[162] As rightly stated by the ECJ in 1995,

> [a]ny weakening, even if only potential, of the uniform application and interpretation of Community law throughout the Union would be liable to give rise to distortions of competition and discrimination between economic operators, thus jeopardising equality of opportunity as between those operators and consequently the proper functioning of the internal market.[163]

A nomination system would ensure central coherence of a single system of law. In this, each Member State 'nominates' an existing national court to sit as a chamber of the Community courts. This proposal is in accordance with judicial subsidiarity as well as recognizing the fact that EU law enforcement should be brought as close as possible to the national legal systems. Consistency in the application and interpretation is paramount and safeguards would need to be imposed to this end.

---

[161] For a detailed discussion of the advantages and disadvantages of this option, see, inter alia, BIICL Report (n 33) 101 ff ('Community Regional Courts and a European High Court of Justice').

[162] See ECJ and CFI, The Future of the Judicial System (n 99) 22, as well as a Report of the Court of Justice on certain aspects of the application of the Treaty on European Union, May 1995, stating as follows:

> The preliminary ruling system is the veritable cornerstone of the operation of the internal market, since it plays a fundamental role in ensuring that the law established by the Treaties retains its Community character with a view to guaranteeing that that law has the same effect in all circumstances in all the Member States of the European Union.

[163] ibid 22.

The proposal is slightly less radical than a fully federal system of courts, such as applies in the US. This has the advantage of being an EU solution to an EU problem. It also reflects the collaborative approach that is a central feature of the EU Reform Treaty.

Components of a nomination system would be as follows:

- The national system nominates a court (existing facilities).
- The national system nominates a presiding judge to the ECJ level of qualification (former Community court judges could automatically qualify).

ECJ procedures would apply and the CFI would have case conference and capacity oversight of workload. The case allocation by the Community courts would reflect the increased capacity of the system and secure a harmonized approach (use of appropriate and modern communications infrastructure would facilitate such an approach).

The national language would apply.

## 4. The benefits of the nomination system

1. The nomination system would be local to the people it makes judgments about and hence would understand their national, social and cultural needs. In other words, the system would be more familiar with the local legal, economic and social systems. The constraints of cultural diversity as they currently exist in front of the Community courts are difficult to define but are nonetheless real.[164]

Differences in culture and in particular legal culture are as important as language as a point of reference for reform. The different legal systems reflect particular national attitudes, which are themselves the product of history and culture. It is not only the general difference between common law and civil law countries,[165] but also differences in attitude or approach,[166] which can affect the day-to-day working and in particular the process of deliberation of the Community courts.

The proposal would ensure that the legal culture and traditions are fully taken into account at all stages in developing and formulating the

---

[164] So stated by Edward (n 74) 13.

[165] However, even this traditional distinction between the common law and Continental systems is not always so profound. Greece, for example, is a Mediterranean country in its administrative habits and political psychology, and comparable to Italy or Portugal in that respect; but its administrative law is very close to the French system, and its Civil Code resembles the German code.

[166] For example, it is well known that German lawyers have a preference for the written procedure, whereas English lawyers prize the oral one.

judgment. As Community court procedures would apply, the 'Community court experience' would need to be transported into the local system.

Also, as a creature of both (the national and ECJ) systems, the proposed judicial system would be closer to the national legal system in which the questions referred to were to be answered than the Community courts.

2. As it would have to be a judge that the local system would nominate, it would have to observe the procedures and disciplines of the Community courts in order to achieve EU level acceptance and coherence.

This proposal fully reflects the provision in the Nice Treaty, which formalized for the very first time the right of each Member State to nominate a judge to the ECJ, thus ensuring representation of all the legal systems in the EU.[167] The key point is that a nominated judge does not need to spend all of his time in the Luxembourg court buildings in order to dispense justice.

The national judges nominated by each Member State would be nominated as members of the Community courts and would be appointed according to clearly defined criteria. These criteria should be qualitative, objective and published. Furthermore, with the Community courts' agreement, former Community court judges would automatically qualify. This would secure a coherent culture.

The proposal that judges would be appointed according to clearly defined qualitative criteria would also deal with the issue that some national legal systems (for example, the German legal system) attach fundamental importance to the principle of 'the legal judge',[168] according to which the rules for composition of the tribunal deciding a case must be known and published in advance.[169]

3. It would operate in the same national language as the country in which it sits but, while looking like a local court, its procedures would be the same as the Community courts. This proposal would particularly afford the widest possible access to the preliminary ruling procedure by avoiding the

---

[167] It is worth mentioning that the British government supported the changes made under the Nice Treaty. See IGC, Reform for Enlargement: The British Approach to the European Union Intergovernmental Conference 2000 (Cm 4595, February 2000), 21. It has always been accepted by the ECJ that there should be one judge from each Member State. In an earlier paper, prepared for the negotiations which led to the Treaty of Amsterdam, the ECJ addressed the considerations which are of paramount importance in this context. See Report of the Court of Justice on Certain Aspects of the Treaty on European Union—Contribution of the Court of First Instance for the Purposes of the 1996 Intergovernmental Conference (May 1995), point 16.

[168] In the German language, 'gesetzlicher Richter'.

[169] In contrast, under English Law it is regarded as normal to allocate cases as judges become available.

congestion resulting from the current need for translation[170] and would also resolve the issue of the status of decision (as heavily discussed in the early 1990's in relation to the proposed Community Regional Courts).[171]

4. The proposed nomination system would consider references to the ECJ in the normal way following the procedural rules and disciplines of the Community courts on cases started in the local courts. Given the fact that the rules of procedure as well as the competence of the nominated courts are already well established in EU law and in light of the doctrine of primacy,[172] this reform proposal does not violate the core of constitutional provisions as reflected in some Member States. In Germany, for example, the transfer of sovereign rights to international institutions, and also the EU, is restricted by a guarantee of identity.[173] A violation of constitutional provisions (for example, democracy) could therefore be identified by the Federal Constitutional Court as an exercise of supranational sovereign power and be declared inapplicable. Furthermore, the CFI (instead of the ECJ) could deal with preliminary rulings on competition cases (under the allocation system and watchful eye of the ECJ if necessary). This idea of providing the CFI with the power to deal with preliminary rulings is also supported by the former CFI President Bo Vesterdorf, who stated that,

[170] See ECJ/CFI (n 102) 26, in which the ECJ supported the 'benefit gained from a substantial reduction in the translation burden borne by the Court of Justice' when 'decentralised judicial bodies responsible for dealing with references for preliminary rulings from courts within their area of territorial jurisdiction' would operate in the language or languages of the State concerned.

[171] The proposal was the introduction of a system of Community regional courts. The central idea of the proposal was that the ECJ remains at the apex of the system, renamed as the European High Court of Justice (EHCJ). Furthermore, the proposal was as follows: (a) four or five regional courts would be created, each to serve a grouping of Member States, to be chosen on the basis of geographical proximity, similar legal traditions and the possibility of having a simplified linguistic regime; (b) direct access would be limited to a number of specific articles of the Treaty; (c) the regional courts would receive preliminary rulings from and issue preliminary rulings to national courts; (d) the CFI would become one of the regional courts; (e) the Commission would retain the right of intervention in all proceedings before the regional courts; (f) the Commission and Member State would be able to request that individual challenges be transferred from a regional court to the EHCJ; (g) decisions or preliminary rulings of the regional courts could be appealed to the EHCJ by any party to the proceedings, and by the Commission, the Council, the Parliament or any Member State as interveners; (h) the EHCJ would have discretion as to whether to admit the appeal; (i) the discretion would be exercised having regard to the importance of the questions raised, a divergence between the case law of the regional courts or a manifest legal error; (j) each regional court would consist of an uneven number of judges (one from each Member State in the region and one or two others from other Member States); (k) oral hearings would take place in the capitals of the Member States in which the case originated; and (l) regional courts would be bound by decisions of the EHCJ. For more details, see BIICL Report, (n 33) 101 ff ('Community Regional Courts and a European High Court of Justice').

[172] See, eg Case 106/77 *Simmenthal* [1978] ECR 629.

[173] Art 23.1 sentence 3 and art 79.3 of the German Basic Law (Grundgesetz).

[I]t may be more coherent to allow the CFI the power to deal with such preliminary rulings as is possible under Article 225(3) EC. This would, however, inevitably increase the workload of the CFI even further and would be an additional factor to be considered in any discussion of changes with the aim of improving speed in the adjudication of competition cases before the Community courts.[174]

Sir Christopher Bellamy also saw merit in the idea, particularly as regards

cases which can be properly identified and isolated as being pure Article 81 and Article 82 cases. Indeed, I think there is some argument for saying that the Court of Justice is not particularly well adapted to doing those kinds of cases in a sort of one-shot way. They tend to be very fact-intensive and the Court of Justice is not geared up really to fact-intensive cases.[175]

Also, Peter Roth QC, Monckton Chambers, was supportive of such an idea, stating as follows:

There is something artificial and discordant in the present structure, whereby appeals from Commission decisions are primarily determined by the CFI whereas references from national courts are determined by the ECJ, when these different procedural routes are common strands in the development of competition law jurisprudence.[176]

As outlined above, preliminary references make up approximately half the cases heard by the ECJ and in practice national courts can expect to wait 20 months for an answer to its questions.

It could also be considered to give the preliminary ruling jurisdiction to the CFI subject to the inclusion of a mechanism for ensuring that the most important questions would always come to the ECJ (after a 'triage' review at the ECJ level) and possibly with an increase in the number of judges at the CFI.[177]

The opportunities for speeding up these proceedings would be considerably improved and the specialist judges at the CFI could be better suited to deal with complex economic questions. It is also important to recall that the CFI was created in part because there was the need for a Community court to review effectively the complex decisions that the Commission adopts in

[174] Vesterdorf (n 41) 27.
[175] See House of Lords Report (n 22) 50, para 181.
[176] See ibid 50, para 180.
[177] In 1999 the ECJ also suggested that the CFI might be given a preliminary rulings jurisdiction (n 99).

the field of competition, hence it was from the start established as a specialist competition law court.

This opinion is also shared by CFI president Mark Jaeger, who recently stated as follows: 'The Court of First Instance was originally created to deal with antitrust cases and relieve the European Court of Justice, the EU's top court. Over the years it has developed expertise in this field and many of its members are now specialists.'[178]

Such a possibility for a preliminary reference to the ECJ, which is either automatically referred to the CFI or is done so after a 'triage' review at the ECJ in order to secure that the ECJ, has the 'first and last word' would therefore appear appropriate.

5. The proposed nomination system would operate under the authority of the Community courts and the coherence and unity of the community legal culture and single legal system would therefore be preserved. In particular, the increased capacity at national level that would be possible in a nomination system would speed up access to justice and more quickly achieve the benefit of enhanced consistency and uniformity of application. The appointment of national Community court judges by the Member States as a whole in accordance with established Community court procedure, as well as through the nomination of a court in a wider network supervised by the Community courts in Luxembourg to which references and/or appeals may be made as appropriate and subject to the authority of the Community courts, would also preserve the coherence and unity of the Community legal system.

The unity of Community law is even more vital and vulnerable since the enlargement of the EU in May 2004. Without this key feature the proposed nomination system could prove politically controversial because of the concern that the nominated courts could adopt, to a degree, a parochial perspective. The proposal respects these concerns and preserves the unity of the Community law by clearly establishing an operation under the authority of the Community courts.[179]

Knowing that it is not for national courts to declare Community acts invalid but that this is a matter exclusively for the Community Court (as the

---

[178] See Jaeger (n 60).

[179] The proposal should not be confused with a proposal made in the past according to which 'regional courts' should be presided over by a 'Superior Supreme Court' (see, eg *The Future of the Judicial System of the European Union, Comments of the Bar European Group of the United Kingdom on the Position Paper of the Court of the Justice of the European Communities* (London, 1999), para 87). Such a construction of a 'Superior Supreme Court' would lead to a substantial delay. In contrast, the proposal foresees that those nominated courts have original jurisdiction and not that parties to a preliminary ruling first litigate domestically and then, if a party chooses, in the ECJ, which would not only require a second round of supplementary translation but also heavily delay the proceedings.

Court also ruled in Foto-Frost),[180] in order to avoid conflicting decisions between the Community and national courts, a nominated court would operate as a chamber of the Community courts and under their authority, and hence address this issue regarding sufficient competence of the nominated courts.

6. It would solve the existing problem of delay and speed up and secure access to justice arising from faster court proceedings, local culture and language, as well as the other benefits outlined above.

7. It avoids the disadvantages of some of the other reform proposals outlined above and, in particular, the difficulty of increasing the community budget would be limited if an existing court was to be nominated, as some of its funding would at least already have been defrayed.

8. It would generally raise the profile of Community law. The proposal would help to resolve any feeling that Community rules are 'foreign laws'. The lack of awareness of European law among the legal profession in the Member States and the resulting danger of conflicting judgments undermining the uniform application of EC law are a key problem of the current judicial system.[181] Needless to say, EU law is part of the national legal order and must be enforced as such; the nomination system would reinforce this principle.
As was stated by the EU Commission in 2001:

> [D]espite longstanding co-operation with the European Court of Justice, national lawyers and courts should be made more familiar with Community law, and assume responsibility in ensuring the consistent protection of rights granted by the Treaty and by European legislation. The Commission will continue to support judicial co-operation and the training of lawyers and judges in Community law, but Member States themselves will have to step up their efforts in the field.[182]

Finally, the nomination system would need to extend more broadly than limited reform of competition issues. This is particularly so because there are only a few Member States with specialist competition law courts and because, as referred to by Sir David Edward, the entire EU treaty, and hence the EU Reform Treaty, is about competition.

---

[180] Case 314/85 *Foto-Frost v Hauptzollamt Luebeck-Ost* [1987] ECR 4199.
[181] Commission of the European Union, Reform on European Governance (Office for Official Publications of the European Communities, Luxembourg, 2003) 37.
[182] Commission of the European Union, European Governance: A White Paper, Brussels, 25 July 2001, Com(2001) 428 final, 25.

A further proposal is the introduction of short-term changes to the current system (in particular in relation to the competition law area) until the above-described long-term solution in the form of a 'nomination system' can be established. Some of the proposed options are not mutually exclusive, though the time required for their introduction and formal preconditions and political sensitivity may differ widely. Generally, the short-term changes outlined below could be introduced as 'quick-fix' solutions; as most of them are in the hands of the European Community courts, they would not result in any change in the judicial structure and would require little, if any, legislative action.

## 4. D. Procedural Improvements for the Short Term—in Particular in the Competition Law Area

### 1. Increased Recourse to Expedition Procedures

Particularly in relation to those areas of the economy which move most quickly, and in the field of competition law, the increased implementation and use of the expedition ('fast track') procedures should be encouraged.[183] In general, the options could be the granting of priority treatment, the accelerated or expedited procedure, the simplified procedure or the possibility of giving judgment without an opinion of the Advocate General. It would be better to look at making the most of the flexibility available within the existing expedited procedure as this possibility has only been introduced recently. Also, recent developments indicate that the time is right to pursue this increased recourse to expedition procedures. For example, in 2003, the CFI reduced the number of judges required to hear a competition case from five to three in order to shorten the average time in which a case is heard.

Furthermore, recent amendments of the CFI Rules of Procedure provide, where the expedited procedure is to be used, applicants with the possibility to structure their pleading so that an abbreviated version may be taken forward on expedition, but with a longer version available as a fall-back in case the expedition application is rejected.[184]

---

[183] Fast-track cases before the CFI are governed by art 76a of the CFI Rules of Procedure (n 75), which came into force on 1 February 2001. The ECJ has also similar rules for a fast-track procedure (art 62a Rules of Procedure, see n 75). The only criteria explicitly stated in the Rules of Procedure are 'the particular urgency' and 'the circumstances of the case', hence leaving the Court a wide scope of discretion.

[184] See amendment of the Rules of Procedure of the CFI adopted on 12 October 2005 [2005] OJ L 298/1. Art 76a, para 1, second subparagraph states as follows:

That application may state that certain pleas in law or arguments or certain passages of the application initiating the proceedings or the defence are raised only in the event that the case is not decided under an expedited procedure, in particular by enclosing with the application an abbreviated version of the application initiating the proceedings and a list of the

The CFI Practice Directions[185] already contain one section (G) dealing exclusively with the formal requirements for a fast-track petition. It is particularly required that the application is 'confined to a summary of the pleas relied upon' and that 'its annexes are limited in number'.[186] A current issue is also that where the CFI Practice Directions regarding the volume and presentation of pleadings as well as the conduct of proceedings have not been complied with, the CFI may decide not to continue with a case under the expedited procedure. In general, parties should limit the length of their pleadings as requested by the CFI Practice Directions (to not exceed 20 pages where possible) and make the most of the flexibility available within the existing expedited procedure.

Although the general request for shortness of the briefs is to be supported, a flexible approach of the Court in relation to this requirement should also be encouraged. Reasons for this are two-fold. First, the merger decisions by the Commission have a tendency to be increasingly detailed, which might require a brief by the applicant that is long and precise enough to deliver the message to the Court in the appropriate way and create a full understanding of the complex factual, legal and economic considerations. Secondly, the absence of a second round of briefs can have a negative impact on the chances of the applicant as the Commission has the last word. Hence, this makes it even more important for the Court to apply a flexible approach in this respect and also to not discriminate the applicant against the Commission. This is because the CFI Practice Directions do not currently contain any specific language limiting the length of the Commission's defence brief.[187]

Furthermore, the ECJ has introduced deadlines into its internal procedures which are also likely to be transposed into the CFI. It is worth noting that a recent amendment of the CFI Rules of Procedure has already introduced some deadlines in relation to the expedited procedure. It states that, where the applicant has requested that the case should be decided under an expedited procedure, the period prescribed for the lodging of the defence

---

annexes which are to be taken into consideration only if the case is decided under an expedited procedure.

[185] Practice Directions to Parties [2007] OJ L 232, 7.

[186] According to s G, 61, of the Practice Directions (ibid), 'an application in respect of which the expedited procedure is requested must not in principle exceed 25 pages'. Experience under the preceding 2002 Practice Direction shows that this requirement can be taken quite seriously by the Court, requiring the briefs to be much shorter than they would be in ordinary proceedings. For example, in the judgment of 21 September 2005 of Case T–87/05 *Energias de Portugal v Commission (EDP)* [2005] OJ C 281, 22, the applicant was required to drop all procedural pleas and to reduce its application to less than 50 pages. See also MF Bay, JR Calzado and A Weitbrecht, 'Judicial Review of Mergers in the EU and the 'Fast Track' Procedure' (2006) The European Antitrust Review 38, 39.

[187] See Bay et al, ibid 39.

shall be one month. In case the CFI decides not to grant the request, the defendant will be granted an additional period of one month in order to lodge or, as the case may be, supplement the defence.[188] Furthermore, a 'super-fast track' procedure so that the appeal process is completed within six months of the Commissions Phase 2 ECMR Decision could be achieved by, for example, abridging the timetable for pleadings, or by not granting an automatic extension to the Commission to the original period of one month allowed for its defence.

Applicants who request the expedited procedure should also have the possibility to include in their application for expedition a request that the language of their case (for example, English instead of the working language of the Community court) should be used by the Community court in its consideration. If the language of a case was English, it might be possible, provided that the language abilities of the judges permit it, to persuade a chamber to use English as the working language, which would save time and the cost of translation.[189]

These changes would hopefully resolve the issues that the fast track procedure may not be appropriate or available in all merger appeal cases and that the fast track procedure is currently not the complete answer to improving the level and speed of effective judicial oversight in merger appeal cases.[190]

Also, the CFI might need additional resources for the fast track procedure to work efficiently and in order to avoid the diversion of resources to fast track procedure cases that will inevitably slow down the review of other cases pending before the Court. Increasing the number of judges in the CFI may raise budgetary problems within the more general Community, but it does not generate the same issues of principle as does an increase in the judges of ECJ (ie impact on the unity), nor is the link between nationality and judges as important as it is in the ECJ.[191]

---

[188] See amendment to the Rules of Procedure of the CFI (n 184) art 76a, para 2, second subpara states as follows:

> By way of derogation from Article 46(1), where the applicant has requested, in accordance with paragraph 1 of this Article, that the case should be decided under an expedited procedure, the period prescribed for the lodging of the defence shall be one month. If the Court of First Instance decides not to allow the request, the defendant shall be granted an additional period of one month in order to lodge or, at the case may be, supplement the defence. The time-limits laid down in this sub-paragraph may be extended pursuant to Article 46(3).

[189] For further reform proposals with regard to the language issues see section III.D.2.
[190] See, eg Cases T–209/01 *Honeywell v Commission* [2006] OJ C 48, 26 and T–210/01 *General Electric v Commission* [2006] OJ C 18, 26.
[191] So also Craig (n 35) 192.

Furthermore, an enabler for the CFI to use the expedited procedure more frequently and more effectively in cases which merit it could be the increased attempt to remove the CFI's jurisdiction from specific areas such as, for example, trademark cases (see also above, section III.D.5). I therefore appreciate the recent creation of the EU Civil Service Tribunal,[192] as I expect this tribunal to reduce approximately 25 per cent of the current caseload of the CFI, or around 170 cases a year.[193]

It is unlikely, however, that any of these procedural changes go far enough to make a material impact on speeding up the process whilst retaining consistency in the application of EU rules. This is particularly apparent in the field of mergers. Furthermore, staff cases are of relatively short duration and are normally scheduled between the major cases handled by the CFI. Furthermore, the statistics of the CFI for 2006 indicate that the Court experienced a rise of 33 per cent over all of its cases under its new competence (hence, excluding staff cases). It therefore becomes clear that, despite the creation of the Civil Service Tribunal, the issue is still the same as the CFI still has to deal with almost exactly the same number of cases as before.[194]

## 2. Language

The choice of the language of a case in the Community courts is a politically sensitive issue, but access to justice should be regarded as a higher priority. Any steps and reform proposals to reduce procedural delays in case the Community courts have a working language that is different to the language of the case, especially in English language cases, which form a significant proportion of the caseload, should be encouraged.

As mentioned before, on average, translation consumes about seven months of the total time taken to process a reference. The amount of time and money wasted by translating the submissions of a case into the working language of the Court should be eliminated wherever practicable.

Considerable savings could be made by sensible expansion and use of the Court's internal languages. Currently (at least) one chamber of the CFI

---

[192] On 2 November 2004 the Council adopted a decision establishing the European Union Civil Service Tribunal. This new specialized tribunal, composed of seven judges, would hear and determine at first instance disputes involving the European civil service. Its decisions would be subject to a right of appeal before the CFI on points of law only. Decisions given by the CFI in this area could exceptionally be subject to review by the ECJ. The European Union Civil Service Tribunal was duly constituted into law on 2 December 2005.

[193] This figure is based on the number of pending cases at the end of 2004, which were 20 per cent, as well as the number of judgments and orders rendered in 2004, which were almost 30 per cent. See Vesterdorf (n 41) 26.

[194] See also Vesterdorf (n 22) oral evidence on 17 January 2007, answer to questions 364 and 370, 89.

already works in English for the practical reason that much of the documentation may be in English. The wider adoption of such a flexible approach should be very much endorsed. It is worth pointing out that neither the International Court of Justice nor the European Court of Human Rights seem to experience any great difficulty from the fact that their deliberations are in both French and English, and even the Vatican (though not a court, certainly one of the most conservative establishments) has abandoned Latin as the sole language of debate (whilst still retaining its official status).[195]

Furthermore, the expansion of the EU and creation of 12 additional working languages has not only 'entrenched the dominance of English'[196] as the working language of all European institutions but also led to the fact that English is already the 'unofficial' working language of the Community courts. I would very much endorse the practice to advocate a wider adoption of such a flexible approach. This would also be in line with the already existing acknowledgment that 'English is the language of business'.[197]

As Margot Horspool stated:

There is a need to strike a balance between democratic and cultural needs for multilingualism and practical and realistic considerations of language in a world which is increasingly 'globalised' and where the general language of communication is inevitably English. This would call for concessions on the part of the Member States which may be politically difficult to make, but should not be impossible if a realistic attitude prevails over outdated procedures and if, in particular, economic considerations are not forgotten.

My practical proposal would be that other languages should be adopted as second, parallel working languages in the CFI and ECJ where:

1.   the documentation suggests this is appropriate; and
2.   the linguistic abilities of the judges permit it.

Furthermore, proposals from parties to adopt the language which both parties have agreed should be allowed, again under the condition that the judges have the linguistic abilities to deal with it. The confinement to either one or two languages as the working language(s) in a particular case, whilst reducing both the cost and delay, does not mean that, where deemed either

---

[195]  Horspool (n 78).

[196]  See 'Chirac Flees Summit' (n 80).

[197]  See ' "Deeply Shocked" Chirac Defends Summit Snub of English Speech'; EU Business, 24 March 2006; 'Chirac Flees Summit', ibid.

necessary or desirable, the case documents cannot be translated into the other official languages. The only difference would be that the proceedings are not held up by the translation process.

The savings in terms of the cost to the public purse from reduced translation of documentation would be significant.[198]

## 3. Tighter case management

One logical and realistic option for speeding up the process is tighter case management. With rigorous case management, the European Community courts would be able to deal with cases speedily despite language complexities and even third-party interventions. This option can be achieved within the existing Rules and essentially involves stricter appliance of the time limits by the European Community courts (in particular the judge-rapporteur).

## 4. Creation of one or more chambers within the European Community courts for a certain class of proceeding

A further alternative option for the short-term future would not involve a change to the existing structure but the creation of one or more chambers for a certain class of proceeding, such as those with significant economic consequences, in terms of the established political goals of the Lisbon agenda, or perhaps for competition cases with three or five judges specialized in and focusing on competition cases alone.

Such a proposal is very much supported by industry and legal practitioners[199] and preferred over the creation over the establishment of a new court as it is thought to be 'comparatively simple, and carries both legal and practical advantages over the creation of a separate competition court'.[200] It is also supported by some witnesses to the recent House of Lords investigation, which stated that 'the move allowing the Council to set up judicial panels ... is to be welcomed'.[201]

---

[198] See also comments of the Bar European Group of the UK on the position paper of the Court of Justice of the European Communities, *The Future of the Judicial System of the European Union* (London, October 1999) para 46.

[199] Both the BDI and the Confederation of Swedish Enterprise took the view that the creation of specialist competition chambers in the CFI would be preferable to the establishment of a new court. See 'Minutes of Evidence' in House of Lords Report (n 22) 118 and 157.

[200] See the memorandum by the Working Group of the Antitrust Committee of the International Bar Association in 'Minutes of Evidence' in House of Lords Report (n 22) page 137.

[201] See M Heim, in House of Lords, European Union Committee, 3rd Report of Session 2005–2006, The Constitutional Treaty: Role of the ECJ: Primacy of Union Law—Government Response and Correspondence (7 July 2005), point 16.

A key advantage is that such a solution could be unilaterally determined by the European Community courts (ie without the need for unanimous agreement in the Council of Ministers), hence such specialized chambers could relatively easily be established within the existing structure of the European Community courts, would not create an additional level or review (and therefore extend the avenues of appeal) and could therefore certainly improve the speed of treatment of (competition) cases. The current Rules of Procedure could be applied without needing to be changed or tailor-made for these specialized chambers, which would save a lot of time as well as cost.

Furthermore, the International Chamber of Commerce and UNICE considered such a specialist chamber to be a 'sensible interim solution',[202] with the Competition Law Association adding that the creation of a specialist chamber 'would be a step in the right direction and should be instigated immediately'.[203]

A disadvantage is certainly that, in the competition law area, for example, it could be difficult to resist a general pressure to allocate non-competition cases to the specialized chambers in times of underutilization or not to allocate competition cases to other chambers in times of overutilization.[204]

Nevertheless, the creation of a specialist chamber is an attractive option, but only if additional judges are allocated to the Community courts. Appointing more judges would be a 'more economical and satisfactory solution', especially 'if the alternative is the creation of a new court'.[205] Also, the former CFI President Bo Vesterdorf was only recently of the opinion that extra judges on the court would be 'evidently something that would be useful'.[206]

## 5. Removal of trademark cases to a judicial panel

This idea was included in the Commission Work programme for 2005[207] and is also supported by the new CFI president Mark Jaeger, who said in a recent interview that he does not think that creating a separate competition

---

[202] In 'Minutes of Evidence' in House of Lords Report (n 22) 144 and 163.

[203] ibid 127.

[204] See Vesterdorf (n 44) 26. From a historical perspective it is interesting to note the criticism of the creation of specialized courts/tribunals or specialized chambers made in the BIICL Report summarized above (see above section III.B.1). The report considered there to be a number of disadvantages, including the difficulty of defining a structured relationship between all the different tribunals, and a concern that specialist tribunals would proliferate and ultimately jeopardize the uniform interpretation and application of Community law.

[205] See Roth (n 22) para 139.

[206] See Vesterdorf (n 22) oral evidence on 17 January 2007, answer to question 389, 93.

[207] COM(2005) 15 final.

court would significantly cut procedures but that 'there are other areas, such as trademarks, that could be moved to a separate court more easily'.[208]

Furthermore, the recent House of Lords report came to the conclusion that 'far better' than setting up a new competition court would be 'reducing the amount of business of the CFI, principally by transferring trademark cases to a judicial panel'. Finally, trademark cases were one of three types of cases originally envisaged (by the 1999 Committee of Reflection, preceding the Nice Treaty) as being suitable for transfer to a judicial panel (the other two being staff cases and competition cases).[209]

The increase in trademark cases in recent years is significant, and it is therefore clear that there would not only be sufficient workload for a judicial panel but that it would also help in speeding up the procedures in front of the CFI. In 2006 the CFI experienced a 46 per cent increase, receiving 143 trademark cases (and was expecting around 170 in 2007);[210] and in 2005 there were more than twice as many new applications (98) as regards trademark issues than competition law cases (42). Excluding staff cases and 'special forms of procedure' cases, 33.7 per cent of all total claims in front of the CFI were trademark cases, 13.7 per cent were competition, 9.6 per cent were in relation to the law governing the institutions and 8.6 per cent were regarding state aid.[211]

To quote former CFI president Bo Vesterdorf: 'Removal of trademark cases would enable it [the CFI] to use the expedited procedure more frequently and more effectively in cases which merit it, including competition and, in particular, merger cases'.[212]

## IV. CONCLUSIONS

The establishment of a nomination system[213] and the implementation of short-term solutions[214] could enable the streamlining of European Community court procedures by overcoming obstacles such as language and translation issues, increased workload, budget hurdles and procedural delays.

Safeguards will be required to ensure consistent application of EU Law. In particular, given the modernization and decentralization of European

---

[208] Jaeger (n 60).
[209] See also Vesterdorf (n 22) oral evidence on 17 January 2007, answers to questions 377 and 379, 90.
[210] So also House of Lords Report (n 22) para 168.
[211] Highlighted by Roth in his written evidence to the House of Lords enquiry (n 22) 153 ff.
[212] Vesterdorf (n 22) 26.
[213] See section III.C.
[214] See section III.D.

competition law and the policy of giving priority to deterrence and consumer welfare (including compensation), the increased role of national courts in private enforcement militates in favour of their active participation in public enforcement as appellate or referral courts. Implementing a structure parallel to that of the European Competition Network and in line with the EU Reform Treaty should not only enhance the competition culture required to improve the competitiveness of European industry to meet the goals of the Lisbon Agenda but should also guarantee over time a structural uniformity in the system of European law.

The nomination system outlined above should not be regarded as a form of renationalization of the Community courts, but should be understood as a responsible mechanism for ensuring consistent enforcement in the interests of policy objectives and, more generally, the economic future of the EU. In this regard, it is potentially an attractive 'halfway house' mechanism that may appeal to a wide audience.

If it were to be regarded as a reform that provided speedier access to justice and swifter enforcement at local level, as well as providing greater political engagement with a supra-national legal framework within a multi-domestic setting, the proposed nomination system might achieve a number of ends through the same means.

Limited reform is preferable to no reform. It is widely recognized that the current system is too slow. Streamlining the European judicial system could provide the impetus needed to foster progress in Europe following on from the Lisbon Treaty, which reinforces the respect for national interests and promotes Member States' coordination towards the EU's common goals.

# CHAPTER 5

# *Checks and Balances: European Competition Law and the Rule of Law*

*Philip Marsden*

The rule of law is an eminently European concept. It may well have been exported around the world, achieving constitutional status in some jurisdictions, but it was first discussed by Aristotle and Plato, formed the basis of the Magna Carta, has been enunciated by Blackstone and Dicey, and motivates the thinking of senior Law Lords to this day.[1] The issue that this paper seeks to introduce, is the degree to which European competition law accords with the rule of law.

## I. QUIS CUSTODIET IPSOS CUSTODES?

The fundamental issue that the rule of law seeks to address is: 'Who guards the guardians?' Who ensures that they use the powers we have granted them to protect us, in an appropriate, just and fair manner, and that we never need to be protected from them? In the context of competition law, much centres on the use of both the power and the discretion that we have given the authorities. Where are the guarantees that they will be accountable, independent and fair? At the same time, how do we ensure that the courts accord competition authorities the appropriate degree of deference due an expert body, while still holding the authorities to both the *acquis communautaire* and the rule of law?

Do we tell a 'noble lie'—as Plato argued—and trust those in power to guard themselves against themselves? Competition officials are after all, experts, and often part of agencies that are independent from ministries. They are public servants, and will keep this responsibility well in mind. Wisely, we do not have that kind of faith. For example, for various reasons over the years, safeguards have had to be introduced into the decision-making process at the European Commission's DG-Competition. As there

---

[1] Lord Bingham, 'The Rule of Law' (2007) 66 CLJ 67.

is no requirement that the European Union's Competition Commissioner be an expert in competition law or economics, we rely on the expertise and analysis of case teams. These are made up of more lawyers and economists than ever before. Their investigations are in turn reviewed internally by a 'fresh pair of eyes': colleagues who act as devil's advocate panels to ensure that the evidence supports the particular theory of harm. This peer review is also supplemented by the rigour and scepticism of the Office of the Chief Economist, which hopefully tempers the fire that we want the case team to have, with added intellectual rigour and objective analysis. There is also obviously the to and fro between the case teams and the parties; added to which independent Hearing Officers monitor oral proceedings to try to ensure both due process, and that the rights of defence are adequately protected. They are also increasingly getting involved in more substantive areas. The Legal Service reviews draft decisions, with an eye on EU law, and the very real pressure that they may have to defend the decision in court some day. Then there is the fact that major decisions go to the College of Commissioners, which, while bowing to the Competition Commissioner's point of view, also provides another layer of review. Then we have possible appeals to the Courts, and the court of public opinion as well: the reporters, and the academic community.

After this exhaustive review, are there not more than enough 'checks and balances' in the system? Let us see. Dicey's three principles of the rule of law require:

- the absolute supremacy of the law over arbitrary power/*discretion*
- *equality* before the law; and that
- the law be defined and enforced by the *courts*.

How does EU competition law match up to these standards? The EU *acquis* is a unique and impressive achievement: uniting civil and common law regimes through public international law, and applied through a unique form of administrative law. It tries to bring together different cultures with different backgrounds, legal traditions, stages of economic development and concentration, and resulting different views on competition, wrongdoing and enforcement.

So we must ask, in such a system, with such obvious opportunities for divergent decisions, is EU law indeed supreme? What is the extent of discretion that we want competition authorities to exercise and to what extent is it controllable? Is there sufficient official guidance for undertakings to understand what conduct is permissible? Are case-selection, re-allocation and decision-making consistent and accountable? Is the law really being interpreted and enforced by the courts? Or is it the authorities that are making the greatest strides in this area? Does this raise any problems, and if so, how are these controlled?

I will address these areas by looking first at the European Commission, particularly DG-Competition; the European Competition Network; and finally the EU Courts.

<br>

II. THE EUROPEAN COMMISSION—LINGERING PROCEDURAL CONCERNS

DG-Competition investigates, prosecutes and decides on competition law matters, subject to appeal to the courts. The various checks and balances outlined above constrain the discretion of the enforcers, as do detailed regulations.

Since these many safeguards have been introduced, however, the OECD has undertaken a peer review of DG-Competition, and found that its multiple roles raise 'serious doubts' about the absence of checks and balances.[2] This is curious; one can understand why, at the level of rhetoric, it might be difficult to accept an authority acting as prosecutor, judge, jury and executioner. But most authorities have multiple roles. Only a very few have to convince a judge of their case—as the United States Department of Justice does—before enforcement action can be taken. The way to ensure that what might otherwise appear to be intolerable accords with fundamental justice is precisely through the kinds of safeguards that the Commission has introduced, and greater transparency in the system. But that can only be the start.

The OECD report focused on a few particulars which make clear that there is still rather a lot of room for improvement. Generally speaking, these all fall within a category of a greater 'judicializing' of the system. The OECD noted that there was no right of undertakings to cross-examine witnesses or leniency applicants. Also, they found the Commission to be the only competition authority where the ultimate decision-maker—the College—is not required to attend the oral hearing, nor is the Competition Commissioner, nor even the Director-General. Despite all the checks in the system, questions have been raised about the extent to which this procedure complies with the right to a fair hearing. Article 6 of the European Convention on Human Rights holds that rights, obligations, and penalties, particularly those not of a minor nature, should be determined at first instance by an 'independent and impartial tribunal' and a right to a subsequent review by an appellate body is not enough. While the OECD recognized that this issue had arisen before, in the 1980s, it clearly thought it worth reconsideration. The severity of recent fines, and the fact that they are obviously punitive, may have played a part. Perhaps the system is begin-

<br>

[2] OECD, European Commission—Peer Review of Competition Law and Policy (OECD, Paris, 2005)

ning to require a degree of separation of powers, and greater judicial involvement. At the very least, some functions within DG-Competition might be separated, formalizing the division between the case teams and the devil's advocate panels. Certainly senior staff—at the Director General or Deputy level—should be more evident at hearings, if such proceedings are to remain an important and credible part of the system. Finally, could DG-Competition investigate and prosecute and then bring their findings to the CFI for review? Of course, the EU Courts are over-burdened as it is, but perhaps given the punitive and quasi-criminal nature of the penalties involved, and the fact that almost every fine gets appealed to the court anyway, it is time for a separate chamber to consider such cases, or a separate European Cartel Court.

## A. Revisit Guidance?

The high fines for violations make it all the more important that undertakings know where they stand ex ante. The removal of the notification system was not supposed to leave them entirely in the dark, and it does not. Informal guidance from the Commission is still available. To date, however, there have only been a few requests for such guidance and no formal findings that article 81 EC does not apply. Perhaps undertakings are happy with their legal advice and just self-assessing. The experience of in-house counsel, however, appears to be that the Commission is reluctant to provide informal guidance. There appears to be a widely held impression that guidance will be difficult to obtain, and perhaps this is why it is so rarely sought. Given the possibility that a non-compliant agreement might be nullified, companies might avoid concluding borderline agreements, even if their potential benefits outweigh their anti-competitive effect. Chilling pro-competitive arrangements is in no one's interest; so it would be good for the Commission to make its thinking clear in this regard to dispel the growing impression—whether ill founded or not—that it is not really minded to provide such guidance.

### III. EUROPEAN COMPETITION NETWORK—TIME FOR MORE DISCLOSURE

The European Competition Network (ECN) was created by the Modernisation Regulation[3] to improve European competition law enforcement by making it quicker, more targeted and closer to the ground, so to speak. The ECN itself is a mechanism for authorities to exchange information and re-allocate cases. DG-Competition benefits because it can apply its

[3] Council Regulation (EC) No 1/2003 of 16 December 2002 on the implementation of the rules on competition laid down in Article 81 and 82 of the Treaty [2003] OJ L1/1.

limited resources to a smaller caseload, ideally involving a truly European interest. A more effective and efficient enforcement regime is thus created, and one which accords more closely with the principle of subsidiarity. As ever with all things 'EU' it is a unique experiment, and one that seems to be working well.

'Seems' is the operative word, because that is all outsiders really have to go on. The network is only for the authorities, and thus is viewed by practitioners as a 'black box'. The unknown naturally attracts suspicion. This is unfortunate because the principles that guide the ECN are sensible and clearly stated in Regulation 1/2003. Generally, the Commission deals with cases affecting more than three EU Member States; the rest go to one or more Member States, based on which is most affected; with the Commission reserving the right to take back some multi-State cases of particular importance, as has happened in the energy and telecoms sectors.

Headline results are reported. The authorities have noted that over 800 cases have been notified within the ECN, and more than 300 reported to the Commission. A great deal of knowledge and—perhaps more importantly—appreciation for each others' competences has developed.

As the central node, the Commission is responsible for maintaining a degree of consistency. So far it has taken a soft approach, ringing authorities, writing letters, or submitting amicus briefs to try to ensure that decisions are broadly consistent with EU standards.[4] This is good and respectful, but it is not going to catch everything. The process depends primarily on the interests and resources of the ECN unit at DG-Competition, which has to monitor more cases in more languages than ever before. Furthermore, it is not always clear that sufficient reporting from national courts is reaching the Commission. Inevitably, there has been divergence, which is to an extent permitted for some aspects of competition law, particularly abuse of dominance.

### A. Inconsistency at the ECN—at the Margins

Resale price maintenance arrangements have been approved in Spain, but banned in Italy and Holland.[5] The infamous *Michelin II* rebates scheme— that attracted such opprobrium and penalties at the European level—has been approved in France. Similarly, British Airways' commissions to travel agents were banned and fined at the EC level, while cases involving similar arrangements of BA were closed by the UK Office of Fair Trading.

---

[4] K Wright, 'European Commission Opinions to National Courts in Antitrust Cases: Consistent Application and the Judicial-Administrative Relationship' CCP Working Paper 08-24, ESRC Centre for Competition Policy, University of East Anglia

[5] Comments of the Global Competition Law Center on the Functioning of Regulation 1/2003 (2008).

The sky is clearly not falling, but cases like these do show the limits of the system and the inevitable uncertainty this provides businesses with pan-European product offerings. The same is true of the analysis the authorities use more generally. Of course each authority has different enforcement priorities, resources, and functions within a different legal 'operating system', whether it is common law, civil law or something else. They also function in different markets, with different degrees of privatization, economic development and concentration, to name but a few variables. This can lead to different approaches in the ways authorities define markets, identify anti-competitive problems, prioritize cases, and intervene.

All of this is not surprising in such different economies. When articles 81 and 82 EC are enforced, though, consistency is not necessarily the hobgoblin of mediocre minds. At the very least a greater effort at transparency would be welcome so we can understand *why* divergences are happening. Where it is possible, historical data from the ECN intranet of cases should be made public. Equally, authorities should be encouraged to publish non-confidential versions of non-infringement decisions and any informal guidance that they issue.

Greater publication of this sort would also save public resources, and be of indirect benefit to business, if it can help authorities with their analysis, and ensure that they do not re-invent the wheel, or reach conflicting conclusions about similar arrangements. Public statements of reasoning behind all decisions—including case-closures—will be more effective in 'spreading the gospel' than relying on the Network operating solely through internal checks.

## IV. THE EU COURTS

Recalling Dicey's third principle, there is no doubt that the EU Courts are the ultimate interpreters of the law. But that does not mean there are not problems en route to justice. The main one is how long that journey is. Back in 1996, the European Court of Justice (ECJ) was found to be largely a victim of its own success, due to its wide jurisdiction, the large volume of case law upon which it was the sole interpreter and the relatively effective enforcement of its judgments.[6] Delay is still the primary problem.[7] Cases can take an average of two-and-a-half to five years, and sometimes eight to

---

[6] British Institute of International and Comparative Law, 'The Role and Future of the European Court of Justice', A report by members of the EC Section of the British Institute's Advisory Board chaired by the Rt Hon the Lord Slynn of Hadley (1996).

[7] T Cowen, '"Justice Delayed is Justice Denied": The Rule of Law, Economic Development and the Future of the European Community Courts' (2008) 4 European Competition Journal 1, and reprinted in this volume (Chapter 4).

nine years from initial decision to final appeal. This is too long, and various initiatives have been suggested to speed things up.

Translation issues are still a major factor in the delay, and it really must be asked whether the court's system of holding internal deliberations in French, with the necessary translation, makes sense, where the majority of judges now will have English as their second language and French as a distant third, if that.

Should there be a separate EU court purely for competition issues? A House of Lords subcommittee said it was not yet the right time for such a body.[8] But something should be done to give appropriate consideration to what is really such an important pillar of EU law, and in which quite important economic interests are at stake. Roving circuit judges or national panels of the EU Courts have also been suggested, particularly if populated by retired members of the ECJ or the EU's Court of First Instance (CFI). This is certainly a most pragmatic suggestion, and while it may take a while to set up, and might mean that some circuits are busier than others, is worth consideration.

The most pressing area is always mergers of course, as this is the most time-sensitive of any aspect of competition law. If a merger tribunal is not yet timely at the EU level, then we should explore more ways to free up the CFI in other areas, so that it can apply its expertise to more quickly rule on mergers. Here again, consideration might be given to a separate panel or court dealing solely with relatively straightforward, though no less important, cartel cases.

## A. Dissents Please

A word of concern about the role of the courts, though. Of course they should continue to rule on the most complex and controversial cases. But how best should they do that? CFI Judge John Cooke, the Judge Rapporteur in the *Microsoft* case, recently revealed, 'I tell my clerks that these (Article 81 and 82) cases are 20 percent fact, 20 percent law and 60 percent policy'.[9] We will never know how much of the case was decided on policy grounds, rather than on the facts or the law itself. It might be viewed simply as following EU case law quite closely, but expanding its scope in some areas to accommodate the Commission's view of the facts. Or it may be yet-another judgment[10] representing an out-dated ordoliberal view of competition, that is also starkly at odds with the Commission's stated aim

---

[8] House of Lords, European Union Committee, 15th Report of Session 2006–2007, An EU Competition Court—Report with Evidence (London, The Stationery Office, 2007) HL Paper 75.

[9] See P Marsden and S Bishop, 'Intellectual Leaders Still Need Ground to Stand on' Editorial (2007) 3 European Competition Journal 2 315

[10] See Case C-95/04 P *British Airways v Commission* [2007] ECR I-2331.

of only intervening when there is clearly identified and likely consumer harm.[11] Can we be sure that the judges understand the economic points being made before them, and can take an appropriate view; or is it sometimes all too difficult, and so their default is more often than not to defer to the Commission? Is that appropriate?

There is no doubt that overturning a Commission decision—or finding it manifestly unsupported—can deal a severe blow to the agency. We do not know how much this is in the minds of the judges, or how much it is discussed in their deliberations. Hopefully though—and Judge Cook's comments aside, policy considerations are not determinative, as judgments must rest on sound and *current* law first and foremost. Where different motivations are behind some rulings, however, then this should be made clear.

Isn't it time to finally allow dissents at the European Courts? The Commission seems confident in leading the world intellectually and through cases. The Courts should be too. It is highly unlikely at this stage that dissents would destabilize the *acquis*. Judges who speak their minds, should not fear national retribution when they retire. Dissents would help make rulings more transparent, reasoning more clear, and help allow new ideas to be discussed and considered.

## B. The Standard of Review

The CFI reviews Commission decisions against a 'manifest error of assessment' standard which supposedly entails ascertaining whether the facts on which the Commission's assessment was based were correct, whether the conclusions drawn from those facts were not clearly mistaken or inconsistent and whether all the relevant factors had been taken into account. The limited standard of review is of course a deferential bow to the relevant agency's expertise, the technical and economic issues at hand, and its discretion. But it is not a full appeal; nor even judicial review.

Is this the appropriate balance, of the Commission's expertise and discretion, and the CFI's duty of review? The CFI has not at all been shy of rebuking DG-Competition when it has not argued its cases carefully enough. The three judgments in *Airtours, Tetra Laval,* and *Schneider* and 'were scathing in their criticism of the Commission's appreciation of the facts and treatment of evidence' and eventually forced the Commission to introduce the very safeguards discussed earlier.[12]

---

[11] P Marsden, '*Microsoft v Commission*—With Great Power Comes Great Responsibility' Competition Law Insight (October 2007).

[12] Case T-342/99 *Airtours v Commission* [2002] E.R. II-2585; Case T-310/01 *Schneider Electric v. Commission* [2002] ECR II-4071; and Case T-5/02 *Tetra Laval v Commission* [2002] ECR II-4381. See N Levy, 'EU Merger Control: From Birth to Adolescence' (2003) World Competition 195, 211.

Nevertheless it can be argued that in very complex economic cases, the CFI's limited standard of review leads it to rely too heavily on the findings of the Commission. There is also the problem that in the legal tradition of Continental Europe—which predominates at the EU Courts—'opinions' and agency findings can often end up being treated as if they are 'facts'. Thus, the Commission's decision might not be as thoroughly tested as it would be, for example, in a British court.

Given this, do Europeans and others really understand the limited nature of the CFI's review of the Commission's decisions? The CFI is only looking at the adequacy of the decision. Judgments are reported as if they were full appeals; as if a hearing was held of all the issues, witnesses examined, arguments heard in full, in a public forum. The reality of course is quite different. There may be judges' questions—which are starting to grow in significance—but there is no in-depth questioning of officials, witnesses, complainants, and the majority of the work has been done in unavailable written pleadings which are protected from public scrutiny. More could be opened up, and thereby provide greater oversight.[13] How much more credibility would the process have if reporters could genuinely write 'today the Court upheld the Commission's decision', rather than what should be: 'today the Court found that the Commission was not manifestly wrong'?

## V. CONCLUSION—'A MORE ECONOMIC APPROACH' MAY LEAD THE WAY

This article has argued for more openness and more legal and procedural guarantees. But perhaps the solution will come from another quarter entirely: the rule of reason. As the Commission pursues its 'more economic approach', it will inevitably have to explain its decisions more thoroughly—whether in providing informal guidance, non-infringement decisions, or actual prohibitions. This too will help authorities around Europe better understand, share and benefit from this self-discipline. It also means that cases will be more thoroughly reasoned, and hard-fought, and thus better tested as they pass through the various existing checks and balances. The recommendation I have made is that greater disclosure of agencies' reasoning, access to ECN data, some separation of the investigative and adjudicative functions, allowing full hearings and dissents, and above all greater transparency, would all help the continued development of EU competition

---

[13] D Lawsky, 'Information Please: Opening Antitrust to the Public—Why More European Union Court and Commission Documents and Hearings Should No Longer Be Secret' in P Marsden (ed), *Handbook of Research in Trans-Atlantic Antitrust* (Edward Elgar, Cheltenham, 2006).

law. Ironically though, the reliance on more economics, and balancing tests like the rule of reason may be what allow EU competition law to better accord with the rule of law. This can only happen though if judges are themselves able and willing to undertake more rigorous evaluation, rather than rely on precedents that were never informed by economic analysis.

# CHAPTER 6

# Investment Protection and the Rule of Law: Change or Decline?

*L Yves Fortier*

## I. A FEW WORDS OF WELCOME

Distinguished guests, dear colleagues, chers amis:

Thank you to the organizers of this conference for the invitation to speak today. I am both honoured and flattered to participate in this event celebrating the golden anniversary of the British Institute of International and Comparative Law. Since its inception, the Institute has been singularly influential in promoting the rule of law in international affairs. It has been devoted to encouraging the understanding, development and practical application of international and comparative law.

I have been asked to share with you today my thoughts on international investment protection: past, present and future and the rule of law. In so doing, my mission is two-fold. First, to highlight the dramatic, and I would add rapid, change that has taken place in the international legal investment landscape. And second, to consider some of the recent challenges and areas of debate in the field with a view to reaching some conclusions, however tentative, about where investment protection is going in the future and whether or not in its journey, it will continue to be influenced by the rule of law.

By way of introductory remarks, I observe that the Institute itself has dutifully taken on a leadership role in the field by establishing a centre for investment treaty research and policy discussion—the Investment Treaty Forum. As may be gleaned from the Forum's mission statement, it builds upon the Institute's existing activities in the fields of public international law and international commercial arbitration. Considering the remarkable pace at which international investment protection continues to evolve, we are all keenly aware of the importance of serious debate and the need for authoritative comment in the field. The Forum has set out to achieve this by, in its words, 'sharing the reputation enjoyed by the Institute for independence, even-handedness and academic rigour, and by drawing on the expertise of Forum and Institute members'. Its Director, Norah Gallagher, accepted to lead this initiative in early 2008, and as a Patron of the Forum, I wish to congratulate Norah on her awesome contribution in the short year since she has been at the helm.

## II. THE BIRTH AND DEVELOPMENT OF THE INTERNATIONAL INVESTMENT PROTECTION SYSTEM: GRADUAL CHANGE OR QUANTUM LEAP?

It will not have gone unnoticed that the Institute shares its golden anniversary with that of the New York Convention on the Recognition and Enforcement of Foreign Arbitral Awards, one of the countless gems in the United Nations' legal crown. The role of the New York Convention, in fulfilling the promise of international arbitration generally and investment arbitration in particular, speaks volumes about a theme close to my heart, the United Nations as an agent of progress in the international legal field. It is by no means a coincidence that the UN Charter itself defines its mandate in a manner that is reminiscent of the Institute's own *raison d'être*, encompassing 'the progressive development of international law and its codification'. With 143 signatory States and counting, the adoption of the New York Convention 50 years ago has proven immensely fruitful in this regard, even if the UN's wider task in relation to peace and security continues to evolve and take shape.

In preparing for this address, I was reminded of a paper entitled 'The International Rule of Law' written in the early 1990s by our dear friend and colleague, the late Sir Arthur Watts, one of the most highly regarded, and widely liked, British international lawyers of his time. Arthur observed in 1993 that '[t]he transition from the establishment of international order by the hegemonic power of one, or a few States, to the full establishment of the international rule of law is a still-continuing process'.[1] And so it has, and continues to be, in the field of international investment protection.

Along similar lines, my friend and colleague, Steve Schwebel, in a recent piece aptly entitled 'A BIT about ICSID', reminds us of how far we have travelled by asking that we '[c]onsider where the law of foreign investment has been not only for the last twenty-five years but the last fifty, from the time when Western imperialism expired and the ranks of capital-importing independent States expanded essentially from Latin America to include Asia and Africa'.[2] Steve adds: 'If we recall the constellation of countries circa

---

[1] Sir A Watts, 'The International Rule of Law' (1993) 36 German Yearbook of International Law 15, 45.
[2] SM Schwebel, 'A BIT about ICSID' (2009) (to be published in the ICSID Review—Foreign Investment Law Journal) 1.

1960, there was a legal as well as economic gulf between capital-exporting States and capital-importing States. There was a great gulf on the substance of the governing law—if any. There was a great gulf on international legal process—if any.'[3]

Whilst it is true that expropriation claims have been a live issue in international law 'since antiquity'[4], it is equally true that the protections afforded to foreign investors with expropriation grievances today are of an unprecedented magnitude, in large part due to the ever-growing network of investment treaties, in particular bilateral investment treaties or BITs. In a mere 50 years, the number of BITs has gone from 0 to nearly 3000 by some accounts—a quantum leap in historical terms. And there is no turning back: The emergence of BITs, coupled with 'dethroning the State from its status as the sole subject of international law',[5] have fundamentally altered the international investment landscape.

In these brief remarks, I will elaborate on examples which illustrate, in my view, how the emergence of BITs has fostered a far more secure and fair investment environment and, indeed, a greater respect for the rule of law. A few well-known facts need to be recalled.

As we all know, the very first BIT was concluded between Germany and Pakistan 50 years ago this year, in 1959. The number of BITs grew at a slow pace in the years that followed, but surged in the late 80s and early 90s from approximately 500 to over five times that number today. No less than 179 countries have entered into one or more such agreements.[6] It is projected that investment inflows worldwide will be close to US$1.5 trillion by 2010.[7] By any measure, and whatever may be the impact of the present economic turmoil, such figures are startling.

Just as telling is the pace at which international investment treaty arbitration has evolved. One recent empirical study surveyed a sample of reported investment treaty claims, of which over 90 per cent had proceeded under the Arbitration Rules established pursuant to the Washington Convention. When one considers that only 10 years ago, the ICSID Secretariat had handled but a handful of cases since its creation in the 1960s, and that in the last 10 years, nearly 300 treaty claimants have elected to proceed under the ICSID Rules, one can only observe with amazement how far we have come in terms of establishing an effective

---

[3] ibid.

[4] T Ginsburg, 'International Substitutes for Domestic Institutions : Bilateral Investment Treaties and Governance' (2005) International Review of Law and Economics 107 109.

[5] SM Schwebel, 'A BIT about ICSID' (2009) 23 ICSID Review 1, 4.

[6] UNCTAD's World Investment Report 2008.

[7] SD Franck, 'Empirically Evaluating Claims About Investment Treaty Arbitration' (2007–2008) 86 North Carolina Law Review 1, 7, quoting the Economic Intelligence Unit, World Investment Prospects to 2010: Boom or Backlash 6 (2006).

framework for the resolution of investment disputes.[8] At this juncture, I cannot help but share with you my pride as a Canadian at the recent appointment of Ms Meg Kinnear as ICSID's first full time Secretary General. I am confident that Meg will continue to foster ICSID's success.

Statistics aside, an informed observer of what some have called the 'movement toward treatification'[9] will know that BITs were initially entered into between an industrialized country on the one hand, and a developing country on the other. The goal, at least initially, was to refrain host country action against the interests of the investors by ensuring that legal commitments made to investors could resist the forces of change often demanded by the political and economic life in host countries. Thus, the first generation of BITs were structured to achieve this goal by (i) subjecting the host State to a set of international legal rules applicable to its dealings with foreign investors and (ii) giving the foreign investors themselves the right to bring a claim in international arbitration against the host country in the event of a violation of those rules. In the absence of BITs, foreign investors were limited to the host country laws alone for the protection of their investments, which was considered by many to be an impediment to global economic development.[10] Indeed, for many investors, the risks were simply too great:

> Host governments can easily change their own domestic law after a foreign investment is made, and host country officials may not always act fairly or impartially toward foreign investors and their enterprises. Investor recourse to local courts for protection may prove to be of little value in the face of prejudice against foreigners or governmental interference in the judicial process. Indeed, these fears were realized in the 1960s and 1970s when numerous instances of interference and expropriation of foreign investments by host country governments occurred.[11]

The BIT movement, and its incorporation of international arbitration as a mechanism for the resolution of treaty disputes, is, in essence, a movement beyond the Calvo doctrine in the sense that, whilst the principle of non-intervention among States has been respected, the companion principle of

---

[8] B Appleton, 'Comparing ICSID and *Ad Hoc* Treaty Arbitration' (2007) 2 Global Arbitration Review 3, 11.

[9] JW Salacuse, 'The Treatification of International Investment Law' (2007) 13 Law and Business Review of the Americas 156.

[10] JW Salacuse and NP Sullivan, 'Do BITs Really Work?: An Evaluation of Bilateral Investment Treaties and Their Grand Bargain' (2005) 46 Harvard International Law Journal 1 67, 75.

[11] ibid.

absolute equality between foreigners and nationals in respect of recourse to local national courts has not.[12]

Since the first generation of BITs between capital-exporting countries and capital-importing ones, there has been a flurry of 'BITs amongst equals', so to speak. This has been the source of some debate—particularly in relation to the impending Lisbon Treaty—to which I will return in a moment, but it bears mentioning at this juncture that most BITs today, regardless of the particular status of the country parties thereto, share similar if not identical substantive and procedural protections. Does this mean that all BITs are the same? I have tackled this question elsewhere, inspired in my answer by the writings of Christoph Schreuer who refers to such factors as the presence of model BITs and the comparative bargaining power of the negotiating parties:

> BITs are typically based on model treaties. Many States have model BITs which serve as a starting point for negotiations with a prospective treaty partner. To what extent the final product will resemble a country's model will depend on the relative weight of the negotiating partners, on whether the other country also has a model BIT that it wants to promote and on the general circumstances of the negotiations.[13]

Be that as it may, prior to the advent of the BIT, international investment protections were essentially the product of customary international law, whereas today, 'treaties have become the fundamental source of international law in the area of foreign investment'.[14] Naturally, this has been pivotal in the encouragement and protection of foreign investment, and indeed BITs often make this explicit in the very title and preamble of the instrument. It has also heightened the importance of international investment law, which is now considered to be 'of immense practical concern to a much wider audience, including the practicing bar, environmentalists, nongovernmental organizations, multinational companies, and governments, both industrialized and developing, who sometimes question the consequences of what they have created over the last four decades'.[15] To be sure, investment treaties can no longer be ignored when embarking upon

---

[12] M Calvo, 'Comments on the 7th Geneva Global Arbitration Forum' (1999) 16 Journal of International Arbitration 2 130.

[13] C Schreuer, 'Diversity and Harmonization of Treaty Interpretation in Investment Arbitration' (7 February 2006) available at http://www.univie.ac.at/intlaw/pdf/cspubl_85.pdf, 8 (quoted in Yves Fortier, 'The Canadian Approach to Investment Protection: How Far Have We Come?' in C Binder (ed), *International Investment Law: Essays in Honour of Christoph Schreuer* (OUP, Oxford, 2009).

[14] JW Salacuse, 'The Treatification of International Investment Law' (2007) 13 Law and Business Review of the Americas 155, 157.

[15] ibid 163.

international investment transactions. As a result, 'participants adjust their behaviour to avoid or minimize the costs of non-compliance, thereby restoring equilibrium in investment arrangements, bolstering international investment law's credibility and promoting international investments'.[16] And so the wheel turns, at least in principle.

The emergence of BITs has not occurred in isolation: the creation of organs such as the European Court of Justice and the World Trade Organization, as well as multilateral instruments such as NAFTA and the Energy Charter Treaty, and of course the Washington Convention, to name but a few, have all contributed to a multiplication of the 'voices' now heard in international law.[17] Some might say that with all these voices, the room has grown noisier or, to quote my friend Professor Reisman, the system has become somewhat more complex. Which brings me to share with you his keen observations in this regard:

> In international law, as elsewhere, the whole is not greater than the sum of its parts. The international legal system is not a unified and coherent decision-maker. It is a complex and modular process in which governments, the secretariats of inter-governmental organizations and an array of private actors operating within and outside of states pursue interests genuinely common to all of them. [...] In this complex process, everyone is seeking increased trade and investment and appreciates their centrality in the achievement of many other development and political transformation goals. But they often disagree on the fine print. International law must balance claims for respect for the special requirements of national communities, which is their very *raison d'être*, and concern for which is one of international law's central postulates, against the need for sustaining the international Rule of Law so that economic activity can continue to flow freely about the globe. International law must accomplish this in an environment in which short-term political interests, often driven by intense domestic constituent pressures as well as by power considerations, may lead to critical states actors to try, in cases of special concern to them to set aside the law for *raison d'état*.[18]

As an arbitrator who has seen his fair share of international investment disputes, I can assure you that the task of accommodating the competing

[16] T-H Cheng, 'Power, Authority and International Investment Law' (2005) 20 American University International Law Review 465, 467.
[17] AK Scheider, 'Not Quite a World Without Trials: Why International Dispute Resolution is Increasingly Judicialized' [2006] Journal of Dispute Resolution 119, 128.
[18] M Reisman, 'Economic Development, National Sovereignty and International Arbitration' paper prepared for delivery to the Arbitration Congress in Santa Fe de Bogotá, Columbia (3 November 2005) 11 and 13.

interests described by Professor Reisman is a challenging one indeed, to be undertaken one case at a time, on the merits of each claim, as argued by the parties and deliberated upon by the tribunal. But as pointed out by Judge Schwebel, given the 'immense number of treaties, the virtual universality of their adherence, and the predominant consistency of their terms, there is room for the view that they have reshaped the body of customary international law in respect of the treatment and taking of foreign investment'.[19] Judge Schwebel in fact surmises that certain core features of BITs, such as those regarding fair and equitable treatment as well as prompt, adequate and effective compensation, 'have seeped into the corpus of customary international law, with the result that they are binding on all States including those not parties to BITs'.[20] That is an interesting observation which may be deserving of another conference someday.

I will leave it to Judge Schwebel to defend his views, but I will take the opportunity to share with you some thoughts on the relationship between investor-State arbitration and the development of the rule of law. However trite, the investment arbitration community must remember, first and foremost, that an arbitral tribunal's duty is to apply the law. It is not to play politics. In fact, 'depoliticizing' investment disputes goes to the very essence of BITs and other international investment agreements, to insulate them from the political playing field and address them as part of the commercial arbitration one. This is not only essential to ensuring greater enforceability of international investment awards, but also key to ensuring that 'the infrastructure of international law can sustain a robust global economy'.[21]

And this, I put to you, has a heightened resonance today amidst the global recession we all face. Will the global recession mean more or fewer investor-State arbitrations? I think that we are likely to see more investor-State arbitrations, not fewer, and that the nationalization, whether complete or partial, of financial institutions may give rise to a new form of investor-State disputes. It is, therefore, all the more pressing that we turn our minds to the health of the investment treaty system, and its ability to deliver practical, meaningful solutions, through a legitimate process, to today's investment disputes.

Many have emphasized that '[t]he rule of law is essential to those participating in the global economy'.[22] I could not agree more. The issue, fundamentally, is one of legitimacy, as Professor Susan Franck has astutely explained:

---

[19] Schwebel (n 2) 5.

[20] ibid.

[21] DP Price, 'Chapter 11—Private Party vs. Government, Investor-State Dispute Settlement: Frankenstein or Safety Valve?' (2000) 26 Canada-United States Law Journal 107, 112.

[22] SD Franck, 'The Legitimacy Crisis in Investment Treaty Arbitration : Privatizing Public International Law Through Inconsistent Decisions' (2004–2005) 73 Fordham Law Review 1521, 1584.

*Without the clarity and consistency of both the rules of law and their
application, there is a detrimental impact upon those governed by the
rules and their willingness and ability to adhere to such rules, which can
lead to a crisis of legitimacy.* Legitimacy depends in large part upon
factors such as determinacy and coherence, which can in turn beget
predictability and reliability. Related concepts such as justice, fairness,
accountability, representation, correct use of procedure, and opportunities for review also impact conceptions of legitimacy. When these factors
are absent individuals, companies and governments cannot anticipate
how to comply with the law and plan their conduct accordingly, thereby
undermining legitimacy.[23] (emphasis added).

As an arbitrator, I might add that while there is certainly room for improvement in the international investment area, the field remains a relatively new
terrain which is maturing exponentially. But, it is still flexible and adapt-
able. The time is ripe for a look at possible means of improving the development of the rule of law in the field of investor-State arbitration, and I will
share a few musings with you in this regard.

### III. THE SUSTAINABILITY OF THE INTERNATIONAL INVESTMENT PROTECTION SYSTEM: THE NEXT FIFTY YEARS AND BEYOND

I take as my starting point some of the criticisms levelled at the international investment protection framework and, in particular, the investment
treaty arbitration process. I propose to consider whether and, if so, how
these criticisms are being addressed, in order that we may have a better
understanding of the 'critical path' towards enhanced legitimacy and
sustainability of the international investment protection system as a whole.

   None of these criticisms will come as a surprise to any of you. Indeed,
the words 'transparency', 'consistency' and 'equity' ring loudly in the ears
of all actors in the system. And whether or not you agree with a particular
criticism, I submit that the concerns expressed cannot be ignored, lest we
truly imperil the system.

### A. Beginning with Transparency

The lack of transparency in investment treaty arbitration is perhaps the
most widely shared criticism of the system—and the area in which the most
progress has been made to date.[24] As I have said elsewhere, parties, arbi-

---

[23] ibid.
[24] M Kinnear, 'Transparency and Third Party Participation in Investor-State Dispute

trators and arbitral institutions have begun to grapple with the tension between the traditional closed-door model of international commercial arbitration and the arbitration of disputes involving governments accountable to their citizens.

This is not to say that this issue has been easy or uncontroversial among the core participants in investment treaty arbitration. Many parties, both States and investors, continue to insist on confidentiality in disputes under various institutions and rules frameworks.[25] This reality is critical to understanding the landscape against which the trend towards transparency is taking shape. The ground *is* indeed shifting toward greater transparency.[26]

Transparency initiatives are taking place in both an *ad hoc* and an institutional environment, and involve efforts to open the arbitral process to the public through various mechanisms, such as the participation of third parties or *amici curiae*, the holding of open hearings, and the publication of awards as well as other documents prepared in the course of an arbitration proceeding. The new ICSID Arbitration Rules, which entered into force in 2006, are an excellent example of progress on all of these fronts. If one also considers the developments within the NAFTA Chapter 11 framework and the growing body of arbitral awards dealing with different aspects of the transparency issue, the gains made towards greater transparency in a very short period of time are remarkable.

It bears recalling at this juncture that the investment protection system is, at its core, based on consent. This consent encompasses not only consent to arbitrate in the narrow sense of this term, but consent to the entire system of investment treaty arbitration, its evolution and future developments. It follows that increased transparency could, in certain situations, require a new definition of the scope of State consent to investment treaty arbitration.

In this connection, my friend Professor Brigitte Stern has observed that developments in transparency, and in particular the involvement of *amici curiae*, are changing the very model on which the system is predicated. In her words:

Settlement', a paper presented at the symposium organized by ICSID, OECD and UNCTAD, titled 'Making the Most of International Investment Agreements: A Common Agenda' in Paris (2 December 2005).

[25] K-H Bockstiegel, 'Transparency and Third-party participation in Investment Arbitration' in R Hoffman and C Tams, (eds), *The International Convention on the Settlement of Investment Disputes (ICSID): Taking Stock after 40 Years* (Nomos, 2007) 209.

[26] L Yves Fortier, 'Arbitrating in the Age of Investment Treaty Disputes' (2008) 31 University of New South Wales Law Journal 1, 290–291. See also C-S Zoellner, 'Third-Party Participation (NGOs and Private Persons) and Transparency in ICSID Proceedings' in R Hoffman and C Tams, (eds) *The International Convention on the Settlement of Investment Disputes (ICSID): Taking Stock after 40 Years* (Nomos, 2007) 197.

> [T]here has been a progression from a consensual commercial arbitration
> system between two parties connected by contractual links to a
> completely different quasi-obligatory international arbitration system to
> which investors may seek recourse, once they deem that an action by the
> state, on whose territory they have invested, poses a serious threat to
> their economic interests. It is therefore clear that not only problems
> involving disputes between contracting parties are at stake, but also that
> issues related to various regulatory State actions directly related to the
> public interest may be raised in this new type of arbitration. [...][T]he
> participation of the *amici curiae* in investor-state arbitration is [...]
> consistent with the changing nature of investor-state arbitrations and the
> complex issues of public policies that tribunals are increasingly being
> called upon to address. [...][T]his system, which was traditionally based
> on private legitimacy arising from the consent of the parties, seems to
> now be in search of public legitimacy, which it is thought can be obtained
> from a certain degree of openness to civil society.[27]

We must not forget, in the momentum carrying us towards greater transparency, that there are costs to this trend, and the question of who bears
those costs is as relevant to the legitimacy of the system as the goal of transparency itself.[28] The cost-benefit analysis of increased transparency ought
not to prevent the arbitration community from adopting proposals that are
likely to improve the system's functioning and enhance its legitimacy.
However, as Noah Rubin recently observed, the costs of various transparency measures are not necessarily apportioned equally among the
system's participants, nor are their benefits.[29]

Returning to the point I made earlier in respect of the de-politicization
of disputes through use of the arbitral model of dispute resolution, a
concern with 'pre-award transparency', that is the participation of *amici
curiae*, the publication of pre-award decisions, and open hearings, among
other measures, is that both claimants and respondents can use this kind of
access as a weapon, contrary to the very principle of neutral, non-political
dispute resolution.[30] And so it follows that '[p]oliticized disputes are less
predictable in outcome than legal disputes, and therefore hinder FDI flows
by making them more expensive'.[31]

---

[27] B Stern, 'Civil Society's Voice in the Settlement of International Economic Disputes'
(2009) ICSID Review—Foreign Investment Law Journal 280, 347.
[28] N Rubins, 'Opening the Investment Arbitration Process: At What Cost, for What
Benefit?' in R Hoffman and C Tams (eds), *The International Convention on the Settlement of
Investment Disputes (ICSID): Taking Stock after 40 Years* (Nomos, 2007) 217–222.
[29] ibid 220–221.
[30] ibid 222.
[31] ibid.

## B. *Turning Now to Consistency*

This leads me to the second area of criticism levelled at the international investment protection system—consistency in arbitral decision-making. Interestingly, the source of this call for greater coherence has been ascribed by some to the very transparency of many investor-State arbitrations.

The implications of such inconsistency for investors and States are fundamental. As Professor Franck has explained, '[s]ome public international law rights have been articulated for the first time in investment treaties—such as the right to 'fair and equitable treatment' and a Sovereign's obligation to 'observe its commitments'.' Tribunals, she says, 'have applied these standards differently and made divergent findings on liability. Rather than creating certainty for investors and Sovereigns, the process of resolving investment disputes though arbitration is creating uncertainty about the meaning of those rights and public international law.'[32]

There are suggestions in some quarters that participants in the international investment protection system are unable to know or determine with any certainty their rights and obligations in a given situation. The criticism has given rise to a call for the establishment of an appellate system or body to remedy this perceived situation. Such a system or body would, as the theory goes, reduce the risk of inconsistent decisions, lend legitimacy to and institutionalize the process of investor-State dispute settlement and contribute to the system's overall sustainability.[33] Taking these and other elements into consideration,[34] every now and then critics clamour for the creation of an appellate structure within the international investment protection system which they aver would ensure predictability, clarity and coherence in the interpretation of investor and State obligations.[35]

The proponents of an appellate system recognize that a proper appeals arrangement will not be implemented easily. Nearly 20 years ago, Eli Lauterpacht, after having reviewed the options before the international society concluded that:

[32] Franck (n 22) 1521–1523.

[33] D Bishop, 'The Case for the Appellate Panel and its Scope of Review' a paper delivered at the Second Conference of the BIICL's Investment Treaty Forum on 'Appeals and Challenges to Investment Treaty Awards: Is it Time for an International Appellate System?' (7 May 2004) 9.

[34] Such as the success of the WTO Appellate Body in the global trade context.

[35] See eg V Hughes, 'The WTO Appellate Body: What Lessons Can be Learned?' a paper delivered at the Second Conference of the BIICL's Investment Treaty Forum on 'Appeals and Challenges to Investment Treaty Awards: Is it Time for an International Appellate System?' (7 May 2004); J Alvarez, 'Implications for the Future of International Investment Law' in K Sauvant and M Chiswick-Patterson (eds), *Appeals Mechanism in International Investment Disputes* (OUP, Oxford, 2008) 29–30, in which Mr Alvarez notes that the WTO 'inspires the envy of investment lawyers' in part through an appeals mechanism that can correct errors of law and direct remedial compliance, where appropriate.

The solution to this question is so fraught with difficulties that we may find that, despite its idealistic appeal, a proper appeal's arrangement was not a practical alternative.[36]

Without dismissing the very real concern of consistency in arbitral decision-making—or the lack thereof—this suggests that we ought to reflect for a moment on the model against which the investment arbitration system is judged. Is coherence—perfect coherence—a feature of any national judicial system? The short answer is, quite clearly, no. This has implications both for the kind of concerns recognized in the coherence debate as requiring some type of systemic reform and the manner in which we undertake that reform. Jan Paulsson has suggested that '[w]hen critics of international arbitration bemoan the lack of consistency and coherence, they are blaming the process for failing to achieve the impossible—and proposing solutions which would fare no better'.[37] In this regard, Jan reminds us that '[a]djudication of matters of public law is everywhere a constraint on collective sovereignty' and '[s]uch is its nature and function'.[38] As a result, the 'promised land' of coherence in his view is not an appellate court of investment adjudicators, as some have suggested.

Jan Paulsson's conclusion that an appellate court falls short of a complete panacea for coherence concerns in the investment protection system is shared by other well respected jurists, although, in some cases, for different reasons. Dr Tams, for example, has suggested that, in the particular context of the ICSID system, there is virtue in simply highlighting the risk of inconsistent decisions, or to make use of two existing alternatives: consolidating cases, or seeking ICJ decisions.'[39] Like others, I find this solution quite compelling because 'the factors causing a perceived need for an appellate structure are diverse. They affect only some ICSID matters and not others. They are in part a sign of the times which may change over the next few years.'[40]

Professor Qureshi, approaching the question from a 'development perspective', comments that the consistency arguments for an appellate

---

[36] E Lauterpacht, Aspects of the Administration of International Justice (Hersch Lauterpacht Memorial Lectures (No. 9), 1991) 111, cited in ibid 18.

[37] J Paulsson, 'Avoiding Unintended Consequences' in K Sauvant and M Chiswick-Patterson (eds), *Appeals Mechanism in International Investment Disputes* (OUP, Oxford, 2008) 245.

[38] ibid.

[39] Dr C Tams, 'Is There a Need for an ICSID Appellate Structure?' in R Hofmann and C Tams (eds), *The International Convention on the Settlement of Investment Disputes (ICSID): Taking Stock after 40 Years* (Nomos, 2007) 250.

[40] R Kreindler, 'Inconsistent ICSID Awards: Is There a Need for an ICSID Appellate Structure?' in R Hofmann and C Tams, (eds) *The International Convention on the Settlement of Investment Disputes (ICSID): Taking Stock after 40 Years* (Nomos, 2007) 226.

system should not be placed on 'such a high pedestal as other objectives—particularly the development objective'.[41] He explains that:

> [F]rom a development perspective a treaty specific appeal system is favoured. A principal concern about the efforts for introducing a non-ring fenced appellate system in the investment sphere is that it seeks to add to the conference and development of international investment law through a somewhat non-transparent route. Further, the need to inject the development dimension in any proposed appellate system is important. A development friendly appellate system requires in particular a focus on its apparatus of interpretation; on participatory rights and technical assistance.[42]

So, the jury is still deliberating. In the meantime, I venture to conclude that the system, whilst not perfect, serves all users well.

### C. This Brings us to Equity

This brings me, quite naturally, to the last area of criticism I wish to address and which I refer to as 'equity'. By equity, I mean, generally, the disparate experience that developed and developing countries may have as participants in the investment treaty system This experience may be shaped by their respective relationships with investors (ie investor-State equity), as well as their relationships with each other (ie inter-State equity).[43]

It has been observed that developing nations bear a disproportionate burden of defending investment treaty claims.[44] The United Nations Conference on Trade and Development, 'UNCTAD', estimates that of the approximately 73 governments involved to date in the defence of investment treaty claims, two thirds have been developing country governments.[45] In 2007 alone, UNCTAD estimates that 24 of the 35 new

---

[41] A Qureshi, 'A Development Perspective to the Introduction of an Appellate process in International Investment Arbitration' in R Hofmann and C Tams, (eds), *The International Convention on the Settlement of Investment Disputes (ICSID): Taking Stock after 40 Years* (Nomos, 2007) 252.

[42] ibid.

[43] Tai-Heng Cheng, 'Power, Authority and International Investment Law' (2005) 20 American University International Law Review 465, 505–512. See also O Schachter, *International Law in Theory and Practice* (Martinus Nijhoff, Dordrecht/Boston/London, 1991) 1–9 (I refer in particular to Mr Cheng's discussion of the relationship between power and the law and, in particular, the ability of powerful States to influence and shape legal rules more so than weaker States and to impose limits on the equal application of the law).

[44] E Gottwald, 'Levelling the Playing Field: Is it Time for a Legal Assistance Center for Developing Nations in Investment Treaty Arbitrations?' (2007) 22 American University International Law Review 237, 250.

investor-State cases brought pursuant to international investment treaties were filed against developing country governments and transitional economies in South-Eastern Europe and the Commonwealth of Independent States.[46]

I will not deal today with the political dimension of these statistics. Rather, I will recall the practical issues which arise from these realities. First, developing countries are more likely to suffer from a lack of adequate resources and expertise to mount a vigorous defence to an investment treaty claim. Second, the lack of transparency in the system, which I have already discussed, can serve as a barrier, in particular to new participants, to fully understand the process and potential risks associated with an investment treaty arbitration. And third, the indeterminacy of meaning in many BIT standards, as also discussed, may result in a correlative uncertainty as to what is required of developing country governments to comply with the treaty.[47]

While these issues are not unique to developing countries, their resolution by least developed country governments are particularly acute '[i]n view of the potentially high amount of damages awarded and the complexity of the issues involved, developing countries require ongoing technical assistance and capacity-building on these matters'.[48]

One proposal to address these and other related issues is the creation of a legal assistance center similar to the Advisory Centre on WTO law, which was established in 2001 to provide legal training, support and advice to developing country governments on WTO law and dispute procedures.[49] This call for technical assistance was reiterated by UNCTAD in its 2008 report on international investment agreements.

In this context, it is interesting to note that developing country governments have not sat idly by waiting for the international investment community to reach consensus on a solution to these issues. Rather, governments from around the world seized the initiative in 2007 and organized what has become an annual forum of developing country investment negotiators to discuss and share experiences in connection with investment treaty arbitration.[50] The challenge for all of us is to ensure that such efforts become part

[45] UNCTAD, Latest Developments in Investor-State Dispute Settlement, IIA Monitor No. 1 (2008), International Investment Agreements, UNCTAD/WEB/ITE/IIA/2008/3, 2.
[46] ibid 1.
[47] E Gottwald, 'Levelling the Playing Field: Is it Time for a Legal Assistance Center for Developing Nations in Investment Treaty Arbitrations?' (2007) 22 American University International Law Review 237, 252–260.
[48] UNCTAD, Latest Developments in Investor-State Dispute Settlement, IIA Monitor No. 1 (2008), International Investment Agreements, UNCTAD/WEB/ITE/IIA/2008/3, 12–13.
[49] Gottwald (n 47) 265–274
[50] See First Annual Forum of Developing Country Investment Negotiators, Singapore, 1–2

of a holistic solution to improve the system for all participants—investors
and States, developed and developing countries alike.

IV. CONCLUDING REMARKS

After this litany of criticisms, one may be inclined to despair and conclude
that the usefulness of the international investment protection system has
been short-lived. I bid you to take heart. As we know from our respective
domestic experiences, '[n]o system of dispute resolution is perfect'.[51]
Indeed, I share the philosophy of eminent colleagues and scholars that we
are living through a period of 'growing pains' and that this period was
inevitable.[52] As Susan Frank has eloquently explained, '[t]here are
inevitably challenging transitions which require a re-examination of the
bedrock principles upon which the system was founded. Investment arbitration is now at this critical juncture.'[53]

Furthermore, as may be gleaned from the rigorous debate engaged in
respect of these issues, a fair criticism will also recognize the complexity and
interdependence of transparency, consistency and equity-related concerns.
The fact that these issues are being debated in a concerted, organized
manner, is legitimacy enhancing itself. While debate alone will not suffice
where action is required to ensure that the international investment protection system continues to meet its aims of fostering a more secure and fair
investment environment and promoting greater respect for the rule of law,
in my view, users of the investor-State arbitration system are on the right
path and I have every confidence that the system will emerge from this
period of 'growing pains' with even greater vitality.

I foreshadowed a few moments ago that I would revert to the issue of the
Lisbon Treaty,[54] which has not yet entered into force, and its portents for

October 2007, co-hosted by the International Institute for Sustainable Development and the
Centre on Asia and Globalisation, Lee Kuan Yew School of Public Policy at the National
University of Singapore, http://www.iisd.org/investment/capacity/dci_forum_2007.asp; Second
Annual Forum of Developing Country Investment Negotiators, Marrakesh, 2-4 November
2008, co-hosted by the International Institute for Sustainable Development, the South Centre,
and the Moroccan Department of Investment, http://www.iisd.org/investment/capacity/
dci_forum_2008.asp.

[51] Franck (n 22) 1521, 1610.
[52] See ibid. See also D Bishop, 'The Case for the Appellate Panel and its Scope of Review' a
paper delivered at the Second Conference of the BIICL's Investment Treaty Forum on 'Appeals
and Challenges to Investment Treaty Awards: Is it Time for an International Appellate System'
(7 May 2004).
[53] Franck (n 22) 1521, 1610–1611.
[54] Treaty of Lisbon amending the Treaty on European Union and the Treaty establishing the
European Community, signed at Lisbon, 13 December 2007.

the international investment protection system. In my view, this is one of those transitions that may require a re-examination of bedrock principles. I am pleased to note that this re-examination is already well underway and that the British Institute of International Law's Investment Treaty Forum is actively involved in debating the 'grey areas' between European law, on the one hand, and the international investment protection system, on the other.[55]

However, the issues raised by the Lisbon Treaty, to my mind, present challenges of a slightly different nature than those I have just discussed. The Treaty does not challenge or question the legitimacy of the international investment protection system per se. Rather, it reflects a new governance arrangement and legal order not contemplated by the current system, that is the localization of exclusive competence over the negotiation and conclusion of international agreements, including investment treaties, in a central body, the European Community, representative of all EU Member States. As Peter Ondrusek observed recently at the Investment Treaty Forum on this subject: '[T]here are not necessarily any real obstacles in principle for the EC to become a party to an international investment-dispute arbitration system. However, there are some obstacles on the part of the current international investor-State arbitration system to be able to accommodate reliably the EC.'[56]

One question arising from this development is, in the context of intra-EU BITs, which law applies? And relatedly, are intra-EU BITs incompatible with the 'European legal order'.[57] I note, in this regard, that a highly respected panel of arbitrators, recently addressed this question in the *Eastern Sugar* case.[58] *Eastern Sugar* involved a claim brought by a Dutch investor against the Czech Republic under the 1991 BIT between The Netherlands and the Czech Republic. The Czech Republic challenged the tribunal's jurisdiction in part on the ground that the BIT was inapplicable beyond the date of the Czech Republic's accession to the EU, that is, beyond May 1, 2004.

---

[55] BIICL, Investment Treaty Forum, 'European Law and Investment Treaties: Exploring the Grey Areas' 4 December 2008.

[56] P Ondrusek, 'EC and Investor-State Dispute Settlement System: Some Thoughts' a paper delivered at the BIICL, Investment Treaty Forum, 'European Law and Investment Treaties: Exploring the Grey Areas' (4 December 2008) 2. Mr Ondrusek identified several obstacles, by reference to the State-State dispute resolution model of the WTO, including the following: an increase in disputes; systemic considerations not present in investor-State disputes; individual access to justice; a risk that the arbitration tribunal 'gets it wrong'; and detailed and developed legal standards.

[57] C Soderlund, 'Two Case Studies Involving Intra-EU BITs' paper delivered at the BIICL, Investment Treaty Forum, 'European Law and Investment Treaties: Exploring the Grey Areas' (4 December 2008) 4.

[58] *Eastern Sugar BV v The Czech Republic*, SCC No. 088/2004, Partial Award (27 March 2007). The Final Award in this case was issued on 12 April 2007, with a Partial Dissenting Opinion on the merits by Arbitrator Volterra.

The tribunal ultimately concluded that 'EU law has not *automatically* superseded the BIT as a result of the accession of the Czech Republic to the EU'.[59] In addition, the tribunal stated that the BIT and the EU Treaty were not incompatible.[60] The final word has not been written in this context and it remains to be seen how additional challenges will be resolved in the future, in particular once the Lisbon Treaty has entered into effect, if it ever does. These challenges will undoubtedly form part of the 'growing pains' experienced by the international investment protection system and the EU in the coming years.

[59] ibid para 172.    [60] ibid para 168.

# CHAPTER 7

# The Rule of Law and Investment Protection

*Norah Gallagher*

## I. INTRODUCTION

The rule of law has been central to the work of the British Institute for many years. In 1959 the *International and Comparative Law Quarterly* (ICLQ) noted that:

> [I]t is intended that the Institute will become in time the principal British organisation for the encouragement of research and for exchange of views in the whole field of international and comparative law, and that it will be used as a source of objective data by all those concerned— lawyers, government officials, business concerns and others—both in this country and abroad ... [And] make a useful and indeed important contribution to international peace and understanding.[1]

These are lofty ambitions and we can only strive to achieve these goals. This 50th anniversary lecture series, of which this evening forms part, seems to re-enforce some of the principle objectives of the Institute. The diverse array of lectures in this series go some way to achieving the aim of the founders of the Institute all those years ago. We are delighted to have been able to entice Mr Fortier, one of the most experienced arbitrators of investment claims today, to share his thoughts on our topic of investment protection. Unconvinced that I can engage, like Aristotle to Plato in their peripatetic debate, I have confined myself to making a few short observations on this evening's discussion on the developments in investment treaty law in recent decades.

---

[1] (1959) 8 ICLQ.

## II. RULE OF LAW

First, let us consider what we understand by the rule of law. Lord Bingham has just completed an entire book on the rule of law which had its genesis in a lecture he gave in Cambridge in 2006. He identified eight sub-rules many of which will sound warmly familiar to you including:

- That the law must be accessible, clear and predictable
- The law should be applied equally to all save when objective differences justify it
- Ministers and public officers at all levels must exercise the power conferred on them reasonably and in good faith
- Judicial and other adjudicative procedures must be fair and independent
- The eighth and final sub-rule identified was that the 'existing principle of the rule of law requires compliance by the State with its obligations in international law whether derived from treaty or international custom...'[2]

Lord Bingham looked more recently at the 'Rule of Law in the International Order' on 17 November 2008 at the Annual Grotius lecture. He endorsed the view that the 'international rule of law may be understood as the application of rule of law principles to relations between states and other subjects of international law.'

Dr Philip Marsden, Director of the Competition Law Forum, noted in a recent article on Lobbying, Climate Change and Competition that the British Institute of International and Comparative Law 'focuses on promoting the rule of law, which attempts to ensure that the discretion that officials exercise on individual cases is applied objectively, transparently and in accordance with the law.'[3]

What then in the context of investment treaty arbitration does the rule of law mean? Indeed the question is often asked by my students at Queen Mary whether there can be a rule of law in a system that has no principle of precedent? Where each tribunal is hermetically sealed and authorized to decide only the particular dispute brought before it by the parties.[4]

In my opinion the two are not mutually exclusive. Yes certainly there are some areas of difficulty in scope and application. For example this was pointed out recently by the tribunal in the *Wintershall* case where it noted

---

[2] Lord Bingham, 'Rule of Law' (2007) Cambridge Law Journal, 67, 81
[3] P Marsden, 'Lobby for Climate Change in EU Competition Policy: Just Don't Talk about the Weather (2009) 1 Concurrences 11.
[4] See eg C Schreuer and M Weiniger (eds), *Special Issue On Precedent In Investment Arbitration* (2008) 5 Transnational Dispute Management 1 and Y Banifatemi (ed), *Precedent In International Arbitration, 5 IAI Series On International Arbitration* (JurisNet, 2008).

at para 189 the 'welter of inconsistent and confusing dicta of different tribunals' on the application of the MFN clause.

As Jan Paulsson, another popular international investment arbitrator noted at an ITF conference two years ago, all awards are equal; but some are more equal than others! 'Some awards are influential, other best forgotten. There are awards that have been annulled and awards which have resisted annulment applications. There are awards which have not been tested at all.'[5]

So even in a system that has no precedent, as Judge Greenwood pointed out in passing at the Energy Charter Treaty Conference last September, most tribunals will not seek to diverge with earlier findings unless compelled to do so. Tribunals attempt to apply the rules applicable to the investment regime, be it based on treaty or customary law. In a way, tribunals take some comfort in knowing that the principles they are looking at have been applied in a certain way by previous tribunals in similar circumstances.

So the question is whether there is a sufficiently clear, identifiable system relating to foreign investment. At the risk of pre-empting some of the comments that Mr Fortier will make I believe there is. The regime has evolved from the protection of aliens and their property abroad, from diplomatic actions by their own State to investors having certain rights which they can directly enforce against host States. Multilateral investment treaties such as the ECT refer expressly to the rule of law. The introductory note to the ECT confirms that the 'fundamental aim of the Energy Charter Treaty (ECT) is to strengthen the rule of law on energy issues...' Judge Buergenthal was not convinced that 'respect for the rule of law has kept up with the proliferation of disputes and dispute settlement procedures.' He suggested in his after dinner speech in Geneva in 2006 that: 'The proliferation of international disputes and international dispute resolution mechanisms requires that the International community pay much closer attention than in the past to the ethical standards necessary to ensure that the rule of law is observed in the settlement of international disputes.'[6]

So despite all the criticism heaped on the system; the calls for consistency, cohesion, an appellate body and even more transparency there is still a recognized legal regime governing the relationship between investors and States, in effect a rule of law. Granted it may be in a state of flux or development. The extent and application of relatively new concepts such as fair and equitable

---

[5] J Paulsson, 'Avoiding Unintended Consequences' in KP Sauvant, *Appeals Mechanism in International Investment Disputes* (OUP, Oxford, 2008) 241, 247.

[6] Judge Thomas Buergenthal, International Court of Justice, 'The Proliferation of Disputes, Dispute Settlement Procedures and Respect for the Rule of Law'; After-dinner speech at the Colloquium on Consolidation of Proceedings in Investment Arbitration organized by Geneva University and PICT (April 21–22, 2006) available online at www.transnational-dispute-management.com.

treatment are being set. The very concept of what comprises an investment under the ICSID Convention 1965 has come in for intense scrutiny in the past decade starting with the *Fedax* case and the *Salini* test to more recent awards that challenge the criteria set down to identify what comprises an investment but nonetheless there is an identifiable legal regime for investment.


III. CHANGE


What we have seen is a dramatic change in this particular area of public international law. From post-World War II where there were major moves to create international economic stability, resulting in the creation of the International Monetary Fund, and the World bank, followed by GATT (General Agreement on Trade and Tariffs) by the WTO. Peter Muchlinski has considered these changes and their impact on the 'development of policy in the field of international foreign investment law.'[7] These early changes impacted the further development of the investment regime but for the purposes of this evening I do not propose to repeat Professor Muchlinski's detailed review. Suffice to point to some developments that I see as significant in the evolutionary path to the system we have today:

- **Emergence of a New World Order**

  We see a shift towards what is often referred to as the New Economic World Order in resolutions adopted by the General Assembly from the 1950s with GA Resolution 523(VI) of 1952[8] up to the Charter of Economic Rights 1974 which noted in its preamble that they were '[f]irmly convinced of the urgent need to evolve a substantially improved system of international economic relations...'[9] The Charter in Chapter 1 sets out a list of fundamental principles which apply to international economic relations. It then continues in Chapter 2 to clearly and unequivocally vest all sovereignty of natural resources—an investment of enormous political and financial significance—in each State.[10] Article 2 (2) gives the state the right to (a) regulate foreign investment in its jurisdiction in accordance with its national objectives and laws (b) to regulate and supervise the activities of transnational corporations in its

---

[7] P Muchlinski, 'Policy Issues' in P Muchlinski, F Ortino and C Schreuer, *The Oxford Handbook of International Investment Law* (OUP, Oxford, 2008) 44

[8] For other similar General Assembly Resolutions see, GA Resolution 626 (VII) of 1952, GA Resolution 1314 (XIII) of 1958, GA Resolution 1803 (XVII) of 1962.

[9] Charter of Economic Rights and Duties of States GA Res. 3281(xxix), UN GAOR, 29th Sess, Supp No 31 (1974) 50.

[10] ibid art 2 provides: 'Every State has and shall freely exercise full permanent sovereignty, including possession, use and disposal, over all its wealth, natural resources and economic activities.'

country and ensure they comply with its laws, rules and regulations and conform with its economic and social policies and (c) '[t]o nationalize, expropriate or transfer ownership of foreign property, in which case appropriate compensation should be paid by the State adopting such measures, taking into account its relevant laws and regulations and all circumstances that the State considers pertinent.'[11]

• **The Creation of ICSID**

A Broches in his Note of 28 August 1961 identified several factors that made the creation of a specialized dispute resolution option between 'foreign investors' and the host State essential. These included, (i) the fact that absent any other agreement the investment was subject to local law and any redress for an investor was also subject to that law; (ii) the complexities of relying on diplomatic protection—an investors' home State may not be willing to submit to international jurisdiction (iii) inequality emerging among investors as mostly large corporations were able to negotiate an arbitration agreement in their concession contract; and (iv) the lack of a suitable international conciliation and arbitration machinery frustrated attempts to agree a method of dispute resolution. In 1965 after much work and consultation[12] the ICSID Convention was adopted, setting up an important international institutional mechanism within which investor-State disputes could be resolved. It accepted that mere ratification of this treaty did not result in a right of an investor to direct recourse against a State. This was intentional, as the drafters agreed to leave the control to consent to the arbitral process in the hands of the States. The ICSID system has been criticized by States, NGOs and aggrieved investors, yet all it is designed to do is provide a neutral and specialized institution where investors and States can arbitrate their dispute. It does not contain any substantive protections, nor does the secretariat have any power to influence how the concession contracts or investment treaties are interpreted and applied by each tribunal.

---

[11] Art 2(2)(c) which continues: 'In any case where the question of compensation gives rise to a controversy, it shall be settled under the domestic law of the nationalizing State and by its tribunals, unless it is freely and mutually agreed by all States concerned that other peaceful means be sought on the basis of the sovereign equality of States and in accordance with the principle of free choice of means.'

[12] Four regional Consultative meetings took place in Addis Ababa, Santiago de Chile, Geneva and Bangkok. The outcome from these and work from a special legal committee in Washington DC resulted after four years in the adoption of the text of the ICSID Convention See ICSID, *History of the ICSID Convention: Documents Concerning the Origin and the Formulation of the Convention on the Settlement of Investment Disputes between States and Nationals of Other States*, Vol 1.

142 *Norah Gallagher*

- **BIT Explosion**

Since the 1980s, there has been rapid change in BITs, not just in the dramatic increase in numbers of treaties but also in their scope, in particular in relation to rights given to investors.[13] I had occasion to randomly flip through the 10 or so Oceania Loose-leaf Volumes compiled by ICSID checking BITs for dispute resolution provisions. There was no discernable pattern other than most of the BITs from the 1970s and early 1980s did not provide for investor state arbitration. In the new book on Law and Practice of Investment Treaties Andrew Newcombe and Luis Paradell must have completed a more comprehensive review as they assert that the first BIT providing for investor-State arbitration was in 1968 the Indonesia/Netherlands treaty. In this early incarnation though it was an agreement to '*assent to any demand*' for arbitration and not a clear standing offer to arbitrate all disputes. Yet since then, it is now as Eli Lauterpacht noted in the Foreword to Schreuer's commentary on the ICSID Convention, almost commonplace for investment treaties to provide a clear consent to arbitrate. The provisions often give the investor a choice what is referred to as a palette of options, for example the Mexico/Netherlands BIT (1998) gives the investor a right to choose between ICSID, ICSID Additional Facility and UNCITRAL Arbitration with a three member tribunal. Similar provisions providing the investor with such a choice appear in NAFTA article 1120 and the Energy Charter Treaty article 26.[14] It is the proliferation of investment treaties that has impacted the growth of investment claims and as a direct result the development of jurisprudence.

- **Substantive Protections**

There has most definitely been a dramatic change to investment protection in the past 50 years most notably in the past decade. As Professor Schreuer points out in the Introduction to the recently published book *Standards of Investment Protection:* 'The upsurge of investment arbitration in the last 10 years or so has made a strong impact on the substantive standards provided by investment treaties. Practice has shifted remarkably.' [15] There has been a shift away from expropriation as the central protection for foreign investors. As Schreuer confirms that

---

[13] See generally, A Newcombe and L Paradell, *Law and Practice of Investment Treaties. Standards of Treatment* (Kluwer, The Hague, 2009) ch 1 and C Mclachlan, L Shore, and M Weiniger, *International Investment Arbitration: Substantive Principles* (OUP, Oxford, 2007) chs 1 and 2.

[14] It should be noted that not all treaties given the exclusive right to choose the forum to the investors, see for example art 9(3) China/Mayanmar BIT which, in line with China's first two Model form BITs, permits either party to submit a claim to arbitration.

[15] C Schreuer, 'Introduction: Interrelationship of Standards' in A Reinisch, *Standards of Investment Protection* (OUP, Oxford, 2008) 1.

recently 'the practice relevance of expropriation in investment disputes has receded. Direct expropriations have become rare. Cases involving claims for indirect expropriations through regulatory measures are much more prevalent.' Today, the 'pivotal position, once occupied by protection from expropriation, has been taken over by fair and equitable treatment.'[16] As seen more recently in the merits award in *National Grid v Argentina* where the tribunal acknowledged Judge Schwebel's statement that 'the meaning of what is fair and equitable is defined when that standard is applied to a set of specific facts.'[17] Also, FA Mann may then have been correct when he wrote his article in the British Yearbook in 1981 that the fair and equitable treatment was an overriding obligation and suggested that 'arbitrary, discriminatory or abusive treatment is contrary to customary international law, unfair and inequitable treatment is a much wider conception which may readily include such administrative measures in the field of taxation, licences and so forth, as are not plainly illegal in the accepted sense of international law.' There have also been divergent views on how the Most Favoured Nation clause is applied in relation to procedural rights. There are some cases that follow and endorse the *Maffezini* approach that permits, subject to some exceptions, the MFN to be used to avail of a more favourable dispute resolution option in another BIT. On the other hand there is the more restrictive application of the MFN that does not permit a 'better' dispute resolution option to be chosen eg Plama. In the Wintershall v Argentina award the tribunal applied the MFN in the Argentina-Germany BIT in the restrictive way contrary to the earlier case in *Siemens* where the exact same treaty provision was in issue. It is clear that there is a rule of law applied in investment arbitration but it is also true that it is still in its infancy with the limits yet to be determined.

- **NAFTA Factor**

Although as Todd Weiler noted in his NAFTA book, Chapter Eleven was not a revolutionary document in 1994. However, the way it has been applied has had a 'paradigmatic shift in the way international economic law is conceived.'[18] The scope of the substantive investment protections under NAFTA have also been controversial; starting with the first NAFTA case in *Metalclad* where the award was set aside in part as the judge in British Columbia disagreed with the tribunal on the scope of

---

[16] ibid 2. See also B Kingsbury and S Schill, 'Investor-State Arbitration as Governance: Fair and Equitable Treatment, Proportionality and the Emerging Global Administrative Law' in AJ van den Berg (ed) *50 Years of the New York Convention* Kluwer (2009) 5.

[17] *National Grid plc v Argentina*, UNCITRAL Award, 3 November 2008 para 169.

[18] T Weiler, *NAFTA Investment Law and Arbitration; Past Issue Current Practice Future Prospects*, (Transnational Publishers, New York, 2006) 3.

article 1105 on minimum standard of treatment and expropriation and whether it included the concept of transparency referred to in the NAFTA preamble. In fact Article 1105 of NAFTA and the manner in which is was being applied by tribunal's prompted the Free Trade Commission to issue a statement clarifying—some say amending—the NAFTA provisions. Article 1105 requirements of fair and equitable treatment[19] and full protection and security were not additive to the minimum standard of treatment in customary international law. The NAFTA cases have contributed to the development of international investment law both in terms of procedure (amicus curia, confidentiality, transparency, crown privilege) as well as substance ('in like circumstances' for national treatment, the fair and equitable treatment standard and whether it is tied to the minimum standard of treatment at international law, indirect expropriation).[20]

- **Transparency**

Following on from the NAFTA influence we have seen a steady march towards greater transparency in this area largely supported by the North American influence.[21] It is now no longer just NAFTA claims where we are seeing applications from third parties to make a submission; it has penetrated ICSID arbitration also. This is not something I would have predicted. In fact several years ago after the *AdT v Bolivia* case where applications by environmental NGO's were refused, I predicted to my students that *amicus curie* were unlikely to be accepted by an ICSID tribunal! Yet change comes quickly in investment law and even before the ICSID Arbitration Rules were revised to accommodate exactly that

---

[19] S Schill, 'Fair and Equitable Treatment under Investment Treaties as an Embodiment of the Rule of Law' IILJ Working Paper 2006/6. He states on page 10 that 'In this sense, fair and equitable treatment can be understood as a rule of law standard that the legal systems of host states have to embrace as a standard for the treatment of foreign investors. While this may not seem much of a concretization given different historic developments and thrusts of the rule of law in different national legal systems and in light of the fact that the exact content and the requirements of the rule of law are often debated, it nevertheless seems to constitute a viable approach to explain the normative content of fair and equitable treatment.'

[20] For the NAFTA awards and submissions see www.naftaclaims.com. For a full commentary see M Kinnear, A Bjorklund and JFG Hannaford, *Investment Disputes Under NAFTA: An Annotated Guide To NAFTA Chapter 11* (Kluwer, The Hague, 2006) and R Weiler, *International Investment Law and Arbitration: Leading Cases from the ICSID, NAFTA, Bilateral Treaties and Customary International Law* (Cameron May, London, 2005) and *NAFTA Investment Law and Arbitration: Past Issues, Current Practice, Future Prospects* (Transnational Publishers, New York, 2004). See also the Canada (2004) and USA (2004) Model BITs where they have sought to limit the application of some of the treaty provisions; eg Annex B.13(1) and Annex A and B respectively.

[21] Canada and the USA have been particularly active in calling for greater transparency of the investment arbitration process. So much so that they have both included specific transparency provisions in their Model BITs, see Article 19 Canadian Model BIT (2004) and Article 29 USA Model BIT (2004).

the tribunal in *Suez, Sociedad General de Aguas de Barcelona SA, and InterAguas Servicios Integrales del Agua SA v Argentina* accepted an application for *amicus curie* submissions. This was a significant step going some way to appease the detractors of investment arbitration which has a public interest element in the types of disputes, the impugned government actions and the impact on the host State of any adverse award. Since that first case, there have been many other applications to submit *amicus* briefs and the ICSID Arbitration Rules were amended in April 2006 to accommodate third party interventions. There have also been cases where the pleadings have been made available online and others where the hearings are open to the public. These are dramatic and recent changes to the investment regime.

- **Ethics and Arbitrator Challenges**

There has of course been much focus on the independence and impartiality of arbitrators acting within this system. Recent cases addressing questions of multiple appointments include financial interest, issue conflict and lawyers in the same chambers as a tribunal member. The recent decision by a predominately common law tribunal in *Hrvatska Elektroprivreda DD v Republic of Slovenia* is noteworthy. Lawyers for the claimant challenged the disclosure a week before a hearing that lawyers for the respondent State, Allen & Overy, had instructed a barrister from Essex Court Chambers, the same chamber at which the President of the tribunal David AR Williams (New Zealand) was a door tenant. The tribunal ordered that Mr Mildon QC could not participate as counsel in the case. This is in stark contrast to the judgment Rix J gave in the English High Court in *Laker Airways* where he commented that 'it remains the case in my view that chambers are made up of their individual barristers with their separate reputations, each working on their own papers for their own client, and sharing neither career nor remuneration.'[22] The judge dismissed the challenge, though noting that he had tried not to overlook or underestimate the concerns of the applicant who was a foreign party. There have been a welter of challenges both to counsel and arbitrators on various grounds in the past few years

---

[22] Laker Airways Inc v (1) FLS Aerospace Ltd (2) Stanley Jeffrey Burnton (1999) 2 Lloyd's Rep 45. Although when commenting on the decision it was noted that 'This decision was specific to its facts. It is not the final word on this issue as the judge was not fully addressed on the issue as the complaining party did not attend the court.' J Lew, LA Mistelis, SM Kröll, *Comparative International Commercial Arbitration* (Kluwer, 2003) para 11–24.

[23] *The Rompetrol Group NV v Romania*, ICSID Case No. ARB/06/3 Decision on the Participation of a Counsel, 14 January 2010. See also *Alpha Projektholding GMBH v Argentina* ICSID Case No ARB/07/16 Decision on Respondent's Proposal to Disqualify Arbitrator Dr Yoram Turbowicz 19 March 2010 and *ICS Inspection v Argentina* UNCITRAL Arbitration, Decision on Challenge to Arbitrator 17 December 2009 for two different outcomes.

with limited success. As noted by the tribunal in *Rompetrol v Romania* 'control of that kind would fall to be exercised rarely, and they only in compelling circumstances.'[23]

- **A Standing Appellate Body**

And whether or not you are persuaded by the assertion made by Gus van Harten that 'untenured arbitrators (ie private contractors in an adjudicative market) should not finally determine the legality of sovereign conduct and the entitlement of individuals to receive public compensation for sovereign wrongs that lead to business loss ...'[24] does this lead inevitably to the conclusion that an appellate body is required similar to the WTO? In my view this is not the solution nor do I see much international political appetite for such a body. In fact, I also entirely agree with Dev Krishan's view of why have an appellate body at all; if we go that route let us have a first instance only reducing cost and time for parties.

- **The EU Element**

There have been recent changes and added complexities of regional arrangements; for example this month's decision by the ECJ in infringement proceedings under article 226 EC Treaty[25] against both Austria and Sweden held that:

> By not taking appropriate steps to eliminate incompatibilities concerning the provisions on transfer of capital contained in the investment agreements ... the Republic of Austria [Kingdom of Sweden] has failed to fulfil its obligations under the second paragraph of Article 307 EC.[26]

This result may not be that surprising in light of the Annual EFC Report to the Commission and the Council on Movement of Capital and the

---

[24] G van Harten, *Investment Treaty Arbitration and Public Law* (OUP, Oxford, 2007).

[25] Christoph Sobotta, European Commission, Environment Directorate-General explained that 'Under Article 226 the Commission can apply to the Court of Justice to find that a Member State has failed to fulfil an obligation under the Treaty. If the Member States fails to comply with the judgment the Commission can again apply to the Court to impose a lump sum or a penalty payment under Article 228.' C Sobotta, 'Legal procedures related to non-compliance with the EC Treaty and European Environmental legislation'. Art 226 provides: 'If the Commission considers that a Member State has failed to fulfil an obligation under this Treaty, it shall deliver a reasoned opinion on the matter after giving the State concerned the opportunity to submit its observations. If the State concerned does not comply with the opinion within the period laid down by the Commission, the latter may bring the matter before the Court of Justice.' Available online at: http://eur-lex.europa.eu/en/treaties/dat/12002E/htm/C_2002325EN.003301.html.

[26] Case No C-205/06 *Commission v Austria* Judgment of the Court (Grand Chamber) 3 March 2009, para 45 and Case No C-249/06, *Commission v Sweden* Judgment of the Court (Grand Chamber) 3 March 2009, para 45.

Freedom of Payments which noted that the Member States seemed reluctant 'to review the need for such BITs agreements.'[sic] The EU Commission will reconsider its option relating to the 190 odd intra-EU BITs in light of the ECJ rulings in these cases. The EU Commission, now that the Lisbon Treaty is in force, is considering the importance of its provisions on FDI. Will this mean the end of competence for Member States to negotiate their own BITs with States outside the EU? Is it conceivable that the Commission itself might end up as a respondent instead of an EU member states in a future investment dispute. These questions do not have a clear and ready answer but the Commission is watching developments carefully see for example the letter the European Commission wrote in *Sugar v Czech Republic* and its application to submit an *amicus* brief in *AES v Hungary*. The Lisbon Treaty came into force on 1 December 2009 and the Commission is actively engaged in the process of determining how investment protection will be dealt with in the future by EU Member States no doubt portending further change.

IV. DECLINE

In short, not yet. Although there is some empirical evidence from the fall off in cases filed at ICSID in 2008 reported by Richard Walck (he estimated a 43 per cent drop between 2007 when 37 cases were filed and 2008 with just 21). There has been an increase in State actions in the energy industry for example by Venezuela[27] and Bolivia. Denunciation of ICSID may be other signs of erosion of decline. [28]

I hear from informal discussions with government officials that they are not terribly keen to continue to sign BITs. However, there seems to be no let up as yet in actual treaty practice with States continuing to sign FTAs, BITs and other regional agreements for example the new ASEAN Comprehensive Investment Agreement 2009. China has for instance signed a NAFTA style BIT last July with Mexico. So rather than a decline in

---

[27] 'Venezuela is not the only country that has taken measures to increase the government take and the role of the national oil company as a whole, especially in Latin America. In fact, the government goals per se appear legitimate as a matter of policy. The key question for readers is to understand whether the process occurred legally or whether the rule of law was somewhat put into question. The development of international law in the area of protection of investments is still evolving and investors learn from every situation, from one country to the next, to become wiser in protecting their investments from the start'. E Eljuri, 'Venezuela's Exercise of Sovereignty over the Hydrocarbon Industry and Preventive Protections to be considered by Investors' Vol 5(2) TDM (April 2008).

[28] On 6 July 2009, the World Bank received a written notice of denunciation of the Convention on the Settlement of Disputes between States and Nationals of Other States (the ICSID Convention) from the Republic of Ecuador. The denunciation took effect on / January 2010 Bolivia had already denounced ISCID Convention effective from 3 November 2007.

reliance on the existing regime, I see development and changes. States will most likely continue to sign treaties but I predict there will be a greater balance between investor and States rights, including obligations on environmental, labour, and social rights seen in the failed Norway Model 2008. In addition, I believe that States will begin to reconsider the scope of BITs perhaps by limiting the definition of 'investment' and 'investor' or including a clause whereby the treaty parties can agree how the provisions should apply which would bind a future tribunal. In this way regaining an element of control over the process.

To alter significantly the current position would be slow given the difficulties in renegotiating or terminating the large network of treaties. The single speedy option open to States to remove the existing legal structures would be to adopt one multilateral treaty that superseded all earlier investment treaties. This requires political appetite and global enthusiasm, which I just do not sense right now given that most States are entirely focused on the financial crisis. In fact, it seems that very few politicians have focused on the potential for investment claims down the line if continued protectionist actions were taken. The aim is solely on economic recovery and stability while pointing out that there was no modern equivalent to the current financial meltdown.

Indeed, it is hard to predict whether there will be a huge surge in investment treaty arbitrations. I am not alone; Professor Schreuer at an ITF Roundtable last month also felt it was hard to be definitive on the actual number of treaty claims arising from the financial crisis. I think we both agreed that there would be an increase given some of the protectionist actions being implemented by States worldwide, but maybe not as many as people would expect or as resulted after the Argentinean crisis.

Perhaps what will happen is that the emphasis will shift and regional organizations; NAFTA, ASEAN, ECOWAS, MERCOSUR, CARICOM and the EU will become more significant actors which no doubt will please my friends in the European Commission.

V. CONCLUSION

And so to conclude, I would like to go back to where we started; to the 50th anniversary of the British Institute of International and Comparative Law. It continues its activities in international and comparative law; promoting the rule of law in these fields. Fifty years ago the first BIT was signed and we have evidenced much change in the investment regime since. The system is still young and evolving slowly. To predict exactly what developments will occur in the next 50 years is a challenge too great but no doubt there will be some interesting times ahead for all of us.

# CHAPTER 8

# Benefits of Comparative Tort Reasoning: Lost in Translation*

*Jane Stapleton*\*\*

Few Americans, even clever and ambitious ones, feel a need to inform themselves about abroad.[1]

## I. INTRODUCTION

Every year I shuttle between three continents: perhaps this is why I have been asked to reflect on the value of 'comparative tort law.'[2] This is a huge and enriching field. A decade ago when I was writing about good faith in private law, Reinhard Zimmermann kindly alerted me to how in the 1920s German courts had used the general provisions of the German Civil Code to engage in 'far-ranging juridical interventionism,'[3] and how, starting in 1933, German courts exploited this technique to imbue the traditional German legal order with Nazi ideology. It was obvious that unless I took a greater interest in comparative law and comparative legal history, I would not address critical issues nor face some of the most important dilemmas presented to a legal system; and that it is a poor legal education that does not expose students to the intellectual riches to be found in a contemplation of how other legal systems work across all levels—doctrinal, procedural,

* Reprinted and included in this volume with kind permission from the Journal of Tort Law, where this article was originally published in Volume 1, No 3 (2007).
** Thanks to Leslie Zines, John Blackie, Martin Hogg, Jens Scherpe, Reinhard Zimmermann, John Keeler, Peter Handford, Ronen Perry, Harold Luntz, Mads Andenas and Peter Cane. This work was supported by a Discovery Grant from the Australian Research Council.
1 M Hastings, Comment & Debate, *The Guardian* (London England May 4 2006) 32.
2 In this article, 'tort law' covers both judge-made common tort law as well as statutes in fields that were traditionally governed by the common law of torts (for example, defamation statutes). By 'tort law,' I also mean 'the law of delict.'
3 R Zimmermann, '"Was Heimat hieb, nun heibt as Hölle": The Emigration of Lawyers from Hitler's Germany: Political Background, Legal Framework and Cultural Context' in J Beatson and R Zimmerman (eds), *Jurists Uprooted: German-Speaking Émigre Lawyers In Twentieth-Century Britain* (OUP, New York, 2004) 1, 58

social, historical and so on. Comparative tort law stretches from theoretical issues such as the possible relationship of a tort system's vitality and prominence with the relative paralysis of its legislature,[4] to procedural matters such as how facts are discovered and dealt with, to empirical issues such as how the judicial use of comparative tort reasoning has varied over time and between jurisdictions.[5] So I must be extremely selective.

The argument I will make in this paper is that the noble cause of comparative law as an intellectual activity is undermined by those who focus on its forensic utility. Specifically, I will examine the practical value to practitioners and judges in the court of final appeal in an English-speaking jurisdiction of paying attention to how tort issues are analysed in a different jurisdiction when the subject matter of the domestic case at hand does not positively *require* it. Why would a tort lawyer in Kansas be interested in how tort law operates in England? Of what value might an appreciation of the tort case law of the Tasmanian Supreme Court be to a lawyer in New Zealand? What dangers lurk for the Canadian judge tempted to dip into the Scots law of delict?

The paper is divided into three Parts. Part I looks at possible benefits that a practitioner or judge in an English-speaking jurisdiction might find in considering tort materials from other English-speaking jurisdictions. I will argue that the benefits of resorting to 'comparative tort reasoning' vary greatly according to the focus of the legal analysis in issue: outcomes; arguments; principle; or conceptual arrangement. For example, an awareness of the outcomes of similar fact situations in other jurisdictions has pragmatic value in relation to forum shopping. When the focus is on legal argument, a grasp of comparative materials yields its richest intellectual rewards for the practitioner and judge because 'it is arguments that influence decisions'.[6] What about where the focus is on principle, that is where the balance of competing arguments has crystallized into legal principle? Because that balance is contingent on cultural context, the value in considering which legal principles have been accepted in other jurisdictions is also contingent: for example, in the US it seems to be a principle that a defendant in the tort of deceit cannot be liable for coincidental consequences; but that principle is rejected in England. Finally, where the focus is on conceptual arrangements, that is on how principles are organized, there is typically very little utility in considering the structures of other systems.

---

[4] For a fine starting point containing more theoretical perspectives with an American focus see D Nelkin, 'Beyond Compare? Criticizing "The American Way of Law"' (2003) 28 Law & Soc Inquiry 799.

[5] For an outstanding short account in a much-to-be-recommended collection on this topic see H Patrick Glenn, 'Comparative Legal Reasoning and the Courts: A View from the Americas' in G Cavinet, M Andenas, and D Fairgrieve (eds), *Comparative Law Before The Courts* (BIICL, London, 2004) 217, as well the outstanding essays in M Reimann and R Zimmerman (eds), *The Oxford Handbook of Comparative Law* (OUP, Oxford, 2006).

[6] *White v Jones* [1993] WLR (AC) (Civ. Div.) (UK) per Steyn LJ

In short, I argue that, tort materials from other English-language jurisdictions may be of value in the work of the domestic practitioner and judge
but that by far the potential for enrichment is greatest in the context of
comparative tort *argumentation*. Moreover, when a comparativist asserts
that 'comparative law and methodology ... should be used by all [legal
academics] when teaching their own topics of national law,'[7] we need not
be dismayed. In all English-speaking jurisdictions tort practitioners and
judges routinely *do* use comparative materials, that is material from outside
their domestic jurisdiction,[8] most notably the fundamental concerns and
arguments that courts in other English-speaking jurisdictions have thought
of legitimate weight. California cites concerns and arguments from New
Jersey judgments, Australia cites Canada, England cites New Zealand, and
we all cite Scottish law on a daily basis![9] Indeed, cross-jurisdictional
comparison is central to legal training in the US where the typical torts
teacher uses far more out-of-state material concerning legal arguments than
in-state. Among English-speaking jurisdictions the real question, therefore,
is simply whether the future resort to even more comparative material
would be worth the candle.

But in Part II, I address a very strange phenomenon about which we must
not be coy: when many people refer to 'comparative law' they mean the study
of law across, not just jurisdictional but language barriers. I will call this
'comparative foreign-language law.' There are a number of reasons why
comparative law has been seen as a cross-language study. One has been the
popularity in recent decades of the search for the 'common core of legal solutions throughout the world ... [wherein] the focus has been on the similarity
of practical results.'[10] This, of course, required comparison across language
barriers. There has been a lot of abstract writing on the 'methodology' of
comparative foreign-language law which I will not address since much of it
seems tediously to state the obvious: the most effective comparative method is
to compare the legal treatment of factually equivalent situations; always read
foreign law in its full social, legal, cultural, political and economic context;
beware assuming that the law in the books coincides with the law in action
and so on. My argument here is that the practitioner and judge in an English-
speaking jurisdiction should, for a variety of reasons, exercise extreme caution
in using comparative materials from foreign-language systems.

---

[7] BS Markesinis, *Foreign Law And Comparative Methodology: A Subject And A Thesis*
(Hart, Oxford, 1997) 2
[8] For example, see the immense influence of the great comparative torts text JG Fleming,
*The Law of Torts* (9th edn, Law Book Co, Sydney, 1998).
[9] Namely, *Donoghue v Stevenson*, [1932] AC 562 (HL) (appeal taken from Scot)(UK).
[10] E Jayme, *Multicultural Society And Private Law German Experiences* (1999) 9–10.
Jayme notes reasons for this such as 'the needs for collaboration in international commerce,
the idea of an international community and the anthropological view of human beings as
having equal needs.'

152                              *Jane Stapleton*

Finally, in Part III, I turn to a body of material I call 'coordinated' tort materials: materials that seek to expound tort law across multiple intra-national tort jurisdictions, such as restatements of law by the American Law Institute, or across multiple national tort jurisdictions such as Helmut Koziol's 'Principles of European Tort Law' published in 2005.

## II. BENEFITS OF COMPARATIVE TORT MATERIALS FROM ENGLISH-LANGUAGE JURISDICTIONS

### A. Basic Contributions

So what can a comparison between the tort systems of English-speaking jurisdictions bring us? There is no doubt that tort tourism can be an entertaining end in itself. It can simply be very amusing to appreciate the quaint doings of foreigners.[11] Beyond mere intellectual curiosity, we should ask in what general ways might an appreciation of the tort systems of other English-speaking jurisdictions illuminate the work done by domestic lawyers? The diversity of experience suggests a number of ways. First, it is often the case that fact situations have been the subject of tort litigation and given rise to the testing of doctrine in other jurisdictions but not yet locally. A knowledge of such phenomena arms domestic lawyers with some very effective tools with which to examine their domestic tort doctrine and may lead to the conclusion that there is a gap, ambiguity or incoherence in such doctrine.

---

[11] We can learn, for example: that in some cultures a clan has standing to sue for damages but not in Scotland; that New Zealanders cannot sue each other in tort for accidental personal injuries; that Australia no longer has a *Rylands v Fletcher* rule; that Canadians no longer have a tort of breach of statutory duty; that breach of fiduciary duty is a tort in the US; that in the Scots law of defamation no distinction is made between written and oral communication, nor does the defamatory statement have to be communicated to a third party; that in the United States there are native American legal systems and courts such as the Navajo Supreme Court which resolve cases on principles that include specifically Navajo norms; that there is at least one English court in technical existence that is, arguably, a civil law court and can proceed only in accord with that law [from 1737 the High Court of Chivalry lay dormant until reconvened in 1954 for *Manchester Corp v Manchester Palace of Varieties Ltd*, [1955] 1 All ER 387 (C.Chiv.) (UK)]; that in Scotland, Shetland and Orkney still retain Udal law derived from the Norse law brought by the Vikings in about 800 AD [for a modern acknowledgement of Udal law see definition of 'owner' in § 2(1) of the Housing Benefit Regulations 2006 No. 213 (United Kingdom); major differences between Udal and Scots Law include shore ownership rights, important for pipelines and cables]; most US employees cannot sue their employer in tort for negligently inflicted injuries; that judgments of the Judicial Committee of the House of Lords are never joint because, technically, they are speeches to the House of Lords Chamber of the Westminster Parliament; and that until the 1960s there was only one judgment issued by the Judicial Committee of the Privy Council because, technically, it is the 'advice' of the Privy Councillors to the Queen (on the members' experience of their unanimity rule see Alan Paterson, The Law Lords 98–99 (1982).

For example,[12] the Canadian case of *London Drugs Ltd v Kuehne and Nagle International Ltd.*[13] highlighted the fact that no common law system has yet formulated a general approach to the question of where, when, and why a defendant to a tort claim can rely on a contractual term, such as an exclusion clause, in a contract which is not between the plaintiff and that defendant. Another example is recovery in negligence for pure economic loss. While this is a backwater in US tort law, it has generated a vast case law in non-US common law systems. An appreciation of the factual scenarios of these cases and how courts dealt with them would definitely enhance the perspective of US tort lawyers. As Justice Posner notes, 'just as our states are laboratories for social experiments from which other states and the federal government can learn, so are foreign nations laboratories from whose legal experiments we can learn.'[14]

Of the other general ways in which comparative tort law might assist domestic lawyers, perhaps the most important is that it helps remind domestic lawyers and courts that the local results of cases, the arguments used to support them and the conceptual arrangements of principles are not some unique and universal order ordained by inexorable 'logic' or legal 'science.' They are culturally and temporally contingent and therefore may be open to forensic re-evaluation.

Now, if we look in detail at how comparative tort law might illuminate the work of domestic lawyers, and so obtain an idea of what future research might be interesting, it is helpful to deal separately with the different types of focus such lawyers may adopt.

---

[12] Yet another example involves the issue of a pharmaceutical manufacturer's tort liability for unforeseeable side effects of prescription drugs, which the Thalidomide disaster squarely presented to the tort systems of a number of English-speaking jurisdictions, notably the United Kingdom and Australia in the 1960s. Had US products liability lawyers been sufficiently sensitive to this issue, they may have more quickly realized that in tort claims against drug manufacturers for unforeseeable risks, despite deploying the rhetoric of 'strict' liability found in § 402A of the Second Restatement of Torts, US courts were scarcely ever prepared to impose such tort liability: a situation that became patent after the hostile furore that followed the extraordinary imposition of such strict liability in *Beshada v Johns-Manville Products Corp* 447 A.2d 539 (1982). Conversely, tort lawyers in English-speaking jurisdictions that have enacted the 1985 European Directive on product liability (namely, England, Scotland and Eire) or clones of it (such as Australia) would today do well to test their interpretation of that Directive with the type of claim known as the 'classic' US products liability case: a crashworthiness claim involving the adequacy of the strength of a car's side panels, truck axle, chair and so on.

[13] *London Drugs Ltd v Kuehne and Nagle Int'l Ltd* [1992] 97 DLR 261 (Can).

[14] R Posner, 'No Thanks, We Already Have Our Own Laws' LEG AFF, July–August 2004, http://www.legalaffairs.org/issues/July-August-2004/feature_posner_julaug04.msp.

## B. A Focus on Outcomes

There is no doubt that parties attempt forum-shopping.[15] It is important to note why this can happen even within a federal system such as Australia where there is only one final court of appeal on matters of judge-made 'common law': it is because the states have legislative capacity in areas in which the common law of torts has been active. For example, until 2006 Australian states had divergent statutes with respect to liability in defamation. So while Australia has a unified 'common law,' its 'tort law' may diverge on a particular issue:[16] hence forum shopping can be attractive.[17]

Forum shopping arises where more favourable outcomes may be produced because of differences in doctrine,[18] procedural rules[19] or other

---

[15] See eg *BHP Billiton Limited v Schultz* (2004) CLR 61 (Austl) (South Australian asbestosis plaintiff seeking to sue employer and asbestos suppliers in New South Wales for, inter alia, negligence and breach of statutory duty).

[16] See L Zines, 'The Common Law in Australia: Its Nature and Constitutional Significance' (2000) 32 Fed Law Rev 337; F Trindade and P Cane, *The Law Of Torts In Australia* (4th edn, OUP, Oxford, 2006) ch 7.

[17] Conversely, in the US, the 'common law' element of tort law is a state matter but certain aspects of 'tort law' may be unified by constitutional principles laid down by the Supreme Court and federal legislation, either by direct action or pre-emption. See S Issacharoff and Catherine Sharkey, *Backdoor Federalism: Grappling with the 'Risk to the Rest of the Country'* (2006) 53 UCLA L Rev 6. Compare § 23 of the Marriage Amendment Act (Comm of Austl No 209, 1976) abolishing the action for breach of promise.

[18] For example, the unique trust law of the Cayman Islands provides tight asset protection that in combination with strict bank secrecy and lack of local income taxes has made this jurisdiction one of the most popular for offshore trusts. Recent examples of forum-shopping in the field of defamation include *Dow Jones & Co Inc v Gutnick* (2002) 210 CLR 575 which held that words published on the Internet overseas, that are accessible in Australia, can amount to a defamation committed in Australia; and *Berezovsky v Michaels* [2000] 1 WLR 1004 (HL) (UK) where the plaintiff, a Russian, brought a libel action in England in respect to an article in the magazine Forbes. 98.9 per cent of the issue in question was sold in the USA, Canada or to US forces while the English circulation was only about 2000 copies. Lord Hoffmann noted:

> ... the notion that Mr Berezovsky, a man of enormous wealth, wants to sue in England in order to secure the most precise determination of the damages appropriate to compensate him for being lowered in the esteem of persons in this country who have heard of him is something which would be taken seriously only by a lawyer. An English award of damages would probably not even be enforceable against the defendants in the United States. ... The common sense of the matter is that he wants the verdict of an English court that he has been acquitted of the allegations in the article, for use wherever in the world his business may take him. He does not want to sue in the United States because he considers that *New York Times v Sullivan*, 376 US 254 (1964) makes it too likely that he will lose. He does not want to sue in Russia for the unusual reason that other people might think it was too likely that he would win. He says that success in the Russian courts would not be adequate to vindicate his reputation because it might be attributed to his corrupt influence over the Russian judiciary ... The plaintiffs are forum shoppers in the most literal sense. They have weighed up the advantages to them of the various jurisdictions that might be available and decided that England is the best place in which to vindicate their international reputations. They want English law, English judicial integrity and the international publicity which would attend success in an English libel action. (1023–1024)

[19] On the importance of the distinction for forum-shoppers see *Harding v Wealands* [2006] UKHL 32 (UK).

aspects of the legal environment. Other factors may be the attraction of a more specialized judiciary,[20] more compassionate juries and trial judges, or better access to the courts and so on. The greater a lawyer's awareness of the pattern of outcomes in other jurisdictions and the reasons for them, the better will be his advice to his client and the arguments on forum that he can put to the relevant court. Thus, for example lawyers for a group of more than 3,000 South African asbestos victims, most black and of modest means, overcame a claim of *forum non conveniens* before the House of Lords by, inter alia, bringing extensive evidence of the unavailability of funding for their claims in South Africa and the absence, as yet, of developed procedures for handling group actions there.[21] Similarly, settlements and bankruptcy reorganization plans that seek to cover plaintiffs from different jurisdictions depend on knowledge about the varying domestic doctrinal and process environments as they actually play out.[22]

Another potential role for an appreciation of outcomes in tort cases in other jurisdictions is as a 'good example or terrible warning.' For example, based on cogent analysis the Australian High Court has held that the builder of a dwelling may owe a duty of care in the tort of negligence to a remote purchaser.[23] This result contrasts starkly with the earlier refusal of such a duty by the House of Lords[24] and may usefully remind litigants in Britain that the exposition of this refusal by the Lords was extremely weakly reasoned. My argument here is not that the mere fact of the Australian decision provides a reason to doubt the Lords decision: we should reject justice by head-count. My point is that it might remind us that the reasoning of the Lords does not withstand scrutiny and that their refusal to recognize a duty *may* therefore be vulnerable to attack.

Outcomes in other jurisdictions may also serve as terrible warnings. For example, 'no one can pretend that the existing law [on recovery in negligence for nervous shock] ... is founded upon principle.'[25] In Britain, for example, the development of the 'bright-line' rules in this field arrived at the

---

[20] As we can see in the case of US corporate bankruptcy law, eg M Cole, ' "Delaware is not a State": Are We Witnessing Jurisdictional Competition in Bankruptcy?' (2002) 55 Vand L Rev 1845, 1863–64 http://www.bepress.com/jtl/vol1/iss3/art6.

[21] *Lubbe v Cape Plc* [2000] UKHL 41; [2000] 1 WLR1545 (U.K.).

[22] See H Luntz, 'Heart Valves, Class Actions and Remedies: Lessons for Australia?' in N Mullany (ed), *Torts In The Nineties* (1997) 72 and HW Baade, Foreign Oil Disaster Litigation Prospects in the United States and the 'Mid-Atlantic Settlement Formula' (1989) 7 J Energy & Nat Res L 125.

[23] *Bryan v Maloney* (1995) 182 CLR 609 (Austl.). But see *Woolcock Street Investments Pty Ltd v CDG Pty Ltd* (2004) HCA 16, 205 ALR 522 (Austl).

[24] *D & F Estates v Church Commissioners* (1989) AC 177 (Austl) on which see J Stapleton, 'Duty of Care Factors: a Selection from the Judicial Menus' *in* P Cane and J Stapleton (eds), *The Law Of Obligations: Essays in Honour of John Fleming* (OUP, Oxford, 1998) 58, 65

[25] *White v Chief Constable of South Yorkshire*, [1998] UKHL 45, [1999] 2 AC 455, 511 (per Lord Hoffmann) (UK).

bizarre point where they would prevent recovery by a mother who suffers psychiatric injury after finding her child's mangled body in a mortuary on the grotesque basis that 'her child's blood [was] too dry to found an action.'[26] Once one jurisdiction has held 'thus far and no further,'[27] as the House of Lords has done in this area, this might remind other jurisdictions that it is both legitimate and sensible to abandon hope that the common law could ever lay down coherent and respectable boundaries to such liability, or confirm a jurisdiction in its refusal to allow any such claim.[28]

On the other hand, it seems clear, at least to me, that the *mere* fact that a domestic lawyer can show that a party in a comparable suit prevailed in another jurisdiction provides no weight for his client's claim: again, law should not turn on head counts (see below).

## C. A Focus on Doctrine

### 1. Outline

In standard judicial analysis in tort a consideration of various 'legal concerns,'[29] often in tension, and the arguments based on them lead to the formulation of 'principles' which are then arranged in a 'conceptual framework.' For example, most common law jurisdictions have crystallized a principle that a person is not liable for failing to rescue a stranger: here the legal concern with the victim's interest in his person is judged to be outweighed by other legal concerns such as the libertarian concern that individuals should be free to do whatever they wish with their person or property, as long as they do not infringe the same liberty of others.[30] In most common law jurisdictions this principle is lodged within the conceptual device known as 'duty': there is no duty in the tort of negligence to rescue a stranger. At each of these three levels of doctrinal focus—arguments, principles and conceptual arrangement—an appreciation of comparative tort may be illuminating.

---

[26] J Stapleton, 'In Restraint of Tort' in P Birks (ed) *The Frontiers Of Liability* (OUP, Oxford, 1994) 83, 84.

[27] *White v Chief Constable* [1999] 2 AC 455, 500 (per Lord Steyn).

[28] US jurisdictions that have taken a hard line on such claims include Arkansas, Georgia, Kentucky and Oregon: see N Mullany, P Handford and P Mitchell, *Tort Liability For Psychiatric Damage* (2nd edn, Law Book Co, Australia, 2006) ¶¶ 1.250–1.280, ch 1, fn 143 and DJ Gilsinger, 89 ALR 5th 255.

[29] The term 'policy' is too limiting: see J Stapleton, 'Legal Cause: Cause-in-Fact and the Scope of Liability for Consequences' 54 Vand L Rev 941, 985–86 (2001).

[30] There are also economic concerns that support the rule: see A Harel and A Jacob, 'An Economic Rationale for the Legal Treatment of Omissions in Tort Law: The Principle of Salience' (2002) 3 Theoretical Inquiries In Law (Online Edition) 2, art 4.

## 2. Concerns and arguments

Let me first take concerns and the arguments based on them. Mainstream domestic legal analysis seeks to excavate the legal concerns embedded in, perhaps masked by, the legal reasoning published by courts. As Justice Posner has acknowledged,[31] the form and substance of legal concerns and arguments excavated from judgments and tort discourse in other jurisdictions can also be valuable to the domestic lawyer by widening his palette of ideas. This can be true even where those judgments originate from a tort system with different general principles arranged within a different conceptual superstructure. It may be that a very specific legal concern is raised in a foreign case but has a parallel application domestically: a particularly important example here being the concern that tort rules should not tend positively to encourage abortion.[32]

A more general example[33] of an emerging dual-concern for many of our systems is whether the tort law of our domestic communities should respond as those communities become increasingly multi-cultural, and if so what form that response should take.[34] As Erik Jayme asserts, 'difference as

[31] Posner (n 14) for the proposition that it is entirely appropriate for a US court 'to cite a decision by a foreign or international court not as a precedent but merely because it contains persuasive reasoning (a source or informational citation), just as one might cite a treatise or a law review article because it was persuasive, not because it was considered to have any force as precedent or any authority.' http://www.bepress.com/jtl/vol1/iss3/art6, 8.

[32] See the decisions of the Court of Appeal of England and Wales in *Emeh v Kensington AHA* [1985] QB 1012, 1021 (UK) (where the concern weighed in favour of the recognition of a duty of care in the context of a birth following a negligent sterilization) and of the Supreme Court of Canada in *Winnipeg Child and Family Services (Northwest Area) v G (DF)* [1997] 152 DLR 4th 193, ¶ 44 (where the concern weighed against recognizing the right of a foetus to an order detaining its pregnant mother whose addiction to glue sniffing threatened to damage its developing nervous system) both cited by the High Court of Australia in *Harriton v Stephens* (2006) HCA 15, ¶¶ 73, 133 and 248.

[33] Legal concerns also arise in relation to how legal reasoning should be presented. Take the unanimous House of Lords decision in *Fairchild v Glenhaven Funeral Services Limited* [2003] 1 AC 32 (UK), on which see J Stapleton, 'Lords a'leaping Evidentiary Gaps' (2002) 10 Torts Law J 276. This allowed claimants, who had contracted mesothelioma after several parties had wrongly exposed them to asbestos, to recover from each even though it was not possible to prove that the exposure of any particular defendant was a factual cause of the cancer because of medical ignorance of the aetiology of that disease. All but one of the Law Lords were concerned to avoid using legal fictions when presenting the new rule being created. They explicitly refused to present this new rule in terms of the legal fiction that 'on the evidence' factual causation was sufficiently established. An awareness of these *Fairchild* judgments should galvanize American tort lawyers to appreciate that, although it has gone virtually unremarked, most US asbestos cases have so far proceeded on the basis of legal fictions. See J Stapleton, 'Two Causal Fictions at the Heart of US Asbestos Doctrine' (2006) 122 Law Q Rev 189 Similarly, Australian courts which have so far sanguinely allowed such mesothelioma claims must now accept that in doing so they have resorted to the very legal fiction wisely deprecated by the Lords.

[34] For a useful introduction to many general issues, see A Dundes Rentelln, *The Cultural Defense* (OUP, New York, 2005).

such has emerged as a value in itself,'[35] and this concern with multiculturalism presents many diverse challenges to tort law. The statement that X
was seen drinking beer would not be shameful or 'defamatory' in most
Anglo-Saxon Christian circles; but how is such an issue to be treated in
Muslim sub-communities such as those of Leicester (where one third of the
population is Asian) and Bradford (where 22 per cent of the population are
from ethnic minority groups, particularly from Pakistan)? What is not
reasonably foreseeable behaviour in one sub-community may be reasonably
foreseeable in another.[36] What is an acceptable lifestyle choice in one sub-
community (loud music, scanty or otherwise revealing attire, religious calls
to prayer,[37] cooking odours, or slaughter of cows) is a gross nuisance in
another. If a reasonable Christian would wear a crash helmet, is it unreasonable conduct (contributory or comparative fault) when a Sikh does not?
When tort law requires a warning to be given, say on a product, what
languages should be used?[38] When parties seek to resolve such conflicts
within the bilateral form of tort law, bald notions of 'accommodation,'
'mutual respect,' and 'tolerance' may well be useless platitudes. Courts will
need to isolate and enunciate the specific legal concerns at play in such
cultural-clash cases, a task in which the experience of the tort systems of
other multi-cultural societies would be especially valuable. [39]

Next we might ask whether material from another jurisdiction can be
legitimately deployed to *attack* a legal concern enunciated by a domestic
judge. Suppose in his reasons for judgment a domestic judge in the court of
final appeal cites the alleged socio-economic consequences of a certain legal
principle: perhaps he has refused to impose negligence liability on, say, a
medical provider or public authority on the basis, inter alia, of his concern
with the possibility of 'defensive medicine' or the 'distortion' of public

---

[35] Jayme (n 10) 4. See also 'a new order based on differences which are accepted and are no
longer levelled down by resort to national public policy ... is the very essence of private law in
a multicultural society' (at 25). *And* the equally splendid analysis by G Calabresi, *Ideals,
Beliefs, Attitudes And The Law: Private Law Perspectives On A Public Law Problem* (The
Berkeley Electronic Press, 2006) 9

[36] See eg *Kavanagh v Akhtar* (1998) NSWCA 779 (Austl). See also *Mustapha v Culligan of
Canada Ltd* [2005] 138 ACWS 3d 767, where the Ontario Superior Court of Justice at ¶ 211
noted 'the background of Mr. Mustapha in the Middle East, where the devotion to and
concern for the family is at a higher level than is found in North America ... predisposed Mr.
Mustapha for the reaction that occurred,' namely psychological injury from observing a fly in
an unused bottle of commercially supplied water.

[37] Church bells; Muslim call to prayer broadcast over loudspeakers; etc.

[38] See eg J Fulbrook, 'Cycle Helmets and Contributory Negligence' (2004) 3 J Pers Inj Law,
171–91.

[39] Of course some nations do not embrace their multiculturalism in the same way. In a
highly perceptive comparative analysis, Chief Justice McLachlin of the Supreme Court of
Canada noted that 'the American ethic is basically one people, one language, one culture.
Canada, by contrast, is not a melting pot but a mosaic.' The American Law Institute, Remarks
and Addresses at the 78th Annual Meeting, May 14–17, 2001.

budgets. Might a comparativist legitimately attack such economic intuitions on the basis that they are undermined by the absence of these effects in other jurisdictions?[40] There are three reasons to think such an attack is not legitimate.

First, the possibility that empirical evidence about the social effects of a specific law in a foreign jurisdiction exists in an adequately rigorous and refined form is vanishingly small:[41] and it is highly unlikely that sufficient funds will be allocated in the future to designing and carrying out the research required to collect and appropriately analyse statistically significant data. Even in the US, where a great effort has been put into empirical analysis of the tort system, we find that the most reliable results are merely impressionistic and do not address the sort of fine-tuned issues at stake in individual cases.[42] Second, even if such empirical evidence of another tort regime were available, there may be social, economic or cultural reasons why that experience cannot be translated to the domestic context.

Third, while it is a valid objection to the domestic judge in the court of final appeal merely asserting 'unconfirmed' economic intuitions, he can easily cure the problem and put his reasoning on a sound basis by expressing his concern in terms of the *risk* that these socio-economic consequences *might* flow from a finding of liability.[43] Such a concern is legitimate and it

[40] For example see the attack on Lord Hoffmann by BS Markesinis and J Fedtke, Authority or Reason? The Economic Consequences of Liability for Breach of statutory Duty in a Comparative Perspective' (2007) 5 EBLR. Also see BS Markesinis, 'Judicial Style and Judicial Reasoning' (2000) CLJ 294, 304. http://www.bepress.com/jtl/vol1/iss3/art6, 10.

[41] See D Dewees, D Duff and M Trebilcock, *Exploring The Domain Of Accident Law: Taking The Facts Seriously* (OUP, New York, 1996) 414: 'The great disappointment is that the deterrent effect of tort is limited and uneven or cannot be established by existing studies ...'; C Harlow, *State Liability—Tort Law And Beyond* (OUP, New York, 2004) 28 'Studies of the effect of tort law on public decision-making are uncommon, inconclusive and sometimes unreliable, and such information as we do possess is fragmentary'; BS Markesinis et al, *Tortious Liability Of Statutory Bodies: A Comparative And Economic Analysis Of Five English Cases* (1999) 117: 'the testing of hypotheses using empirical research techniques ... is expensive and rarely done'; SJ Carroll, 'Asbestos Litigation: Costs And Compensation' (2005) available at http://www.rand.org/pubs/documented_briefings/DB397/DB397.pdf; and P Cane, 'Consequences in Judicial Reasoning' in J Horder (ed), *Oxford Essays In Jurisprudence* (4th edn, OUP, Oxford, 2000) 41.

[42] Ironically, the best recent illustration of the inadequacy of empirical data from foreign systems is provided in Markesinis and Fedtke (n 40) 59–60 and 72. The authors seek to persuade British courts to expand the liability of public authorities into new fields such as exercising a statutory power to order the removal of an object obstructing vision at an intersection, see *Stovin v Wise* [1996] 3 WLR 388. In support, these authors cite some what dated surveys which investigated the financial burden of liability on German public authorities between 1974–1977 and 1993–1995. Yet, as the authors themselves concede, not only did these surveys not provide a 'price-tag' for the administration of these liabilities, but the surveys did not even differentiate the new fields in issue such as that in *Stovin's* case (for example the surveys merely state that 73.4 per cent of payments were made in relation to 'traffic accidents').

[43] As Lord Hoffmann put it in 'Human Rights and the House of Lords' (1999) 62 Mod L Rev 159 at 162 'the payment of compensation *might* in fact be detrimental to good policing, because it *might* make the police defensively unwilling to take risks' (emphasis added). (Published by The Berkeley Electronic Press, 2006) 11

is up to such a judge to place a value on the concerns he legitimately identifies, including a preference for any doctrinal shifts that occur within the
law to be incremental if possible. If the judge thinks there is even a mere
chance that doctors or public authorities might indulge in wasteful defensive measures he might well assess that risk as one that weighs very heavily
against the imposition of liability. The same is true of the mere risk that
imposition or failure to impose liability might positively encourage abortion. As an individual we might not agree with the judge's assessment of the
relevant risk but it is not incoherent. We must acknowledge that judges'
valuations may have deep cultural roots that are not the same as those of
other jurisdictions,[44] producing different judicial responses even if the risks
could be assessed as identical. In short, it is not incoherent for a domestic
court to ignore 'evidence' of how a legal principle operates elsewhere.

Finally, even though it is in the area of legal concerns and basic argument
(for example about abortion,[45] indeterminacy of liability, self-help, or encouragement of rescue, etc)[46] that comparative tort reasoning offers its richest
rewards, a domestic court must be selective in its use of tort material from
other English-speaking jurisdictions. The human mind has 'bounded rationality': gathering and processing information is costly so not all material can
be addressed. Given there must be limits on what the domestic court can look
at, it needs some sort of rule of thumb by which to select the sources which
may be of most value. For example, within the group of nations consisting of
the UK and the 'Old Commonwealth'[47] (Canada, Australia and New
Zealand) the de facto rule of thumb seems to be that, while much may be of
value in one another's jurisprudence, explorations of comparative materials
from farther afield is probably not cost efficient.[48]

---

[44] For example, in France extensive liability is imposed on public authorities and the justification given is that since the collective benefits from the activities of these bodies the burden
of those activities should be shared, while in stark contrast, in England such liability is much
narrower, and this is explained by a philosophical emphasis on the collective benefit that flows
from having the individual yield to the wider public interest: D Fairgrieve, *State Liability In
Tort: A Comparative Law Study* (OUP, Oxford, 2003) 265–266.

[45] Posner (n 14): 'Suppose a judge happened to read a decision of the German
Constitutional Court concerning the right to an abortion and found in it an argument against
abortion (or perhaps facts about the motives for or procedures of abortion) that he hadn't seen
before and that he found persuasive. ... All these are examples of unexceptionable citation to
foreign decisions.'

[46] Dozens of such concerns are identified and evaluated in Jane Stapleton, *Duty of Care
Factors: A Selection from the Judicial Menus*, in P Cane and J Stapleton (eds), *The Law Of
Obligations: Essays In Honour Of John Fleming* (OUP, New York, 1998) 59.

[47] This informal term describes that subset of the (British) Commonwealth of Nations
comprising the pre-1945 Dominions. The less diplomatic term is the 'white commonwealth'.

[48] Within the UK-Old Commonwealth group there exists a vigorous email discussion group:
the Obligations Discussion Group run by Jason Neyers of the University of Western Ontario.
To be added to the list send a message to obligations-request@uwo.ca. http://www.bepress.
com/jtl/vol1/iss3/art6, 12.

This is not a surprising approach: the legal concerns, principles and conceptual arrangements of tort law are closely related to the cultural values and legal structures of a society;[49] and there is little doubt that lawyers and judges within this group of nations tend to think there is a greater affinity with each other in all these respects than with other, even English-speaking, jurisdictions. This is, at least, a more palatable explanation for their Western neglect of comparative English-language legal materials from outside this 'white Commonwealth.'[50] It is also an explanation why courts in this group of nations rarely venture into US tort law in any fully engaged manner.[51]

Moreover, within this group of nations, we often see domestic courts being even more selective on the basis of the relative intellectual utility[52] of the materials from other jurisdictions. Not unexpectedly a domestic court finds greater illumination in material from other jurisdictions which: attempts to provide general guidance rather than to decide a case on the narrowest possible grounds; provides succinct reasoning about the case in hand rather than an exhaustive survey of previous case law or an academic discourse on the general area of law; and above all contains lucid reasoning raising sound and persuasive legal concerns, crystallized where possible into general principles that are presented in a simple transparent conceptual arrangement. When one or more of these qualities is lacking the domestic court is unlikely to gain much from the material from another jurisdiction.[53]

[49] Even among those who accept that tort law is conditioned by cultural context, there is disagreement about the nature and extent of that influence. See N Roos, 'NICE Dreams and Realities of European Private Law' in M Van Hoecke (ed), *Epistemology And Methodology Of Comparative Law* (Hart Publishing, Oxford, 2004) 197, 202–213 comparing the 'culturalist' approaches of Reinhard Zimmermann and Pierre Legrand.

[50] For example, legal materials from the world's largest democracy, India, are available at www.commonlii.org but are rarely referred to in the West. But see M Kirby, 'The Supreme Court of India and Australian Law' in BN Kirpal et al (eds) *Supreme But Not Infallible: Essays in Honour of The Supreme Court of India* (OUP, Oxford, 2000).

[51] It is more common for such a court selectively to cite only those US cases that accord with the result the British or Commonwealth court intends to adopt locally.

[52] And therefore prestige. These characteristics are not static but wax and wane. There was a time when John Fleming, the 'doyen' of Commonwealth torts scholars (according to Lord Cooke of Thorndon in *Hunter v Canary Wharf Ltd* [1997] AC 655, 717 (UK)), vividly contrasted the intellectual power of the Supreme Court of Canada and the House of Lords (J Fleming, 'Employee's Tort in a Contractual Matrix: New Approaches in Canada' (1993) 13 Oxford J Legal Studies 430, 439; see also J Fleming, *Economic Loss in Canada* (1993) 1 Tort L Rev 68 concluding that the former clearly eclipsed the latter. Today I am sure John would say the current House of Lords had more than made up the lost ground.

[53] See, alas, the prolixity of some recent decisions of High Court of Australia such as: *Cattanach v Melchior*, (2003) 199 ALR 131 with 69,493 words supported by 606 footnotes; *Perre v Apand* (1999) 164 ALR 606 (68,900 words, 539 footnotes); and *Brodie v Singleton Shire Council* (2001) 180 ALR 145 (61,918 words, 599 footnotes). The barriers such length presents to courts in other jurisdictions is reflected in how rarely these landmark Australia decisions have been cited by British courts. *Cattanach* twice, *Perre* three times; and *Brodie* only twice. (Published by The Berkeley Electronic Press, 2006) 13.

## 3. Principles

At the level of the crystallization of tort principles there is some potential for fruitful cross-fertilization. There are, of course, classic examples of this from the past. When in *MacPherson v Buick* (1916)[54] a US court re-analysed the balance of legal concerns in the tort of negligence, it swept away the privity fallacy and ushered in the modern era of that dominant and voracious tort. Sixteen years later the House of Lords also swept the fallacy aside, expressly drawing support from the principle found in *MacPherson*, with Lord Atkin famously formulating it as the 'neighbour principle'. This principle of law recognized in *Donoghue v Stevenson*,[55] formally an appeal on the Scots law of delict, went on to be adopted throughout the rest of the common law world. While on Scots law, we might note that, being an English-speaking 'mixed system'[56] of law, the influence of its civil law heritage can be studied free of the distortion of translation. For example, we can see that in Scots law precedents tend often to be used more to illustrate principle and 'rights' than to provide a close factual analogy.[57] By an appeal to principle, specifically to the general principle of reparation for loss wrongfully caused, *damnum injuria datum*, it may therefore be possible to create new entitlements in delict more freely than in England and Wales where the focus is on (the availability of) remedies under specific 'nominate' wrongs or 'torts'. Since the highest court of appeal for delict claims from Scotland, the House of Lords, is the same body as the highest court of appeal for tort claims from England and Wales, the development of principle in Scotland has the potential to influence the tort law of the latter jurisdiction in significant ways.[58] A future example here might be personality rights.[59]

---

[54] *MacPherson v Buick Motor Co* 217 NY 382, 111 NE 1050 (1916).

[55] *Donoghue* [1932] AC 562.

[56] Other mixed systems include: Quebec, Louisiana, Puerto Rico, The Philippines, Sri Lanka, and Israel. South Africa and Scotland are particularly interesting examples for English-speaking lawyers: see eg R Zimmermann and D Visser (eds), *Southern Cross: Civil Law And Common Law In South Africa* (Clarendon Press, Oxford,1996); R Zimmermann, K Reid and D Visser, *Mixed Legal Systems In Comparative Perspective Property And Obligations In Scotland And South Africa* (OUP, Oxford, 2005).

[57] M Hogg, *Obligations* (Avizandum, Edinburgh, 2003); 73 See Also J Thomson, *Delictual Liability* (3rd edn, 2004). Indeed in Scotland certain law texts, written principally in the 17th, 18th and 19th Centuries, are regarded as a source of law. A Rodger, 'Savigny in the Strand' (1995) 28–30 The Irish Jurist 1, 14 argues that 'any generalisations ventured by the Scottish judges themselves tend to be drawn from the convenient quarries of the institutional writers.'

[58] Nonetheless, this strong informal tendency to 'coordination' and convergence between the two jurisdictions in tort/delict operates formally on an opt-in basis.

[59] On which, see http://www.law.ed.ac.uk/ahrb/personality, part of 'Privacy, Property, Personality,' a project of the Arts and Humanities Research Council Research Centre for Studies in Intellectual Property and Technology Law based in the School of Law at the University of Edinburgh. For example, at a highly stimulating conference on rights of personality rights at the Law School, University of Strathclyde in May 2006 I was delighted to witness

A final lesson from Scots law of delict is that the value of comparative law to the domestic lawyer is in inverse proportion to the density of local case law. If, as in Scotland, that density is low there will be more perceived need and enthusiasm to search for ideas from other systems. And if, as in Scotland, the local system is a mixed one this comparative law strategy has a double potential to be fruitful.

But we should not ignore the fact that, though there has long been considerable comparative communication and cross-inspiration between English-speaking common law systems, their *principles of tort law now diverge in many ways*.[60] The cultures, legal cultures[61] and legislative environments within which tort law operates are not equivalent and such differences, though not necessarily apparent, may profoundly influence how tort principles are shaped, applied and perceived: the concerns of tort law are culturally and historically[62] contingent. As Justice Windeyer of the High Court of Australia noted, 'too much store can be put upon uniformity of law when it operates in conditions that are not uniform.'[63]

For example, determination of important tort issues such as duty, standard of care, vicarious liability and immunities are influenced by domestic cultural attitudes, for example to medical practitioners[64] and patients' rights, insurance, commercial product suppliers such as bars, the profit motive in general, employers, the home and family,[65] lawyers, the press, organized religion[66] and public authorities.[67] There are even differences between English-speaking jurisdictions in relation to which torts are actionable per se, and this may signal quite significant variations in how the

---

a debate on whether dwarf tossing might be a tort and, if so, owed by whom to whom and under what circumstances!

[60] A dynamic fuelled by the gradual abolition of appeals to the Privy Council.

[61] See generally J Webber, 'Culture, Legal Culture and Legal Reasoning' (2004) 29 Austl J Leg Phil 27; D Nelken and J Feest (eds), *Adapting Legal Cultures* (Hart, Oxford, 2001); M Rosaria Ferrarese, 'An Entrepreneurial Conception of the Law? The American Model through Italian Eyes' in D Nelken (ed), *Comparing Legal Cultures* (Dartmouth Publishing Group, 1996) 157; and J Bell, *French Legal Cultures* (CUP, Cambridge, 2001).

[62] The modern Western concern with privacy is an example here. In medieval times European travellers shared their hostelry bed with strangers, often with up to 10 strangers, and the practice of sleeping several to a bed, usually naked, was not considered demeaning. N Ohler, *The Medieval Traveller* (C Hillier trans, Boydell, Press, 1989) 93.

[63] *Skelton v Collins* (1966) 115 CLR 94, 136 (Austl).

[64] Contrast *Arndt v Smith* [1997] SCR 539 (Can.) with *Hollis v Birch* [1995] SCR 634 (Can.). See J Stapleton, 'Legal Cause: Cause-in-Fact and the Scope of Liability for Consequences' (2001) 54 Vand L Rev 941, 964 fn 57.

[65] Lord Cooke of Thorndon in *Hunter v Canary Wharf Ltd* [1997] AC 655: 'The reason why I prefer the alternative ... is that it gives better effect to widespread conceptions concerning the home and family.'

[66] Is circumcision a battery?

[67] See D Fairgrieve, *State Liability In Tort: A Comparative Law Study* (2003) (The Berkeley Electronic Press, 2006) 15.

respective cultures value the underlying interest at stake.[68] Judicial perceptions of such 'instincts and traditions of the people' and 'common law
rights'[69] are sometimes asserted in proud terms. For example in one case
Lord Goff of Chieveley stated:

> [W]e may pride ourselves on the fact that freedom of speech has existed
> in this country perhaps as long as, if not longer than, it has existed in any
> other country in the world ... we in this country (where everybody is free
> to do anything, subject only to the provisions of the law) proceed ...
> upon an assumption of freedom of speech ...[70]

Even bolder were the comments of Lord Hoffmann in a recent case:

> Freedom from arbitrary arrest and detention is a quintessentially British
> liberty, enjoyed by the inhabitants of this country when most of the
> population of Europe could be thrown into prison at the whim of their
> rulers.[71]

More generally Lord Hoffmann has emphasized 'the real differences ... in
the history, cultures, and political structures of' the United States, Germany
and the United Kingdom, and concluded that in the latter: '... confident
democracy ... we have our own hierarchy of moral values, our own cultur-
ally-determined sense of what is fair and unfair, and I think it would be
wrong to submerge this under a pan-European jurisprudence of human
rights'.[72]

---

[68] See eg S Balganesh, *Property Along the Tort Spectrum: Trespass to Chattels and the Anglo-American Doctrinal Divergence* (2006) 35 Common Law World Review 135.

[69] On which see for example R Cooke, *The Road Ahead for the Common Law* (2004) 53 ICLQ 273.

[70] *Attorney-General v Guardian Newspapers* (No 2) [1990] 1 AC 109, 283 (UK). See also *Derbyshire County Council v Times Newspapers Ltd* [1993] AC 534 (UK).

[71] In *A & Ors v Secretary of State for the Home Dept* [2004] UKHL 56, ¶ 88. See also: '... a power to detain people indefinitely without charge or trial ... Nothing could be more anti-thetical to the instincts and traditions of the people of the United Kingdom.'(¶ 86); '... such a power in any form is not compatible with our constitution. The real threat to the life of the nation, in the sense of a people living in accordance with its traditional laws and political values, comes not from terrorism but from laws such as these.' (¶ 97). Similarly strident were His Lordship's comments in *A & Ors v Secretary of State for the Home Dept* [2005] UKHL 71, ¶ 82: 'When judicial torture was routine all over Europe, its rejection by the common law was a source of national pride and the admiration of enlightened foreign writers such as Voltaire and Beccaria. In our own century, many people in the United States, heirs to that common law tradi-tion, have felt their country dishonoured by its use of torture outside the jurisdiction and its practice of extralegal "rendition" of suspects to countries where they would be tortured.' See J Waldron, *Torture and Positive Law: Jurisprudence for the White House* (2005) 105 Colum L Rev 1681, 1681–1750.' http://www.bepress.com/jtl/vol1/iss3/art6 16.

[72] Lord Hoffmann, *Human Rights and the House of Lords* (1999) 62 Mod L Rev 159, 160, 165.

Examples of divergences abound.[73] For example the judge-made law of torts in England and Wales: did not develop analogues of the tort set out in §402A of the Second Restatement or the US tort of retaliation against an employee in violation of public policy; and, despite its abolition in another part of the common law world, has retained the tort of breach of statutory duty. Perhaps the most prominent recent example of divergence from within the Commonwealth is when the Privy Council acknowledged that the common law of New Zealand appropriately embraced a principle of negligence liability[74] which the House of Lords, drawn from the same pool of Law Lords, has refused to admit to the common law of England and Wales.[75] Lord Lloyd of Berwick, speaking for the Privy Council, noted 'whether circumstances are in fact so very different in England and New Zealand may not matter greatly. What matters is the perception.'[76] Similarly, though Australia and New Zealand are extremely close in many socio-economic and cultural ways, aspects of their tort systems could not be in starker contrast. Finally we have seen that even when a federal system such as Australia has a unified 'common law,' the 'law of torts' will diverge where the states have legislative capacity in the field traditionally addressed by common law of torts.[77]

We might speculate about the causes of this divergence of principles within the Common Law world. What is clear, however, is that modern Commonwealth tort lawyers do not regard this phenomenon as objectionable per se. Indeed, most would probably argue that it is the inevitable and healthy manifestation of the adaptability of the common law to local circumstance and its ability to fashion appropriate principles. As Lord Cooke has remarked:

[I]t has become widely appreciated that there may be more ways than one in which national common law systems, starting from the same

---

[73] As an Australian my favourite illustration of this has to do with bush hospitality: since 1914 the Australian High Court has rejected the special *ignis suus* rule (which makes the landowner vicariously liable for such escapes caused by the negligence of mere licensees) on the explicit basis that 'contemporary conditions in this country have no real similarity to urban conditions in medieval England where the escape of domestic fire rivalled plague and war as a cause of general catastrophe' and that such a liability rule would have been an intolerable restriction on 'the tradition of hospitality in the bush and would have been a disincentive to pastoralists to allow Aboriginal communities to camp on their holdings.' *Burnie Port Authority v General Jones Pty Ltd* (1992)179 CLR 520, 534, 566. See also *Whinfield v Lands Purchase and Management Board* (1914) 18 CLR 606, 616 (per Griffiths CJ).

[74] That a local government inspector owed a duty of care to avoid economic loss to the plaintiff when he inspected the foundations of a building. *Invercargill City Council v Hamlin* [1996] 1 NZLR 513 (PC); [1996] AC 624.

[75] *Murphy v Brentwood District Council* [1991] 1 AC 398 (UK).

[76] *Invercargill City Council v Hamlin*, [1996] UKPC 56, 56 ¶ 31 (Appeal taken from New Zealand).

[77] See (n 16).

roots, may justifiably go. Different chains of reasoning and weightings of values may be reasonably open ... national ethos is allowed its own weight.[78]

In short, while legal argument is easily transferred across jurisdictional boundaries because the concerns on which argument rest are foundational and simply expressed, the same cannot be said for principles crystallized by a local evaluation of legal concerns.

Finally, we must acknowledge that the role of the court of final appeal is to 'judge,' not provide some intellectual survey of world law. Suppose a court of final appeal in one jurisdiction is reliably informed that another English-language jurisdiction resolved the exact tort issue in dispute in favour of the plaintiff on the basis of principle X. Suppose further that both jurisdictions are extremely similar in all cultural parameters and share the same range of legal concerns and conceptual arrangements. Besides prompting extra care in the evaluation of the issues, even 'anxious review,'[79] does the existence of principle X in the other jurisdiction have any legitimate role in the resolution of the case? I do not think so. In my view it is not an incoherent or necessarily objectionable situation that: a barrister's immunity from suit in negligence is wider in Australia than in New Zealand, Canada and the UK; British local authority building inspectors do not owe the duty of care to building owners that New Zealand ones do; US lawyers who carelessly fail to lodge a client's private law claim within the limitation period are not liable to the client if that claim had a less than even chance of success while in a parallel situation the British lawyer would be liable; and so on.

Accepting Lord Steyn's view that 'tort is not underpinned by a single overarching rationale ... it is a mosaic of interwoven principles of corrective and distributive justice,'[80] I argue that the tort principles embraced by courts staffed by reasonable people may legitimately be different, and therefore produce different results between jurisdictions. The reason the courts of final appeal diverge may not even be based on different circumstances but merely on 'an intellectual preference for one outcome over another.'[81]

---

[78] R Cooke, 'The Dream of an International Common Law' in C Saunders (ed), *Courts Of Final Jurisdiction: The Mason Court In Australia* (Federation Press, Sydney, 1996) 138, 143.

[79] *Fairchild* [2003] 1 AC 32, ¶ 32 (per Lord Bingham).

[80] Lord Steyn, 'Perspectives of Corrective and Distributive Justice in Tort Law: the John Maurice Kelly Memorial Lecture' (2002) 7–8. http://www.bepress.com/jtl/vol1/iss3/art6 18

[81] A Mason, 'Old and New–Commonwealth Final Courts of Appeal and Their Perspectives on the Common Law' 18 (13th Commonwealth Law Conference, Melbourne 16 April 2003). My favorite example of this concerns two US cases involving the same defendant and the same allegedly defective intra-uterine device: the first court, a federal appellate court applying Arkansas law, found for the plaintiff; two days later the second court, the Delaware Supreme Court, reached the opposite conclusion. Juries were not involved at any stage of either case.

It is, therefore, dangerous to argue that a determination of tort entitlements in another jurisdiction '*must* also have some bearing in giving concrete effect to the vague notions of 'fair' and 'reasonable'.'[82] I see no reason for such an extraordinary conclusion. But what if a considerable number of other jurisdictions have adopted the same principle X? Even here I believe there is a slippery slope from the argument that material describing the position in other legal systems 'provides a check . . . that the problem identified in these appeals [by the Appellants] is genuine'[83] to the separate assertion that it 'is one that *requires* to be remedied'[84] in the Appellants' favour. A 'head-count of decisions and codes adopted in other countries around the world, often against a background of different rules and traditions'[85] should be irrelevant. What is critical is the judge's '*basic sense of justice*'.[86]

## 4. Conceptual

Arrangement of Principles Two systems of tort law might embrace identical principles and produce identical results, but these may not be arranged in the same conceptual architecture. Even more rarely than in the case of principles of tort law will a comparison with the different conceptual arrangement in another jurisdiction be fruitful for the local practitioner or judge. For example, unusually in the common law world, breach of fiduciary duty is a tort in the US, yet it is hard to see how an awareness of this arrangement would in itself be of assistance to a non-US judge or practitioner.[87]

But there may be occasions when a domestic court of final appeal might fruitfully be prompted to reconsider the structural form of local tort law on the basis that it is less intellectually 'convenient' for some reason than that in another system. Take the area of causation in the law. Historically many common law jurisdictions have used causal language to capture two quite distinct legal questions: was the tortious conduct of the defendant historically

M Corr, *Problems with the EC Approach to Harmonization of Product Liability Law* (1990) 22 Case W Res J Int'l L 235, 242. The cases are: *Hill v Searle Labs* 884 F.2d 1064, 1070 (8th Cir. 1989) and *Lacy v GD Searle & Co* 567 A.2d 398 (Del 1989).

[82] Markesinis (n 7) 352 emphasis added.

[83] *Fairchild* [2003] 1 AC 32, ¶ 165 (UK) (per Lord Rodger).

[84] ibid. (emphasis added). Also see *Macfarlane v Tayside Health Board* [1999] UKHL 50; [2000] 2 AC 59 at 81 (per Lord Steyn): 'the discipline of comparative law does not aim at a poll of the solutions adopted in different countries. It has the different and inestimable value of sharpening our focus on the weight of competing considerations. And it reminds us that the law is part of the world of competing ideas markedly influenced by cultural differences.'

[85] *Fairchild* [2003] 1 AC 32, ¶ 32 (per Lord Bingham).

[86] ibid. (emphasis added).

[87] See also the structural line between contract and tort: in Scotland consideration is not a requirement for contract; English courts are well aware of this structural difference but see no advantage in adopting the Scottish position. Needless to say, the feeling is mutual. (Published by The Berkeley Electronic Press, 2006) 19.

involved in any way with the injury of which complaint is made? And if so, is that consequence of the tortious conduct judged to be within the (normatively) appropriate scope of liability for the particular cause of action? Thus in some US jurisdictions we have the twin labels of 'factual cause' and 'proximate cause'; in others 'legal cause' is used for the former enquiry; while in yet others it is used for the latter. To make the situation even more fractured the First and Second Restatements used the term 'legal cause' to refer to the amalgam of both enquiries! Meanwhile, in the past some Commonwealth courts have tried to distinguish the enquiries by saying that they are concerned respectively with the search for 'a cause' and 'the cause.' Others have referred to the latter enquiry as a determination of whether the damage was 'too remote,' a bizarre term given that it does not refer in any way to physical or spatial proximity!

Many of us have argued that this is an obfuscatory state of affairs. Now the American Law Institute's *Draft Restatement (Third)* has adopted a much more transparent conceptual arrangement:[88] causal language is to be restricted to the first enquiry which is termed 'factual causation' and the second enquiry is to be labelled 'scope of liability.' Henceforth the factual nature of the former enquiry and the normative nature of the second will be patent. Old terms such as 'proximate cause' and vacuous 'fudges' such as 'substantial factor' are to be abandoned, and the relevance of a factor intervening between tortious conduct and injury, such as lightning or a criminal act by a third party, will be seen for what it is: relevant, not to the factual issue of whether the tortious conduct was involved in the history leading to the injury of which complaint is made, but relevant to the normative issue

---

[88] The Draft Restatement arrangement also allows us to identify issues more accurately. Take coincidences. A coincidental consequence of a course of conduct is a consequence the risk of which is *not generally* increased by the occurrence of that type of conduct. For example: D carelessly speeds along a road and this happens to bring the vehicle to a position where a tree falls on the vehicle injuring a passenger. It is well settled that speeding is careless and it is foreseeable that trees sometimes fall onto vehicles passing along a road. But, although in this freakish event the speeding was historically involved in the injury to the passenger (because but for the speeding, the tree would have missed the passenger), in general speeding does not increase the risk of trees falling on vehicles. The fact that speeding resulted in such an outcome on this particular occasion is a coincidence. The current assumption in the US seems to be that a tortfeasor is never held legally responsible for a coincidence, but this is not the case in other common law jurisdictions (see eg *Smith New Court Securities Ltd v Scrimgeour Vickers Ltd* [1997] AC 254 (UK)). It is therefore misleading to mask the coincidence issue as one of whether there is, what Justice Calabresi calls, a 'causal linkage' between tortious conduct and injury (G Calabresi, 'Concerning Cause and the Law of Torts: An Essay for Harry Kalven, Jr' (1975) 43 U Chi L Rev 69, 71–72; *Liriano v Hobart Corp* 170 F.3d 264, 271–72 (2d Cir.1999)). Far more convenient, because it allows more future flexibility in the development of the common law, is to identify this issue as a straightforwardly normative one. The Draft Restatement does this by treating coincidences as raising an issue going to the scope-of-liability. Other common law jurisdictions would greatly benefit from this conceptual arrangement because coincidental consequences are a common problem in tort cases. http://www.bepress.com/jtl/vol1/iss3/art6.

of whether the tortfeasor should be liable for this particular consequence of his tortious conduct. Lawyers in non-US common law systems would benefit from examining this new conceptual arrangement. For example, the current jurisprudence of the Supreme Court of Canada continues to deploy 'substantial factor' in just the sort of incoherent and indefensible ways that are rightly condemned in the Draft Restatement. Similarly, important decisions of the House of Lords and High Court of Australia would have been much clarified and simplified had such a conceptual arrangement as that of the Draft Restatement been used.[89]

Finally, we must note that, while in jury-free tort systems the debate about which conceptual arrangements are preferable is not skewed by institutional competition between judge and jury decision-making, this has a profound influence in the US. There is a deep fracture in US tort law that divides the loud rhetoric of the importance, almost sanctity, of jury decision-making[90] and the typically covert manoeuvres made by US courts and advocated by tort academics to prevent issues from reaching the jury.[91] Fundamental structures of US tort doctrine reflect this fracture, which is most nakedly exposed in cases where courts seek to restrain liability in negligence. The polarization between two crystallized duty *rules of law* with which the judge governs access to the jury (namely: a duty-owed-to-the-whole-world; and no duty to rescue a stranger) is unique to US tort law and a fine illustration of this schizophrenic attitude to jury decision-making. The most astute US tort lawyers are prepared candidly to concede that 'whether we are better served by giving juries or judges more or less normative work to do ... is largely a political judgment, not a legal one';[92] but it is clear that any analysis of the conceptual arrangements adopted in US tort law would be incomplete without reference to this normative context.

### D. A Digression on Theory

Though my focus in this paper is on the utility of comparative tort law for practitioners and judges, I want to digress at this point to say something

---

[89] See J Stapleton, 'Occam's Razor Reveals an Orthodox Basis for Chester v Afshar' (2006) 122 LQ Rev 426.

[90] A conceptual arrangement that allocates the decision on an issue to the jury has important consequences: the decision will be unelaborated; it will be heavily protected from appellate review; and it will not provide any precedent in the future.

[91] J Stapleton, 'Controlling the Future of the Common Law by Restatement' in M Stuart Madden (ed), *Exploring Tort Law* (CUP, Cambridge, 2005) 262. Contrast the 'subterfuge' of allocating to the jury, which 'can give results without reasons of explanations', tragic choices that we wish to 'paper over.' G Calabresi, *Ideals, Beliefs, Attitudes And The Law: Private Law Perspectives On A Public Law Problem* (Syracuse University Press, Syracuse, 1985) 88.

[92] W Powers, Jr, 'Judge and Jury in the Texas Supreme Court' (1997) 75 Tex L Rev 1699, 1715 (Published by The Berkeley Electronic Press, 2006) 21.

about theory. US tort scholars now embrace 'high theory' with an enthusiasm their peers in other English-speaking jurisdictions do not. Indeed, it has been asserted that today 'tort scholarship in the United States veers from one universal solvent to another...,'[93] while Posner, in noting the antitheoretical tradition of the common law, observes that 'suspicion of theory is a bright thread in the tapestry of English thought.'[94] It was not always thus in the US In 1907, James Coolidge Carter wrote:

> In nothing is human vanity more largely displayed than in the love of a theory. The simple and beautiful forms in which consequences develop themselves when a sufficient cause is assumed . . . furnish a pleasure which the mind desires to hold in its grasp, and it recoils from any scrutiny into facts from a secret fear that the possession will be endangered, and turns back to revel in the delights of the theory.[95]

Later, in 1930, Karl Llewellyn also did not see great merit in constructing a general theory of law:

> [T]he difficulty ... is that there are so many things to be included, and the things to be included are so unbelievably different from each other. Perhaps it is possible to get them all under one verbal roof. But I do not see what you have accomplished if you do.[96]

There is, no doubt, an intriguing cultural history behind why, in the closing decades of the 20th century, there was this 'flight from doctrine'[97] to theory in US legal academia. Certainly it has its critics, one of whom noted:

> [T]he obsession of United States torts theorists with superficially attractive simplifying arguments, which, after being denounced by the partisans of some other simplifying argument, seem inevitably to end up more complex than the material they set out to simplify. If, as I believe, there is an irreducible complexity in most important problems, then a strategy which accepts complexity from the start is more likely to avoid disaster

---

[93] D Howarth, 'O Madness of Discourse, That Cause Sets Up with and Against Itself!' (1987) 96 Yale LJ 1389, 1423.

[94] Posner (n 14) 418. See also AC Hutchinson, *Evolution and the Common Law* (CUP, Cambridge, 2005) for the argument that no grand theory will satisfactorily explain the dynamic interactions of change and stability in the common law.

[95] J Coolidge Carter, *Law: Its Origin Growth And Function* (GP Putnam's Sons, 1907) 217.

[96] KN Llewellyn, 'A Realistic Jurisprudence—The Next Step' (1930)30 Colum L Rev 431. http://www.bepress.com/jtl/vol1/iss3/art6 22.

[97] Comment to the author made by Geoffrey Hazard (Thomas E Miller Distinguished Professor of Law at the University of California, Hastings School of Law), at the Council Meeting of the American Law Institute in New York City, October 2006.

than one which starts with impossible simplifications. But the cost of such a strategy is the inevitable disappointment for those who seek 'breakthroughs.'[98]

There seem to me to be structural as well as cultural reasons for the popularity of tort theory in the US. Within the one nation of the United States there is a multiplicity of tort-law jurisdictions and therefore a diverse range of persuasive precedents by which a court may be influenced. Added to the resultant phenomenon of doctrinal fragmentation, there is the fact that within any one US jurisdiction lower courts are subjected to weak control by appellate courts, thanks in great part to the reverence paid to that institutional buffer or 'black-box,' the jury. This means that courts enjoy greater freedom from the shackles of precedent, and therefore greater freedom to make law than that enjoyed by courts in non-US common law systems.[99] A 'theory' of 'US tort law' must, like a 'restatement' of it, seek some abstract, common denominator account and thereby may falsely suggest some convergence dynamic. In addition, the career profile of US tort scholars requires an output that addresses more than the tort materials of their State jurisdiction. In such an environment theory can be expected to flourish.

But if we contrast the common law systems of the England and Wales, Canada, Australia, and New Zealand we find that doctrinal development of the judge-made common law of torts is formally unified: nationally there is only one final court of appeal on such issues. So while in the US there may be dozens of final pronouncements on a point of common law torts, in non-US common law jurisdictions there will only be one and, unlike Continental courts labouring under the formal supremacy of a private law Code, these pivotal judgments of the final court of appeal in non-US common law jurisdictions can be and are noticeably more candid in their reasoning. Yet the reasoning in these final courts of appeal is, for theorists claiming descriptive legitimacy, embarrassingly pluralistic and uninfluenced by legal philosophers.[100] Tort law is revealed to be generated by a melange of legal

---

[98] Howarth (n 90) 1423. See also CJ Robinette, *Can There be a Unified Theory of Torts? A Pluralist Suggestion from History and Doctrine* (2005) 43 Brandeis LJ 369; and Hutchinson (n 94) who argues that no grand theory will satisfactorily explain the dynamic interactions of change and stability in the common law.

[99] RS Summers and PS Atiyah, *Form And Substance In Anglo-American Law* (Clarendon Press, Oxford, 1987) (Published by The Berkeley Electronic Press, 2006) 23.

[100] 'There is little overt sign ... that the work of legal philosophers has yet greatly shaped the opinions of our judges.' A Rodger, 'Savigny in the Strand' (1995) 28–30 The Irish Jurist 1, 8. Note also Lord Rodger's view that 'precisely because the law has evolved in thousands of cases, there may be no completely satisfying principles to be discovered' in the common law, just as 'the texts of Roman Law which have come down to us do not on the whole contain statements of general legal principles' (14–15).

concerns, some moral, some economic, some symbolic, some distributive:[101] quite impossible to capture by rarefied mono-theory.

There are other reasons besides descriptive failure why I think lawyers in non-US common law jurisdictions eschew tort theory. In England and Wales, Canada, Australia and New Zealand the common law of torts is not only unified, as it is in say Germany and France, but it consists of the pronouncements of one final court of appeal, the judges of which enjoy pre-eminence and great prestige within the national legal system. Legal academics in these jurisdictions therefore have a realistic hope of affecting, quite directly and quite soon, the development of the common law of torts: their work is not a source of law but many seek as their audience the few judges sitting on that final court of appeal and the intermediate courts that feed that court. In such an environment theory tends to be a less attractive career strategy than providing this audience with a compelling, doctrinally thorough and precise, critique of a quite small body of relevant precedent, not least when these appellate judges openly tell academics that 'we are ... helping each other to make law.'[102]

In this connection I should report that at the Conference at which this paper was delivered in the fall of 2006, a number of participants offered another reason why theory was popular in the US legal academy and not in the rest of the Western world. The argument, as one person expressed it, is 'that theoretical research may present a higher level of thinking, and that perhaps American scholars are simply ahead of their counterparts in Europe and other places.' Moreover, it was pointed out that tort theory has recently become popular in a few non-US elite institutions such as Toronto and in Israel. Unsurprisingly, I prefer not to conclude that tort scholars in the US, Toronto and Israel are somehow simply intellectually 'ahead' of those elsewhere. Rather my experience suggests to me that, for non-academic reasons, Israelis and some Canadians tend to seek respect, success and even jobs in US legal academia. In contrast, Britons and Australasians tend not to do so. They confine their ambition to directly influencing the creation of tort law in their jurisdictions, and anywhere else courts are open to doctrinal analysis with a high level of precision.

---

[101] J Steyn, 'Perspectives of Corrective and Distributive Justice in Tort Law: the John Maurice Kelly Memorial Lecture' 7–8 (Faculty of Law University College Dublin, 2002). Such a corrective justice lens also ignores what the most eminent judges tell us: that in cases determined by the court of final appeal reasons of distributive justice may well be 'decisive' and that more generally 'tort is not underpinned by a single overarching rationale. It is a mosaic of interwoven principles of corrective and distributive justice.' In short, when we look to restate the actual lawmaking performed by courts, theory is of little use in identifying sufficiently clear standards let alone the appropriate overarching architecture.
[102] Lord Hope, 'Opening Remarks, at Conference on Rights of Personality in Scots Law' (The Law School, University of Strathclyde, 5 May 2006). http://www.bepress.com/jtl/vol1/iss3/art6. (Published by The Berkeley Electronic Press) 2006.

Once we understand why a certain theoretical account of tort law has influence in one jurisdiction and not in another, we might then ask what value might comparative law be to theorists? One obvious advantage is that it provides yet wider landscapes against which to test descriptive theories. An acknowledgement of the significant divergences between superficially comparable English language jurisdictions would push economic theorists to accept the weight given by courts to socially-contingent values incommensurable with money; and press certain corrective justice theorists to acknowledge the cultural and temporal relativity of 'rights'. Normative theories might also find the comparative perspective chastening to the extent that a comparative sensibility carries with it a norm of respect for cultural difference and an acknowledgment of socially-validated legal change; and it can challenge the myopia of a theory with its implicit assumptions and static bias. For example, the corrective justice standard of justification of private law might itself be revealed as no more than a Western cultural artefact, the norms of which ignore the phenomenon of societies elsewhere that happily base core socio-legal relations on group standing and group responsibility.

## E. The Special Case of the United States

### 1. Non-US English-speaking lawyers looking at US tort doctrine

It is worth addressing the United States specifically at this point not least because there is a marked, if unreciprocated, enthusiasm by many non-US tort lawyers to delve into US tort doctrine. For academics attraction lies, understandably, in the domestic and international prestige of acquiring an understanding of the diverse legal environment in the world's current superpower, and getting published in one of its law reviews! This appreciation can also sometimes advantage non-US practitioners, for example when a reference to the US phenomenon of market-share liability prompts the domestic court to create a similar liability or draw support for a finding of proportionate liability for an indivisible injury.[103] But, as in all comparative 'borrowings,' such reference to US tort law is impressionistic, merely illustrative and scarcely qualifies for the description of 'legal transplant.' Tort law cannot simply be 'exported' because there will always be structural and cultural features which cannot be ignored and which have no equivalent in the potentially 'importing' system. Not least of these in the US system is the 'constitutionalization' of tort law by the Supreme Court.

---

[103] Compare the House of Lords decision in *Barker v Corus* UK Ltd, [2006] UKHL 20, 2 AC 572 (UK) with the decision of the Hoge Raad of October 9, 1992 on which see Ewoud Hondius, *A Dutch DES Case—Pharmaceutical Producers Jointly and Severally Liable* (1994) 2 Eur Rev Priv L 409.

So we should ask, of what perils should a non-US lawyer looking to US tort materials be aware? US tort law is certainly the outrider within the English-language jurisdictions for reasons that may not be easily adjusted for by non-US practitioners and judges.[104] For example, though tort law is overwhelmingly a state matter, state legislatures are relatively paralyzed when it comes to enacting comprehensive private law reform and this has effects that the non-US tort lawyer may not appreciate. For example, she may be shocked to discover that contributory negligence was a complete defense to US tort claims until relatively recently, and that in many jurisdictions the abandonment of this bar was only achieved by judicial decision. Without this comparative insight the non-US lawyer would fail to understand the crucial subtext of many US tort cases dating from before this change.

Indeed, the non-US lawyer must be alert to the general fact that in the US it is culturally accepted that courts can be considerably more adventurous with doctrine and the boundaries between causes of action than non-US common law courts can.[105] For example, the new tort recorded in §402A *Restatement (Second) of Torts (1965)* arguably had its origins in a 1913 case[106] where a single trial judge simply abandoned the doctrine of privity and decided that a commercial buyer of food should be able to sue the distant seller in warranty. Today, just as the various state enactments of the Uniform Commercial Code have made the US law on warranty quite complex, so too the state common law versions of the rule in § 402A are riddled with variables that are daunting for the non-US lawyer.[107]

But there is also a trap for the unwary non-US lawyer who believes that US judges say what they mean in authentic 'legal realist' style. For example, the emergence of § 402A was uniformly accompanied by ringing pro-consumer judicial rhetoric of 'strict liability' for defective products.[108] But in fact, when push came to shove and courts were faced with cases in which the relevant product danger was unforeseeable at the time of supply, US courts refused to impose strict liability in design and warning cases: they refused to require manufacturers to conform to impossible standards. For example, out of the thousands of design defect cases brought against product manufacturers over the past few decades there seem to be, at most, only three[109] where a US court was prepared to follow the logic of its strict liabil-

---

[104] See J Stapleton, 'Bugs in Anglo-American Products Liability' (2002) 53 SC L Rev 1225, 1256–1257.

[105] Summers (n 94).

[106] *Mazetti v Armour & Co* 135 P 633 (Wash 1913).

[107] And, of course, results can diverge even where the law is identical: see the two US cases (n 78).

[108] See (n 12).

[109] DG Owen, *Products Liability Law* (Thomson West, 2005) 700 fn 167. Owen states 'the two pillars of modern products liability law in America' are 'that manufacturers must guard

ity rhetoric and impose that liability. Not one involved a pharmaceutical! Had Europeans been more sensitive to this it may have alerted them to the fundamental political and doctrinal dilemmas of imposing strict tort liability on manufacturers for unforeseeable risks, and they may have balked at agreeing to the ambiguous 'all-things-to-all-parties' wording of the notorious 1985 Directive on Products Liability.[110]

Process and procedure are also culturally contingent in ways that may not be obvious. The non-US lawyer might not appreciate fundamental features of US tort doctrine, for example, that most US employees injured at work are unable to sue their employer because workers' compensation is their 'sole' remedy. The non-US lawyer will, therefore, fail to understand why the emergence of the common law rule in §402A of the *Restatement (Second) of Torts (1965)* had such an impact on US tort law: it provided employees with a route to tort-level damages if they could identify some product with which they worked and successfully allege that its 'defective' condition caused their injury. Though rarely remarked on in the US, the results can seem bizarre to the non-US lawyer. For example, where an employer buys an unguarded cutting machine and later his employee is severely injured by the blade, the employer escapes any tort sanction. The loss either remains on the victim[111] or is shifted to a, perhaps entirely innocent, non-manufacturing party in the chain of supply of the machine such as a wholesaler or retailer.[112]

Also, as I noted earlier, a tort lawyer from outside the US may not appreciate that a covert concern with jury decision-making in the US generates a pronounced tendency to crystallize rules of law with which the trial judge can govern access to the jury. Conversely, in the United States access to a jury trial is so much taken for granted as a right, that it evokes scant comment. Yet in other jurisdictions there is far more ambivalence: for example in the recent Scottish case of *Heasman v JM Taylor & Partners*[113] a person suffered personal injuries in a car accident and sued the defender in delict; thereupon the defender challenged the use of a jury on the basis that it would contravene his right to a fair hearing under article 6 of the

---

against risks only if they are *foreseeable*, and that manufacturers must guard against those risks only by precautions that are *reasonable*' (38).

[110] How can a product be defective for failing to warn of something no one could have known about? Why is the state of the art of substitutes relevant but not the state of the art of discovering the need for a substitute? See also J Stapleton, 'Liability for Drugs in the US and EU: Rhetoric and Reality' (2007) 26 Rev Litigation 991.

[111] This is the result in jurisdictions that evaluate design defect using consumer expectations. See Owen (n 104) 296 and 490.

[112] This is typically the result in jurisdictions that evaluate design defect using risk-utility: on the basis that the removability of the guard meant the machine's risks outweighed its utility. See Owen, (n 104) 302 and 315. (Published by The Berkeley Electronic Press, 2006).

[113] 2002 SC 326, [2002] ScotCS 63 (Inner House, Court of Session).

Convention for the Protection of Human Rights and Fundamental Freedoms! Indeed, it is a striking feature of the US tort system that lawyers seem to find little if anything to object to in two juries reaching opposite outcomes in cases of identical facts. In non-US systems the ideal of like cases being treated alike is much more in evidence.

Similarly, the nature and degree of concern over rates of litigation is culturally contingent. For example, to establish that American resort to tort litigation is far greater than in economically comparable countries does not establish that its litigation system is in need of reform.[114] There is no doubt, for example, that the role of tort law in the US is not the same as in New Zealand where for decades tort claims for personal injury by accident have been excluded in favour of a state-run comprehensive accident compensation scheme. Clearly, empirical findings may also be highly location-dependent. For example, the landmark work of Lloyd-Bostock,[115] that suggested individuals' attribution of responsibility for accidents in England was influenced by what they knew of the law's attribution, may well be specific and not generalizable to the US which was outside her empirical frame of reference.

## 2. US lawyers looking at tort materials from other English-speaking jurisdictions

Bounded rationality explains and partially justifies the indifference of US legal practitioners and judges to otherwise-relevant non-US English-language materials. In US tort law the palette of domestic tort ideas and arguments is probably sufficiently rich not to require or justify looking farther afield unless, of course, the case has some overt foreign element such as a *forum non conveniens* claim. Moreover, there will be important aspects of US tort law that have no close parallels elsewhere, such as the specific constitutional constraints on it recognized by the US Supreme Court. So, each year as I teach[116] US products liability in Texas, I do not find much

---

[114] See D Nelkin, 'Beyond Compare? Criticizing "The American Way of Law"' (2003) 28 Law & Soc Inquiry 799.

[115] See Sally M Lloyd-Bostock, 'Common Sense Morality and Accident Compensation' in DP Farrington et al (eds), *Psychology, Law, And Legal Processes* (MacMillan, London, 1979) 93, 101 (noting that accident victims may first determine a right to compensation and then attribute fault to justify compensation); and S Lloyd-Bostock, 'Fault and Liability for Accidents: The Accident Victim's Perspective' in D Harris et al (eds), *Compensation And Support For Illness And Injury* (OUP, New York, 1984) 139, 150–51

[116] Remember I am only concerned in this paper with the value of comparative tort law to practitioners and judges. Those engaged in academic projects such as legal history and theoretical comparative studies must address the wider world where the international circulation of ideas can be a fascinating phenomenon: how Roman law affected legal systems down the ages (R Zimmermann, *The Law Of Obligations: Roman Foundations Of The Civilian Tradition* (Clarendon, Oxford, 1996); P Stein, *Roman Law In European History* (CUP,

need to trawl non-US case law for ideas additional to those available within US material: not least because the comparative palette of tort ideas presented to US law students is drawn from across the country, not merely the state of tuition.

There is, however, one area in which US lawyers would benefit from a comparative perspective on tort law. An awareness of the issues presented to courts of final appeal in other English-speaking jurisdictions can fruitfully expose them to types of claim, and thereby to legal issues, that have either not yet been litigated in a US jurisdiction[117] or have been 'fudged' in local jurisprudence. As we noted early on, this appreciation can challenge, illuminate, and enrich a lawyer's grasp on his or her own system of tort law. Though an individual US lawyer may not have the resources to engage in such research, the Restatement projects of the American Law Institute, of which the torts restatements have by far been the most used and influential, provide one valuable avenue by which notice of useful non-US English-language developments can be given to domestic lawyers. Restatements are, however, only reconsidered after long interludes. Other avenues need development: perhaps the American Law Institute might consider some electronic technique for notifying highly relevant tort cases from other English-speaking jurisdictions?

III. BENEFITS OF COMPARATIVE TORT MATERIALS FROM FOREIGN-LANGUAGE JURISDICTIONS

*A. For US, Canada, Australia and New Zealand*

Next we need to consider whether in their work a legal practitioner or judge in an English-speaking jurisdiction outside the European Union would be assisted by a consideration of the tort law of a foreign language jurisdiction?

---

Cambridge, 1999); how from Mediterranean mercantile customs the law merchant spread to English law, thereafter to the United States and then into treaty law (see T Plucknett, *A Concise History Of The Common Law* 663 (5th edn, CUP, Cambridge, 2001) and R Coquillette, 'Legal Ideology and Incorporation II: Sir T Ridley, 'Charles Molloy, and the Literary Battle for the Law Merchant1607–1676' (1981) 61 BULRev 315; how the special tort liability for commercial suppliers of defective products spread from the US to the EU and thereupon to other nations; and how non-Western legal systems deal with the issues we call tort or delict (see for example, the alternative to the 'winner takes all' litigation rule of the Tiv tribe of Northern Nigeria discussed in E Hondius, 'The Supremacy of Western Law' in L De Ligt et al (eds), *Viva Vox Iuris Romani: Essays In Honour Of Johannes Emil Spruit* (Brill, Leiden, 2002) 337, 340: Arguing that the idea of the supremacy of Western law is basically flawed. In general See H Patrick Glenn, *Legal Traditions Of The World: Sustainable Diversity In Law* (2nd edn, OUP, New York, 2004)).

[117] See for example the pure economic loss claim in *Perre v Apand* [1999] HCA 36 (Austl). In general see Jane Stapleton, 'Comparative Economic Loss: Gary Schwartz and Case Law Focussed 'Middle Theory' (2002) 50 UCLA Law Review 531.

Apart from the general advantages of perhaps being alerted to novel types
of factual dispute and formulations of legal argument, is it likely, for example, that a Supreme Court judge in a New Zealand tort case would find
significant further illumination by seeking to understand the relevant
Spanish law on the contentious issues? Were the Supreme Court of
California[118] and the High Court of Australia[119] in some sense wrong or at
least unwise not to refer to the German concept of contract with protective
benefit for a third party when they found that a claim lay in the tort of
negligence when due to a lawyer's carelessness the intended beneficiary of a
will failed to inherit? Certainly the case law suggests that courts in the US,
Canada, Australia and New Zealand do not find any advantage in a regular consideration of the tort law of foreign-language jurisdictions. Why
might this be?

## 1. The multi-linguist's problems

Assume our common law judge or practitioner is perfectly multi-lingual:
she would still face a number of problems handling foreign-language *law*.
First, consider concepts and conceptual arrangements: once we leave the
common law world, as we do when we enter foreign-language jurisdictions,
we find highly sophisticated legal environments within which we will search
in vain to find direct parallels of certain distinctive legal categories that
common lawyers use such as trustee, consideration and estoppel.
Conversely, we will find concepts with no direct parallel in the common
law, and though these can be of use in English-speaking jurisdictions with
a mixed heritage such as Louisiana[120] and Scotland, their transplantation
into simple common law systems is perilous. Again take the German
concept of a contract with protective benefit for a third party, a construct
that Germans exploit to deal with the perceived inadequacies of tort law as
codified in the German Civil Code: why on earth would California or
Australia want to address this foreign phenomenon when local tort law
suffers from no such inadequacy?

---

[118] *Biakanja v Irving* 49 Cal.2d 647, 650 (1958) held that a notary public who negligently
failed to direct proper attestation of a will became liable in tort to an intended beneficiary
damaged because of the invalidity of the instrument. See also *Lucas v Hamm* 56 Cal.2d 583
(1961) which extended the *Biakanja* rationale to the attorney-client relationship and held that
an attorney who negligently drafted a will could be held liable to a person named in the will
who suffered deprivation of benefits as a result of the negligence.
[119] *Hill v Van Erp* (1997) 188 CLR 159 (Austl).
[120] There are 'many cases where common law judges employ the concepts of the civil law in
order to assist them in their interpretation of the common law.' W J Zwalve, 'Ryall v Rolle and
the Commune, Canon Law, and Common Law in England' (1992) 66 Tul L Rev 1745, 1755.
On mixed systems see fn 54). *Civilian Tradition* (1995) 56 La L Rev 437, 439. See also Charles
Donahue, Jr, *Ius*.

There may also be many structural features of a foreign jurisdiction that need to be understood: thus a recent decision of the House of Lords has been attacked for its referring to German tort law while apparently neglecting the allegedly relevant fact that, like most US employees, German workers cannot sue their employer in negligence.[121]

More generally, there are broad contrasts in legal style between Old and New World jurisdictions. For example, reference to common Roman law origins can help deflate trivial or artificial differences between jurisdictions within the Old World.[122] In contrast, amongst judges and practitioners in the New World jurisdictions of North America and Australasia there is a pronounced indifference to Roman law,[123] perhaps based not merely on their common law rather than civilian heritage (Quebec and Louisiana excepted) but also on an embarrassment about Roman law's tolerance of slavery and a repulsion for a legal system that had been accessible only to a Latin-comprehending Christian elite.[124]

Another vital contrast relates to the status and form of judicial reasoning. Though it is widely known in the common law world that the status of case law is different in Code systems, it is not widely known what that status is for individual foreign-language jurisdictions and how, for example, it might vary between areas of tort law and over time.[125] Moreover, not all tort doctrine is derived from the Code and later statutes: there is a great deal of judge-made tort law, some of which exhibits a spirit that is antithetical to that originally associated with the Code.[126] Indeed the great John Fleming noted that 'the modern law of torts in all of the principle civil law countries is today judge-made, a vast gloss overlaying a few exiguous Code articles.'[127]

---

[121] T Weir, 'Making it More Likely v Making it Happen' (2002) Cambridge L J 519, 521 'The *tour d'horizon* was admittedly superficial. Omitted is the salient fact that in almost none of the jurisdictions glanced at would the claimants in *Fairchild* have succeeded: in most places an employee simply cannot sue his employer in tort, since workmen's compensation or social security takes its place.'

[122] But see (n 164).

[123] Even in US academe, there may be open hostility. For example, John G Fleming who had escaped the holocaust as a schoolboy noted Roman law, has a 'curious, almost neurotic, fascination for British scholars' and that 'the whole retention [in a modern comparative law text] of this Roman law relic [of the Lex Aquilia] surely owes more to nostalgia than to functional justification.' JG Fleming, 'Comparative Law of Torts' (1984) 4 Oxf J Leg Studs 235.

[124] The exclusion of Jews from the Western legal world slowly eroded during the 19th century. Zimmermann, (n 3) 16–17.

[125] E Hondius, 'Precedent in East and West' (2005) 23 Penn St Int'l L Rev 521. An interesting question is whether the recent development of electronic resources, making case law more accessible across the Continent may lead judicial analysis to converge as judges cite and engage with a wide pool of cases.

[126] Such as the right of personality and privacy in German law. See H Beverley-Smith, A Ohly and Agnès Lucas-Schloetter, *Privacy, Property And Personality—Civil Law Perspectives On Commercial Appropriation* (CUP, Cambridge, 2005) ch 4, 10. On This 'Decodification' Dynamic See Fleming (n 123) 235, 238–39

[127] Fleming ibid 241.

Yet how intellectually accessible is that case law to the common lawyer? In the New World legal realism urges courts to provide reasoning that is not only coherent and rigorous, but also candid and transparent in identifying and evaluating the underlying values in tension. While it is true that, within the subtle and rich jurisprudence surrounding a Civil Code, civilian courts sometimes treat Code text as an impassable obstacle, narrow tram-tracks that allow only a very limited amount of manoeuvre and adaptation to new challenges, often such courts covertly manipulate the Code's provisions. Typically adopting the direction pointed to by some eminent jurist, these courts are willing to be highly 'creative' in their manipulation to reach the desired result,[128] far more creative than (at least non-US) common law courts tend to be in their respectful approach to statutory interpretation. Such nuances are not a simple matter for the practitioner or judge in an English-speaking jurisdiction to grasp.

The importance of this for our purposes is that a common lawyer looking for inspiration from the legal values in play in Continental judgments will often be disappointed because the latter can be 'absorbed with ways to outflank the Code without taking us into their confidence why these manoeuvres are thought desirable. German, no less than French, courts are articulate about means but not ends.'[129] Furthermore, even where the court in a foreign-language jurisdiction

does enunciate values, the weight put on them is culturally contingent in ways that are complex and hard for the outsider to appreciate. For example,[130] in one society there may be a long tradition of expecting young adults to assume responsibility and care for the elderly which is supported by an expectation that people will be supported in their old age.[131]

---

[128] Using 'surreptitious techniques ... [and] covertly through subtle manipulation' of the Code text. M Bussani and V Palmer (eds), *Pure Economic Loss In Europe* (CUP, Cambridge, 2003) 124. *See also* Koziol's paper for this conference.

[129] Fleming (n 123) 242. Consider also the 'inscrutable language in which the [European Court of Justice] traditionally clothes its judgments': A Rodger, 'Savigny in the Strand' (1995) 28–30 The Irish Jurist 1, 10. For an enlightening general study of the contrasting approaches to judicial discourse and accountability between the US Supreme Court, the French Cour de cassation and the European Court of Justice, see M De S-O-L'é Lasser, *Judicial Deliberations: A Comparative Analysis Of Transparency And Legitimacy* (OUP, Oxford, 2004).

[130] Another example is the absolute protection to human dignity enshrined in Article 1 of the 1949 post-Nazi Constitution (Basic Law, Grundgesetz) of Germany.

[131] Contrast the social functions of adoption in the US with those in Turkey where adopters must be over 35, adoptees are mostly over 30 and usually remain part of their natural family. D Nelken, Book Review of E Orucu 'The Enigma of Comparative Law: Variations on a Theme for the 21st Century' (2006) 26 Legal Stud 129, 134

In short, the general indifference of North American and Australasian courts and practitioners to the tort law of foreign-language jurisdictions seems a wise response to inescapable phenomena. For them there is no more to be *reliably* derived from foreign-language jurisdictions than from English-speaking ones, namely notice of novel types of factual dispute and formulations of legal argument: moreover, there are added perils of misinterpretation. The common law world seems, at least to me, to be rich enough for most needs of tort practitioners and judges in English-speaking jurisdictions, and claims that they should also address foreign-language legal materials, let alone that they should routinely do so, are not supported by compelling argument. Indeed we should be mightily relieved that our North American and Australasian judges are not tempted to acquiesce to the pressure of such claims.

## 2. The mono-linguist's problems

But of course the perils involved when tort practitioners and judges in English-speaking jurisdictions resort to foreign-language legal materials are even graver because most common law judges and practitioners are fully fluent only in English: access to foreign-language legal materials will be second hand. For that reason, the legal and linguistic capacity of the translator is crucial, but so too is availability and quality of the translated materials. As we all know from experience of our domestic tort system; some judges, legal commentators and empiricists are more gifted than others; and even between gifted lawyers there are large disagreements about the law. I have no doubt that the percentage of gifted lawyers in foreign-language jurisdictions is at least as high as that in English-language ones. But how confident can a domestic practitioner or judge be that it is the output of these foreign lawyers that are put up for translation into English?

This problem is especially acute in Code systems where certain academic commentaries on tort law both within and outside the Civil Code have influence and authority far beyond any academic materials in English-speaking jurisdictions,[132] except for the US Restatements. The fact that, whereas the English legal tradition treats judges as the senior partners in law-making, the Continental tradition recognizes legal academics in this role, partly explains why some Continental jurists make statements that such and such is the 'correct' 'solution'[133] to a legal issue. Such language

[132] Indeed, Continental jurists are sometimes mandated reading for common law judges! See Civil Jurisdiction and Judgments Act 1982 (United Kingdom, ch 27), § 3(3) as amended.
[133] Another reason is the limits of language. English has words that convey the 'resolution', 'remedy' or 'resolution' of a problem without the implication that this is the only 'solution' that may be possible. Languages other than English may not have this diversity of expression so that a translation into the term 'solution' may mislead the English reader into thinking the writer means something more normatively loaded than merely 'a resolution.'

can shock lawyers in common law jurisdictions where it is customary to couch normative arguments with greater reserve, unless they appreciate that these Continental lawyers seek to have their academic commentaries accepted as law. The legal cultural reasons for this difference in the role of jurists are fascinating in their own right, especially in comparison to US and other common law systems.[134] But the point I want to make here is that of the six or so most authoritative and extensive commentaries on the German Civil Code and extra-code law of obligations, none has been translated into English. This means that English speakers do not have these texts available so as to provide the necessary foils for the one extensive text on German tort law that has been written in English.[135] Moreover, to my knowledge there are no other texts, written in English or in translation, that deal in detail[136] with tort law in other foreign-language jurisdictions.

This raises a further problem, that of appropriate selection. Faced with the practical limits of adjudication and bounded rationality, even the most enthusiastic advocate of the use of foreign-language legal materials in common law courts could not support a comprehensive survey of all such materials from all foreign-language jurisdictions: no sane Taxing Master would approve the costs a party would have to expend to marshal the necessary experts in such material.

Nor could such an advocate defend a selection that was random. But there seem to be little debate about possible methodologies of selection.[137]

It is true that Basil Markesinis and Jorg Fedtke have recently asserted that when, in following their direction to address the law of foreign juris-dictions, we make our selection: [A] single one can be enough, provided it is an advanced system, with a roughly comparable socio-economic envi-ronment and offers reasonable accessibility to its sources and experience.[138]

Accordingly, in their campaign to persuade British courts to expand the liability of public authorities into new fields, they select Germany as their favoured foreign jurisdiction. This is not simply because they believe that the German legal system deserves lavish praise: 'structure, system, and internal consistency are attributes highly valued by German lawyers; and

---

[134] On the comparative role of the academic, judge and practitioner in a legal system see W Twining, W Farnsworth, S Vogenauer and F Téson, 'The Role of Academics in the Legal System' in P Cane and Mark Tushnet (eds), *The Oxford Handbook of Legal Studies* (OUP, Oxford, 2003) 920; A Rodger, 'Savigny in the Strand' (1995) 28–30 The Irish Jurist 1. Few common lawyers seem to appreciate the extent of the role of the civilian judge in discovering the relevant law, rather than relying on the submissions of counsel.

[135] BS Markesinis and H Unberath, *The German Law o f Torts: A Comparative Treatise* (4th edn, Hart, Oxford, 2002).

[136] Contrast For Example Jo Bell, S Boyron and S Whittaker, *Principles Of French Law* (OUP, Oxford, 1998).

[137] J Beatson, *Book Review* (2004) 120 Law Q Rev 175, 178.

[138] BS Markesinis and J Fedtke, 'Authority or Reason? The Economic Consequences of Liability for Breach of statutory Duty in a Comparative Perspective' (2007) EBLR 5 66–67.

their Civil Code ... has adopted them to perfection'.[139] They select Germany on the basis of their belief that 'Germans have masses of'[140] the kind of raw empirical data relevant to the liability of public authorities. The flaw in their approach is that these data are in no way adequate to the purpose Markesinis and Fedtke seek to put them: they are simply too crude. Moreover, it is extremely unlikely that the research and analysis needed to produce compelling socio-legal data in the future from any jurisdiction will receive the necessary funding.

So we are left without an obvious criterion of selection. This is problematic since there would seem to be a number of different possible criteria. For example, the United States has more citizens of German descent than of French; New Zealand has more citizens of Scottish descent than Spanish; Australia has more citizens of Greek descent than of German. Should this affect the selection? What about language pools within the domestic jurisdiction? In which case US courts should presumably prioritize materials from Spanish-speaking jurisdictions.[141] What about a traditional comparativists' device, the 'legal family'? In which case England should look to Singapore rather than Germany.[142] What about the relationship between 'parent' systems and 'colonies' or 'derivatives'?[143] In which case India and many African nations should look to England rather than culturally closer jurisdictions. What about major trade partners? In which case Australian courts should address Japanese law[144] and US courts will need to look at Chinese law.[145] What about military partners? Should US courts give particular emphasis to the law of those countries that contain most of the overseas US Defense Department installations: Germany (302), Japan (111) and South Korea (106)?[146]

## B. For Eire, Scotland, England and Wales

These three Old World English-speaking jurisdictions share membership of the European Union with a large number of foreign-language jurisdictions and, for some judges in this trio of jurisdictions, this provides a reason to pay attention to foreign-language materials from the individual Member

---

[139] ibid 9.

[140] ibid 67; see (n 41) and accompanying text.

[141] Spanish is the second most common language in the United States after English. According to the 2000 United States Census, Spanish is spoken most frequently at home by about 28.1 million people aged 5 or over.

[142] Materials from the Commonwealth are available on the net at Commonlii.

[143] BS Markesinis and J Fedtke, 'The Judge as Comparativist' (2005) 80 Tul L Rev 11, 68. See also 34, 97.

[144] On which, see H Oda, *Japanese Law* (OUP, New York, 2001).

[145] On which, see for example GW Conk, 'People's Republic of China Civil Code: Tort Liability Law' (2005)5 Private Law Rev 77.

[146] Department of Defense, Base Structure Report, Fiscal Year 2005 Baseline, at 2.

States even where the case at hand involves a purely domestic legal issue of tort law. For example, having specifically asked counsel for material describing the position in European legal systems[147] in a landmark mesothelioma case, *Fairchild*, creating a special rule of proof of causation, Lord Bingham stated that:

> In a shrinking world (in which the employees of asbestos companies may work for those companies in any one or more of several countries) there must be some virtue in uniformity of outcome whatever the diversity of approach in reaching that outcome.[148]

Must there be? One by one, jurisdictions will confront an issue. When are there enough resolutions so that a sufficient 'uniformity' of outcome can be detected and exercise this normative pull on the undecided? What if the early consensus offends a court's sense of justice? What if the source of the foreign-language material or its translator is not reliable? What if, as alleged by Tony Weir in relation to this same decision, the foreign-language material was superficially 'glanced' at without reference to a highly relevant contextual fact?[149]

Significantly, in this same case the Lords also looked at English-language materials to which they wisely paid very much greater attention. In the decision of the Supreme Court of California of *Rutherford v Owens-Illinois Inc.*[150] the Lords found a range of pertinent arguments in a familiar common law conceptual framework and in their own language the subtle nuances of which presented no barrier to understanding.[151] Again in the subsequent case addressing the issue of whether liability under *Fairchild* should be *in solidum* or proportionate, no member of the House of Lords referred to the material concerning foreign-language jurisdictions that had been proffered by counsel but three members[152] used arguments found in a variety of materials from the US[153] In short, the practice of the judges in

---

[147] See J Stapleton, *Lords a'leaping Evidentiary Gaps* (2002) 10 Torts Law J 276, 302.

[148] *Fairchild* [2003] 1 AC 32, ¶ 32 (UK) (per Lord Bingham).

[149] See (n 116).

[150] 67 Cal Rptr 2d 16 (1997).

[151] Lord Rodger has noted that 'our judges can read the cases [from other English-language jurisdictions] for themselves and can assess how their reasoning could be fitted into the existing scheme' which is crucial because 'to be really helpful ... the [foreign] authority would have to be investigated in detail and would have to be capable in some way of application within the framework of our own system.' A Rodger, *Savigny in the Strand*, (1995) 28–30 The Irish Jurist 1, 19.

[152] See *Barker v Corus (UK) Plc* [2006] UKHL 20, per Lord Hoffmann, per Lord Walker of Gestingthorpe at ¶ 111 and Baroness Hale of Richmond at ¶ 122.

[153] Such as *Prosser And Keeton On Torts* (5th edn, West Group, 1984); the Supreme Court of California decision in *Brown v Superior Court* 751 P.2d 470 (1988); and the Court of Appeals of New York in *Hymowitz v Eli Lilly & Co* 539 N.E.2d 1069 (1988).

English-language jurisdictions, even those in the EU, to look to foreign-language materials on tort cautiously and only intermittently is both legitimate and wise. Indeed, were we to accept the extraordinary argument of Basil Markesinis, that once a judge does refer to foreign material in one case, he must explain why he is not using it in each and every case thereafter,[154] a new judge would have a real incentive not to refer to that material in any case ... ever!

IV. BENEFITS OF 'COORDINATED' TORT MATERIALS: RESTATEMENTS, EU 'PRINCIPLES'

### A. Intra-National Coordination by Restatement of Tort Law

A final possible source of comparative tort materials for the practitioner and judge in an English-speaking jurisdiction are what I will call 'coordinated' materials: those that seek to capture or review tort law across more than one formal judicial or legislative jurisdiction. American lawyers are completely familiar with ALI restatements.[155] Restatements exist for and are funded by US practitioners, judges and other users: they are in this sense 'bottom-up' projects. The general motive for these intra-national projects is apolitical, in the sense that there is no explicit or covert aim to rearrange formal law-making power.[156] Rather the aim is to provide a fulcrum for the dissemination of information about divergences and convergences among the dozens of jurisdictions that operate within one nation and one national market place. That such divergences have grown up after a relatively short

---

[154] BS Markesinis, 'Judicial Mentality: Mental Disposition or Outlook as a Factor Impeding Recourse to Foreign Law' (2006) 80 Tul L Rev 1325, 1361–62: 'If that same judge had, on an earlier occasion, himself resorted to foreign law, one would expect him to tell his audience why in this newer case the foreign experience was of no relevance.' (Markesinis also asserts that where one judge mentions foreign law 'would it not be reasonable, constructive and courteous to expect [his colleagues in the same decision] to try and counter in a specific manner this material rather than pass it by in silence?' (at 1371).) Justice Scalia asserts a similar point to attack *any* citation of foreign law: 'to invoke alien law when it agrees with one's thinking, and ignore it otherwise, is not reasoned decision-making, but sophistry.' *Roper v Simmons* 543 US 551, 627 (2005) (Scalia J, dissenting).
[155] See eg 'The Restatement (Third) of Torts: Liability For Physical Harm' (Proposed Final Draft No. 1, 2005).
[156] There are however debates about the degree to which the ALI processes are or can be politically neutral. See eg FJ Vandall, 'Constructing a Roof Before the Foundation is Prepared: The Restatement (Third) of Torts: Products Liability Section 2 (b) Design Defect' (1997) 30 U Mich JL Reform 261, 279, 'the ALI's mission is no longer to restate the law, but rather to issue pro-manufacturer political documents'; RA Posner, Address to the American Law Institute, 18 May 1995, 'who would have imagined that the special interests would place the Institute under siege, as if it were a real legislature ... the increasing political character of American law [means] ...it is more and more difficult for the Institute to engage with important questions ... without crossing the line that separates technical law from politics.'

time since they developed from a common source in England (Louisiana excepted) is testament to the centrifugal tendencies of the common law method, it not being tied to any Code text.[157] In addition, US tort law is further fragmented by local state legislative reforms, perhaps most notoriously in the area of joint and several liability.[158] As noted earlier, this doctrinal fragmentation is, I suspect, one reason why tort theory is much more popular in the US than in other English-speaking jurisdictions: it allows academics to write for a national audience which activity is attractive both intellectually and because it enhances career prospects. In contrast, academics in English-speaking jurisdictions with unified tort law need only deal with a relatively small set of appellate cases before their doctrinal analysis can be attractive to a national academic, practitioner and judicial audience. Moreover it can directly influence the judicial development of a tort law that is national.[159]

Three features of US tort restatements are important in comparative perspective, especially in light of the moves to unification in the European Union. First, the Reporter's Notes of the recent third round of torts restatements have a much increased citation of non-US cases and secondary materials, virtually all of which refer to the law in other English-speaking jurisdictions. Second, non-US tort lawyers should appreciate that the black-letter format of restatements provides an institutionalized way of crystallizing potential rules of law with which the judge can govern access to the jury.[160] This crystallization is not required in jury-free systems.

Third, non-US tort lawyers should understand how a restatement might seem to encourage convergence. A restatement consists of three types of text: the black-letter section, comments on the black-letter, and Reporter's Notes. In virtually all restatements the black-letter does not record divergences between jurisdictions:[161] this is discussed in the comments and actual cases are only recorded in the Reporter's Notes. By elevating an

---

[157] Legal history can illuminate the socio-politico-economic reasons for broader centrifugal fashions such as the rise of post-revolutionary French interest in reflecting national identity and culture in their law, and a comparable concern in other Continental countries after the collapse of Napoleonic empire. See F Wieacker, R Zimmermann and T Weir, *A History Of Private Law In Europe With Particular Reference To Germany* (1996); and (n 163) Contrast the 'top-down' politically motivated centripetal projects in the EU today, see below.

[158] The resultant state of disarray, set out in Restatement (Third) Of Torts: Apportionment Of Liability 153–159 (2000), has been described by Tony Weir as 'such a trackless morass, Dismal Swamp, and Desolation of Smaug that surely a very wrong turning must have been taken in order to reach them.' T Weir, 'All or Nothing?' (2004) 78 Tul L Rev 511, 524 fn 63.

[159] Or in the case of England and Wales, and Scotland, can be if the decision on an appeal from one jurisdiction is stated to apply to or is later accepted in the other.

[160] See text at (n 87–89) above.

[161] A notable exception is The Restatement (Third) of Torts: Apportionment of Liability (2000).

approach which has only so far been taken by a few jurisdictions to the status of a black-letter 'rule,' a Reporter can promote that approach across the nation: this is the story of the rule in §402A of the Second Restatement which was, subsequent to its publication, adopted by US courts in virtually all jurisdictions.

Conversely, by including within the black-letter a requirement the Reporter believes is imposed by a majority of jurisdictions, he can encourage the minority of states to follow suit: an example is the requirement of a reasonable alternative design in §2(b) of the Third Restatement on Products Liability.[162] However, this appearance that restatements promote convergence is highly deceptive: as US practitioners know only too well. State courts have, for example, interpreted the special tort liability in §402A differently and so today state regimes of products liability manifest considerable variations. This confirms that US tort law, even when it stems from a common text such as §402A, will diverge because there is no single court of ultimate appeal on tort matters.

### C. Inter-National Coordination by Harmonization/Codification of Tort Law

The European Union began to issue uniform laws relating to private law with the 1985 product liability Directive which, albeit described as a harmonization measure, bizarrely introduced an *additional* layer of potential liability on product suppliers across all Member States.[163] Since then there has been increasing interest in comparing private law regimes within the Union. For example, the projects of the Trento Group[164] seek to identify divergences as well as the convergent 'common core' of European private law: these projects have no political goal. The Group has produced a number of works in English such as a volume on economic loss in which Mauro Bussani and Vernon Palmer provide profound insights into the divergences and convergences of the law in this field across jurisdictions.[165]

---

[162] Restatement (Third) of Torts: Products Liability (1998). Section 2(b) reads:

A product is defective when, at the time of sale or distribution, it contains a manufacturing defect, is defective in design, or is defective because of inadequate instructions or warnings. A product: (b) is defective in design when the foreseeable risks of harm posed by the product could have been reduced or avoided by the adoption of a reasonable alternative design by the seller or other distributor, or a predecessor in the commercial chain of distribution, and the omission of the alternative design renders the product not reasonably safe.

[163] For a list of the relevant measures see O Radley-Gardner, H Beale, R Zimmermann and R Schulze (eds), *Fundamental Texts on European Private Law* (Hart Publishing, Oxford, 2003) Sub I.

[164] On which, see M Bussani, 'Current trends in European Comparative Law: The Common Core Approach' (1998) 21 Hastings Int'l & Comp L Rev 785.

[165] M Bussani and V Palmer (eds), *Pure Economic Loss In Europe* (CUP, Cambridge, 2003).

A similar political agnosticism is manifest in recent comparative studies on public authority liability[166] and in the monograph on European tort law by Cees van Dam[167] who doubts, rightly in my view,[168] that pro-active harmonization of tort law across the Union is authorized by the Treaty of Rome. The EU has no direct power as such to enforce harmonization, let alone codification, across tort law.[169] There is simply no evidence that the real differences across tort systems appreciably distort trade or competition, which according to the European Court of Justice is a Treaty pre-requisite for any EU legislative initiative to harmonize tort law. Moreover, such a move arguably offends the EU's alleged commitment to 'preserving diversity and ensuring that decisions are taken as close as possible to the citizens.'[170] Indeed there are profound philosophical arguments in favour of diversity of law as a source of enrichment of a community's identity.[171] Nonetheless, there has been quite an embarrassing amount of work published that asserts, not merely that there is much harmony already between the tort law of European systems, but also that they are rapidly converging. Where 'convergence' authors do not declare their political motivations,[172] such work must be treated as deeply suspect. But there is also much recent material in English on European tort law that is more or less candid in its politically-motivated enthusiasm for pro-active harmonization[173] across existing jurisdictions, a dynamic that can be assisted,

---

[166] See D Fairgrieve, M Andenas and J Bell (eds), *Tort Liability Of Public Authorities In Comparative Perspective* (CUP, Cambridge, 2002); and D Fairgrieve, *State Liability In Tort: A Comparative Law Study* (OUP, Oxford, 2003) Which Is A French-English Law Comparison. Contrast BS Markesinis et al, *Tortious Liability Of Statutory Bodies: A Comparative And Economic Analysis Of Five English Cases* (Hart Publishing, Oxford, 1999).

[167] C Van Dam, *European Tort Law* (OUP, Oxford, 2006) 133–135.

[168] J Stapleton, *Product Liability* (Butterworths, London, 1994) 53–58.

[169] J Mance, 'Is Europe Aiming to Civilise the Common Law?' (2006) 7 EBLRL.

[170] See http://europa.eu/abc/panorama/index_en.htm. On the 'difficulty in a budding federal system of setting pragmatic limits to centralising idealism and giving real meaning to 'subsidiarity',' and Mance (n 161).

[171] 'At the end of the 18th century, in reaction against the rationalism of the Enlightenment, it was recognised that nations and peoples also had an individuality of their own, which found expression in, among other things, their laws, and that these national individualities were valuable, and ought to be cherished. Scots law is different from English law. Not only may it be none the worse for that … but it is a positive merit, contributing a further thread to the web of Scottish identity. Although there are advantages in a uniform Code Napoleon or Whitehall-drafted Statute Law, these are usually purchased at too high a price of impersonality and alienation. The diversity of peoples ought to be reflected in a diversity of laws, in order that we may all feel at home in our own laws; the anomalies of devolution are a small price to pay for our all being able collectively to do our own thing.' JR Lucas, 'The Nature of Law' (1979) 23 Philosophica 37, 43.

[172] Contrast the admirably explicit declaration of political motivation in his emphasis of similarities among EU jurisdictions by Markesinis (n 7) (1997).

[173] See M Van Hoecke and F Ost (eds), *The Harmonization of European Private Law* (Hart, Oxford, 2000); F Cafaggi (ed), *The Institutional Framework Of European Private Law* (OUP, Oxford, 2006); G Bruggemeier, *Common Principles of Tort Law: A Pre-Statement of Law* (BIICL, London, 2004).

albeit superficially,[174] by appeal to the 'common heritage' of civilian systems in Roman Law, the Corpus Juris Civilis and the European Ius Commune.[175] Though we can expect 'distortion as the price of uniformity,'[176] support for full codification is also now fashionable among many academics.[177] For example, Christian von Bar has published large volumes on the 'common European law of torts'[178] and heads the 'Study Group on a European Civil Code'[179] which is drafting common European principles for the most important aspects of the law of obligations and certain aspects of the law of property in movables. So far, however, only Helmut Koziol's group, the European Group on Tort Law,[180] has published in hard copy its model tort rules, the 2005 'Principles of European Tort Law' (PETL).

Such principles may lead to a future EU Code and so they may be of some current value to the practitioner or judge in Eire, Scotland, England and Wales: so long as they clearly understand the political motivation and compromise nature of the Principles and take account of the large variation between Member States in how a common text will be perceived and applied.[181] But are such principles of value for the non-EU practitioner or

---

[174] See eg Fleming (n 123) 'True it certainly is that many of the still recalcitrant problems were already identified by the Roman jurists (omissions, economic loss, etc), but the modern law of torts in Europe bears few discernible traces of that heritage.'

[175] See eg K Luig, 'The History of Roman Private Law and the Unification of European Law' (1997) 5 ZEUP 405 Roman Law, as it was systematized in the Corpus Juris Civilis (the collection of laws initiated by the Emperor Justinian I around 530), was rediscovered, interpreted and reshaped by medieval jurists with elements of canon law and of Germanic custom, especially feudal law. Some argue that by the middle of the 16th century, there had resulted a European Ius Commune that was common to all continental Europe (and Scotland). This era of apparent unity of legal system ended when national codifications were adopted beginning with the French Civil Code in 1804. For a strident critic of the notion of a 'ius commune which previously existed,' see P Legrand, Book Review: Walter van Gerven (ed), *Torts* [1999] CLJ 439, 440 A more nuanced account is H Patrick Glenn, *On Common Laws* 16–20 (2005).

[176] HLA Hart, *The Concept of Law* (2nd edn, Clarendon, Oxford, 1994) 38.

[177] A Hartkamp et al (eds), *Towards A European Civil Code* (3rd edn, Kluwer, The Hague, 2004); MW Hesselink (ed), *The Politics Of A European Civil Code* (Kluwer, The Hague, 2006).

[178] C Von Bar, *The Common European Law Of Torts, Vol 1* (OUP, Oxford, 1998); C Von Bar, *The Common European Law Of Torts, Vol 2* (OUP, Oxford, 2000).

[179] The first volumes of this project began to appear in 2006.

[180] European Group on Tort Law, *Principles of European Tort Law: Text And Commentary* (2005). The home page of the Study Group on a European Civil Code, http://www.sgecc.net, has the text of its articles on tort law in the version dated December 2005.

[181] For legal-cultural reasons it might be, for example, that French courts will read a common text as merely a broad guideline (requiring only 'soft convergence') within which they can exercise considerable discretion (using devices such as the opaque French approach to causation. See (n 123), but English courts will read such a text in terms of hard convergence requiring a rigorous attempt to accommodate other member states' applications of the text. More generally there is a school of thought, prominently represented by Pierre Legrand that argues that harmonization is impossible because people from different legal cultures may understand the same legal text in quite different ways. See P Legrand, 'The Same and the Different' in P Legrand and R Munday (eds), *Comparative Legal Studies: Traditions And*

judge in, for example, the US, Canada, Australia, and New Zealand? There are a number of reasons to suggest not. First, there are all the reasons why such lawyers would be wise to avoid a consideration of the law of individual foreign-language jurisdictions.[182] Second, at least in relation to the 2005 PETL, the format of the text follows, understandably given the vast majority of EU members with civilian legal systems, the layout of civilian Codes and does not map easily onto the common law landscape. Third, the future standing of the black-letter articles is problematic. Even were an EU Code of tort principles to be adopted, it is unlikely to be accompanied by mechanisms sufficiently thorough to prevent the divergences of interpretations and development we see in common law systems.[183] The reality seems to be that the European Court of Justice could never exercise the control of tort doctrines that is currently possible in domestic systems with tight adherence to precedent and a single court of final appeal on matters of judge-made common law such as Australia, Canada and, subject to reciprocal acceptance of House of Lords' decisions, the United Kingdom.

Finally, there is still some doubt about how stable the EU will prove in the long term as a political, as opposed to economic, union. Before its dissolution into 15 nations in 1991 the population of the USSR was 293 million: today the EU has 27 Member States and 490 million people; and it uses 23 official languages.[184] If tort law does manifest features that are culturally specific, how much might the social fabric of local jurisdictions be damaged by elimination of such features in a unifying 'code'? For example, unlike French parents, British parents are not vicariously liable for their underage offspring who live with them: were a future EU Civil Code to impose such liability, would there be an outcry in Britain? Would this and similar frustrations contribute to a future collapse of the political union? It is a shame

---

*Transitions* (CUP, Cambridge, 2003); P Legrand, 'European Legal Systems Are Not Converging' (1996) 45 ICLQ 52; P Legrand, 'Against a European Civil Code' 60 Mod L Rev 44 (1997). Thus 'even if there are identical legal rules, the legal cultures will still be different, a fact which may ultimately lead to different practical results.' E Jayme, 'Multicultural Society And Private Law German Experiences' (1999) 10. See also S Weatherill, 'Why Object to the Harmonization of Private Law by the EC?' (2004) 12 Eur Rev Priv Law 633; S Weatherill, 'Harmonisation: How Much, How Little?' [2005] EBLR 533; G Teubner, 'Legal Irritants: Good Faith in British Law or How Unifying Law ends up in New Divergences' 61 MLR 11 (1998); and the Manifesto or Study Group on Social Justice in European Private Law (see Study Group on Social Justice in European Private Law, 'Social Justice in European Contract Law: A Manifesto' 10 EUR L J 653 (2004)) which produces material that seeks to highlight the political dimensions of the effort to Europeanize private law and the cultural embeddedness of law which can produce divergences in the application of an identical legal rule.

[182] Compounded when, as here, the legal materials rely on translations from *many* languages.

[183] There is an important parallel here with the divergences that past empires and monarchies had to tolerate. See HP Glenn, *On Common Laws* (OUP, Oxford, 2005).

[184] *New York Times* (1 January 2007). The United Nations has only 6 official languages.

that we do not seem to know or care whether frustrations in the private law area played any part in the agitation that produced the collapse of the USSR, let alone the extent to which the private law systems of the resultant separate nations have diverged since that collapse.

But, whatever the fate of the EU, there is of course one use to which materials such as the 2005 PETL might fruitfully be put: namely, as yet another source of plausible arguments and legal concerns. The admirable commentaries on the Principles adopt a 'flexible system'[185] which allows a variety of differing concerns and arguments to be spelt out. Thus, in the unlikely event that a practitioner and judge in an English-speaking jurisdiction is in need of yet further inspiration beyond that available in the pool of English-language jurisdictions, these commentaries would be a valuable additional resource.

### V. CONCLUSION

Comparative law is a vast field. I believe it is one that provides a crucial enrichment of the lawyer's perspective and understanding. It invites a deep respect for difference even across shared values.

In this paper I have only focused on one dimension of comparative tort law: its utility for courts of final appeal and practitioners in cases where the subject matter does not positively *require* knowledge of a foreign system (as it would require, for example, when EU law or the judgments of the European Court of Human Rights are in issue). My conclusion is that comparative tort law can enrich the palette of ideas, concerns, perceptions—in short, arguments—that a judge brings to bear on the matters in dispute, since 'it is arguments that influence decisions.'[186] Moreover comparative law provides the insight that there is nothing inevitable about current domestic conceptual arrangements, and so can ease the path of the tort lawyer who is inviting a domestic court to alter those arrangements because it can show that others are at least intellectually viable. This is well-appreciated in English-speaking jurisdictions where, except in the United States, tort practitioners and courts have always regarded each other's national systems as an important source of readily accessible and intelligible ideas. In the US it is arguable that, in a nation as large and litigious as it is, there may be sufficient diversity of arguments to oust a role for comparative non-US English-language law given the practical constraints when practitioners advise and courts decide cases. Even so, the experience

---

[185] European Group On Tort Law, *Principles Of European Tort Law: Text And Commentary* (2005) 15.

[186] *White* [1993] 3 WLR 730 (U.K.) it is arguments that influence decisions rather than the reading of pages upon pages from judgments' per Lord Steyn L J.

of other English-speaking jurisdictions is not identical to the US and as Justice Posner notes: US lawyers can learn from the social laboratories of other nations.[187]

In contrast, foreign-language comparative tort law is fraught with dangers: how to select resources, their degree of reliability and so on. It is rightly unpopular with courts and practitioners in English-speaking jurisdictions, which typically have sufficiently rich resources from within their own language pool.[188]

Finally, comparative tort law can give a court of final appeal no guidance on the justice of a case—how the law should be applied to the facts. In English-speaking common law jurisdictions it makes no sense for a legal academic baldly to attack a decision of the final court of appeal as 'wrong' on the mere basis that it is not the same as that of another jurisdiction or set of jurisdictions. To do so misunderstands the core role of such courts: to determine the weight of arguments in a case and reach a reasoned decision. Legal reasoning can be incoherent, inconsistent or facile, and rightly attacked on those grounds. But even if an academic could identify all the relevant coherent, consistent and perceptive concerns in a case, she cannot claim that, by virtue of some objective 'legal science,' she has deduced the correct 'conclusions about the proper policy for the law to adopt,'[189] or more generally the 'best answer to [tort] problems,'[190] let alone that the foreign idea is 'superior.'[191] Such claims seem more common among Continental comparativists than among common lawyers who accept that 'in the nature of things, there is no 'right' answer.'[192] In short, while the normative rhetoric of the 'correct' or 'best' or 'superior' solution fits the accepted role of the Code commentator, the perceptive comparativist should, from his sensitivity to comparison and context, see that it is simply inappropriate usage in a common law system, unless he clearly acknowledges that it merely signifies his personal subjective preference.

[187] Posner (n 14).
[188] The same is probably true of the pool of Spanish speaking jurisdictions and that of the Chinese.
[189] K Zweigert and H Kotz, *An Introduction To Comparative Law* (3rd edn (Tony Weir trans, OUP, Oxford, 1998) 6.
[190] BS Markesinis et al, *Tortious Liability of Statutory Bodies: A Comparative And Economic Analysis of Five English Cases* (Hart, Oxford, 1999) 105.
[191] BS Markesinis and J Fedtke, *The Judge as Comparativist* (2005) Tul L Rev 11, 54, 80.
[192] A Rodger, *What Are Appeal Courts For?* (2004) 10 Otago L Rev 517, 535 'Whatever the decision and whatever the reasons, critics will always be able to question them if only because, in the nature of things, there is no 'right' answer. The court has simply got to choose and, when it does so, it puts forward the best set of reasons it can devise. Those reasons may not be compelling but that does not mean that the decision itself is incorrect.'

# CHAPTER 9

# *Comparing Tort Law: Some Thoughts*

*Duncan Fairgrieve*

## I. INTRODUCTION

Professor Jane Stapleton's stimulating paper[1] raises a host of important issues for comparative law generally and comparative tort lawyers in particular. In this short piece, I would like to take the opportunity to respond to aspects of her paper.[2]

An interest in comparative law has traditionally been seen from a common law perspective as a likeable eccentricity, and comparative tort law sits on the fringes of even that! In truth, however, some form of comparative law has long been part of the judicial process in England and Wales, though it is fair to say that this was predominantly undertaken between common law jurisdictions. The inherent characteristics of the common law have perhaps served to mask the fact that this was indeed a comparative law exercise. The seamless nature of the common law, from its origins in English law, through its permutations across to former colonies and beyond, provided a reason and justification for the courts across the commonwealth to look to each other's jurisprudence, exchange solutions and thereby create a network of persuasive authority.

Nonetheless, there has recently been a major shift in the role that courts play, and the sources which are now applicable in judicial decision-making. Shedding their traditional adherence to 20th century positivist and national paradigms, domestic courts are deliberately and explicitly making use of comparative law to an unprecedented extent. Many factors can of course been seen as having influenced this process.[3] Primarily amongst those is the

---

[1] J Stapleton, 'Benefits of Comparative Tort Reasoning : Lost in Translation' reprinted in this volume (Chaper 8).

[2] This is a text of a paper delivered at the BIICL 50th Anniversary Event Series Seminar on Thursday 23 April 2009.

[3] See more general discussion in M Andenas and D Fairgrieve, '"There is a World Elsewhere" Lord Bingham and Comparative Law' in M Andenas and D Fairgrieve, (eds) *Tom Bingham and the Transformation of the Law: A Liber Amicorum* (OUP, Oxford, 2009).

breakdown of the traditionally closed and hierarchical national legal systems. Another factor is the increasingly complex issues with which modern courts are required to engage, whether they be fundamental rights, constitutional review, international law or emerging areas such as biomedical issues, in which ethical and moral issues are increasingly prominent. The polycentric nature of these issues pose challenges to the traditional judicial approaches and explain a whole host of changes, in terms of procedures, personnel, and outlook. In many ways, the complexity of decision-making has heightened the importance of knowing how other jurisdictions have dealt with similar problems. This has thus opened the door to the use of, and increases in, the utility of comparative law, through the development of formal and informal avenues for judicial dialogues, as well as an increasing engagement with doctrinal literature within the formal decision-making process.

The modern tendency has however meant moving away from the safe harbour of English-language comparison. The use of European law influences, or more generally, and in the terminology of Professor Stapleton, 'foreign-language jurisdictions', are somehow seen as very different and more problematic for a common law audience.

As Professor Stapleton rightly points out, there is of course an issue of language. Whilst this may in certain circumstances be an obstacle, I doubt whether it can now be considered as insurmountable, given the number and richness of the sources that exist, both in academic journals, the relevant literature and electronic sources.[4] According to Professor Stapleton's paper, the essential pre-conditions for a meaningful comparative study would seem to be based on the criterion of an 'English-language jurisdiction' in which the two jurisdictions possess *'similar ... cultural parametres'* and also *'share the same range of legal concerns and conceptual arrangements.'*[5] These seem to be encapsulated by a series of 'Old Commonwealth' countries, with prominent examples of Australia and New Zealand, and Canada. But are these countries in reality so culturally comparable? Personally, I would have thought that there are arguments in favour of an increasing shared cultural context with Europe, and a decreasing core of common experience and values with the cited commonwealth examples.

There are of course pitfalls in drawing from European case law or commentaries, as Professor Stapleton rightly points up in her essay, but I would argue that there are now strong reasons in favour of the use of

---

[4] See eg the University of Texas's Institute for Transnational Law which has a large number of translated decisions, masterminded by Professor Basil Markesinis (http://www.utexas.edu/law/academics/centers/transnational/work_new/); the BIICL Product Liability Database (http://www.biicl.org/plf/database), as well as country-based databases such as http://www.legifrance.gouv.fr/ (France, including translations of the main Codes).

[5] Stapleton (n 1) 166.

sources from outside the traditional hunting grounds of the common law. In the context of the work at the British Institute of International and Comparative Law, I would like to refer to a number of topics drawn from our recent work in relation to tort law, and damages actions more generally.

## II. PRODUCT LIABILITY: WHY COMPARE?

The topic of product liability is one of the core research interests of the Institute, and thus constitutes a good starting point for analysis.[6] This is an area which was long dominated by English-speaking discourse due predominantly to the prominence of US product liability law. Recently, however, comparative law studies have instead shifted towards an analysis of European jurisdictions, as we shall see.

In historical terms, the progression towards product liability as an identifiable subject matter, rather than subsumed within the broader law of obligations, was first made on the other side of the Atlantic, where the appearance of products liability cases in the US law reports coincided with the spread of the industrialization of the late 1800s.[7] The modern era of US products liability law subsequently emerged from a string of 20th century cases,[8] then coalescing in the well-known US restatements.

In contrast, within Europe it was only relatively late in the 20th century that there was a perceptible movement towards products liability as raising distinct legal issues which might require a bespoke regime for compensation. Reform efforts were prompted by consumer products tragedies in the pharmaceutical sphere[9] and the perceived inadequacy of the traditional responses of the law. Comparative law also played a role, initially of a transatlantic origin, with US law having a significant impact upon German law (partly due to renaissance of German comparative studies in the 1960s)[10] as is shown inter alia by the adoption of the manufacturing/design defect dichotomy in Germany.[11] American influence was not however predominant across Europe. Indeed, French law was much less receptive to such influences due to the fact that, as Borghetti notes, until the 1970s, most French lawyers remained ignorant of the developments of foreign product liability in general.[12]

---

[6] See http://www.biicl.org/plf/.

[7] D Owen, *Products Liability Law* (West Law School, 2005) para 1.2.

[8] Eg 1916 decision of *MacPherson v Buick Motor Co* 111 NE 1050 (NY 1916).

[9] Particularly the thalidomide tragedy in the late 1950s and 60s.

[10] J Bell, 'The Development of Tort Law' in H Koziol and B Steininger, *European Tort Law 2007* (Springer, Dordrecht, 2008) 21–22.

[11] See S Lenze, 'German Product Liability Law' in D Fairgrieve (ed), *Product Liability in Comparative Perspective* (CUP, Cambridge, 2005) 103 ff.

[12] Quoted by J Bell, 'The Development of Tort Law' in H Koziol and B Steininger, *European Tort Law 2007* (Springer, Dordrecht, 2008) 20.

Subsequently, European sources themselves increasingly provided reference points,[13] partly through the work of the Council of Europe, but culminating in the introduction of substantive law via the harmonised measures in the Product Liability Directive,[14] thereby giving rise to a European regime of product liability.

The development of a specifically European approach to compensation in this sphere gradually undermined the influence of the North American approach to the topic. It has inevitably taken time for that shift to be made, but it is now clear that, whilst American or commonwealth developments are still of great interest from a comparative perspective, in substantive terms, attention must now be turned in the European Member States. Let us look at that in a little more detail.

Despite the harmonizing objectives underpinning the European Directive, a notion subsequently described by the ECJ as intended to effect a 'complete' and not a 'minimum' harmonization,[15] it must be recognized that certain features of the Directive tend to suggest otherwise, and tend instead to promote diversity of solutions. Due to political compromises, the Directive contains a menu of options and add-ons, including the development risks defence, the exclusion of primary agricultural produce and game[16] and a ceiling on personal injury damages. Moreover, many of the concepts in the Directive were either left undefined (such as the crucial notion of 'putting into circulation')[17] or when they were defined, were given·a very open-textured nature, which of course is notoriously the case with the central notion of 'defect' of a product.[18] Moreover, key elements of a product liability action under the Directive were simply left to domestic law, including areas as fundamental as causation, remoteness of damage, standard of proof, assessment of damages, procedure and rules of discovery.

These lacunae within the Directive clearly present challenges to the objective of harmonization. And yet claimants relying upon the Directive, as well as courts applying the law need to give flesh to the amorphous notions contained therein. How is that to be done? Resort to *travaux préparatoires* and domestic doctrinal discussion is of course important.

---

[13] See eg the work of the Council of Europe as enshrined in : Council of Europe, European Convention on products liability in regard to personal injury and death of 27 January 1977, ETS No. 91.

[14] Council Directive of 25 July 1985 on the approximation of the laws, regulations and administrative provisions of the Member States concerning liability for defective products (85/374/EEC), OJ L210.

[15] See Case C-183/00 *Gonzalez Sanchez v Medicina Asturiana SA* [2002] ECR I-3901; Case C-52/00; *Commission v France,* [2002] ECR I-3827.

[16] Subsequently amended: Directive 99/34 OJ 1999 L 141/20.

[17] See arts 6, 7 and 11 of the Directive.

[18] Defined as when a product does not 'provide the safety which a person is entitled to expect': see art 6 of the Directive.

Arguments by analogy with pre-existing national provisions can assist of course in ensuring that the transposition process is accepted. What about other Member States? There is no obligation as a matter of EU Law for courts of one Member State to consult, still less to be bound by, the case law of other Member States on the interpretation of EU law. That position is at least clear. It is of course the role of the ECJ to ensure the uniform interpretation and application of EU law across the Member States. However, that does not mean that the process of looking to the case law of other jurisdictions is irrelevant. On the contrary, it would be surprising if, on important points of EU law, the decisions of other courts deciding similar points were not accorded some importance as a reference point as to how such issues were dealt with by the judicial process. Would it be going too far to say that such decisions could constitute persuasive precedent, *a fortiori* where there was evidence that *the courts of a significant number* of Member States had decided a particular issue of EU law in one distinct way?

Issues of methodology and scope of course arise. From a potential set of 26 other jurisdictions, where does one look? These however are not insurmountable hurdles despite opinions to the contrary. There can sometimes be a tendency of comparative law sceptics to pose conditions for the use of comparative law which are so stringent as to render the exercise practically impossible. Professor Stapleton raises the issue of 'appropriate selection' in using material from what she refers to as 'foreign-language jurisdictions.' Two extremes are thus contrasted: the exhaustive comparative study of one point of law, and the purely random approach. However, no reasonable comparatist is advocating the need to undertake 'a comprehensive survey of ... foreign-language jurisdictions', which is rightly described by Stapleton as unmanageable. On the other hand, the remaining choice is not simply the purely random resort to materials which happen to be to hand,[19] which Stapleton seems to envisage as the alternative. Certain jurisdictions may be of obvious relevance in terms of subject matter (for instance, in terms of product liability, Germany, given the developed doctrinal commentary, or France and Austria given the ample case law), or alternatively one may undertake a survey of a series of representative jurisdictions.

Let us take an example from the sphere of product liability. The potential role for comparative law are well-illustrated in the seminal product liability case of *A v National Blood Authority*,[20] which gave rise to a judgment which is probably the most extensive judicial analysis of product liability provisions in any of the Member States. Mr Justice Burton drew

---

[19] It must be said that the resort to commonwealth authorities in the past has not necessary given the impression of any particularly structured methodology!

[20] [2001] 3 All ER 289; [2001] Lloyd's Rep Med 187.

extensively upon comparative law as a core aspect of his decision-making.[21] He thus opined that:

> I have had the great benefit of detailed submissions in writing, and some ten days of exegesis and argument orally in opening and closing by leading counsel, just on the law, including authorities and academic writings from France, Germany, Spain, Portugal, Sweden, Denmark, Belgium, Italy, Holland, Australia and the United States, as well as the United Kingdom and the European Court.

The challenges involved in such an approach, and the measures undertaken to surmount these are described by two of the leading counsel in the case, Michael Brooke QC, who has subsequently been elevated to the bench, and Ian Forrester QC:[22]

> The language of Articles 1, 4, 6 and 7 of the Directive as well as its Recitals was reviewed at length. Of the nine European Union languages, the judge was the only person who attempted the modern Greek texts, and the Finnish text was not consulted. Most attention was given to the English, French, German, Italian and Portuguese texts. The Livenote transcribers of the shorthand record of the hearings included linguists who were able to produce accurately typed German, French, Italian or Spanish in the transcript delivered to the judge and counsel at the end of the day. Emphasis was placed on the fact that the explanatory memoranda adopted by other Member States usually made recitals of certain principles relevant to the construction of the Directive.

> The parties were greatly helped by the fact that the judge having the conduct of the litigation, Mr Justice Burton, was known to speak French comfortably and, as it turned out, other European languages very adequately. It was not necessary to go to the expense of preparing translations of all the material in various foreign languages. This was particularly convenient as to French, the language of most of the *travaux préparatoires*. However, translations of the entirety of two of the judgments of the *BGH* were prepared, as well as translations of the Arnhem district court judgment and Swedish *travaux préparatoires* which accompanied the promulgation in Swedish law of the Directive. The full texts of the academic commentators relied upon were made available and

---

[21] See generally M Brooke and I Forrester, 'The Use of Comparative Law in *A & Others v National Blood Authority*' (with postscript by Nicholas Underhill and afterword by Sir Michael Burton) in D Fairgrieve (ed), *Product Liability in Comparative Perspective* (CUP, Cambridge, 2005).
[22] ibid 28.

translations prepared of sentences or paragraphs which seemed particularly relevant.[23]

As these extracts show, no one is under the illusion of course that all the
challenges of using foreign-law materials have been resolved. Indeed, the
methodological discussions are still very much in play,[24] and much remains
to be determined. However, given the importance of the issues, it cannot be
right to say that comparative law should be relegated to play a periphery
role. European law calls for an integrated comparative approach so as to
ensure uniform application of European norms. The Luxembourg court
itself resorts to such an approach as part of its decision-making process.[25]
The European parliament has called for increased use of databases and electronic information to facilitate this process,[26] with the Wallis Report in
particular pointing to the need for the development of Judgment
Databases.[27]

In the sphere of product liability, it is clear that in order to adopt a
harmonized approach to the Product Liability Directive, as required by the
ECJ, national courts need to be able to access the relevant materials, including the national transposing measures, the decisions of national courts, as
well as relevant commentaries. Little has been done to give effect to this at
an EU level, despite repeated calls from interested parties. Certain private
initiatives have been undertaken,[28] and it would seem that the Commission
has expressed its intention to support the improved availability of national

---

[23] ibid 22.

[24] See eg M Andenas and D Fairgrieve, '"There is a World Elsewhere"—Lord Bingham and
Comparative Law' in M Andenas and D Fairgrieve (eds) *Tom Bingham and the
Transformation of the Law : A Liber Amicorum* (OUP, Oxford, 2009).

[25] See eg Judge Koen Lenaerts who has argued that '"comparative law" plays a central role
in the activities of these [Community] courts.' (K Lenaerts, 'Interlocking legal orders or the
European Union variant of "*E pluribus unum*"' in G Canivet, M Andenas and D Fairgrieve,
*Comparative Law before the Courts*, (BIICL, London, 2004, reprinted 2005) 99). He goes on
to note on page 99 that 'For the Court of Justice and the CFI ..., it is one method amongst
other methods of interpretation of the law (such as literal, exegetic, historical, systematic interpretation) and it thus constitutes a tool for establishing the law.'

[26] See *European Parliament resolution of 9 July 2008 on the role of the national judge in
the European judicial system* (2007/2027(INI)): 'Welcomes the Commission's intention to
support the improved availability of national databases on national court rulings concerning
Community law; considers that these databases should be as complete and user-friendly as
possible.' (para 10).

[27] See *Report on the role of the national judge in the European judicial system*
(2007/2027(INI)), 4 June 2008, page 46.

[28] Including the Product Liability Database developed by the British Institute of
International and Comparative Law: http://www.biicl.org/plf or the Jurifast database available
on the website of the Association of the Councils of State and Supreme Administrative
Jurisdictions of the European Union : http://www.juradmin.eu/en/jurisprudence/jurlfast/juri-
fast_en.php.

databases on national court rulings concerning Community law,[29] but much still needs to be done.

III. SPECIFICITY OF COMMUNITY LAW?

In terms of the broader debate about the rationale of engaging with comparative law, the riposte of sceptics would simply be to say that the European law backdrop provides both the *raison d'être* and the vector for comparative law influences in respect of product liability.

Whilst it is true that the Community law context does indeed provide a specific reason for the use of comparative law, this should not be seen as justifying in some way a ring-fencing of those areas including a Community law element as solely receptive to comparative law influences. In many areas, such a division would be impracticable. As an illustration of this point, take a current example from civil procedure, that of the increasing use of group actions in damages claims (referred to as collective redress in a European context).

The European Commission has taken a great interest in this area, identifying it as a key strand of policy in its Consumer Policy Strategy for 2007–2013,[30] with a variety of concrete initiatives flowing from this, including a Green Paper on *Consumer Collective Redress*.[31] From the perspective of comparative law, it is striking that the reform efforts have been accompanied by a heightened awareness of civil procedure reforms within other legal systems. Comparative law has clearly influenced both the policy debate as to the need for reforms as well as the resultant debate about what amendments should be made to civil procedure, with foreign examples featuring prominently in the discussion about the architecture of reform.[32] Any reform of collective redress would clearly impact upon the core areas of EU law such a consumer law, product liability and competition law. It would by no means be restricted to such spheres, and the trans-

---

[29] See *European Parliament resolution of 9 July 2008 on the role of the national judge in the European judicial system* (2007/2027(INI)) para 10.

[30] In its Consumer Policy Strategy for 2007–2013 (adopted in March 2007), the Commission underlined the importance of consumer redress, indicating that it would consider 'action on collective redress mechanisms for consumers both for infringements of consumer protection rules and for breaches of EU anti-trust rules.' (*EU Consumer Policy Strategy for 2007–2013*, COM(2007) 99 Final, page 11).

[31] COM(2008) 794 final.

[32] For two prominent examples see, in relation to England and Wales, the impressive study undertaken by Rachael Mulheron (*Reform of Collective Redress in England and Wales : A Perspective of Need* (a research paper for the Civil Justice Council, February 2008) and the French working group on the reform of group actions (*Rapport sur l'action de groupe* (16 December 2005) both of which rely heavily upon comparative law analysis.

versal nature of civil procedure makes it likely that any reforms would spill-over into, or be replicated by, other areas of civil law.

Another area where a Community law element has contributed to a more general resort to comparative law is that of public authority liability.

IV. PUBLIC AUTHORITY LIABILITY

Let me now refer to another area of tort law in the context of the use of comparative law, that of public authority liability. Over the past 10 years or so, the law has evolved very rapidly in this area, with a plethora of case law at the highest level. I will say a word by way of introduction about two prominent torts, namely the negligence and misfeasance in public office.

The tort most commonly invoked in claims against public bodies remains the tort of negligence. The traditional position of the case law was some-what restrictive. Over a long period of time, the courts repeatedly invoked a series of public policy concerns as militating against the imposition of duties of care on public authorities in the exercise of statutory functions,[33] including the fear that potential liability would prompt authorities to engage in unduly defensive practices, as well as diverting time and resources in repelling speculative claims.[34] This was followed by a perceptible change in attitude of the courts during the 1990s with regard to the liability of public bodies, with indications of a more liberal approach in cases such as the social welfare case of *Barrett v Enfield LBC*,[35] and the education case of *Phelps v Hillingdon LBC*[36] indicating that the courts were less ready to accept the standard policy concerns invoked to deny public authority liability. Whilst there has been a certain retrenchment in recent decisions,[37] the courts undoubtedly countenance public authority liability in broader circumstances now than a decade ago.

[33] See eg *Hill v Chief Constable of West Yorkshire* [1989] AC 53 (liability of the police); *X (Minors) v Bedfordshire County Council* [1995] 2 AC 633.
[34] cf *Yuen Kun Yeu v Attorney General of Hong Kong* [1988] AC 175, 198.
[35] [2001] 2 AC 550.
[36] [2001] 2 AC 619.
[37] See *JD v East Berkshire Community Health NHS Trust* [2005] UKHL 23, [2005] 2 AC 373 (social welfare); *Chief Constable of Hertfordshire Police v Van Colle, Smith v Chief Constable of Sussex* [2008] UKHL 50 (police); *Trent Strategic Health Authority v Jain* [2009] UKHL 4 HL (dismissal of claim for pure economic loss due to revocation of claimants' nursing home's registration by court order after application of by defendant based on misleading information). Note, however, the strong dissent of Lord Bingham in *Smith v Chief Constable of Sussex*, in which he argued that that English law should adopt the 'liability principle' under which 'if a member of the public (A) furnishes a police officer (B) with apparently credible evidence that a third party whose identity and whereabouts are known presents a specific and imminent threat to his life or physical safety, B owes A a duty to take reasonable steps to assess such threat and, if appropriate, take reasonable steps to prevent it being executed.' (at [44])

Misfeasance in public office is the only tort applying *solely* to public bodies and provides a remedy for those who have suffered loss due to the abuse of power by a public officer acting in bad faith. The inherent element of bad faith in this tort allows claimants to circumvent statutory immunities,[38] and there are other reasons why this tort can prove attractive. First, the notion of proximity, a frequent stumbling-block in regulatory cases,[39] would not seem to play any role in respect of the tort of misfeasance in public office.[40] Secondly, the courts' policy of caution as regards the recovery of pure economic loss in the context of negligence claims has not—as yet—been extended to the tort of misfeasance in public office.[41]

To make out the tort of misfeasance, it must be shown that the defendant is a public officer,[42] and that the claim relates to the defendant's exercise of power as a public officer.[43] The crux of the tort, however, is the mental state of the defendant. The position in this regard is not simple,[44] but essentially boils down to two alternative elements. First, the most stringent arm of this tort is known as targeted malice and requires proof that a public officer has acted with the intention of injuring the claimant.[45] The second limb is less strict and in essence is made out when a public officer acts in the knowledge that he thereby exceeds his powers and that this act would probably injure the claimant.[46]

### V. USING COMPARATIVE LAW IN THIS SPHERE

England and Wales is not the only jurisdiction to have grappled with the thorny issue of State liability. As a large number of comparative studies have shown, the modern revolution in remedies against the state has swept along within it the issue of monetary recompense, posing challenges to many legal systems.[47]

---

[38] Due to the 'bad faith' exception in the relevant statutory provisions.

[39] Particularly where the class of the potential claimants to which a duty of care in negligence would be owed, as in this case, is very broad.

[40] See *Three Rivers DC v Bank of England (No. 3)* [2003] 2 AC 1, 193 and 228 (Lords Steyn and Hutton).

[41] See discussion in M Andenas and D Fairgrieve, 'Misfeasance in Public Office, Governmental Liability and European Influences' (2002) 51 ICLQ 757.

[42] *Three Rivers DC v Bank of England (No. 3)* [2003] 2 AC 1, 191.

[43] ibid.

[44] As illustrated by the two House of Lords decisions on this topic: *Three Rivers DC v Bank of England (No. 3)* [2003] 2 AC 1 (House of Lords' first and second decision).

[45] *Bourgoin SA v MAFF* [1986] QB 716, 776. See also *Dunlop v Woollahra Municipal Council* [1982] AC 158, 172.

[46] *Three Rivers DC v Bank of England (No 3)* [2003] 2 AC 1.

[47] There have been a number of comparative law studies of governmental liability:

Debate has arisen about the relevance of such external sources on the development of domestic law.[48] Traditionally, commonwealth authority has often been the primary reference point for the judiciary given the common vocabulary and concepts deriving from the common law heritage.[49] It remains of course an important source of ideas, subject perhaps to the caveat that the very different sources of law now prevailing in England and Wales means that the law in this area has moved in a very different direction to that of the commonwealth jurisdictions.

In other fora, I have argued in favour of comparative law as a guide for reforms in this area. An initial point to make, whilst an obvious one, is the influence of European law. The recent evolution in State liability has undoubtedly been influenced by European law, both Community and human rights law.[50] There have been a number of decisions of the European Court of Human Rights (ECtHR) on the topic of State liability, with the United Kingdom in a number of cases as respondent. The controversial case of *Osman v UK*[51] is of course emblematic,[52] and has been followed by a steady stream of other decisions, re-aligning the Strasbourg's courts position, such as the more nuanced decision in *Z v UK*[53] (which arose from the House of Lords' decision in *X(minors) v Bedfordshire CC*), as well as the more recent case of *RK and AK v United Kingdom*.[54]

Another avenue for the introduction of European influences, and perhaps even the changing of mindsets, is a claim for damages for breach

---

Markesinis, Auby, Coester-Waltjen and Deakin, *Tortious Liability of Statutory Bodies: A Comparative and Economic Analysis of Five English Cases* (Hart, Oxford, 1999); M Andenas and J Bell and D Fairgrieve (eds), *Tort Liability of Public Authorities in Comparative Perspective* (BIICL, London, 2002); Bell and Bradley, *Governmental Liability: A Comparative Study* (London, 1991); Harlow, *Administrative Liability: A Comparative Study of French and English Law* (Thesis, London, 1979); Street, *Governmental Liability: A Comparative Study* (CUP, Cambridge, 1953).

[48] See the particularly lively debate about the relevance of comparative law in this area between Professor Basil Markesinis and Professor Jane Stapleton: BS Markesinis 'Goethe, Bingham and the Gift of an Open Mind' and J Stapleton, 'Benefits of Comparative Tort Reasoning:Lost in Translation' both chapters in M Andenas and D Fairgrieve, (eds) *Tom Bingham and the Transformation of the Law:A Liber Amicorum* (OUP, Oxford, 2009) and the latter reprinted in this volume (Chapter 8).

[49] See eg reference to commonwealth authority in *Stovin v Wise* [1996] AC 923 (House of Lords) and contrariwise *Sunset Terraces* [2010] NZCA 64 (New Zealand Court of Appeal).

[50] See eg Law Commission, *Monetary Remedies in Public Law:A Discussion Paper* (Law Commission, October 2004) para 2.42.

[51] *Osman v UK* [1999] 1 FLR 193.

[52] The reaction of commentators to the case of *Osman v. UK* was somewhat critical of the ECtHR's reasoning in *Osman* : See eg M Lunney, 'A Tort Lawyer's View of *Osman v United Kingdom*' (1999) 10 KCLJ 238; T. Weir, 'Down Hill—All The Way?' [1999] CLJ 4; C Gearty, 'Unravelling *Osman*' (2000) 64 MLR 159. But compare L Hoyano, 'Policing Flawed Police Investigations: Unravelling the Blanket' (1999) 62 MLR 912.

[53] [2001] 2 FLR 612. See J Wright, *Tort Law and Human Rights* (Hart, Oxford, 2001); J Miles, 'Human rights and Child Protection' [2001] CFLQ 431.

[54] See *RK and AK v United Kingdom*, Application No 38000(1)/05. Judgment 30

of the Convention rights enshrined in the Human Rights Act 1998.[55] In formulating the rules governing damages under the HRA, the English courts must take account of the more liberal attitude found in the jurisprudence of the ECtHR on the notion of just satisfaction,[56] such as monetary awards for a wide variety of non-pecuniary loss, as well as taking a broad approach to the recovery of pure economic loss, and lost chances.[57] In a broader sense, it has been argued that the HRA is challenging orthodox common law philosophy of State liability, with the introduction of a rights-based approach, rather than the traditional focus on defining tortuous wrongs by reference to duties, and not rights.[58]

There are other indirect entry points for foreign legal concepts through the influence of State liability for breach of European Community law,[59] which has both focused attention upon the illegality-fault relationship in English law, and provided an example of alternative ingredients for determining State liability, most notably with the 'sufficient seriousness' test. It is interesting to note that not only have the courts adopted the Community law test for State liability with equanimity, avoiding the protectionist language that has often marked the domestic law, but the application of Community law has also led certain judges to go through remarkable metamorphoses.[60] Notable also is the fact that the Law Commission drew upon

---

September 2008 (arising from one of the appeals in the case of *JD v East Berkshire Community Health NHS Trust* [2005] UKHL 23, [2005] 2 AC 373, referred to above). ECtHR found a breach of art 13 ECHR, but rejected a claim based on art 8.

[55] Section 8 of the Human Rights Act 1998 confers upon the courts a power to award damages as a remedy for the breach of a Convention right. On this, see the leading cases of *R v Secretary of State for the Home Department ex parte Greenfield* [2005] UKHL 14; *Anufrijeva v London Borough of Southwark* [2003] EWCA 1406 (CA).

[56] Section 8(4) HRA. See also Lord Bingham's judgment in *R v Secretary of State for the Home Department ex parte Greenfield* [2005] UKHL 14, at [19].

[57] See eg *Allenet de Ribemont v France* (1995) 20 EHRR 557 (compensation inter alia for loss of business opportunities); *Pine Valley Developments Ltd v Ireland* (1993) 16 EHRR 379 (loss of value in land).

[58] See T Hickman, 'Tort Law, Public Authorities and the Human Rights Act 1998' in D Fairgrieve, M Andenas and J Bell, *Tort Liability of Public Authorities in Comparative Perspective* (BIICL, London, 2002).

[59] See for instance the joint dissenting opinion of Lords Bingham and Steyn in *Cullen v Chief Constable of the Royal Ulster Constabulary* [2003] UKHL 39, where, in the context of a purely domestic law claim based upon breach of statutory duty, reliance was placed by their Lordships upon the Community law standard: 'We would hold that a breach of the right under section 15 is actionable *per se*. But, applying the test enunciated by the European Court of Justice, we would be inclined to hold that proof of a serious breach is required for a damages action: Wyatt and Dashwood's *European Union Law* 4th edn 2000 126–127; Craig, *Administrative Law*, 4th edn, (849).' (at [21])

[60] This is illustrated by Lord Hoffmann's views on State liability. Compare his Lordship's judgment in *Stovin v Wise* [1996] AC 923 with that in *R v Secretary of State for Transport ex p Factortame Ltd (No 5)* [2000] 1 AC 524, in which his Lordship boldly declared that 'I do not think that the United Kingdom ... can say that the losses caused by the legislation should lie where they fell. Justice requires that the wrong should be made good.'

the 'sufficient seriousness' standard in its proposed reform of administrative redress, including a scheme contingent upon the claimant proving 'serious fault' on the part of the public body.[61]

Second, over and beyond these formal sources of European law, it is my belief that there is great value in resort to foreign law, even those which happen to be, as labelled by Professor Stapleton 'comparative foreign-language law.'[62] I have dealt with these issues in detailed format in other publications,[63] but would like to take up one point here in more detail, which is the use of comparative law to evaluate the weight of policy concerns by judges in deciding upon the issue of liability of public authorities.

This is a much contested issue. As we have already seen, the courts have often relied upon a series of public policy concerns as militating against the imposition of duties of care on public authorities. It is my view that comparative law can help us to re-evaluate the assumptions underlying domestic law, and the power of the traditional policy concerns may thereby be questioned.

There is judicial support for such an approach. Indeed, in a case concerning the existence and extent of the immunity of advocates, Lord Steyn opined that '[c]omparative experience may throw some light on the question whether in the public interest such an immunity of advocates is truly necessary.'[64] There is no reason why the traditional public policy concerns in state liability cases should not also be subject to similarity scrutiny.

Professor Stapleton is however less persuaded of the value of such an exercise. In her paper, she casts doubt upon 'whether material from another jurisdiction can be legitimately deployed to *attack* a legal concern enunciated by a domestic judge.'[65] She illustrates this by reference to the policy concern that liability may have a negative effect on the activities of public authorities, and gives three reasons why such an approach is not justifiable.[66] First, she states that it is unlikely there would be any empirical evidence on this topic in a foreign jurisdiction of 'an adequately rigorous and refined form.' Setting aside the fact that this broad statement contains questionable assumptions about the state and quality of research elsewhere,

---

[61] Law Commission, *Administrative Redress:Public Bodies and the Citizen* (Consultation Paper N° 187), see explicit parallels draw with EC law in paras 4.4, and 4.15–4.16.

[62] Stapleton (n 48) 775.

[63] See eg D Fairgrieve, *State Liability in Tort : A Comparative Law Study* (OUP, Oxford, 2003).

[64] *Hall v Simons* [2002] 1 AC 615, 680. Note that there was no exclusion of 'comparative foreign-language law.'!

[65] Stapleton (n 48) 782.

[66] ibid 782–783.

this seems to be less a comment about the appropriateness of comparative law references, and more about the (uncontroversial) issue of the difficulty of assembling reliable empirical research in this area.[67]

Second, Professor Stapleton states that even if such empirical evidence were available, there may be social, economic or cultural reasons why that experience could not be translated to a domestic context. Whilst this may of course be true in some contexts, if applied in a blanket manner, this approach would make it quite simply impossible to undertake comparative law at all, given the inevitably different socio-legal circumstances. Moreover, such a statement would seem to apply equally to commonwealth countries, particularly those on the other side of the world, as it would do to other (foreign language) jurisdictions.[68] And yet, this does not seem to have proved a barrier to comparative evaluation of policy concerns from other commonwealth countries.[69]

Third, Professor Stapleton argues that whilst it may be questionable for a judge merely to assert 'unconfirmed' economic intuitions, 'he can easily cure the problem and put his reasoning on a sound basis by expressing his concern in terms of the *risk* that these socio-economic consequences *might* flow from a finding of liability.'[70] With respect, this seems to constitute more a verbal sleight of hand rather than a true shift in reasoning. If there is no actual data to support economic intuitions, then basing a judicial decision on the fact that there may be a *risk* of it occurring seems problematic. The risk in question may in fact be infinitesimally small. Moreover, there may also be the opposite chance of 'positive' reactions to potential liability. Indeed, might not the potential liability result in an improvement of standards than over-cautious defensive attitudes? Such a possibility may explain the uneven application of this policy concern in similar factual circumstances: it was accepted as an argument against a duty of care of the coastguard rescue service,[71] but rejected in the relation to rescue activities of the fire brigade.[72]

A final point is that made by Peter Cane, who describes the 'overkill' policy argument as suffering from 'two grave defects.'[73] Over and above the

[67] See generally on this Law Commission, *Administrative Redress:Public Bodies and the Citizen* (Consultation Paper N° 187).

[68] As Professor Stapleton recognizes, see (n 1) 161.

[69] Amongst the numerous examples, see Lord Steyn's dicta referred to in *Hall v Simons* [2002] 1 AC 615, 680 (cited above).

[70] Stapleton (n 48) 783.

[71] *Skinner v Secretary of State for Transport: The Times* (3 January 1994).

[72] *Capital & Counties PLC v Hampshire County Council* [1997] QB 1004.

[73] P Cane, *Tort Law and Economic Interests* (2nd edn, OUP, Oxford, 1996) page 241. For an outstanding detailed, appraisal of the 'overkill' argument, see P Cane, 'Consequences in Judicial Reasoning' in J Horder (ed), *Oxford Essays in Jurisprudence* (OUP, Oxford, 2000).

fact that where it is used, the concern is 'based on no (or, at least, no reliable) empirical evidence', (an issue we have already examined above), Cane also makes the telling point that the overkill argument is based upon a misinterpretation of the law by the person who benefits from its operation: '*it depends on attributing to potential defendants an ignorance of the requirements of the law (which does not expect the taking of 'unnecessary precautions'), and more seriously, uses this ignorance as a basis for a legal rule.*'[74]

Indeed, it does seem problematic that untested economic intuition should be used shape the contours of tort law. Those that rely upon the policy concerns in question should be required to provide expert evidence to support their contentions on a standard evidential basis.[75] Otherwise, if we are to rely upon judicial hunches, then it is surely unlikely that a principled development of law will be achieved in this area.

### VI. CONCLUSION

Neglecting the use of comparative tort law will mean that doctrinal commentary will—again—fall behind the courts. The reality is that courts are increasingly using comparative law arguments. In jurisdictions where the form of judgments allows it, judges make open reference to comparative law sources, and in particular to judgments by foreign courts.

Whilst the use of comparative law before the courts of course poses challenges, we should not forget that similar challenges have been addressed, and examined, in similar circumstances. One example is the issue of courts dealing with foreign law, within the sphere of Private International Law, in respect of which[76] distinct procedures and safeguards have been devised so as to accommodate this task. No one however would consider the resultant judicial process regarding the use of foreign-language materials as unmanageable or inappropriate. Similarly, the Privy Council has also developed procedures for dealing with foreign law issues in its role as court of final appeal for the UK overseas territories and Crown dependencies, and for certain Commonwealth countries.[77] Moreover, the use of European, foreign

---

[74] P Cane, *Tort Law and Economic Interests* (2nd edn 1996, OUP, Oxford) 241.

[75] As Buxton LJ held in *Perrett v Collins* [1998] 2 Lloyd's Rep 255, 276–277.

[76] See generally S Geeroms, *Foreign Law in Civil Litigation: A Comparative and Functional Analysis* (OUP, Oxford, 2004).

[77] See eg the case of *Snell v Beadle* [2001] UKPC [5] which examined the Jersey law notion of *déception d'outre moitié de juste prix*, deriving from Roman law, Norman customary and the ius commune, and in respect of which much materials were in Norman French.

language materials is by no means an entirely novel, strange concept. European private law has provided a fertile hunting ground for common lawyers in centuries past when cultural differences were far more marked than they are now.[78]

---

[78] The obvious, outstanding example of this is the pioneering 18th century work of Lord Mansfield on English commercial law, which drew on strong influences of the civil law. Ibbetson notes in *A Historical Introduction to the Law of Obligations* (OUP, Oxford, 1999) that 'in the last decade of the eighteenth century there started to appear a steady stream of treatises on the law of contract ... The model from which judges and writers derived their inspiration was the Traité des obligations of the French jurist Robert-Joseph Pothier first published in 1761 and translated into English in 1806.'

# CHAPTER 10

# *International Cooperation and the Modern Prosecutor*

*Keir Starmer*

I. INTRODUCTION: THE ESTABLISHMENT OF THE CROWN PROSECUTION SERVICE[1]

The origins of the CPS are to be found in the Report of the Royal Commission on Criminal Procedure, established in 1978 and chaired by Sir Cyril Philips. The Commission was set up to look at, inter alia, existing arrangements to investigate and prosecute crime in England and Wales and to make recommendations for improvement. The Report, published in 1981, concluded that it was undesirable for the police to continue both to investigate and to prosecute crime, and that the wide differences in prosecution practice throughout England and Wales required a major change in the prosecution process. What was established as a result was a national Prosecution Service headed by the Director of Public Prosecutions and under the superintendence of the Attorney General. The CPS was created by the Prosecution of Offences Act 1985.

This new service, comprising fewer than 3,500 staff, initially found itself squeezed between the police and the courts. The police continued to be responsible for deciding on the charge and for preparing a case file for the CPS. The role of the prosecutor was to review these cases, largely behind the scenes, and prepare them for barristers to represent the CPS at court at the end of the process.

Times have changed. The rapid pace of development in technology and communications, coupled with ever increasing opportunities to travel and cross borders, has significantly altered the way in which crimes are committed and the way in which criminals act in the 21<sup>st</sup> century. The CPS has changed too. Its role has broadened and deepened.

---

[1] Hereinafter CPS.

Today, modern prosecutors engage with their communities to address the issues that matter to all members of society. For example, in serious and complex cases, prosecutors frequently advise and assist the police and other investigating agencies prior to charge. They even have a power of direction in cases involving the Serious Organised Crime Agency. Prosecutors are also responsible for diverting individuals away from the courts in appropriate cases and for deciding the charge in all but the most routine cases. In addition, prosecutors help to ensure that witnesses are able to give their best evidence by conducting pre-trial witness interviews and applying for special measures and witness anonymity orders. Prosecutors also regularly conduct their own cases as advocates, not just in the magistrates' courts, but in the Crown Court as well. Finally, prosecutors play an active and important role in sentencing and on appeal.

The international role of the prosecutor has also changed. One of the first British extradition treaties was the Jay Treaty of 1794, which covered the surrender of fugitives to and from the United States and the British North American colonies. However, only very few fugitives were ever surrendered under it. Today, in addition to extradition agreements with our European partners, the UK has about 80 extradition arrangements with other countries and there are 34 Mutual Legal Assistance treaties between the UK and non-EU countries. International cooperation—once rare—has become commonplace. Cases with an international dimension are being considered on a daily basis in almost every office in the prosecution service. For example, in the year 2008–2009, the CPS was responsible for 797 cases involving extradition/removal from the UK. This translated into over 3,000 extradition hearings in 2008. That number is set to increase. By the end of April 2009, there had been 1,231 hearings, and it is anticipated that there will have been in excess of 3,500 in 2009.

The case of *Zardad*,[2] the Afghan warlord accused of torture and hostage taking in his own country, shows how increasingly sophisticated means to combat crime can make a real and tangible difference to international criminal justice. In this case, the police investigation involved officers making several trips to Afghanistan under armed escort to track down the warlord's victims. At trial, key evidence from Afghan witnesses—many in fear of their lives—was given in a British court via a video link from the UK embassy in Kabul. Zardad was later convicted and sentenced to 20 years imprisonment.

The case of *Hussain Osman*[3] is also a good example of effective inter-

---

[2] *R v Zardad*, High Court,19 July 2005.
[3] *R v Osman*, Crown Court, 9 July 2007.

national cooperation. Osman was one of the suspected bombers in the failed 21 July 2005 attacks in London. He fled to Rome immediately after the events. Using the procedures available in the European Arrest Warrant, our Liaison Magistrate based in Rome worked closely with the police, prosecutors and judges in both Italy and the UK to ensure that the accused was extradited back to the UK in just 58 days.

The case of *Allen Heard*[4] is also worth mentioning. Our Liaison Magistrate based in Madrid approached the Spanish Authorities for the case to be transferred to the UK. Once the proceedings were transferred, she assisted UK-based police in Madrid in obtaining toxicology samples, video footage and photographs of the crime scene to use as evidence in the prosecution in the UK. The defendant pleaded guilty and was sentenced to life imprisonment.

These examples clearly demonstrate how international cooperation has become part of our core business. However, cooperation now goes far beyond formal cooperation in individual cases. As I have just alluded to, the CPS now has Liaison Magistrates in post in Madrid, Paris, Rome, Washington, and more recently Islamabad. Their primary role is to provide practical assistance to UK prosecutors, police and foreign authorities as regards extradition and mutual legal assistance. Their assistance, however, does not stop there. For example, our Liaison Magistrate based in Pakistan not only assists the UK and Pakistani authorities with mutual legal assistance and extradition requests, but he is also available to provide expertise to Pakistani prosecutors, judges and police officers on criminal justice reform.

The role of the prosecution service in protecting the public is no longer confined to our own borders, and it naturally impacts on international cooperation. Making communities safer is a key aim of the prosecution service's programme of international work, in which we support the rule of law and help to build more effective criminal justice systems in other countries. By providing assistance to countries that export serious and organized crime to the UK, we are reducing the threat to our communities posed by such criminal activity. Recent history has demonstrated the gravity of such threats and the need for a firm, effective and transparent response.

The CPS now directly supports wider UK Government efforts abroad to help local prosecutors, police and judiciary improve their criminal justice system and deal with crimes abroad. The threat to our local communities does not start at our borders. Crime transcends borders, therefore we need to support others in their efforts to tackle international crime at its source and protect more effectively the communities we serve in the UK. Doing so not only helps protect people within the UK, it also

---

[4] *R v Heard*, Crown Court, 13 January 2009.

helps protect communities and improves access to justice for many abroad. We can and must ensure that this is done with due regard to fundamental human rights principles. This work is a natural and important development for the 'modern prosecutor'.

Consequently, the CPS is now working with the UK Government and international colleagues in locations as diverse as Africa, Afghanistan and Jamaica. Wherever we work, the CPS seeks to support the UK Government's contribution to international efforts to ensure a robust, transparent and fair criminal justice system, grounded in due process and the rule of law.

This work is a clear illustration of the developing role of the prosecution service of England and Wales. Our work is no longer limited to ongoing cases as and when they arise. Our remit is much wider than this. We need to work strategically with our partners to improve cooperation and reduce threats and we need to do so in innovative ways. Fundamentally, we play a central role in promoting respect for human rights at home and abroad. This is the mark of a strong, effective and forward-looking prosecuting authority.

It is clear that as the prosecuting service for England and Wales, the CPS has come a long way since 1986. As we now position ourselves for the future, we need to anticipate an even greater reliance on international cooperation. Against that background, the next section will describe the fundamental principles that govern international cooperation from the perspective of the modern prosecutor.

### III. FUNDAMENTAL PRINCIPLES THAT GOVERN INTERNATIONAL COOPERATION AND THE PROSECUTION OF CRIME

Those principles are relatively easy to state. First, there is a clear common interest in ensuring that international cooperation is provided in a fast and efficient manner. Second, any international cooperation must be compatible with international human rights guarantees. The early international instruments dealing with international cooperation were not explicit about this, nor indeed was the European Convention on Human Rights.[5]

However, subsequent instruments have made the position very clear. For example, the European Union Mutual Legal Assistance Convention 2000, which aims to encourage and modernize cooperation between judicial, police and customs authorities within the European Union, expressly provides that mutual assistance must be compatible with the basic principles of the national law in Member States and must be in compliance with

[5] Hereinafter ECHR.

the individual rights and principles of the ECHR.[6] Equally, the Framework Decision on the European Evidence Warrant expressly provides for the application of fundamental rights principles.[7]

Alongside these instruments, the European Court of Human Rights (itself celebrating its 50th anniversary) has interpreted the ECHR as very clearly requiring that international cooperation be compatible with international human rights standards. Under article 2 (the right to life) and article 3 (the prohibition on torture and ill-treatment) of the ECHR there is a rule that no government can remove an individual to another country if there is a real risk that he or she will be killed, tortured or subjected to inhuman treatment on his or her return. That rule was first articulated by the European Court of Human Rights in a case called *Soering v UK*.[8]

In the *Soering* case, the then UK Government wanted to extradite the defendant to Virginia, where he would be at risk of the death penalty after many years on death row. When questioned by the European Court of Human Rights about its decision to deport Mr Soering to Virginia to face the death penalty, the UK Government's case was straight-forward. It argued that whatever the authorities do in Virginia is none of our business. That notion may have had some currency in the 1930s when all eyes were on Germany, but it was famously rejected by the European Court on the basis that:

> It would hardly be compatible with the underlying values of the Convention, that common heritage of political traditions, ideals, freedom and the rule of law ... were a Contracting State knowingly to surrender a fugitive to another State where there were substantial grounds for believing that he would be in danger of being subjected to torture, however heinous the crime allegedly committed.[9]

For 17 years this rule has been applied throughout Europe, and hundreds of individuals have been spared death, torture and ill-treatment as a result.

The third fundamental principle that governs international cooperation from the perspective of the modern prosecutor is a particular application of the second, namely that evidence obtained by torture must never be used in legal proceedings. The prohibition on torture is an absolute prohibition, which does not permit exceptions under any circumstances. This prohibition is not only set out in international human rights instruments, but is also a fundamental constitutional principle of the common law. This was clearly recognised by the House of Lords in the case of *A and others*,[10]

---

[6] See Preamble.     [7] See Recitals 8 and 27, and art 1(3).
[8] (1989) 11 EHRR 439.     [9] At 88.
[10] *A (FC) and others (FC) (Appellants) v Secretary of State for the Home Department (Respondent)* (2004); *A and others (Appellants) (FC) and others v Secretary of State for the Home Department (Respondent) (Conjoined Appeals)* [2005] UKHL 71.

where Lord Bingham rightly described the use of torture to obtain evidence as 'unreliable, unfair, offensive to ordinary standards of humanity and incompatible with the principles which should animate a tribunal seeking to administer justice'.[11] It is the duty of the modern prosecutor to adhere steadfastly to these principles.

It will be clear from the articulation of these principles that I fundamentally disagree with those who, in the wake of tragic events such as 9/11, argued that the so-called war on terrorism and respect for and protection of human rights were incompatible, such that the latter should yield to the former. As President Obama has recognized, that is a false choice. It is by keeping our principles intact that we set ourselves apart from those we seek to prosecute.

That is one of the reasons why I am a keen advocate of the Human Rights Act 1998. The Human Rights Act is a carefully crafted piece of legislation intended to strike the right balance between the judicial protection of human rights and the sovereignty of Parliament and a constitutional document of the first importance. Critics of the Human Rights Act would do well to remember the fact that the rights of victims and witnesses—for example, to transparent and fair investigation and prosecution, and to protection at court—are not derived from the common law so prized by Professor Dicey, but from the ECHR. They have become part of our law largely thanks to the Human Rights Act without which the task of the modern prosecutor would be more, not less, difficult.

The fundamental principles that govern international cooperation from the perspective of the modern prosecutor are thus clear enough. However, just as the British Institute of International and Comparative Law has always committed itself not just to the principles of international and comparative law but also to their practical application, so too modern prosecutors must commit themselves to the practical application of those principles.

That is the reason why the Code for Crown Prosecutors, which sets out how we reach our decisions regarding prosecution, requires the modern prosecutor to act in accordance with the Human Rights Act. Later this year I plan to supplement the Code with a revised Statement of Ethical Principles, which will bind all prosecutors. The Statement of Ethical Principles, which will become a core document, obliges our prosecutors to render mutual legal assistance effectively and efficiently to the prosecution services and investigative agencies of other jurisdictions, in accordance with the law and in a spirit of mutual cooperation. It also recognizes that the central role that prosecutors play in the criminal justice process places obligations on them to act at all times in accordance with the highest ethi-

---

[11] ibid, para 51, 41.

cal standards and in the best interests of justice. In particular, it requires prosecutors to 'decline to use evidence you reasonably believe to have been obtained through unlawful methods which constitute torture, inhuman or degrading treatment'.

### IV. CONCLUSIONS

In conclusion, the role of the 'modern prosecutor' is crucial in ensuring that the fight against crime is achieved without diminishing the fundamental human rights we know to be so important. It is in all of our interests to address the threat of serious crime. That is the only way we can protect all members of society, including the most vulnerable. It is also in all our interests that we do so in a way that protects the rights of all those involved.

Modern prosecutors should welcome, value and promote their role at the heart of this process whenever and wherever they can. Prosecutors have a great opportunity to develop a more effective response to serious crime *and* to promote transparent, consistent and fair decision-making. This is why the CPS now has prosecutors at home and abroad playing a significant role in doing just that.

# CHAPTER 11

# International Cooperation: A Challenge for the Modern International Prosecutor

*Sarah Williams*

## I. INTRODUCTION

The contribution of Mr Starmer to this collection focuses on the role of the domestic prosecutor, operating in an often challenging legal environment. This contribution will address a different aspect of international cooperation; that of cooperation between States and the international and so-called 'internationalized' criminal tribunals. Cooperation in this context includes the ability to secure custody of the accused and to access witnesses, victims and physical evidence. Cooperation may include arrangements with States regarding the enforcement of sentences following conviction, relocation of a defendant after acquittal, support of witness protection programmes, and the provision of medical, technical, legal and other forms of assistance. Within such a system, the modern international prosecutor has the often difficult task of securing cooperation from perhaps reluctant States, individuals or international organizations.

Several international criminal tribunals have been established in recent years. These include the International Criminal Tribunal for the former Yugoslavia (ICTY), the International Criminal Tribunal for Rwanda (ICTR) and the International Criminal Court (ICC). Other tribunals—the so-called 'hybrid' or internationalized tribunals—have also been created as a mechanism to achieve accountability. Four such tribunals are currently operational: the Special Court for Sierra Leone (SCSL); the Extraordinary Chambers in the Courts of Cambodia (ECCC); the War Crimes Chamber in the State Court of Bosnia and Herzegovina (WCC); and the Special Tribunal for Lebanon (STL).[1] The Special Panels for Serious Crimes in Timor Leste (SPSC) suspended operations in May 2005, and the international judges and

---

[1] While the author has argued elsewhere that the Iraqi High Tribunal should also be considered an internationalized criminal tribunal, in the interests of space, this institution will not be considered here. See: S Williams, *Hybrid and Internationalized Criminal Tribunals* (Hart Publishing, forthcoming 2011). This contribution was current as at July 2010.

prosecutors programme (IJPP) operated by the United Nations in Kosovo has been transferred to the European Rule of Law mission.[2] The defining feature of these tribunals is that 'both the institutional apparatus and the applicable law consist of a blend of the international and domestic'.[3]

A common feature is that these international and internationalized tribunals recognize the right of the accused to be present during the trial,[4] although this right may be restricted in varying circumstances.[5] This means that in most situations it will be necessary to secure the custody of the accused before a trial can commence. Yet, international and internationalized criminal tribunals have not been endowed with their own enforcement mechanism. Unlike courts operating strictly within the national system, there is no international police force that international courts can call upon to enforce their orders. For the hybrid and internationalized tribunals, the circumstances in which they may expect the support of national law enforcement authorities may be limited.[6] The tribunals cannot arrest persons on the territory of a State and transfer them to the custody of the court. Nor can the tribunals perform search and seizures on the territory of a State if an individual refuses to cooperate, or compel a reluctant witness to testify. The tribunals depend totally on the cooperation of the relevant national authorities for their actions to be effective. In this sense, the tribunals have been compared to 'a giant without arms and legs'.[7]

There are several aspects of cooperation to consider. First, there is cooperation with the affected State; that is the State(s) in the territory of which the alleged crimes have occurred. Second, there is the arrangement with States that may be called 'specially affected', for example States where a number of nationals are accused of committing atrocities, States neighbouring the territorial State, and States where a number of victims or witnesses are located. Third, the cooperation of other States—so-called third States— may be needed. Finally, it may also be necessary to obtain the cooperation of international or regional organizations, other non-state actors (such as insurgent groups) or individuals. As will be discussed below, each aspect of cooperation may be subject to differing arrangements and legal obligations.

[2] The panels have continued to operate within the EU mission.
[3] L Dickinson, 'The Promise of Hybrid Courts' (2003) 97 AJIL 295, 295.
[4] Art 21(d) ICTY Statute; art 20(d) ICTR Statute; art 63(1) ICC Statute; art 17(d) SCSL Statute; art 35(d) Cambodian Special Law; Article 7 Criminal Procedure Code Bosnia and Herzegovina; art 16(4)(d) STL Statute; sections 6(2) and 5(1) of UNTAET Regulation 2000/30. See also UNMIK Regulation 2000/1, On the Prohibition of Trials in Absentia for Serious Violations of International Humanitarian Law.
[5] See, for example, art 61 ICC Statute; Rule 60, RPE SCSL; arts 247 and 242 Criminal Procedure Code Bosnia and Herzegovina; Rule 81, RPE ECCC.
[6] For example, the SPSC and the IJPP could rely on UN peacekeeping and police forces to a limited extent.
[7] A Cassese, 'On Current Trends Towards Criminal Prosecution and Punishment of Breaches of International Humanitarian Law' (1998) 9 EJIL 2, 13.

As outlined in the next section, there are two models of cooperation available to international criminal tribunals: the vertical and the horizontal models. This paper will consider these models and highlight the difficulties encountered by the tribunals in securing cooperation. It will examine how the particular model of international cooperation applicable to a tribunal is linked to the tribunal's legal basis, in particular its method of establishment and its constituent documents. It will also discuss whether the models have been successful in achieving cooperation and the strengths or weaknesses of the enforcement mechanisms adopted, including the potential role of the Security Council. It concludes that even those tribunals with a 'strong' enforcement mechanism have encountered problems with securing cooperation. As a result, various non-legal factors are influential in obtaining cooperation from reluctant States. Moreover, international criminal justice depends to a large extent on willing cooperation from States, rather than enforced cooperation.

## II. MODELS OF COOPERATION

International law recognizes two models of cooperation: the vertical, or supra-state model, and the traditional, state-based, horizontal model.[8] The vertical model is characterized by an international judicial authority, usually established by a decision of an international institution, vested with sweeping powers as regards both subjects within the State and the State itself. The court has the power to issue binding orders and to enforce its orders, and States may not rely on normal exemptions to extradition, such as national security and the prohibition against the extradition of nationals, to withhold cooperation.[9] The vertical model may be implemented in two ways. First, States may authorize (or may be required to authorize) the organs of an international tribunal to conduct independently all investigative, prosecutorial and judicial activities on its territory, other than those activities, such as the execution of arrest warrants, that require the assistance of the national authorities. Second, although States may be legally obliged to cooperate with a request for assistance, all investigative, prosecutorial and judicial activities on its territory are to be carried out by the relevant national authorities, albeit with the assistance or in the presence of representatives of the international tribunal.

---

[8] *Prosecutor v Blaskic*, Judgment on the Request of the Republic of Croatia for Review of the Decision of Trial Chamber II of 18 July 1997, ICTY, 29 October 1997, para 47 (hereafter *Blaskic*).

[9] *Blaskic*, paras 61–65.

In contrast, the horizontal model is based on consensus, and the sovereign equality of States. This model forms the basis of the 'normal' bilateral and multilateral arrangements for judicial assistance and cooperation between States.[10] Cooperation is generally provided for in a treaty and is based on reciprocity. Specified exceptions to extradition apply and cooperation may be refused on the basis of national security and other agreed grounds. Disputes as to the interpretation of the obligation to cooperate are to be resolved by dispute settlement measures, including diplomatic channels.[11] The State requested to provide assistance performs the required functions (for example, arrest of suspects, interviewing witnesses) using its own authorities and processes, and the results are forwarded to the requesting State.

III. TRIBUNALS ESTABLISHED BY THE SECURITY COUNCIL

This section assesses the cooperation models currently used by the international and internationalized tribunals. It seeks to demonstrate that the model adopted is influenced by the legal basis for the establishment of the tribunal and its constituent instruments. Generally speaking, there are three methods of establishing an international criminal tribunal. First, the tribunal could be established by the Security Council acting under its powers for international peace and security under Chapter VII of the United Nations Charter. Second, the tribunal may be established by a treaty, either multilaterally or bilaterally between two States or between a State and the United Nations (or another international organization). Third, the tribunal may be established pursuant to national law, with significant international involvement and assistance, which may or may not be regulated by an agreement between the State concerned and the United Nations or other international actor. Each of these methods of establishment and the implications for cooperation is discussed.

### A. ICTY and ICTR

The ICTY and the ICTR are examples of tribunals created by the first method of establishment. Both were established by the Security Council acting pursuant to its powers under Chapter VII of the Charter.[12] Member States of the United Nations must comply with the orders of the tribunals

---

[10] As set out in the Annual Report of the Special Tribunal for Lebanon, 2009–2010.

[11] G Sluiter, 'Legal Assistance to the Internationalized Criminal Tribunals' in Romano et al (eds) *Internationalized Criminal Courts and Tribunals: Sierra Leone, East Timor, Kosovo and Cambodia* (OUP, Oxford, 2004) 382.

[12] Resolution 827 (1993) (ICTY) and Resolution 955 (1994) (ICTR).

by virtue of article 25 of the Charter.[13] This general obligation to cooperate is confirmed by the terms of the Council resolution establishing each tribunal[14] and in the statute of each tribunal.[15] This obligation reflects the interest of the international community in the tribunals performing their mandate.[16] Exceptions normally found in bilateral or multilateral agreements on extradition do not apply, and do not justify non-cooperation with requests from the ad hoc tribunals.[17] States of the former Yugoslavia are also under additional obligations to cooperate contained the Dayton Peace Agreement and the Paris Accords. Despite the confusion concerning the status of the former Yugoslavia's membership of the United Nations, no State contested the obligation to cooperate with the ICTY on the basis of non-membership of the United Nations.[18]

The ICTY has issued binding orders directed to States,[19] international organizations,[20] individuals[21] and non-state actors.[22] In terms of enforcement of its orders, the ICTY and the ICTR are 'not vested with any enforcement or sanctionary power *vis-a-vis* States'.[23] However, the President of each tribunal may inform the Security Council, its parent body, of a judicial finding of non-compliance by a State. It is then for the Council to take the action (if any) it considers appropriate.[24] Interestingly, the ICTR has

---

[13] Art 25 provides 'The Members of the United Nations agree to accept and carry out the decisions of the Security Council in accordance with the present Charter'.

[14] Para 4, Resolution 827 and para 2, Resolution 955 state that the Council 'decides that all States shall cooperate fully with the International Tribunal and its organs ...'.

[15] Art 29, ICTY Statute; Art 28, ICTR Statute. This provision states that Member States shall cooperate with the ICTY/ICTR in the investigation and prosecution of crimes and shall comply without undue delay with a request for assistance or an order of the ICTY/ICTR.

[16] *Blaskic*, para 26.

[17] For the non-application of legal impediments to the surrender of the accused, see Rule 58, ICTY RPE. Note that national security is a ground for refusing production of documents in limited circumstances: Rule 54*bis*, ICTY RPE.

[18] Contrast the positions adopted in other fora: *Case Concerning Legality of the Use of Force (Serbia and Montenegro v United Kingdom)*, 15 December 2004, paras 53–77; *Case Concerning the Application of the Convention on the Prevention and Punishment of Genocide (Croatia v Serbia)*, 19 November 2008, paras 43-51.

[19] See, for example, *Blaskic*, para 26; and C Warbrick and D McGoldrick, 'Co-operation with the International Criminal Tribunals' (1996) 45 ICLQ 947.

[20] Order for the Production of Documents by the European Community Monitoring Mission and its Member States, *Kordic and Cerkez*, 4 August 2000, ICTY.

[21] The tribunals may only address binding orders to state officials in very limited circumstances; in most situations, requests are to be addressed to the State and not the official: *Blaskic*, paras 43, 49–51. This does not preclude the tribunal requesting information concerning events witnessed in a personal capacity. See: A Chaumette, 'The ICTY's Power to Subpoena Individuals, to Issue Binding Orders to International Organisations and to Subpoena Their Agents' (2004) 4 International Criminal Law Review 357.

[22] Binding Order to the Republika Sprska for the Production of Documents, *Kristic*, 12 March 1999, ICTY.

[23] *Blaskic*, para 33.

[24] Rule 7*bis*, RPE of both tribunals. The Appeals Chamber confirmed that the power to make a judicial finding of non-cooperation is an inherent power of the tribunals: *Blaskic*, para 33.

recently indicated a more limited view of the scope of the obligation to cooperate with the ad hoc tribunals, finding that the duty to cooperate is restricted to the 'investigation and prosecution' stages, and does not extend to matters such as the relocation of persons acquitted by the tribunals.[25]

The ICTY and the ICTR thus fall within the first model of cooperation, the supra-state model. However, securing the cooperation of States has proved to be one of the greatest challenges of the ad hoc tribunals, particularly for the ICTY in relation to the States of the former Yugoslavia. Non-cooperation has included the failure to arrest and surrender those indicted by the ICTY, non-production of documents and evidence, and interference with witnesses and defence council.

The President of the ICTY has in the past reported non-cooperation to the Security Council in relation to Croatia and Serbia.[26] The Bosnian authorities, particularly those of the Republika Sprska, also largely failed to cooperate with the ICTY, [27] although cooperation has improved in recent years. The Security Council responded to the findings of non-cooperation by issuing statements or further resolutions calling for cooperation and by confirming that States are under a general obligation to cooperate with the ICTY.[28] Despite such calls, securing cooperation has remained difficult.

In addition to the Council resolutions calling for increased cooperation, Member States and regional organizations adopted a number of other measures intended to encourage the Balkan States to cooperate with the ICTY. For example, full cooperation with the ICTY was made a prerequisite of closer association and future membership of the European Union and the North Atlantic Treaty Organisation. The EU, which opened stabilization and association agreement (SAA) negotiations with Serbia in 2005, suspended those negotiations in May 2006 due to Serbia's continued failure to arrest General Mladic and Radovan Karadzic. Negotiations were resumed following the adoption of an action plan by Serbia, which led to the arrest and surrender of Karadzic in July 2008. An increased willingness

---

[25] *In Re Andre Ntagerura*, Appeals Chamber, 18 November 2008, para 15. ICTR.
[26] See generally G McDonald, 'Problems, Obstacles and Achievements of the ICTY' (2004) 2 JICJ 558.
[27] The President reported to the Council the failure of the authorities of the Republika Sprska to arrest and surrender Dragan Nicolic: Letter from President Gabrielle McDonald to the President of Security Council 2 November 1999. The Republika Sprska authorities did not surrender a suspect to the ICTY until January 2005.
[28] For example: Resolution 1160 (1998) (noting the FRY is required to cooperate with ICTY investigations); Resolution 1207 (calling upon the FRY to implement its obligation to cooperate with the ICTY into domestic law and condemning the FRY for its failure to execute outstanding arrest warrants); and Statement of the President of the Security Council, 18 December 2002 (reiterating the Council's support for the ICTY and recalling the mandatory obligation of member states to cooperate with the ICTY).

to cooperate and the surrender of several war criminals to the ICTY enabled the adoption of the SAA in November 2007.[29] Serbia has officially been accepted as a candidate for membership of the EU, but its membership is conditional on continued cooperation with the ICTY.[30] Similarly, discussions with Croatia concerning possible EU membership were suspended in 2005 due to Croatia's failure to surrender Ante Gotovina, but were resumed following improved cooperation.[31] Bosnia's negotiations towards a SAA opened in 2005, but were not finalized until 2007, delayed due to concerns regarding police reform and cooperation with the ICTY. An application for EU membership by Bosnia is expected by the end of 2010, and it is anticipated that membership will be conditional on continued reform and cooperation with the ICTY. NATO has also considered cooperation a prerequisite for greater integration, although the organization invited Serbia, Croatia and Bosnia to join Partnership for Peace in 2006. The United States has linked its bilateral financial assistance to Serbia on satisfactory evidence of cooperation with the ICTY, suspending aid on numerous occasions due to Serb non-cooperation.[32]

Although cooperation from these States has improved,[33] there remain outstanding issues. The tribunal's two outstanding fugitives—General Mladic and Goran Hadzic—are believed to be located in Serbia. There is considerable pressure on Serbia to locate and arrest and surrender both men to the ICTY. Arrest of suspects is not the only issue. Litigation in the *Gotovina* trial has concerned the failure of the Government of Croatia to produce military documents related to Operation Storm.[34] Moreover, a criminal investigation in Croatia has possibly caused interference with the conduct of the defence in this trial and led to a Trial Chamber issuing an order requiring Croatia to suspend the associated national proceedings.[35] In Bosnia, an individual referred from the ICTY to Bosnia and convicted by the War Crimes Chamber is at large, after escaping prison while serving his

---

[29] It appears that there may be a significant delay in the SAA entering into force, as both the Netherlands and Belgium have indicated that they will not sign the agreement (signatures of all EU member states are required).

[30] Accession to the EU is also likely to be affected by developments following the declaration of independence by Kosovo in February 2008.

[31] Gotovina was eventually transferred to the ICTY from Spain in December 2005. His arrest was reportedly enabled by information provided to Spanish authorities by the Croatian intelligence services.

[32] For example, the US suspended bilateral assistance in 2004, 2005 and 2006 due to concerns regarding cooperation with the ICTY.

[33] The most recent report on the Completion Strategy notes that Serbia's responses to requests have been 'timely and accurate', Croatia is 'generally responsive' and Bosnia has 'responded adequately': S/2010/270, 1 June 2010.

[34] See: *Gotovina* et al, Order in Relation to the Prosecution's Application for an Order Pursuant to Rule 54*Bis*, 16 September 2008.

[35] *Gotovina* et al, Decision on Requests for Permanent Restraining Orders Directed to the Republic of Croatia, 12 March 2010 (subject to appeal).

sentence.[36] Moreover, there remain ongoing issues concerning witness protection in these States, particularly in Kosovo.[37] These issues have led to further calls by the Security Council for increased cooperation with the ICTY, in particular for the arrest of the remaining fugitives.[38]

In its early stages, the ICTR encountered fewer difficulties with securing cooperation than the ICTY. Rwanda, although having voted in the Security Council against the creation of the ICTR,[39] cooperated with the ICTR in most respects. It entered into a Memorandum of Understanding relating to cooperation with the ICTR in 1999, restating this commitment in 2010. However, there have been a number of issues regarding cooperation. Visa restrictions imposed by Rwanda effectively prevented witnesses travelling to the ICTR (based in Arusha). This led to a formal report to the Council of non-cooperation in 2002[40] and a statement by the President of the Security Council reiterating Rwanda's obligation to cooperate with the ICTR.[41] Following this, the restrictions were eased and cooperation improved.[42] Rwanda also briefly suspended cooperation with the tribunal in 1999, following an order for release of a suspect.[43] There remain some witness protection issues.[44]

In general, the ICTR has received willing cooperation from other Member States, particularly from African States. Fugitives have been surrendered to the tribunal from over 20 States, while several States have agreed to receive both convicted and acquitted suspects. After receiving requests for surrender, there have been instances where States have considered the process as a traditional request for extradition, engaging in detailed analysis of the reasons for and evidence supporting the request, as well as whether national requirements have been satisfied.[45] While the accused in

---

[36] Radovan Stankovic was transferred to the War Crimes Chamber in 2005 and was subsequently convicted. He escaped from a prison in Foca.

[37] For example, the Appeals Chamber noted the unprecedented atmosphere of serious and widespread witness intimidation that surrounded the trial' of Haradinaj et al: *Haradinaj et al*, Judgment, Appeals Chamber, 21 July 2010, para 34 ICTY.

[38] Resolution 1931, 29 June 2010, para 1.

[39] Statement by the Rwandan Representative to the Security Council on 8 November 1994. Rwanda supported the idea of the tribunal in principle, but objected to certain features in the ICTR's Statute and to the removal of the death penalty as a possible sentencing option.

[40] See Letters from the President of the ICTR to the Council dated 26 July 2002 (S/2002/847) and 8 August 2002 (S/2002/923).

[41] A/PRST/2002/39, 18 December 2002.

[42] See E Mose, 'Main Achievements of the ICTR' (2005) 3 JICJ 920.

[43] *Barayagwiza*, Judgment, Appeals Chamber 3 November 1999. The decision was reversed: 31 March 2000, with some of the judges referring to the difficulties in obtaining cooperation from Rwanda.

[44] See eg, M Othman, 'The "Protection" of Refugee Witnesses by the International Criminal Tribunal for Rwanda' (2003) 14 International Journal of Refugee Law 495.

[45] For discussion of the US decisions, see: M Coombs, '*In Re Surrender of Ntakirutimana*' (2000) 94 AJIL 171; J Godinho, 'The Surrender Agreements between the US and the ICTY and the ICTR: A Critical View' (2003) 1 JICJ 502.

question were ultimately surrendered, this reflected a failure on the part of these national courts to recognize the vertical model of cooperation that is applicable to the ICTR.

Several suspects have been (and remain) located in the Great Lakes region, in particular the Democratic Republic of Congo and Uganda. Those States have largely been unable to cooperate with the ICTR due to the ongoing armed conflict in the region and the resulting difficulty in carrying out arrests, as well as a general lack of capacity on the part of national authorities. There has been recent progress in securing arrests in this region, with increased cooperation between the ICTR and prosecutors and national authorities in these States. Arrests of two suspects were made in Uganda and the DRC in late 2009, undertaken with the support of UN peacekeepers.[46]

Other current issues include the arrest and surrender of the remaining 11 fugitives. In particular, a high-profile suspect, Kabuga, is believed to have been at large in Kenya since 1994, with the knowledge of Kenyan officials. Despite repeated requests from the ICTR, Kenya has failed to arrest Kabuga or to provide evidence that he has departed Kenya. This repeated failure led the President to report Kenya's non-cooperation to the Council in May 2010.[47] The Council responded by reiterating its call upon 'relevant States' to increase their efforts to bring Kabuga, as well as other fugitives, to justice.[48] The ICTR is also still struggling to find States willing to relocate three individuals who have been acquitted, including one individual who has been waiting for relocation for four years.

Rwanda has faced greater challenges than the ICTY in referring some of its cases to national jurisdictions, with several States unable to accept referrals due to jurisdictional limits in national legislation.[49] The ICTR has been unable to refer cases to Rwanda due to concerns regarding compliance of the national court system with international standards of due process and fair trial.[50] The Prosecutor has announced that further requests for referral of the cases of eight of the remaining fugitives to the Rwandan courts will be made in 2010, following reforms to the national legal system and the removal of the death penalty as a sentencing option.[51] Both the ICTR and the ICTY are now also facing an increasing number of requests from national authorities for access to their records and the evidence collected.

[46] See S/2010/259, para 23–24.

[47] See S/2010/259, para 69.

[48] S/Res/1932, para 1.

[49] See, for example, the proceedings concerning Michel Bagaragaza, who was transferred to the Netherlands, only to be returned to the ICTR when a Dutch court it could not exercise jurisdiction in the case. Two cases have been successfully referred to France.

[50] Requests were denied in relation to defendants Hategekimana, Kanyarukiga, Munyakazi and Gatete (all in custody) and Kayishema (at large).

[51] Statement by ICTR Prosecutor to the Security Council, 3 December 2009.

This 'reverse' cooperation is partly a result of the completion strategy and a greater willingness on the part of national authorities to initiate prosecutions for serious crimes.

## B. *Special Tribunal for Lebanon*

The Special Tribunal for Lebanon, which commenced operations in March 2009, is a further example of a tribunal established by the Security Council. It differs from the ICTY and ICTR in that it is a hybrid tribunal, consisting of both national and international personnel and applying a mixture of national and international law. It is the first—and so far the only—international or internationalized criminal tribunal with jurisdiction in respect of terrorism. Unlike most other hybrid or internationalized criminal tribunals (discussed below) the STL operates separately from the domestic legal system.

The STL was originally intended to be established by an international treaty.[52] However, the Government of Lebanon was unable to satisfy the domestic requirements for ratification of the agreement.[53] Instead, the STL was unilaterally established by the Security Council pursuant to Resolution 1757.[54] While it is difficult to assess the intention of the Security Council as to the legal basis of the STL, what is clear is that without Resolution 1757 and the binding powers of the Security Council, the STL would not exist. Thus it must be said the STL cannot be considered a treaty-based institution like the ICC and the SCSL, considered below. Instead, its legal basis must lie in Resolution 1757. Either the Council has bound Lebanon as a party to the STL Agreement (without its consent) or it has bound Lebanon to Resolution 1757 by incorporating its terms into the text of a resolution binding upon Lebanon. Both actions require the Council to be acting pursuant to its powers under Chapter VII of the Charter. Therefore, under either option, the STL should be considered a 'Chapter VII tribunal', similar to the ICTY and the ICTR.[55]

Which cooperation model applies to the STL? In relation to Lebanon, the Government is required to cooperate with the STL, as set out in article 15 of the STL Agreement.[56] This obligation was incorporated into

---

[52] The proposed Agreement for the Special Tribunal for Lebanon, between the United Nations and the Government of Lebanon (STL Agreement).

[53] The STL Agreement required that the domestic requirements for entry into force be complied with: art 19. This required that the agreement be ratified by the Lebanese Parliament, in accordance with art 52 of the Lebanese Constitution. This did not occur.

[54] Resolution 1757, 30 May 2007.

[55] For further discussion, see B Fassbender, 'Reflections on the International Legality of the Special Tribunal for Lebanon' (2007) 5 JICJ 1091; and Williams (n 2).

[56] Art 15 requires the Government to cooperate with all organs of the STL and to allow access to sites, persons and relevant documents. The Government is also required to comply, without undue delay, with requests for assistance from the STL.

Resolution 1757 and binds Lebanon as a decision of the Security Council due to article 25 of the Charter. The RPE of the STL provide that the Prosecutor may issue a request for information and cooperation to the Lebanese authorities.[57] Where cooperation is not forthcoming, the Prosecutor may seek an order from the Chamber or a Pre-Trial Judge to compel the assistance sought. If the Lebanese authorities fail to comply with the order, the President is to make a judicial finding to that effect and report the matter to the Security Council.[58] A finding of non-cooperation may also be reported to the Council where the Lebanese authorities have failed to comply with a request for deferral of proceedings.[59] The STL thus adopts a mainly vertical model of cooperation in relation to requests for assistance from Lebanon. The experience of the United Nations International Independent Investigation Commission, the predecessor to the STL, and the early experience of the STL suggest that cooperation from Lebanon will be forthcoming. This is significant as the cooperation of the Lebanese authorities will be vital for the success of the STL.

Of greater potential concern is the relationship between the STL and Syria, whose officials and intelligence services are suspected of involvement in the assassination of President Hariri. Neither the STL Agreement nor Resolution 1757 imposed an obligation to cooperate with the STL in respect of States other than Lebanon, including Syria. This is in contrast to the resolutions establishing the ICTY and the ICTR, which direct States to cooperate fully with the ad hoc tribunals.[60] It is also in contrast to resolutions adopted by the Council with respect to cooperation with the UNIIIC, which required Member States, and specifically Syria, to cooperate fully.[61] The Secretary-General had suggested that a similar obligation to cooperate be considered for the benefit of the STL, however, the Security Council did not act on this suggestion.[62]

It has been suggested that the existing terrorism conventions to which Lebanon or the requested State are a party may give rise to a duty to cooperate with the STL.[63] However, these treaties contain only an obligation to extradite or to prosecute. As Syria has indicated that it will try any of its nationals implicated in the attacks, it would be entitled to refuse to extradite those individuals. Moreover, these conventions are restricted to cooperation between State parties, and do not extend to cooperation with an

---

[57] Rule 16. The Defence Office may also make such requests.
[58] Rule 20.          [59] Rules 17 and 20.
[60] ibid.
[61] Resolutions 1595 (2005), 1636 (2005) and 1644 (2005). In relation to Syria, see Resolution 1636 (2005), para 11.
[62] Report of the Secretary-General on the establishment of a special tribunal for Lebanon, S/2006/893, para 53.
[63] For discussion see B Swart, 'Cooperation Challenges for the Special Tribunal for Lebanon' (2007) 5 JICJ 1153.

international court.[64] The STL could rely on the Security Council's resolutions regarding terrorism as establishing a duty to cooperate in terrorism matters. This approach is suggested by Resolution 1636, which states that, in the context of cooperation with the UNIIIC, 'Syria's continued lack of cooperation to the inquiry would constitute a serious violation of its obligations under relevant resolutions, including 1373 (2001), 1566 (2004) and 1595 (2005)'.[65] However, again it may be argued that such instruments are directed at cooperation between States and not with an international tribunal.[66] As with the terrorism conventions, these resolutions also contemplate prosecution by the State of nationality as an alternative to extradition. It is possible that the Security Council could adopt further resolutions—as it did regarding the UNIIIC—requiring Syria in particular, or Member States in general, to cooperate with the STL. The Security Council has issued such requests for the arrest and extradition of suspects accused of committing terrorist offences in the past.[67]

As a tribunal that operates outside the domestic legal system, the STL is not able to rely on existing agreements between Lebanon and other States or organizations in such areas as extradition or mutual legal assistance. However, as it possesses separate legal personality,[68] the STL is able to negotiate bilateral agreements with States and international organizations as necessary. This possibility is reflected in the RPE, which recognize that the STL may invite a third State or other entity to provide assistance on the basis of an arrangement or to enter into an agreement with the STL.[69] Where there is such an agreement in place, all requests and issues concerning non-cooperation are to be dealt with according to the terms of the agreement.[70] Where an agreement is not in place, and hence there is no obligation to cooperate with the STL, the tribunal is limited to engaging in 'consultations' with the authorities of the State concerned.[71] The STL has entered into agreements with several international organizations.[72] It also

---

[64] The terrorism conventions contain obligations to extradite or prosecute and to afford assistance in investigations and extradition. Lebanon is not a party to the International Convention for the Suppression of Terrorist Bombings or the International Convention for the Suppression of Terrorist Bombings. However, both Lebanon and Syria are party to the Arab Convention for the Suppression of Terrorism.

[65] Resolution 1636 (2005), para 5.

[66] Swart dismisses this option, arguing that the terrorism resolutions create obligations only between states. However, this is a limited interpretation of the obligations imposed, and does not appear to be shared by the Security Council. See: Swart (n 63) 1159.

[67] Resolutions 748 (1992) and 1192 (1998) (Libya), Resolution 1267 (1999) and 1333 (2000) (Afghanistan) and Resolution 1070 (1996) (Sudan).

[68] Art 7 STL Agreement.                                      [69] Rule 13.

[70] Rule 21(A).                                               [71] Rule 21(B).

[72] See Agreement between the Special Tribunal for Lebanon and the International Committee of the Red Cross, 12 June 2009; Cooperation Agreement Between the Special Tribunal for Lebanon and the International Police Organisation—Interpol, October 2009.

circulated a draft agreement on legal cooperation with third States, inviting States to either enter into a formal agreement to cooperate with the STL, or to adopt the terms of the draft agreement as a framework for cooperation.[73] Despite the STL efforts to encourage States to consider the draft agreement, it appears that, as at July 2010, no States have adopted its terms, either formally or informally.

Thus the STL adopts a horizontal model of cooperation in respect of third States and the cooperation of third States with the STL 'depends on three factors: the ability, the duty and the willingness of those states to provide it'.[74]

IV. TRIBUNALS ESTABLISHED BY TREATY

The second method of establishment of an international or internationalized tribunal is by treaty. There are currently two examples of tribunals relying on this legal basis: the International Criminal Court and the Special Court for Sierra Leone. The ICC was established by a multilateral treaty, the Rome Statute,[75] while the SCSL was established pursuant to a treaty between the United Nations and Sierra Leone.[76] The terms of the relevant treaty are significant, as is the principle that a treaty cannot create obligations for States that are not party to the treaty without their consent.[77]

## A. *International Criminal Court*

The ICC adopts a different model of cooperation to the ICTY and the ICTR, one which is 'a mixture of the "horizontal" and the "vertical"'.[78] The ICC relies on State consent, and lacks the support provided by a mandate from the Security Council acting under Chapter VII of the Charter. As Broomhall comments, the 'cooperation provisions reflect a balance between the needs of an effective Court and the prerogatives of the sovereign States whose support for the Statute will underlie its success'.[79] Article 86 of the Rome Statute imposes a general obligation on States to cooperate

---

[73] Special Tribunal for Lebanon, Annual Report 2009–2010.

[74] Swart (n 63) 1157.

[75] Rome Statute of the International Criminal Court, 1998.

[76] Agreement between the United Nations and the Government of Sierra Leone on the Establishment of the Special Court for Sierra Leone, signed on 16 January 2002.

[77] Arts 34 and 35, Vienna Convention on the Law of Treaties 1969.

[78] B Swart,'International Co-operation and Judicial Assistance: General Problems' in Cassese et al (eds) *The Rome Statute of the International Criminal Court* (OUP, Oxford, 2002), 1590. See also V Oosterveld, M Perry, and J McManus, 'The Co-operation of States with the International Criminal Court' (2001) 25 FILJ 767.

[79] B Broomhall, *International Justice & The International Criminal Court* (OUP, Oxford, 2003) 155.

with the ICC, while article 87 enables the ICC to issue requests for assistance—not orders—to States parties. States parties must also provide the necessary procedures under domestic law that are required for cooperation with the ICC.[80] The framework adopted also 'entails that the Contracting Parties may not assume reciprocal obligations that would infringe upon rights of third States under treaties or general international law'.[81] Where a State party has failed to cooperate, and that failure affects the ability of the ICC to exercise its powers and functions, the ICC may make a judicial finding to that effect and refer the matter to the Assembly of State Parties.[82] Where a non-state party refers a situation to the ICC, it is expected to cooperate with the ICC in accordance with the cooperation provisions applicable to States parties.[83]

The position of States parties that have 'self-referred' cases to the ICC is interesting.[84] States have referred situations to the ICC on three occasions: Democratic Republic of Congo; northern Uganda; and the Central African Republic. The ICC Prosecutor has noted that, having referred these cases to the Court, the referring States are under a special obligation to cooperate with the ICC investigation and trial.[85] However, such States may face significant practical problems in fulfilling this obligation. The DRC has largely been unable to cooperate with the Court's requests due to the ongoing civil war in the country, which has rendered the national authorities unable to cooperate.[86] Support from the UN peacekeeping force operating in the DRC has only recently partly overcome this deficit and, of the four arrest warrants issued, one remains outstanding.[87] The situation in northern Uganda has become entangled with the ongoing peace process between the Government and the Lord's Resistance Army. The execution of arrest warrants has been linked to the possibility of amnesty for rebel leaders willing to cease hostilities as well as to a possible request from the Council for a deferral of prosecution to enable the peace process to continue.[88] From the arrest warrants issued in respect of Uganda, four suspects remain at

---

[80]  Art 88, Rome Statute.

[81]  Swart (n 78) 1594, citing articles 73, 90, 93 and 98 of the Rome Statute.

[82]  Art 87(5). The Assembly of State Parties is required to 'consider ... any question relating to non-cooperation', art 112(2)(f). In the case of referral of a situation to the ICC by the Security Council, the ICC will inform the Security Council: art 87(7).

[83]  Art 12(3) Rome Statute.

[84]  Self-referral is provided for by art 14 of the Rome Statute.

[85]  Remarks by the ICC Prosecutor at the 27th meeting of the Committee of Legal Advisers on Public International Law (CAHDI), Strasburg, 18–19 March 2004.

[86]  R Raston, 'The responsibility to enforce—Connecting justice with unity' in C Stahn and G Sluiter (eds), *The Emerging Practice of the International Criminal Court* (Brill, Leiden, 2009).

[87]  The suspect Bosco Ntaganda remains at large.

[88]  Ratson (n 86).

large.[89] These problems with cooperation have not led to formal findings of non-cooperation, so the ASP has not been seized of these issues. The ASP, in the form of the ASP Bureau, has been considering actively how to ensure cooperation with the Court. It is not yet clear, however, how these obligations would be enforced.

It is also necessary to consider the legal framework that will apply when the Security Council, acting under Chapter VII of the Charter, has referred a situation to the ICC in accordance with article 13(b) of the Rome Statute. To date, the only situation to have been referred is the situation concerning Darfur, Sudan, referred pursuant to Resolution 1593.[90] Sudan is not a party to the Rome Statute and, absent Resolution 1593, would have no obligation to cooperate with the ICC.[91] However, Resolution 1593 imposes an obligation on the Government of Sudan, and all parties to the conflict in Darfur, to 'cooperate fully with and provide any necessary assistance to the Court and the Prosecutor'.[92] Thus Sudan is clearly obliged to cooperate with the ICC. States party to the Rome Statute are also obliged to cooperate in accordance with their commitments under that treaty. However, States that are not party to the Rome Statute and international organizations are not required to cooperate with the ICC, although they may chose to do so on a voluntary basis. This is recognized in Resolution 1593, which urges all States and international organizations to cooperate with the court.[93]

The ICC has issued five arrest warrants in respect of the situation in Darfur. Most controversially, in March 2009, a Pre-Trial Chamber of the ICC authorized the issue of an arrest warrant in respect of President Al-Bashir.[94] While the decision raised important issues of State immunity,[95] it also brought into question whether Sudan was required to comply with the arrest warrant, and the obligations of other States—both parties and non-parties to the Rome Statute—to arrest and surrender President Bashir should he travel outside Sudan. The decision on the issue of the arrest warrant noted Sudan's obligation to execute the arrest warrant and the

---

[89] Following the death of Mr Lukwiya, the proceedings against him have been terminated. Proceedings are continuing against Joseph Kony, Vincent Otti, Okot Odhiambo and Dominic Ongwen, all at large.

[90] Resolution 1593 (2005). See R Cryer, 'Sudan, Resolution 1593, and International Criminal Justice' (2006) 19 LJIL 195.

[91] See G Sluiter, 'Obtaining Cooperation from Sudan—Where is the Law? (2008) 6 JICJ 871.

[92] Para 2, Resolution 1593.

[93] Ibid.

[94] Decision on the Prosecution's Application for a Warrant of Arrest against Omar Hassan Ahmad Al Bashir, ICC-02/05-01/09, 4 March 2009.

[95] See D Akande, 'The Legal Nature of Security Council Referrals to the ICC and its Impact on Al Bashir's Immunities' (2009) 7 JICJ 333; S Williams, and L Sherif, 'The Arrest Warrant for President al Bashir: Immunities of Incumbent Heads of State and the International Criminal Court' (2009) 14 JCSL 71.

obligation of States parties to the Rome Statute to arrest and surrender President Bashir if present in their territory. It also recognized that States not party to the Rome Statute and international organizations were not required to assist, but requested them to do so. A recent decision of the Pre-Trial Chamber has included charges of genocide and authorized an additional warrant for arrest in respect of genocide charges.[96] This may enable arguments to be made that States that are also party to the Genocide Convention may have additional obligations to cooperate with the arrest warrant request.[97]

There has been continued difficulty in securing cooperation from Sudan, with the Prosecutor reporting that there has been no real cooperation with the Court from Sudan since 2007.[98] While three suspects have recently voluntarily surrendered to the ICC,[99] all were members of rebel groups, and it is unlikely that the ICC will secure the cooperation of Sudan in the foreseeable future in relation to the three outstanding arrest warrants.[100] The Government of Sudan has indicated that it will not surrender its nationals, least of all its President, to the ICC. The arrest warrant in respect of President Bashir remain outstanding, although there is evidence that the warrant has affected President Bashir's ability to travel. However, in July 2010, authorities in Chad announced that they would not move to arrest President Bashir during a trip to Chad.[101] This was significant, as it is the first time that President Bashir has travelled to a State that is a party to the Rome Statute.

Article 87 of the Rome Statute provides that, in relation to a situation referred to the ICC by the Council, where there has been non-cooperation, the ICC may render a finding of non-cooperation. The Chamber must notify this decision to the ICC President, who must then transmit the finding to the Council and, if so decided, to the Assembly of State Parties. This mechanism parallels the arrangements in place for the ICTY and ICTR, and equates to the supra-state model. In April 2010, the Prosecutor filed a request for a finding on the non-cooperation of Sudan pursuant to article 87 in respect of two of the outstanding arrest warrants (but not the warrant for President Bashir).[102] Pre-Trial Chamber 1 issued a formal finding of

---

[96] *Prosecutor v Al Bashir*, Second Decision on Prosecution's Application for a Warrant of Arrest, 12 July 2010.

[97] G Sluiter, 'Using the Genocide Convention to Strengthen Cooperation with the ICC in the *Al Bashir* Case' (2010) 8 JICJ 365. This argument is based on art VI of the Genocide Convention.

[98] Eleventh report to the Security Council, 17 June 2010.

[99] Mr Garda (surrendered voluntarily in May 2009; charges not confirmed); Mr Nourain (surrendered voluntarily in June 2010); and Mr Jamus (surrendered voluntarily in June 2010).

[100] The outstanding arrest warrants relate to President Al-Bashir, Ahmad Harun and Ali Kushayb.

[101] 'No Question of Chad arresting Sudan President Bashir' *BBC News* (22 July 2010).

[102] *Prosecutor v Harun and Ali Kushayb*, Prosecution Request for a finding on the non-cooperation of the Government of the Sudan' 19 April 2010.

non-cooperation in May 2010, noting that 'the Security Council is vested with the power to address and take any action in respect of Sudan's failure to cooperate with the Court'.[103] The decision was forwarded to the United Nations and to the Security Council in June 2010,[104] but the Council is yet to consider the issue.

## B. SCSL

As noted above, the SCSL was established by an agreement between the United Nations and the Government of Sierra Leone. While the Security Council was involved in the creation of the SCSL,[105] the relevant resolution, Resolution 1315,[106] did not establish the tribunal but merely requested the Secretary-General to negotiate the agreement. The SCSL Agreement states that it is it that forms the legal basis for the tribunal.[107] The SCSL has confirmed its status as a treaty-based institution,[108] as has the Council.[109]

The SCSL is a hybrid tribunal in that it applies a mix of national and international law, and utilizes both national and international personnel. Like the STL, the SCSL is an entity separate to the domestic legal system, and cannot rely directly upon the national authorities of Sierra Leone. Instead, the SCSL Agreement imposes an obligation on the Government of Sierra Leone to cooperate with the court.[110] This includes requests for the arrest, detention and transfer to the SCSL of persons within the territory of Sierra Leone.[111] This obligation was incorporated into national law by the Special Court Agreement (2002) Ratification Act, which also provides the mechanisms for such cooperation. The SCSL RPE also regulate cooperation with the national authorities.[112] There are two mechanisms for obtaining cooperation.[113] First, the SCSL may issue a request to the Attorney-General of Sierra Leone, who is then obliged to ensure the request is satisfied.

---

[103] *Prosecutor v Harun and Ali Kushayb*, Decision informing the United Nations Security Council about the lack of cooperation by the Republic of Sudan, 25 May 2010.

[104] See S/2010/265.

[105] For background to the SCSL, see S Beresford and AS Muller, 'The Special Court for Sierra Leone: An Initial Comment' (2001) 14 LJIL 635; and R Cryer, 'A Special Court for Sierra Leone?' (2001) 50 ICLQ 435.

[106] Resolution 1315 (2000), 14 August 2000.

[107] Art 1. SCSL Agreement.

[108] For example, see discussion in *Prosecutor v Fofana*, Decision on Preliminary Motion on Lack of Jurisdiction Materiae: Illegal Delegation of Powers by the United Nations, Appeals Chamber, 25 May 2004.

[109] See Resolution 1688 (2006), preambular para 2.

[110] Art 17, SCSL Agreement.

[111] Art 17(2), SCSL Agreement.

[112] Rule 8(A), SCSL RPE.

[113] See discussion of the provisions of the Ratification Act in Sluiter (n 11).

Second, the SCSL may issue an order that has a direct binding effect in domestic law. It is the ability to issue such orders binding as a matter of national law that distinguishes the SCSL from the ICTY and the ICTR. In the event of non-cooperation, there is no enforcement mechanism, although the President, after a judicial finding of non-cooperation, may 'take appropriate action'.[114] This may include drawing the matter to the attention of the relevant authority in Sierra Leone, such as the Attorney-General, or notifying the Secretary-General. Any dispute between the Government of Sierra Leone and the United Nations as to cooperation is to be resolved by negotiation between the parties.[115]

In relation to third States, the SCSL Agreement cannot create obligations for non-parties. As a general matter, States are not under an obligation to cooperate with the SCSL.[116] However, the SCSL has separate international legal personality and has been able to negotiate bilateral arrangements with States and international obligations as and when required.[117] It need not rely on the Government of Sierra Leone to issue requests to third States on its behalf. Yet, as a court outside the domestic legal system, it cannot rely on the existing treaty arrangements of Sierra Leone. While the Security Council did not establish the SCSL, it maintains an interest in its activities and has, in resolutions subsequent to Resolution 1315, called upon and urged States to cooperate with the SCSL.[118] Such requests are not binding, but may encourage States to cooperate. The Council has not acted upon suggestions that the Council should 'endow' the SCSL with 'Chapter VII powers' and the ability to bind third States. The Security Council has issued binding resolutions regarding the SCSL on only one occasion, in relation to the transfer of the former President of Liberia, Charles Taylor, to The Hague for trial.[119] The Court had been unable to secure custody of Taylor for several years, with Taylor remaining in exile in Nigeria, which was not under any obligation to surrender Taylor to the SCSL. The surrender of Taylor to the SCSL was only obtained with the support of the Council, and only when it became apparent that his continued presence in Africa was destabilizing the region. Even then, a Chapter VII resolution was only

---

[114] Rule 8(B), SCSL RPE.

[115] Art 20, SCSL Agreement.

[116] This was confirmed in *Prosecutor v Taylor*, Decision on Immunity from Jurisdiction, Appeals Chamber, 31 May 2004, where the Court held that Ghana did not have an obligation to cooperate with the SCSL in relation to the arrest warrant in respect of Charles Taylor.

[117] Art 11, SCSL Agreement. Rules 8(C) and (D) of the SCSL RPE enable the SCSL to request assistance from third states on the basis of an ad hoc arrangement, a bilateral agreement with the State or any other basis.

[118] Resolution 1508 (2003), para 6, and Resolution 1537 (2004), para 9.

[119] Resolution 1688 (2006), paras 7 and 8, deciding that the Netherlands shall not exercise its jurisdiction in relation to Taylor while he is in the custody of the SCSL and that the Netherlands 'shall facilitate the implementation of the decision of the Special Court to conduct the trial of former President Taylor in the Netherlands'.

considered due to requests from the host State, the Netherlands, which required such a resolution for domestic legal reasons, and as the Council had to lift travel restrictions it had imposed in relation to Taylor to allow his transfer to The Hague.

The legal basis of the SCSL has posed a legal obstacle to some States otherwise willing to assist the tribunal, where domestic legislation requires either a treaty basis for extradition or assistance, or a binding decision of the Security Council. For example, the United Kingdom agreed to accept Taylor in the event that he was convicted. Yet the relevant legal basis for such cooperation was not in place[120] and took some time to enact.[121] While the delay was not significant in relation to enforcement of a possible sentence of an accused whose trial had not concluded, it may have been if the request had been for the arrest and surrender of an accused. Similar issues may also arise where cooperation is sought from a State that is not a party to the Rome Statute or has not yet introduced appropriate implementing legislation. The uncertain legal basis of the Special Tribunal for Lebanon may also hinder States seeking to offer cooperation to the tribunal.

### V. INTERNATIONALIZED TRIBUNALS

The third type of tribunal is the so-called internationalized tribunals. While there are some commonalities between these tribunals, each of the international and internationalized tribunals have been established in a different context and have varying features, including the relationship between the tribunal and States, in particular the territorial State. These courts are a mix of the domestic and the international, although the nature and extent of international involvement varies. They operate effectively as national institutions, albeit often with a significant degree of international involvement. Established by national law, these tribunals adopt a mainly horizontal cooperation model, using existing bilateral and multilateral arrangements. Have they fared any better in securing cooperation?

---

[120] The legal basis for cooperation with the ICTY and the ICTR is the United Nations Act 1946, supplemented by the United Nations (International Tribunals) (Former Yugoslavia) Order 1996 and the United Nations (International Tribunals) (Rwanda) Order 1996. The United Nations Act allows the United Kingdom to implement resolutions of the Council under art 41 of the Charter only. The International Criminal Court Act 2001 was limited to cooperation with that institution.

[121] The International Tribunals (Sierra Leone) Act 2007 entered into force on 18 June 2007. See also the International Tribunals (Sierra Leone) (Application of Provisions) Order 2007, which permits the implementation of the sentence enforcement agreement entered into between the United Kingdom and the SCSL.

---

The ECCC is established by a national law, the Special Law.[122] It is supported by an agreement between the Government of Cambodia and the United Nations, which assists in the establishment and operation of the ECCC.[123] However, unlike the SCSL Agreement, this agreement does not establish the ECCC, thus it is not a treaty-based institution.[124] In terms of cooperation with Cambodia, the ECCC Agreement requires the Government to cooperate with the ECCC.[125] This obligation, which was based on the cooperation provisions in the Statutes of the ICTY and ICTR, 'appears to result in the imposition of far-reaching duties on the Cambodian authorities vis-à-vis the Extraordinary Chambers'.[126] It also has direct effect in Cambodian law.[127] Failure to cooperate could result in the United Nations claiming that the ECCC Agreement has been violated, although as there is no third party dispute resolution mechanism the only sanction appears to be the withdrawal of United Nations funding and assistance.[128] The inclusion of a specific provision on cooperation also results in the ECCC having a separate procedure for relying on the national authorities than national courts. This is not necessarily a negative result, as the ECCC may still rely directly on the national authorities, but have a separate means of ensuring that requests for assistance are met.[129] The ECCC thus adopts a fairly robust means of obtaining cooperation from Cambodia.

The position is less clear in relation to cooperation from other States. The ECCC Agreement has not created obligations for States other than Cambodia, consistent with the principle that a treaty cannot create obligations for third States. The ECCC lacks separate legal personality and cannot negotiate agreements with third States to secure their cooperation. Instead, it is dependent on the existing bilateral agreements to which Cambodia is a party and on national authorities to issue the necessary requests for assistance.[130] However, this may not prove to be a major issue, as to date all of the accused have been located within the territory of Cambodia and have been arrested and transferred to the ECCC by the Cambodian authorities.

[122] Law on the Establishment of Extraordinary Chambers in the Courts of Cambodia for the prosecution of crimes committed during the period of Democratic Kampuchea, adopted 2001. For background to the ECCC, see S Williams, 'The Cambodian Extraordinary Chambers—A Dangerous Precedent for International Justice?' (2004) 53 ICLQ 227; S Linton, 'New Approaches to international justice in Cambodia and East Timor' (2002) 84 IRRC 93.

[123] Agreement between the United Nations and the Royal Government of Cambodia concerning the prosecution under Cambodian law of crimes committed during the period of Democratic Kampuchea, dated 6 June 2003.

[124] Art 2 of the Special Law provides that the ECCC is established by the Special Law.

[125] Art 25, ECCC Agreement.     [126] Sluiter (n 11) 398.

[127] Art 31, ECCC Agreement.     [128] Art 28, ECCC Agreement.

[129] Sluiter (n 11) 398.

[130] Note Sluiter's view that while the ECCC Agreement would extend to the Government of Cambodia issuing requests to other states, it would not require the Government to negotiate new bilateral agreements (n 11) 403–404.

The SPSC and the IJPP were created in Timor Leste and Kosovo by the international administrations established by the Council under Chapter VII of the Charter, UNTAET and UNMIK respectively. These missions exercised delegated Chapter VII powers and were responsible for all legislative and executive functions in the territory during the period of international administration.[131] However, both UNTAET and UNMIK acted as a national authority when establishing and operating the SPSC and the IJPP[132] and the panels were not established by the Council acting under Chapter VII.[133] The SPSC and IJPP are therefore best viewed as internationalized tribunals operating under national legal provisions rather than Chapter VII institutions established by the Council.

As the missions were the relevant government authorities within the territory for much of the mission, cooperation issues arose mainly in respect of third States. In relation to individuals located outside Kosovo or Timor Leste, a horizontal model was applied. The obligation upon Member States to assist UNTAET and UNMIK in the performance of their mandate[134] did not extend to a general obligation to cooperate with the SPSC and the IJPP, including extradition and the provision of legal assistance.[135] In Timor Leste, UNTAET entered into a Memorandum of Understanding with Indonesia to govern cooperation on criminal matters.[136] As Sluiter notes, the memorandum was 'not based on the assumption of a full and unconditional obligation incumbent upon Indonesia to provide UNTAET with all necessary assistance'.[137] Ultimately, cooperation with UNTAET was extremely limited, with Indonesia refusing to extradite any suspect for trial.[138] Following independence, Timor Leste entered into negotiations with Indonesia in a number of areas, including cooperation in legal and

---

[131] Resolution 1244 (1999) and Resolution 1272 (1999).

[132] For discussion of the dual nature of the functions of such missions, see R Wilde, 'The Complex Role of the Legal Adviser when International Organizations Administer Territory' (2001) ASIL Proceedings 251.

[133] This argument is developed further in Williams (n 2).

[134] In Resolution 1244 (1999), the Security Council demanded that 'all states in the region cooperate fully in the implementation of all aspects of this resolution', para 18. Resolution 1272 (1999) states that the Security Council 'Stresses the importance of cooperation between Indonesia, Portugal and UNTAET in the implementation of this resolution', para 7.

[135] See Sluiter (n 11) 385–386, noting that it was possible that the Security Council had intended a general obligation to cooperate with the SPSC and the IJPP.

[136] Memorandum of Understanding between the Republic of Indonesia and the United Nations Transitional Administration in East Timor Regarding Co-operation in Legal, Judicial and Human Rights Related Matters, 5 April 2000.

[137] Sluiter (n 11) 391. For detailed discussion of the relevant provisions of the MoU, see 391–393.

[138] Indonesia relied upon the provisions of the MoU itself, which allow for refusal of extradition and cooperation in a number of situations, and on the provision in its domestic law prohibiting the extradition of nationals. By the conclusion of the SPSC's activities, a total of 339 indicted people remained beyond the jurisdiction of the SPSC, many believed to be at large in Indonesia: JSMP, Overview of the Justice Sector, 2005, 30–31.

judicial measures, but the two States are yet to enter into a general bilateral agreement on this topic. UNTAET also exercised its capacity to enter into international agreements and to negotiate agreements with third States if required for judicial cooperation. This process continued after independence.

The position of UNMIK concerning the cooperation of Serbian authorities was more problematic, as until independence, Kosovo remained legally part of Serbia and requests for extradition and judicial assistance technically came from the same jurisdiction.[139] However, both Serbia and UNMIK appear to have treated the court systems as distinct, and adopted a horizontal model of cooperation, entering into arrangements for extradition and legal assistance in criminal matters on an ad hoc basis.[140] The ambiguous legal status of Kosovo during the transitional administration also impacted upon the ability of the IJPP to secure cooperation from other States. UNMIK could request assistance on behalf of the IJPP, but there would be no legal obligation for the requested State to comply. Similarly, without the support of the Serb authorities, the IJPP was unable to rely upon the treaties to which Serbia was a party. Requests to extradite suspects to and from Kosovo were made on an ad hoc basis between UNMIK and the State concerned.[141] UNMIK did negotiate a number of memoranda with States such as Albania, the Federal Yugoslav Republic of Macedonia and Montenegro providing for cooperation in criminal justice matters and bilateral agreements with States to enable extradition.

The WCC was established by the national authorities, in cooperation with the Office of the High Representative in Bosnia, as part of the completion strategy of the ICTY. It focuses on trials referred to it by the ICTY, as well as other significant or sensitive cases arising from the conflict in Bosnia. As a national court, it also adopts a horizontal model of cooperation in relation to third States, including the States of the former Yugoslavia. The WCC relies on requests for extradition and legal assistance

---

[139] Sluiter (n 11) 390.

[140] For example, in 2004, the War Crimes Prosecutor of Serbia entered into an agreement with UNMIK's Prosecutors' Office which enabled the investigation of witnesses located in Kosovo by Serb authorities, with reciprocal access for witnesses located in Serbia. UNMIK has issued requests for extradition to authorities in Serbia. However, both UNMIK and the Serbian authorities maintained that Serbia was not a foreign jurisdiction. See 'UNMIK Requests Serbia to Extradite Serb Leader from Northern Kosovo' *Yugoslav Daily Survey* (22 August 2002).

[141] UNMIK has received requests for extradition from the national authorities of the former Yugoslav Republic of Macedonia and Rwanda. UNMIK has issued requests on behalf of the IJPP for extradition to the national authorities of Austria, which refused extradition. In light of concerns that the law in Kosovo did not provide an acceptable basis for the extradition of suspects, UNMIK introduced UNMIK Regulation 2003/34, Amending the Applicable Law on Procedures for the Transfer of Residents of Kosovo to Foreign Jurisdictions. The Regulation depended on a bilateral agreement between UNMIK and the requesting country being in place prior to transfer.

made by the relevant national authorities either on an ad hoc basis or in accordance with treaties for extradition and mutual legal assistance. Cooperation with other States in the region has improved following ratification by Bosnia of the European Convention on Extradition.[142] Cooperation from the authorities of the Republika Sprska also appears to have improved, and any difficulties in obtaining cooperation with the constituent entities have been considered a matter of domestic law. The WCC also enjoys a relationship with the ICTY and has received several cases referred to it by the ICTY, with the accused transferred from the ICTY to the Bosnian authorities, and then to the WCC. Rule 11*bis* of the ICTY RPE also contemplates the transfer of an indictment to the WCC; that is where the accused is not yet in custody, the ICTY can determine that once the accused is arrested, the arresting State must surrender the accused to the WCC. As Bohlander notes, this potentially allows the WCC to bypass bilateral or multilateral agreements, and to call on the custodial State to transfer the accused even in the absence of a treaty arrangement.[143]

## VI. CONCLUSIONS

As outlined in section II, there are two cooperation models currently applicable to international and internationalized criminal tribunals: the vertical or supra-state model and the horizontal or sovereignty model. Only those tribunals established by the Security Council, the ICTY and the ICTR, rely on the vertical model, although the STL adopts a similar model in relation to the obligation of Lebanon to cooperate with the tribunal. The ICC adopts a mixed vertical and horizontal model, which may approximate a vertical model when considering situations referred to the ICC by the Security Council. Despite its suggested authority and the absence of exceptions, the tribunals adopting the vertical model have still faced significant challenges in securing cooperation from reluctant States. The vertical model depends to a large extent on the enforcement mechanism; in all cases the ability of the tribunal to refer a finding of non-cooperation to the Security Council. There is a marked reluctance to characterize a State as 'non-cooperative'. Even when this step is taken, the Council has to date not taken any steps to enforce an obligation to cooperate with an international tribunal. Instead, it has simply reiterated calls for cooperation or restated that the

---

[142] CETS No. 024. Bosnia ratified on 25 April 2005, with the treaty entering into force for Bosnia on 24 July 2005. Croatia, Serbia, the FRY Macedonia and Montenegro are also parties to this treaty. All are also parties to the European Convention on Mutual Assistance in Criminal Matters, CETS No. 030.

[143] M Bohlander, 'Referring an Indictment from the ICTY and ICTR to another Court—Rule 11*bis* and the Consequences for the Law of Extradition' (2006) 55 ICLQ 219.

State in question is obliged to cooperate. Such resolutions have had limited effect and as soon as any improvement in cooperation is reported, the need for a response is reduced.

However, it is unclear as to what the Council is expected to do in the face of continued non-cooperation. Apart from diplomatic pressure, the most likely options are those under article 41 of the Charter, including embargoes and sanctions against a State or individuals. It has been suggested that the Council could authorize States to apprehend suspects by force. This is perhaps more acceptable when the United Nations or another international or regional organization has a peacekeeping mission in the affected territory, and its mandate could be expanded to include arresting suspects. However, such missions often operate in a complex political context, and may depend on the cooperation—or non-interference—of the national authorities. Instructing such missions to arrest suspects, who may have official positions or significant influence in the State, may undermine the overall objectives of the mission. It is unlikely that the Council would authorize the use of force, outside the context of an existing mandate, to detain suspects, particularly where this would involve action against the territory of a third State.

Aside from the ICTY, ICTR and ICC the other tribunals considered—even those established by the Security Council—have adopted a horizontal cooperation model in relation to third States, and are to an extent therefore dependent on the cooperation of such States to fulfil their mandate. This will not be a significant issue where the majority of accused are located within the territory of the affected State, as in Cambodia. However, it may undermine the effectiveness of the tribunal where the majority of the accused, particularly the senior level accused, are located outside the territory of the affected State, as occurred in Timor Leste. In such circumstances, impunity will only be avoided if the State in which the accused are present is prepared to cooperate by transferring the accused to the internationalized tribunal or is willing and able to try the accused before its own courts, or where there is an international tribunal able to exercise jurisdiction in respect of the accused. The horizontal model is particularly challenging when many suspects are located outside of the territorial State, no real arrangements for extradition and mutual assistance are in place, and the political context is such that the requested State is unlikely to cooperate voluntarily (eg Indonesia). The horizontal model allows no method of forcing a State to comply, even as ineffective as that has proved to be. It is thus vital to consider the potential location of the accused when designing a hybrid or internationalized criminal tribunal.

Perhaps the most important issue is to secure the cooperation of the affected State in which the majority of the accused would normally be located. This may be done in an informal, non-binding manner, by engaging the national authorities in the design and establishment of the tribunal, and allowing normal domestic provisions to govern the assistance provided to the tribunal. This appears to have been the model adopted in Bosnia. This may not be an issue when the United Nations retains control of the territory and the national authorities as in Timor Leste and Kosovo. Alternatively, the obligation may be formalized as a treaty obligation by inclusion in the agreement establishing the tribunal (SCSL) or governing the terms under which assistance is to be provided (ECCC). The final option is to issue a binding order to cooperate addressed to the affected State in a Security Council resolution (STL). Failure of States to comply is often blamed on the lack of a binding Chapter VII mandate for the tribunal. However, the problems of the ICTY and—to a lesser extent—the ICTR in securing cooperation are well-known. Even where such obligations to cooperate are created, they may not be enforced, either because the only option is to withdraw funding, or because there is insufficient political will to take action against the affected State, or limited enforcement options.

Where obtaining custody of the accused looks unlikely, one possible option is to allow trials in absentia in a wider range of circumstances, as has been done in relation to the STL,[144] or adopting a procedure similar to Rule 61 of the ICTY RPE. Another approach is that adopted by the SPSC in its later stages, issuing indictments containing a large number of defendants, so that while there is no prospect of obtaining custody of the defendants, the evidence is available as a matter of historical record. One other option is to apply diplomatic or financial pressure, as was done in relation to cooperation with the ICTY by the Balkan States. While this appears to have been largely successful, it depends on the requested State needing something from the international community.

Obtaining custody of the accused and access to evidence will continue to prove a challenge for the modern international prosecutor and the tribunals in which she or he serves. It is an issue that requires attention when designing a tribunal's legal structure and constituent instruments. It also requires an appreciation of the political context. Activities may require the support of the wider international community, including the Council, regional organizations such as Nato and the EU, as well as States committed to the rule of law and the removal of impunity for serious crimes. Ultimately, the success of international and internationalized criminal tribunals will depend on the voluntary and good faith cooperation of States. The role of the international prosecutor is to create an environment in which this cooperation is forthcoming.

---

[144] Art 22 of the STL Statute is the most expansive provision, as, unlike the other tribunals, the accused is not required to have been present at any stage of the proceedings. For further discussion, see P Gaeta, 'To be (Present) or Not to Be (Present): Trials in Absentia before the Special Tribunal for Lebanon' (2007) 5 JICJ 1165 and C Aptel, 'Some Innovations in the Statute of the Special Tribunal for Lebanon' (2007) 5 JICJ 1107.

# Index

*[all references are to page number]*

**Accessibility**
European courts, and, 56
principles of the rule of law,
and, 28
**Administrative procedures**
principles of the rule of law,
and, 28
*Amici curiae*
investment protection, and,
127–128
**Appeals**
investment protection, and
changes to the system,
144–145
development of system,
129–130
**Application of law**
European courts, and, 56–57
principles of the rule of law,
and, 28
**Arbitration rules**
investment protection, and,
127
**ASEAN Comprehensive Investment
Agreement**
investment protection, and, 146
**Australia**
comparative tort reasoning, and,
177–183

**BIICL Report (1996)**
generally, 78–79
redistribution of jurisdiction to
national courts, 82
refusal of jurisdiction by
Community courts, 82

regional Community courts,
80–81
specialized courts or tribunals,
81–82
two-tier ECJ, 81
US court system, 79–806
**Bilateral investment treaties (BIT)**
business, and, 36–37
comparative tort reasoning, and,
177
investment protection, and
development of system,
121–126
generally, 141–142
**Bretton Woods conference (1944)**
international law, and, 5
**Brussels Protocol (1955)**
carriage of goods by sea, and, 5
**Business**
human rights, and
conclusions, 46–47
counter-terrorism sanctions,
45–46
health products, 41–43
introduction, 39–41
labour rights, 43–45
stabilization clauses, 43–45
sub-rules or principles, 28–30
international rule of law, and,
35–39
introduction, 27–28
overview, 21–26

**Canada**
comparative tort reasoning, and,
177–183

**Caribbean Commercial Community**
international legal order, and, 5
**Carriage of goods**
international law, and, 5
**Case management**
European court procedural
reforms, and, 104
**Charter of the United Nations**
national rule of law, and, 30
war, and, 11
**Clarity**
European courts, and, 56
principles of the rule of law,
and, 28
**CMR Convention (1956)**
carriage of goods by road, and,
5
**Code for Crown Prosecutors**
international cooperation, and,
214–215
**Codification**
comparative tort reasoning, and,
187–191
**Coherent application of law**
European courts, and, 56–57
principles of the rule of law,
and, 28
**Community law**
comparison of tort law, and,
200–201
**Comparative tort reasoning**
Australia, 177–183
benefits of comparative
materials in English language
jurisdictions
basic contributions, 152–153
digression on theory, 169–173
doctrine, 156–169
outcomes, 154–156
United States, and, 173–177
benefits of comparative
materials in foreign language
jurisdictions

Australia, for, 177–183
Canada, for, 177–183
Eire, for, 183–185
England, for, 183–185
New Zealand, for, 177–183
Scotland, for, 183–185
US, for, 177–183
Wales, for, 183–185
benefits of 'coordinated'
materials
codification of tort law, by,
187–191
harmonization of tort law, by,
187–191
restatement of tort law, by,
185–187
Canada, 177–183
codification, 187–191
conclusions, 191–192
*Consumer Collective Redress*
(EC Green Paper), 200
coordination
inter-national, 187–191
intra-national, 185–187
doctrine
conceptual, 167–169
concerns and arguments,
157–161
outline, 156
principles, 162–167
Eire, 183–185
England, 183–185
harmonization, 187–191
inter-national coordination,
187–191
intra-national coordination,
185–187
introduction, 149–152
misfeasance in public office, 202
New Zealand, 177–183
outcomes, 154–156
Principles of European Tort Law,
189–190

restatement, 185–187
Scotland, 183–185
United States, and
comparative materials in
English language jurisdictions,
173–177
comparative materials in
foreign language jurisdictions,
177–183
Wales, 183–185
**Competition Court**
European court procedural
reforms, and, 82–84
**Compliance with state obligations**
principles of the rule of law,
and, 29
**Consistency in decision-making**
investment protection, and,
129–131
*Consumer Collective Redress* (EC
Green Paper)
comparative tort reasoning, and,
200
**Coordination**
comparison of tort law, and
inter-national, 187–191
intra-national, 185–187
**Corporate social responsibility
(CSR)**
business and human rights, and,
40–41
**Counter-terrorism**
human rights, and, 45–46
**Court of First Instance (CFI)**
conclusions, 106–107
decentralization, 74–75
judicial review of decision-
making, 76–77
key policies and goals, and,
60–63
linguistic regime, 72–74
options for reforms, 77–106
procedural delays, 63–72

role within the framework of the
rule of law, 51–60
**Covenant of the League of Nations**
war, and, 10
**Criminal law**
international law, and, 6–7
**Crown Prosecution Service (CPS)**
establishment, 209
role, 210–212

**Decentralization**
European court procedural
reforms, and, 74–75
**Delay**
European court procedural
reforms, and, 63–72
**Delict**
*See also* **Tort law**
benefits of comparative
materials
English language jurisdictions,
152–177
foreign language jurisdictions,
177–185
benefits of 'coordinated'
materials, 185–191
comparing tort law
conclusion, 207–208
introduction, 193–195
product liability, 195–200
public authority liability,
201–202
specificity of Community law,
200–201
use, 202–207
conclusions, 191–192
introduction, 149–152
**Discretion**
principles of the rule of law,
and, 28
**Dispute resolution**
principles of the rule of law,
and, 28

Economic, Social and Cultural
  Rights Covenant (1966)
  international legal order, and, 7
Edward Inquiry report
  European court procedural
    reforms, and, 84–8
Eire
  comparison of tort law, and,
    183–185
Equality
  principles of the rule of law,
    and, 28
Equity
  investment protection, and,
    131–133
Ethics
  investment protection, and, 144
EU Mutual Legal Assistance
  Convention
  international cooperation, and,
    212
European competition law
  conclusion, 117–118
  European Commission, and,
    111–112
  European Competition Network
    generally, 112–113
    inconsistency, 113–114
  European courts
    dissent, 115–116
    generally, 114–115
    standard of review, 116–117
  guidance, 112
  introduction, 109
  *quis custodiet ipsos custodes*,
    109–111
European Competition Network
  generally, 112–113
  inconsistency, 113–114
European Convention on Human
  Rights (ECHR)
  international legal order, and,
    7–8

international cooperation, and,
  212–213
European Court on Human Rights
  (ECtHR)
  international cooperation, and,
    212
  international legal order, and, 7
European Court of Justice (ECJ)
  BIICL Report (1996)
    generally, 78–79
    redistribution of jurisdiction
      to national courts, 82
    refusal of jurisdiction by
      Community courts, 82
    regional Community courts,
      80–81
    specialized courts or
      tribunals, 81–82
    two-tier ECJ, 81
    US court system, 79–80
  case management, 104
  Competition Court, and, 82–84
  conclusions, 106–107
  decentralization, 74–75
  delay, 63–72
  Edward Inquiry report, 84–86
  expedition, 99–102
  House of Lords Sub-Committee
    report, 82–84
  international legal order, and,
    7–8
  international rule of law, and,
    34–35
  judicial review of decision-
    making, 76–77
  key policies and goals, and,
    60–63
  linguistic regime
    generally, 72–74
    short term procedural
      improvements, 102–104
  need for reform
    decentralization, 74–75

judicial review , 76–77
language, 72–74
procedural delay, 63–72
Nice Treaty, and, 90–91
nomination system, and
benefits, 93–999
introduction of, 91–93
Nice Treaty, 90–91
Regulation (EC) No 1/2003,
88–90
options for reforms
BIICL Report (1996), 78–82
Edward Inquiry report, 84–86
HoL Sub-Committee report,
82–84
introduction, 77–78
nomination system, 88–99
overview, 78–88
short term procedural
improvements, 99–106
Vesterdorf submissions,
87–88
procedural delays, 63–72
redistribution of jurisdiction to
national courts, 82
reforms
need, 63–77
options, 77–106
refusal of jurisdiction by
Community courts, 82
regional Community courts,
80–81
Regulation (EC) No 1/2003,
and, 88–90
'Role and Future of the ECJ'
(BIICL, 1996)
generally, 78–79
redistribution of jurisdiction
to national courts, 82
refusal of jurisdiction by
Community courts, 82
regional Community courts,
80–81

specialized courts or
tribunals, 81–82
two-tier ECJ, 81
US court system, 79–80
role within the framework of the
rule of law, 51–60
short term procedural
improvements
case management, 104
expedition, 99–102
language, 102–104
specialist chambers, 104–105
trademark cases, 105–106
specialist chambers, courts or
tribunals
generally, 81–82
short term procedural
improvements, 104–105
trademark cases, 105–106
two-tier ECJ, and, 81
US court system, and, 79–80
Vesterdorf submissions, 87–88
**European Union**
European courts
conclusions, 106–107
decentralization, 74–75
judicial review  of decision-
making, 76–77
key policies and goals, and,
60–63
linguistic regime, 72–74
options for reforms, 77–106
procedural delays, 63–72
role within the framework of
the rule of law, 51–60
international legal order, and, 5
international rule of law, and, 34
introduction, 49–51
investment protection, and,
145
**Exercise of power**
principles of the rule of law,
and, 28

**Expedition**
European court procedural
reforms, and, 99–102
**Extradition**
international law, and, 6
**Extraordinary Chambers in the
Courts of Cambodia (ECCC)**
generally, 236
introduction, 217

**Fair and equitable treatment**
investment protection, and, 129
**Fair procedures**
principles of the rule of law,
and, 28

**General Agreement on Tariffs and
Trade (GATT)**
international legal order, and, 5
**Geneva Convention (CMR) (1956)**
carriage of goods by road, and,
5
**Guantanamo Bay detentions**
international law, and, 11
international rule of law, and, 32

**Hague Conferences (1899 and
1907)**
war, and, 10
**Hague Convention (1955)**
carriage of goods by air, and, 5
**Hague Rules (1924)**
carriage of goods by sea, and, 5
**Harmonization**
comparison of tort law, and,
187–191
**Health products**
business and human rights, and,
41–43
**House of Lords Sub-Committee
report**
European court procedural
reforms, and, 82–84

**Human rights**
business, and
conclusions, 46–47
counter-terrorism sanctions,
45–46
health products, 41–43
introduction, 39–41
labour rights, 43–45
stabilization clauses, 43–45
sub-rules or principles, 28–30
international cooperation, and,
212–214
international law, and, 7–9
principles of the rule of law,
and, 28
**Human Rights Act 1998**
international cooperation, and,
214
**Hybrid tribunals**
ECCC, 236
generally, 235
IJPP, 237–238
introduction, 217
SPSC, 237–238
WCC, 238–239

**Independence**
principles of the rule of law,
and, 28
**Intelligible**
European courts, and, 56
principles of the rule of law,
and, 28
**International carriage of goods by
sea**
international law, and, 5
**International Centre for the
Settlement of Investment
Disputes (ICSID)**
business, and, 37
creation, 141
international legal order, and,
5

investment protection, and,
121–122
**International cooperation**
challenges for the 'modern
prosecutor'
conclusions, 239–241
internationalized tribunals,
235–239
introduction, 217–219
models of cooperation,
219–220
treaty tribunals, 229–235
UN Security Council
tribunals, 220–229
Code for Crown Prosecutors,
214–215
conclusion, 215
cooperation models, 219–220
Crown Prosecution Service
establishment, 209
role, 210–212
EU Mutual Legal Assistance
Convention, 212
European Convention on
Human Rights, 212–213
Extraordinary Chambers in the
Courts of Cambodia (ECCC)
generally, 236
introduction, 217
governing principles, 212–215
horizontal model of cooperation,
220
Human Rights Act 1998, 214
hybrid tribunals
ECCC, 236
generally, 235
IJPP, 237–238
introduction, 217
SPSC, 237–238
WCC, 238–239
International Criminal Court
(ICC)
establishment, 229

generally, 229–233
introduction, 217
International Criminal Tribunals
(ICT)
generally, 220
former Rwanda, for, 220–226
former Yugoslavia, for,
220–226
introduction, 217
Special Tribunal for Lebanon,
226–229
international judges and
prosecutors programme
(IJPP)
generally, 237
introduction, 217–218
internationalized tribunals
ECCC, 236
generally, 235
IJPP, 237–238
introduction, 217
SPSC, 237–238
WCC, 238–239
models of cooperation,
219–220
'modern prosecutors'
challenges for, 217–241
conclusion, 215
introduction, 209
principles, 212–215
role, 210–212
mutual legal assistance treaties,
210
role of prosecutors, 210–212
Security Council tribunals
generally, 220
ICT for former Rwanda,
220–226
ICT for former Yugoslavia,
220–226
introduction, 217
Special Tribunal for Lebanon,
226–229

Special Court for Sierra Leone (SCSL)
generally, 233–235
introduction, 217
Special Panels for Serious Crimes in Timor Leste (SPSC)
establishment, 229
generally, 237–238
introduction, 217
Special Tribunal for Lebanon (STL)
generally, 226–229
introduction, 217
state-based model of cooperation, 220
supra-state model of cooperation, 219
treaty tribunals
establishment, 229
generally, 229
International Criminal Court, 229–233
introduction, 217
Special Panels for Serious Crimes in Timor Leste, 233–235
UN Security Council tribunals
generally, 220
ICT for former Rwanda, 220–226
ICT for former Yugoslavia, 220–226
introduction, 217
Special Tribunal for Lebanon, 226–229
vertical model of cooperation, 219
War Crimes Chamber in the State Court of Bosnia and Herzegovina (WCC)
generally, 238–239
introduction, 217

International Court of Justice (ICJ)
international rule of law, and, 33
jurisdiction, and, 11
International Covenant on Civil and Political Rights
international legal order, and, 7
International Covenant on Economic, Social and Cultural Rights
business and human rights, and, 41
international legal order, and, 7
International Criminal Court (ICC)
establishment, 229
generally, 229–233
introduction, 217
International Criminal Tribunals (ICT)
generally, 220
former Rwanda, for, 220–226
former Yugoslavia, for, 220–226
introduction, 217
Special Tribunal for Lebanon, 226–229
International judges and prosecutors programme (IJPP)
generally, 237
introduction, 217–218
International law
generally, 1–10
war, 10–19
International Monetary Fund (IMF)
international legal order, and, 5
Internationalized tribunals
ECCC, 236
generally, 235
IJPP, 237–238
introduction, 217
SPSC, 237–238
WCC, 238–239
Investment protection
*amici curiae*, 127–128
appeals

changes to the system, and,
144–145
development of system, and,
129–130
arbitration rules, 127
arbitrator challenges, 144
ASEAN Comprehensive
Investment Agreement, 146
bilateral investment treaties
development of system, and,
121–126
generally, 141–142
consistency in arbitral decision-
making, 129–131
equity, 131–133
ethics, 144
European Union, and, 145
fair and equitable treatment, 129
ICSID
creation, 141
development of system, and,
121–122
most favoured nation clauses,
138
multilateral investment treaties,
139
NAFTA, and, 143
'New Economic World Order',
140
New York Convention, and, 120
origins and development of the
system
conclusions, 133–135
generally, 120–126
introduction, 119–120
sustainability, 126–133
pre-award transparency, 128
regional arrangements, 145
rule of law, and
change, 140–145
conclusion, 147
decline, 146–147
generally, 137–139

introduction, 137
sub-rules, 138
substantive protections, 142–143
sustainability of the system,
126–133
transparency in arbitral decision-
making
changes to the system, and,
143–144
development of system, and,
126–128
Treaty of Lisbon, and, 134
**Iraq war**
international law, and, 11–16

**Judicial procedures**
principles of the rule of law,
and, 28

**Kellogg-Brand Pact (1928)**
war, and, 10–11

**Labour rights**
business and human rights, and,
43–45
**Language**
European court procedural
reforms, and
generally, 72–74
short term procedural
improvements, 102–104
**Law of nations**
international law, and, 1

**Millennium Declaration (UN)**
international law, and, 2–3
international rule of law, and, 32
**Ministerial Code (July 2007)**
international law, and, 1
**Misfeasance in public office**
comparison of tort law, and, 202
**Montreal Convention (1999)**
carriage of goods by air, and, 5

Most favoured nation clauses
  investment protection, and, 138
Multilateral Investment Guarantee
    Agency
  international legal order, and, 5
Multilateral investment treaties
  investment protection, and, 139
Mutual legal assistance treaties
  international cooperation, and,
    210

NAFTA
  investment protection, and, 143
'New Economic World Order'
  investment protection, and, 140
New York Convention
  investment protection, and, 120
New Zealand
  comparison of tort law, and,
    177–183
Nice Treaty
  European court procedural
    reforms, and, 90–91
Nomination system
  benefits, 93–999
  introduction of, 91–93
  Nice Treaty, 90–91
  Regulation (EC) No 1/2003,
    88–90

*Pacta sunt servanda*
  international rule of law, and, 32
Predictability
  European courts, and, 56
  principles of the rule of law,
    and, 28
Principles of European Tort Law
    (PETL)
  comparison of tort law, and,
    189–190
Product liability
  comparison of tort law, and,
    195–200

Public authority liability
  comparison of tort law, and,
    201–202

Realizing Rights
  business and human rights, and,
    26
*Rechtsstaat*
  generally, 28
Red Flags report
  business and human rights, and,
    22–23
Redistribution of jurisdiction
  European court procedural
    reforms, and, 82
Refugees
  international law, and, 9–10
Refusal of jurisdiction
  European court procedural
    reforms, and, 82
Regional Community courts
  European court procedural
    reforms, and, 80–81
Regulation (EC) No 1/2003
  European court procedural
    reforms, and, 88–90
Restatement
  comparison of tort law, and,
    185–187
'Role and Future of the ECJ'
    (BIICL, 1996)
  generally, 78–79
  redistribution of jurisdiction to
    national courts, 82
  refusal of jurisdiction by
    Community courts, 82
  regional Community courts,
    80–81
  specialized courts or tribunals,
    81–82
  two-tier ECJ, 81
  US court system, 79–80

Rule of Law Index
  generally, 28

Scotland
  comparison of tort law, and,
    183–185
Security Council tribunals
  generally, 220
  ICT for former Rwanda,
    220–226
  ICT for former Yugoslavia,
    220–226
  introduction, 217
  Special Tribunal for Lebanon,
    226–229
Special Court for Sierra Leone
    (SCSL)
  generally, 233–235
  introduction, 217
Special Panels for Serious Crimes in
    Timor Leste (SPSC)
  establishment, 229
  generally, 237–238
  introduction, 217
Special Tribunal for Lebanon (STL)
  generally, 226–229
  introduction, 217
Specialist chambers, courts or
    tribunals
  generally, 81–82
  short term procedural
    improvements, 104–105
Stabilization clauses
  business and human rights, and,
    43–45
Supremacy of the law
  generally, 28–29

Tort law
  Australia, 177–183
  benefits of comparative
    materials in English language
    jurisdictions

basic contributions, 152–153
  digression on theory,
    169–173
  doctrine, 156–169
  outcomes, 154–156
  United States, and, 173–177
benefits of comparative
  materials in foreign language
  jurisdictions
  Australia, for, 177–183
  Canada, for, 177–183
  Eire, for, 183–185
  England, for, 183–185
  New Zealand, for, 177–183
  Scotland, for, 183–185
  US, for, 177–183
  Wales, for, 183–185
benefits of 'coordinated'
  materials
  codification of tort law, by,
    187–191
  harmonization of tort law, by,
    187–191
  restatement of tort law, by,
    185–187
Canada, 177–183
codification, 187–191
Community law, 200–201
comparing tort law
  conclusion, 207–208
  introduction, 193–195
  product liability, 195–200
  public authority liability,
    201–202
  specificity of Community law,
    200–201
  use, 202–207
conclusions, 191–192
*Consumer Collective Redress*
  (EC Green Paper), 200
coordination
  inter-national, 187–191
  intra-national, 185–187

doctrine
 conceptual, 167–169
 concerns and arguments,
  157–161
 outline, 156
 principles, 162–167
 Eire, 183–185
 England, 183–185
 harmonization, 187–191
 inter-national coordination,
  187–191
 intra-national coordination,
  185–187
 introduction, 149–152
 misfeasance in public office, 202
 New Zealand, 177–183
 outcomes, 154–156
 Principles of European Tort Law,
  189–190
 product liability, 195–200
 public authority liability,
  201–202
 restatement, 185–187
 Scotland, 183–185
 specificity of Community law,
  200–201
 United States, and
  comparative materials in
   English language jurisdictions,
   173–177
  comparative materials in
   foreign language jurisdictions,
   177–183
 Wales, 183–185
Trademark cases
 European court procedural
  reforms, and, 105–106
Transparency in decision-making
 investment protection, and
  changes to the system, and,
   143–144
  development of system, and,
   126–128

Treaty of Lisbon
 European courts, and, 61
 generally, 49–51
 investment protection, and, 134
Treaty tribunals
 establishment, 229
 generally, 229
 International Criminal Court,
  229–233
 introduction, 217
 Special Panels for Serious Crimes
  in Timor Leste, 233–235
TRIPS Agreement
 business and human rights, and,
  41–43

UK government Ministerial Code
 (July 2007)
 international law, and, 1
UNCITRAL rules
 business, and, 37
UNCLOS
 international rule of law, and, 33
United Nations
 international cooperation, and
  generally, 220
  ICT for former Rwanda,
   220–226
  ICT for former Yugoslavia,
   220–226
  introduction, 217
  Special Tribunal for Lebanon,
   226–229
 war, and, 11–16
United States
 comparison of tort law, and
  materials in English language
   jurisdictions, 173–177
  materials in foreign language
   jurisdictions, 177–183
Universal Declaration on Human
 Rights (1948)
 international legal order, and, 7
 overview, 21–22

Wales
  comparison of tort law, and,
    183–185
War
  international law, and, 10–19
War Crimes Chamber in the State
    Court of Bosnia and
    Herzegovina (WCC)
  generally, 238–239

introduction, 217
Warsaw Convention (1929)
  carriage of goods by air, and,
    5
World Bank
  international legal order, and,
    5
World Trade Organisation (WTO)
  business, and, 37